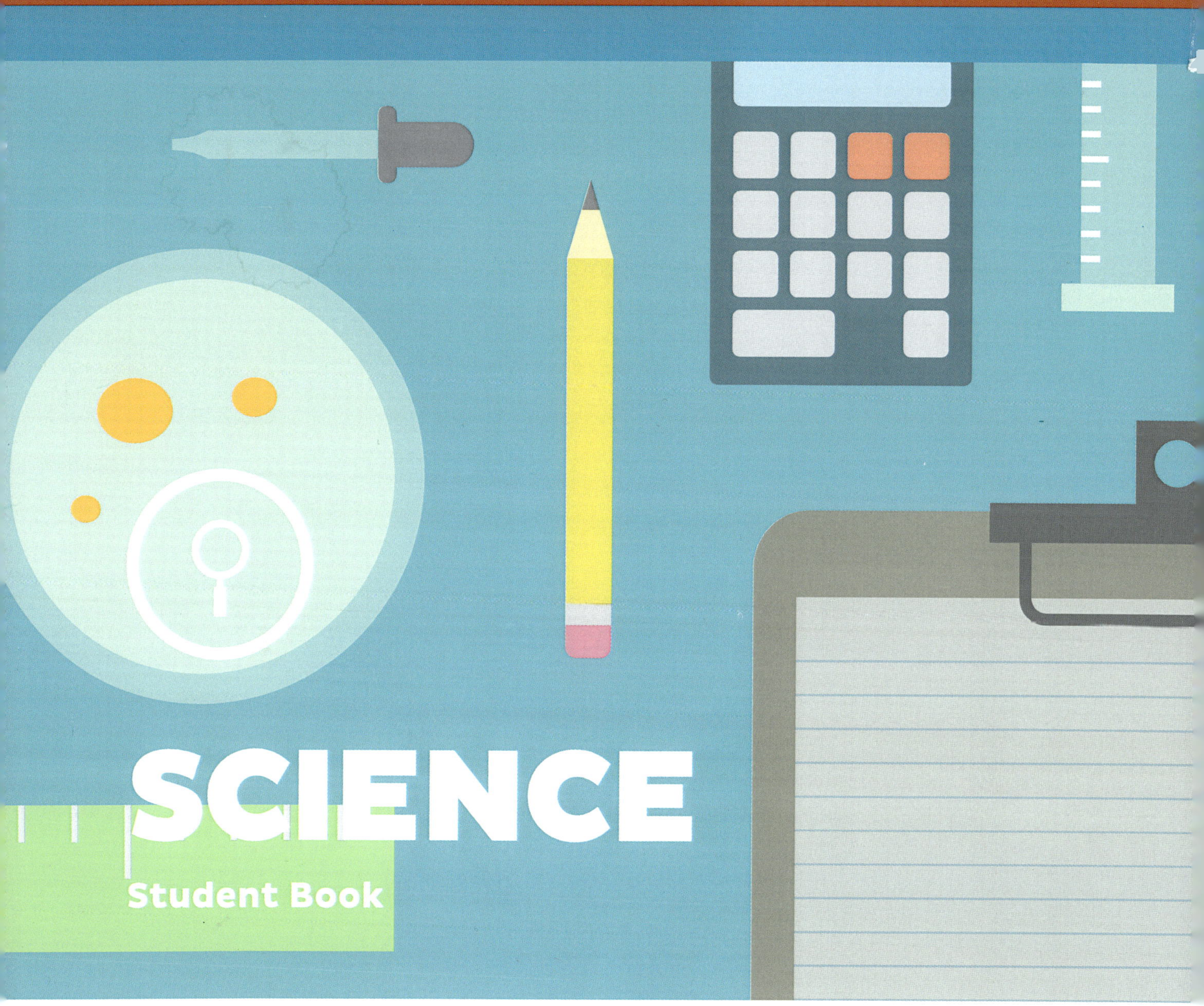

SCIENCE

Student Book

5th Grade | Unit 1

SCIENCE 501

CELLS

Author:
Barry G. Burrus, M.Div, M.A., B.S.

Editor:
Alan Christopherson, M.S.

Editor:
Brian Ring

Illustrations:
Brian Ring

Media Credits:
Page 3: © Adrian Neal, Photodisc, Thinkstock; **6:** © Zoonar RF, Thinkstock; **8:** © somersault18:24, iStock, Thinkstock; **11:** Jeff Metzger, Hemera, Thinkstock; **19:** ©jimmyan, iStock, Thinkstock; **23:** John Schwegel, iStock, Thinkstock; **27:** Sashatigar, iStock, Thinkstock; **38:** © harmpeti, iStock, Thinkstock; **39:** © colematt, iStock, Thinkstock; **45:** © Jupiterimages, liquidlibrary, Thinkstock; **48:** © Bigandt Photography, iStock, Thinkstock; **51:** © Andy Dean, iStock, Thinkstock; © Thawatchai Tumwapee, iStock, Thinkstock.

804 N. 2nd Ave. E.
Rock Rapids, IA 51246-1759

CELLS

In the Book of Genesis, we read that God created everything, including all living things. In this LIFEPAC®, you will explore the tiny unit that God made part of all living things. This tiny unit that is part of all living things is called a cell. All living things that God has created contain cells.

Because most cells are so tiny, they can only be seen with the aid of a microscope. Therefore, it was only after microscopes were invented that men and women were able to explore the tiny world of cells. In 1665, an Englishman named Robert Hooke examined a slice of cork under a crude microscope. He noticed that the cork was made up of small chambers that were similar in appearance. He called these small units "cells." Later, other people discovered more information about cells. They discovered new information about the make-up of cells, the types of cells, and the ways that cells grow and divide. They discovered much about the work and energy processes that take place within cells. Scientists are still making new discoveries today about cells and the fascinating things that happen in them.

In this LIFEPAC, you will also learn much about the make-up, types, and growth of cells. As you explore the fascinating world of cells, think about the wonderful work of God in making such tiny, complex, and orderly units to be part of all living things. Like King David in Psalm 143:5, you can think about the wonderful work of God's hands in creating such a great variety of cells: "I meditate on all thy works; I muse on the work of thy hands."

Before beginning your study of cells, write below some things that you have heard or read about cells. ____

____

____

List below some questions that you have about cells. ______________________

____

____

____

____

Objectives

Read these objectives. The objectives tell you what you will be able to do when you have successfully completed this LIFEPAC. Each section will list according to the numbers below what objectives will be met in that section. When you have finished this LIFEPAC, you should be able to:

1. Give a basic definition of a cell and explain what a cell is.
2. Use a microscope to examine examples of different types of cells.
3. Label the different basic parts of a cell.
4. Identify different types of cells.
5. Explain in more detail the make-up of the cell membrane, cytoplasm, and nucleus.
6. Examine some unique characteristics of plant and animal cells.
7. Examine types of plant and animal tissues.
8. Define what energy is and explain how plants and animals receive and produce energy.
9. Explain how cells reproduce and grow.

Science 500 Supplies

Many of the things that you will need to perform the experiments in Science 500 can be found around the home. For instance, instead of using test tubes, you may substitute baby-food jars and lids. Instead of a beaker, you may use a mayonnaise jar. Some of the things you will need to successfully perform the experiments you will just need to borrow or buy. There are resources in your area where you may be able to find these materials. Your local school may lend you a microscope or perhaps you can buy an older one from them when they purchase new ones. There may be discount department stores in your area that sell these things for low cost. Ordering science material through the mail or over the internet is also a possibility. With each complete boxed set of science curriculum, you should receive an order blank from a trusted supplier for science supplies in the sizes and amounts that you will need to successfully perform the experiments.

If you did not receive an order blank, call the Alpha Omega Publications Customer Services Department for more information.

A suggested support item for this course is the 5th Grade Science experiments video, SD0501. The video includes presentations of many of the experiments in this course. Several of the experiments that require special equipment or materials are demonstrated on these videos. They can either be used for answering the questions of the lab report or as a demonstration of the procedure prior to performing the experiment. A notice is included with each experiment in the LIFEPAC where the video is available.

Remember, it is the supervisors' or parents' responsibility to make sure that all students follow proper safety procedures for experiments and lab work. Any questions that you have about chemicals or supplies should be directed to the supplier of those materials. It cannot be assumed that all necessary warnings and precautions are contained in this material.

As a Christian school curriculum publisher, we discuss what is taught and believed regarding the creation and origins of life on our planet from the Christian point of view. It is the responsibility of the family to decide what they desire to be learned by their students in the school and the home, and whether or not the biblical view is what they want to be taught. There are a number of Christian websites on the internet, however, that may be examined to get further information on the origins of life from a biblical point of view. One of them is the Creation Research Institute website.

1. THE BASIC UNIT OF LIVING THINGS: A CELL

What is a Cell?

Definition. A **cell** is the basic unit of all living things. It is the unit of life. Some living things consist of only one cell. They are called **unicellular** (one-celled). Other living things consist of more than one cell. They are called **multicellular** (many-celled). All plants and animals are multicellular. God provided his creation with a great variety of cells! Yet, as you will learn, all cells have some things in common.

Objectives

Review these objectives. When you have completed this section, you should be able to:

1. Give a basic definition of a cell and explain what a cell is.
2. Use a microscope to examine examples of different types of cells.
3. Label the different basic parts of a cell.
4. Identify different types of cells.

Vocabulary

Study these new words. Learning the meanings of these words is a good study habit and will improve your understanding of this LIFEPAC.

bacteria (bak tir′ ē ə). Simple organisms that consist of one cell. They are a type of prokaryote cells (no nucleus). Bacteria are among the smallest living things.

cell (sel). The basic unit of all living things.

cell membrane (sel mem′ brān). The thin-layer outer structure of each cell that completely surrounds the cell and holds the other contents of the cell within it.

cell wall (sel wôl). A non-living chemical produced by the plant's cells. It surrounds the cell outside the cell membrane. It is harder than the cell membrane.

columnar (kō lum′ năr). Column shaped.

cytoplasm (sī′ tō plaz′ um). The fluid material (mainly water) within the cell membrane that does not include the nucleus.

elongated (i lông′ gāt id). A long, stretched-out shape.

eukaryote (yū kar′ ē ot). The type of cell that contains three basic parts: the cell membrane, the cytoplasm, and the nucleus.

microscopic (mī′ krə′ skop′ ik). Very small. A microscope is needed to see something microscopic.

multicellular (mul′ tī sel′ yū lur). Contains more than one cell, usually many cells.

nucleus (nü′ klē us). The command center that controls the life and activity of the cell. It is located within the cytoplasm of the cell.

prokaryote (prō kar′ ē ot). The type of cell that contains only two basic parts: the cell membrane and protoplasm. It does not have a nucleus. Bacteria are an example of this cell.

protoplasm (pro′ tə plaz′ əm). The inner fluid material within the cell membrane.

unicellular (yü′ nə sel′ yə lur). One-celled. Living things that have only one cell.

Note: *All vocabulary words in this LIFEPAC appear in* **boldface** *print the first time they are used. If you are unsure of the meaning when you are reading, study the definitions given.*

Pronunciation Key: h**a**t, **ā**ge, c**ã**re, f**ä**r; l**e**t, **ē**qual, t**ė**rm; **i**t, **ī**ce; h**o**t, **ō**pen, **ô**rder; **oi**l; **ou**t; c**u**p, p**u̇**t, r**ü**le; **ch**ild; lo**ng**; **th**in; /ŦH/ for **th**en; /zh/ for mea**s**ure; /u/ or /ə/ represents /a/ in **a**bout, /e/ in tak**e**n, /i/ in penc**i**l, /o/ in lem**o**n, and /u/ in circ**u**s.

Write the answers on the lines.

1.1 All living things that God has created contain ______________ .

1.2 An Englishman named Robert Hooke examined ______________ under a crude microscope and called the small chambers "cells."

1.3 A cell is the ____ of all living things.

1.4 A one-celled living thing is called ________________________ .

1.5 A many-celled living thing is called ________________________ .

Basic parts of a cell. All cells have at least two basic parts: (1) a **cell membrane**, and (2) an inner material called **protoplasm**. This inner material called protoplasm is usually a fluid or jelly-like substance, although in some cells it is harder than jelly. Cells that contain *only* these two parts—an outer membrane and the inner protoplasm—are called **prokaryote** cells. The living things called **bacteria** are examples of these two-part prokaryote cells.

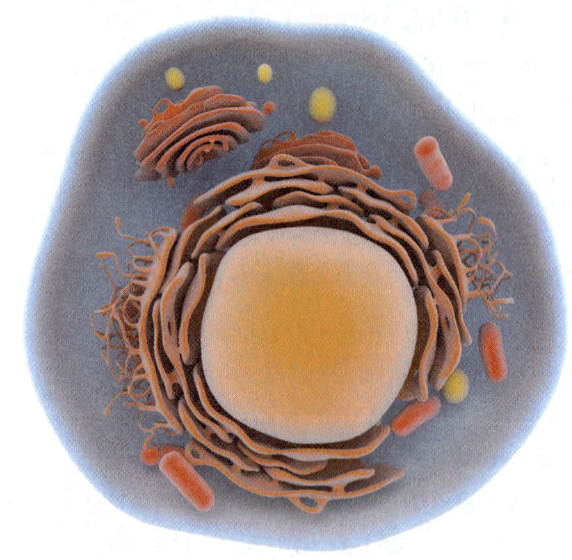

| Structure of the human cell

Many other cells contain a third basic part: a **nucleus**. The nucleus is part of the protoplasm of the cell and is located within the cell membrane. It usually looks like a little dark ball or dot within the cell. When a cell contains a nucleus, then we call the part of the protoplasm outside the nucleus the **cytoplasm**. The cytoplasm is the liquid or jelly-like substance within the cell membrane and outside the nucleus, while the nucleus consists of harder living substances. Therefore, these cells with a nucleus contain three basic parts: (1) an outer membrane, (2) the cytoplasm, and (3) the nucleus. Cells with three basic parts are called **eukaryote** cells. There are many unicellular living things that consist of a single eukaryote cell; that is, they are a three-part cell. *All* the cells in multicellular living things are eukaryote cells. Therefore, all the cells in your body are eukaryote cells. There is a fourth basic part of cells found in plants and fungi. This is called the **cell wall**. The cell wall surrounds the cell membrane. It helps give support to the plant. Animal cells do not contain cell walls.

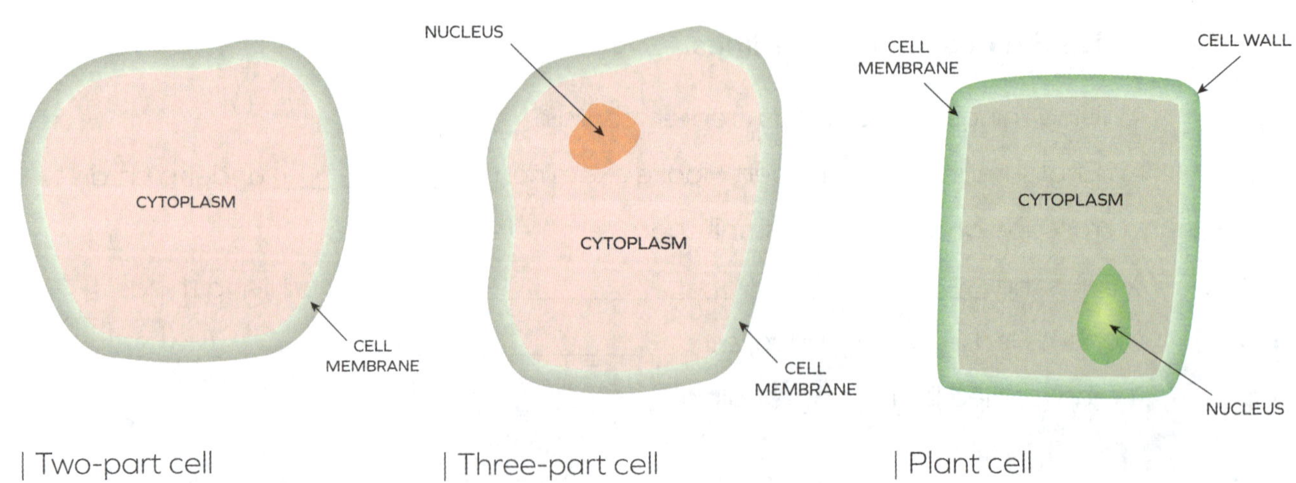

| Two-part cell | Three-part cell | Plant cell

Match these items.

1.6 __________ protoplasm

1.7 __________ prokaryote

1.8 __________ eukaryote

1.9 __________ nucleus

1.10 __________ cytoplasm

1.11 __________ cell wall

a. contains three basic parts of the cell: cell membrane, cytoplasm, and nucleus

b. inner fluid material within the cell membrane

c. a fourth part of a cell found only in plants

d. found within the protoplasm and looks a little like a dark ball or spot

e. part of a microscope

f. contains only two basic parts of the cell: cell membrane and protoplasm

g. fluid material within cell membrane and outside the nucleus

Complete this activity.

1.12 Draw a typical three-part cell on a separate sheet of paper and label the three basic parts of a cell.

INTERNET NOTICE: There are many good resources on the Internet giving information about cells and the life of cells. A lot of these internet sites have excellent drawings, illustrations, and animations showing the detailed parts of cells. You can use keywords like "cells" and "nucleus" to find out more details on cells. We will cover more details on cells in Section 2 of this LIFEPAC.

Size. Almost all cells are **microscopic**. This means that most cells are so tiny that they require a microscope to be seen. In fact, the period at the end of the last sentence would hold about 500 average-sized cells! These average-sized cells would be about 1/1000 of an inch in diameter (0.0025 centimeter).

The human body has more than 10 trillion (10,000,000,000,000) cells!

However, other cells can be larger. The largest cells are the yolks of birds' eggs. The largest cell of all is the yolk of an ostrich egg. It is about 3 inches in diameter (7.6 centimeters), yet it consists of only one cell!

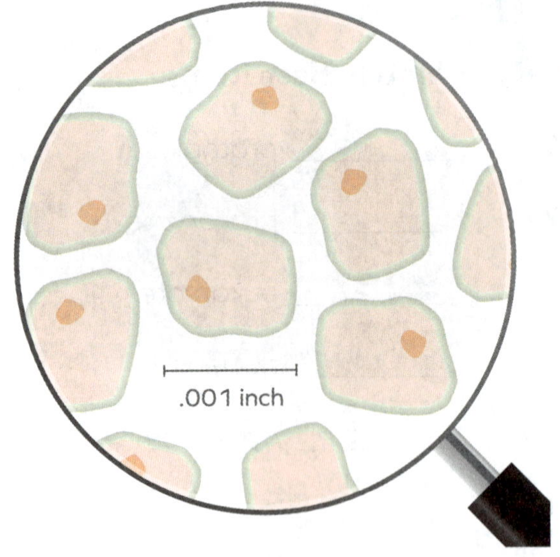

Shape. Cells also come in a variety of shapes. There are round cells, oval cells, cubed cells, **columnar** cells, **elongated** cells, and irregular cells. Other cells are shaped like doughnuts or pancakes. There are even cells shaped like hearts and commas and corkscrews! There is no typical cell shape.

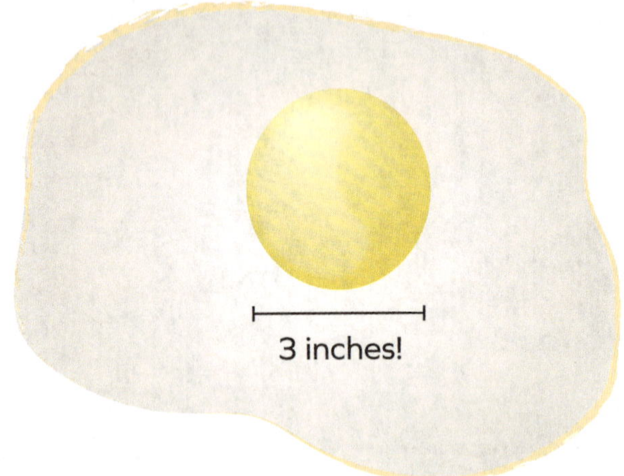

Viewing Cells

The only way to view most cells is to use a microscope. There are different types of microscopes. An *optical microscope* is the one you will normally see and use. It can magnify a cell up to about 2,000 times so that we can easily see the basic parts of the cell. However, some cells are too small to be seen by an optical microscope. For these, an *electron microscope* is needed. An electron microscope can magnify a cell by one million times! These electron microscopes not only allow us to see the smallest of cells, they also allow us to view the tiny subparts of cells. (We will cover some of these subparts of cells in Section 2 of this LIFEPAC.)

It is also helpful to use dyes to view cells. The dyes stain certain parts of the cell—such as the cell membrane and the nucleus—so that they stand out more clearly when we view the cells under a microscope. (You will use iodine as a dye in some of the experiments in this LIFEPAC.)

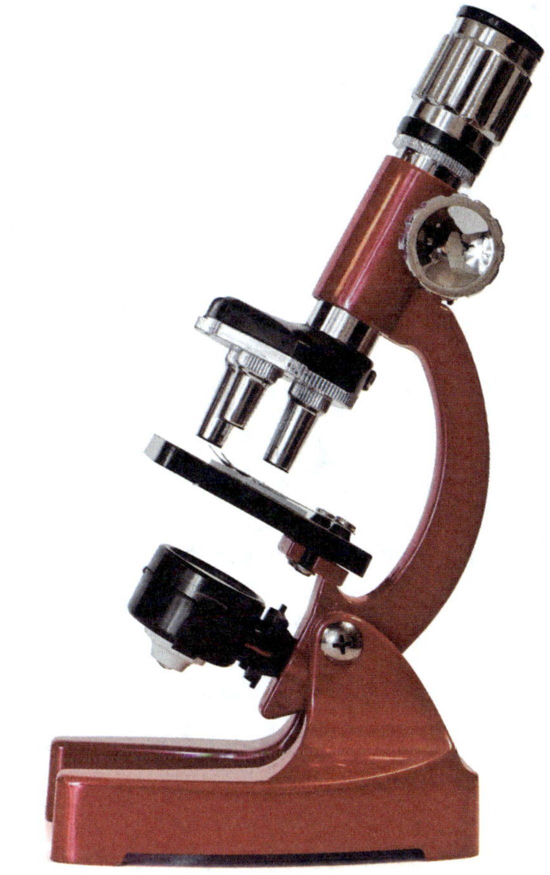

| Optical microscope

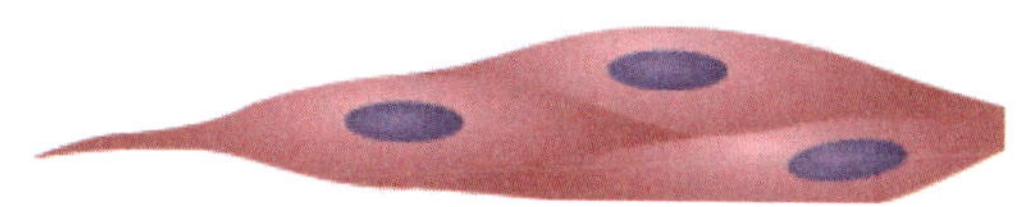

| Muscle cells

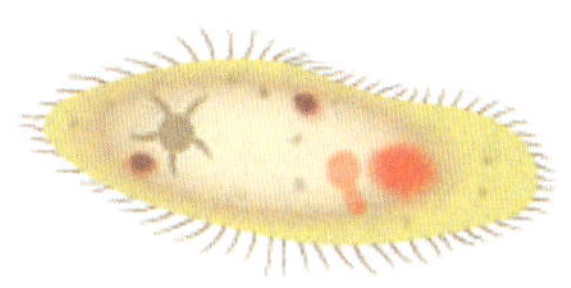

| Paramecium

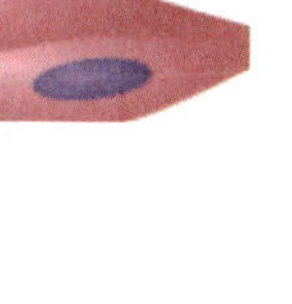

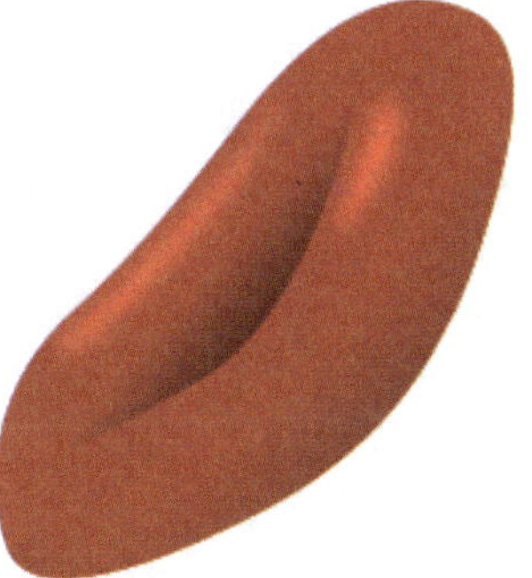

| Red blood cell

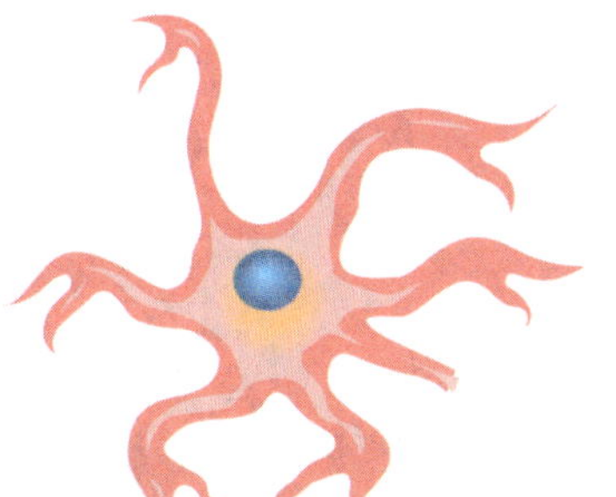

| Nerve cell

| Diatom

| Leaf pore guard cell

Answer *true* or *false*.

1.13 ____________ Almost all cells are "microscopic."

1.14 ____________ The smallest cell is the yolk of an ostrich egg.

1.15 ____________ The human body has more than 10 trillion cells.

1.16 ____________ Cells come in a great variety of shapes.

1.17 ____________ All cells are the same size.

Answer this question.

1.18 What things help us to view cells? ____

____

____

____

____

____

____

501.A SKIN CELLS

View 501
SKIN CELLS:
Grade 5 Science experiments video

Overview. You will use an optical microscope to observe some skin cells from the palm of your hand.

These supplies are needed:

- optical microscope
- diluted iodine solution
- slide
- knife or scalpel
- slide cover
- small eyedropper or toothpick

Follow these directions carefully. Place a check mark in the box as you complete each step in these directions.

☐ 1. Have the teacher show you how to use the optical microscope. (If this has already happened, go to step 2.)

☐ 2. Ask your teacher to be present. When the teacher is with you, ***CAREFULLY*** use the edge of the knife or scalpel blade to lightly scrape some skin cells from the palm of your hand. (**NOTE:** You will be able to get a lot of cells from just a little material, so you will not have to do a lot of scraping.)

☐ 3. Place the scraped skin cells on the slide.

☐ 4. Use the small eyedropper or a toothpick to place a small drop of diluted iodine solution on the skin cells while they are on the slide. (**NOTE:** This will stain parts of the cells and make them easier to view in the microscope.)

☐ 5. Cover the stained skin cells with a slide cover.

☐ 6. Place the prepared slide of skin cells under the microscope for viewing.

(continued on the following page)

☐ 7. Adjust the microscope settings until you can see the skin cells clearly. (**NOTE:** If you have trouble adjusting the microscope to view the slide, have your teacher assist you.) The picture below should help you see what to look for. There may be some bubbles of air present along with the skin cells.

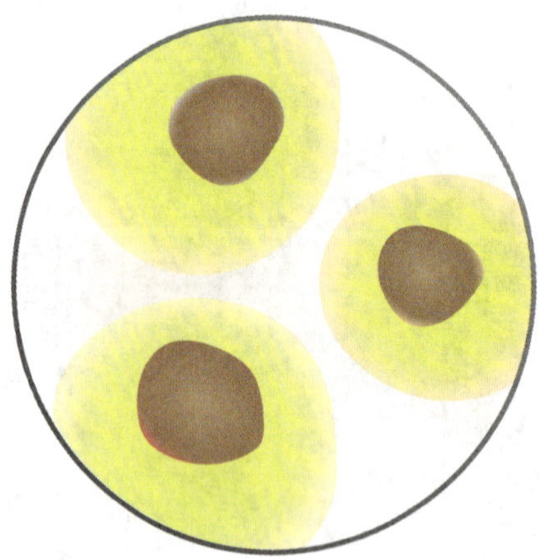

Record your observations.

1.19 Draw the view you have in the microscope in the large circle below. Label the cells (and the basic cell parts, if you can see them) and also label what may be air bubbles.

| Skin Cells

(continued on the following page)

1.20 Record any other information about this experiment that you found interesting or surprising! ______________________________

____

____

____

____

____

____

____

____

____

____

____

Teacher check:

Initials ______________ Date ______________

Review the material in this section to prepare for the Self Test. The Self Test will check your understanding of this section. Any items you miss on this test will show you what areas you will need to restudy in order to prepare for the unit test.

SELF TEST 1

Match these items (each answer, 3 points).

1.01 __________ cell
1.02 __________ cytoplasm
1.03 __________ unicellular
1.04 __________ protoplasm
1.05 __________ prokaryote
1.06 __________ eukaryote
1.07 __________ nucleus
1.08 __________ Robert Hooke
1.09 __________ cell wall
1.010 __________ God

a. inner fluid material within the cell membrane
b. Englishman who discovered cells by looking at cork
c. contains only one cell
d. contains three basic parts of the cell: membrane, cytoplasm, and nucleus
e. basic unit that is part of all living things
f. a fourth part of a cell found only in plants
g. found within the protoplasm as a dark ball or spot
h. part of a microscope
i. contains only two basic parts of the cell: membrane and protoplasm
j. contains many cells
k. fluid material within cell membrane and outside the nucleus
l. discovered the shapes of cells
m. created all living things

Write the letter of the correct answer on the blank line (each answer, 3 points).

1.011 All living things that God has created contain __________.
a. the nucleus b. chloroform c. cells d. a cell wall

1.012 Scientists are still making new __________ today about cells.
a. computer programs b. textbooks
c. discoveries d. names

1.013 Living things that contain only one cell are called __________.
a. bacteria b. unicellular c. microbes d. none of these

1.014 Eukaryote cells contain (1) a cell membrane, (2) cytoplasm, and (3) ________ .

a. a nucleus
b. prokaryote
c. protoplasm
d. elongated cells

1.015 An ________ is normally used to view cells and can magnify up to about 2,000 times.

a. overhead projector
b. iodine solution
c. electron microscope
d. optical microscope

1.016 Some of the shapes of cells include ________ .

a. round and oval
b. hearts and corkscrews
c. cubed and columnar
d. all of these

1.017 The largest cell of all is the ________ .

a. amoebae
b. yolk of an ostrich egg
c. elephant foot
d. palm cell

Write your answer (each answer, 10 points).

1.018 What is a cell? ____

____

____

____

1.019 Explain why it is helpful to use dyes (such as iodine) to view cells in a microscope.

____

____

____

____

Draw a picture below (5 points) **and label it** (4 points).

1.020 What are the four basic parts of a typical plant cell? Label each part.

Teacher check: Initials ____________

Score ____________________ Date ____________

64/80

2. THE LIFE AND ACTIVITY OF CELLS

Objectives

Review these objectives. When you have completed this section, you should be able to:

2. Use a microscope to examine examples of different types of cells.
3. Label the different basic parts of a cell.
4. Identify different types of cells.
5. Explain in more detail the make-up of the cell membrane, cytoplasm, and nucleus.
6. Examine some unique characteristics of plant and animal cells.
7. Examine types of plant and animal tissues.

Vocabulary

Study these new words. Learning the meanings of these words is a good study habit and will improve your understanding of this LIFEPAC.

antibodies (an′ ti bod′ ēz). Proteins that destroy bacteria, viruses, and other invaders of the body, or make them harmless.

cellulose (sel′ yə lōs). A substance that forms the walls of plant cells.

chlorophyll (klôr′ ə fil). The green pigment in a plant cell chloroplast that gives the plant a green color.

chloroplast (klôr′ ə plast). An organelle found in the cytoplasm of plant cells that contain chlorophyll and is involved in energy production in the cell.

chromatin (krō′ mə tin). The long strands of material within the nucleus made up of DNA, RNA, and other proteins.

chromosome (krō′ mə sōmz). The orderly strands of chromatin that form when a cell is going to reproduce.

DNA, or *Deoxyribonucleic Acid* (dē ŏk′sē rī′ bō noo klē′ ĭk ăs′ ĭd). A very large, complex molecule that forms a double-helix shape and is contained in the chromatin of cells.

epidermal (ep′ ə der′ mul). The outside layer of cells covering plants.

epithelial (ep′ ə thē′ lē ul). A layer of cells that form the skin and the linings of various inner organs and glands.

genes (jēnz). Part of the DNA within the cell. Genes are like "recipes" for making specific types of proteins in the cell.

nuclear membrane (nü′ klē ər mem′ brān). An outer, double-membrane covering for the material within the nucleus.

nucleolus (nü′ klē′ ō lus). A small part within the nucleus that is very condensed chromatin and consists mainly of RNA and other proteins.

organelles (ōr′ gə nelz′). Tiny subparts of material within the cytoplasm of a cell that produce proteins, energy, or perform a specialty function.

phospholipid (fos′ fō li pid). A molecule that forms most of the material for the cell membrane and the nuclear membrane. It forms a double layer to make the cell membrane and four layers on the nuclear membrane.

photosynthesis (fō′ tō sin′ thə sis). A very important process in plants that takes energy from sunlight and the chlorophyll in the plant and forms oxygen and sugars from carbon dioxide and water.

proteins (prō′ tēnz). Large, complex molecules made up of smaller units called amino acids. All proteins contain carbon, hydrogen, nitrogen, and oxygen. They may also contain other elements. Proteins are important in the life and activities of cells.

protozoan (prō′ tə zō′ un). One-celled animals.

RNA, or *Ribonucleic Acid* (rī′ bō noo klē′ ĭk ăs′ ĭd). A complex molecule similar to DNA that plays an important role in making the proteins within cells.

tissues (tish′ üz). A group of similar cells connected together that perform similar work.

white blood cells (wīt blud selz). Colorless blood cells that protect the body against infection by attacking germs and diseased cells.

xylem (zī′ lum). The connective tissues in plants that help carry materials through the plant.

Pronunciation Key: hat, āge, cãre, fär; let, ēqual, tėrm; it, īce; hot, ōpen, ôrder; oil; out; cup, pu̇t, rüle; child; long; thin; /ŦH/ for **th**en; /zh/ for mea**s**ure; /u/ or /ə/ represents /a/ in **a**bout, /e/ in tak**e**n, /i/ in penc**i**l, /o/ in lem**o**n, and /u/ in circ**u**s.

More Details of Cells

Introduction. In Section 1 of this LIFEPAC, you learned about the *basic* parts of cells. In Section 2, we will look in more detail at each of the basic parts of cells: the cell membrane, cytoplasm, the nucleus, and (for plants) the cell wall. God made cells with a lot of details! We will examine the various subparts of cells and explain what goes on there. Then we will discuss some specific things about plants cells and animal cells. Finally, we will discuss how various cells make up tissues. You will also do some more experiments involving cells in this section of the LIFEPAC.

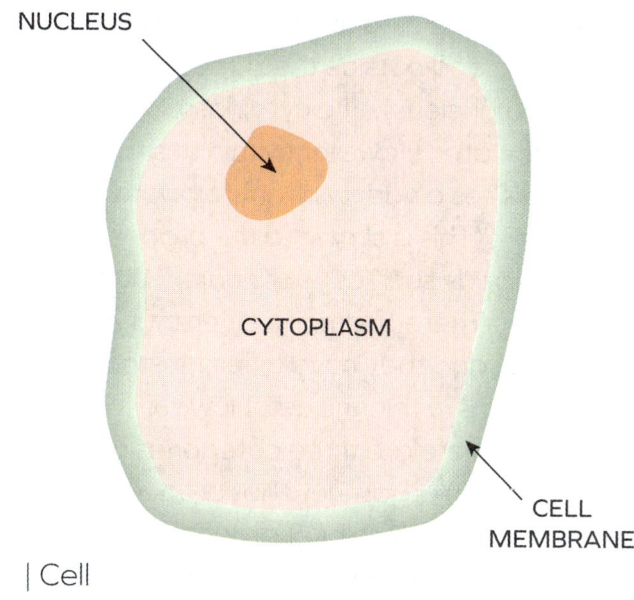

| Cell

Cell membrane. The cell membrane is the outer structure of each cell. It is a continuous membrane that completely surrounds the rest of the cell and holds the other contents of the cell within it. The membrane also controls what goes in and out of the cell. The membrane controls the entry or exit of various kinds of molecules that are either used by the cell or are given off by the cell.

The cell membrane consists of two different parts: (1) a **phospholipid** double layer of molecules and (2) **proteins** that are scattered within the phospholipid layer of the membrane. The *phospholipids* are molecules that form most of the material for the cell membrane. Two layers of these phospholipid molecules are used to provide the main thickness of the membrane. The *proteins* in the cell membrane generally are of three types. They may be *carrier proteins* that regulate what enters and leaves the cell. The second type of proteins is *marker proteins* that identify the cell to other cells. The third type of proteins located in the cell membrane is *receptor proteins,* which allow the cell to receive instructions and communicate with other cells. It's amazing how much ability God placed in the tiny membrane of a cell!

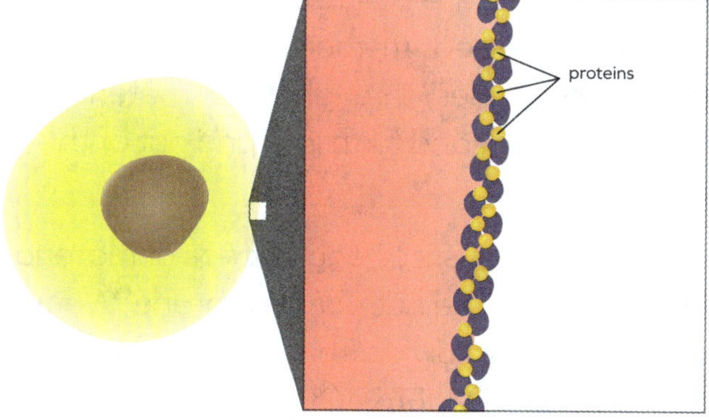

| Phospholipid double layer

Cytoplasm. The cytoplasm is within the membrane and outside the nucleus (if the cell contains a nucleus). The cytoplasm consists mainly of water. However, within this fluid part of the cells lies a variety of tiny subparts called **organelles**. (This is similar to the *organs* in your own body such as your heart, lungs, liver, and so on.) There are many different types of organelles, and they have different structures and functions within the cell. However, in general, there are three categories of organelles: (1) organelles that produce proteins within the cell; (2) organelles that produce energy in the cell; and (3) specialty organelles. All of these organelles are active within the cytoplasm to help make the cell function correctly.

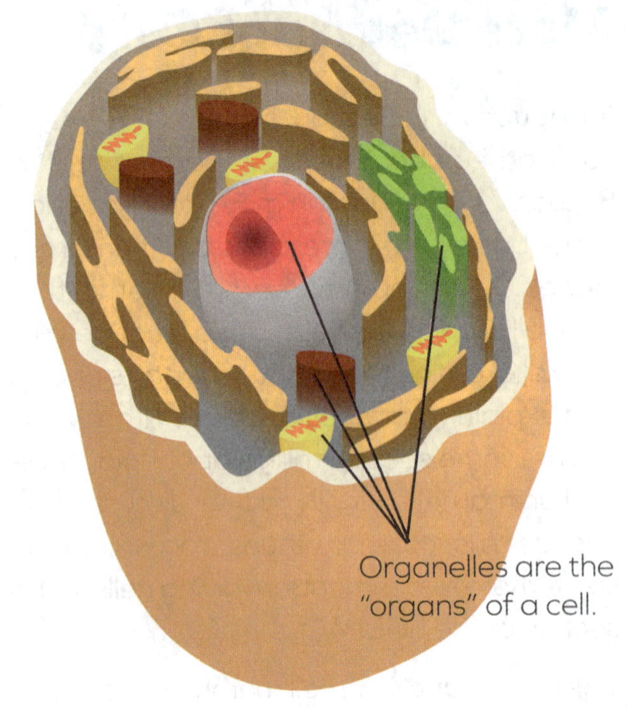

| Organelle

Nucleus. The nucleus is like a "command center" or headquarters for the activity and life of the cell. It regulates all activity of the cell. The nucleus has three basic parts: (1) the **nuclear membrane**, (2) **chromatin**, and (3) the **nucleolus.**

The *nuclear membrane* is an outer covering for the material within the nucleus. It is a double membrane that has four phospholipid layers. The nuclear membrane also has large pores (open holes) through which materials may pass back and forth into and out of the nucleus.

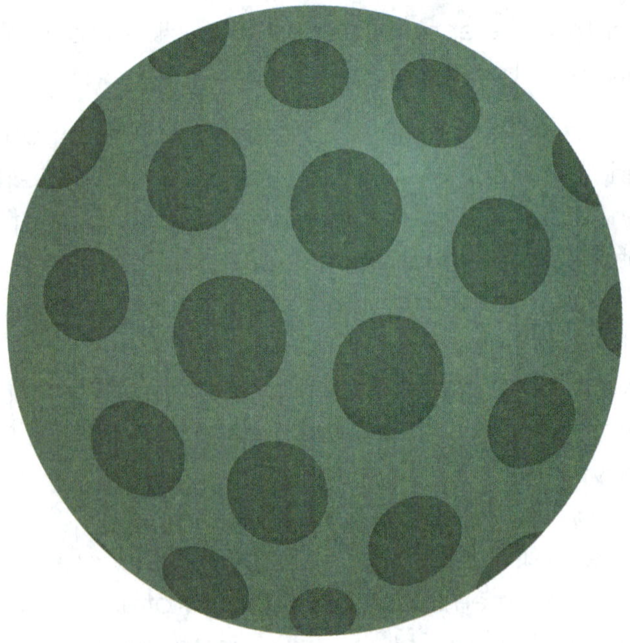

| Nuclear membrane

Chromatin consists of long strands of material located within the nuclear membrane. When a cell is going to divide (more on that in Section 3 of this LIFEPAC), the chromatin rearranges and condenses into orderly strands called **chromosomes**. Chromosomes (which consist of chromatin) are very important to the life of the cell when it is going to reproduce (more on this in Section 3 of this LIFEPAC). There are different and specific numbers of chromosomes in different cells. For example, there are 23 pairs of chromosomes in human cells.

The *chromatin* (the material of the chromosomes) within the nucleus is made up of **DnA** (***Deoxyribonucleic Acid***), **RnA** (***Ribonucleic Acid***), and other proteins. You have probably heard of DNA. DNAs are very large, complex molecules that look like a "twisted ladder" (called a "*double helix*" shape). DNA contains **genes**. The genes are like "recipes" for making specific types of proteins in the cells. The DNA and genes contain the molecular information to make the cells and the groups of cells within a living thing what it is to be. For example, the DNA in your body determines the color of your hair and eyes. Your DNA is specific to you. The DNA is what makes the offspring of a living thing resemble the parent. DNA is what makes a dog produce another dog rather than a fish.

God designed the DNA in living things to produce other living things similar to them.

The third part of a nucleus is the *nucleolus*. The nucleolus looks almost like a little "nucleus" within the nucleus! It is very condensed chromatin that contains mainly *RNA* (*Ribonucleic Acid*) and other proteins. RNA is similar to DNA and plays an important role in making the proteins within cells.

Wow! God provided a lot of detail in the make-up of all living things, especially human beings! Along with King David, we can say, "I will praise thee; for I am fearfully and wonderfully made: marvellous are thy works" (Psalm 139:14).

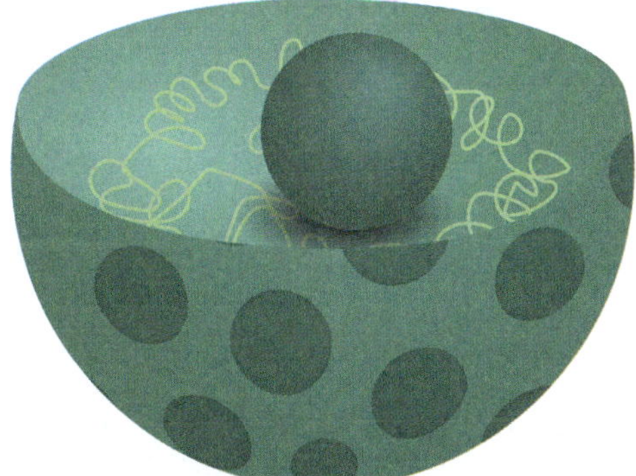

| The nucleolus inside the nucleus.

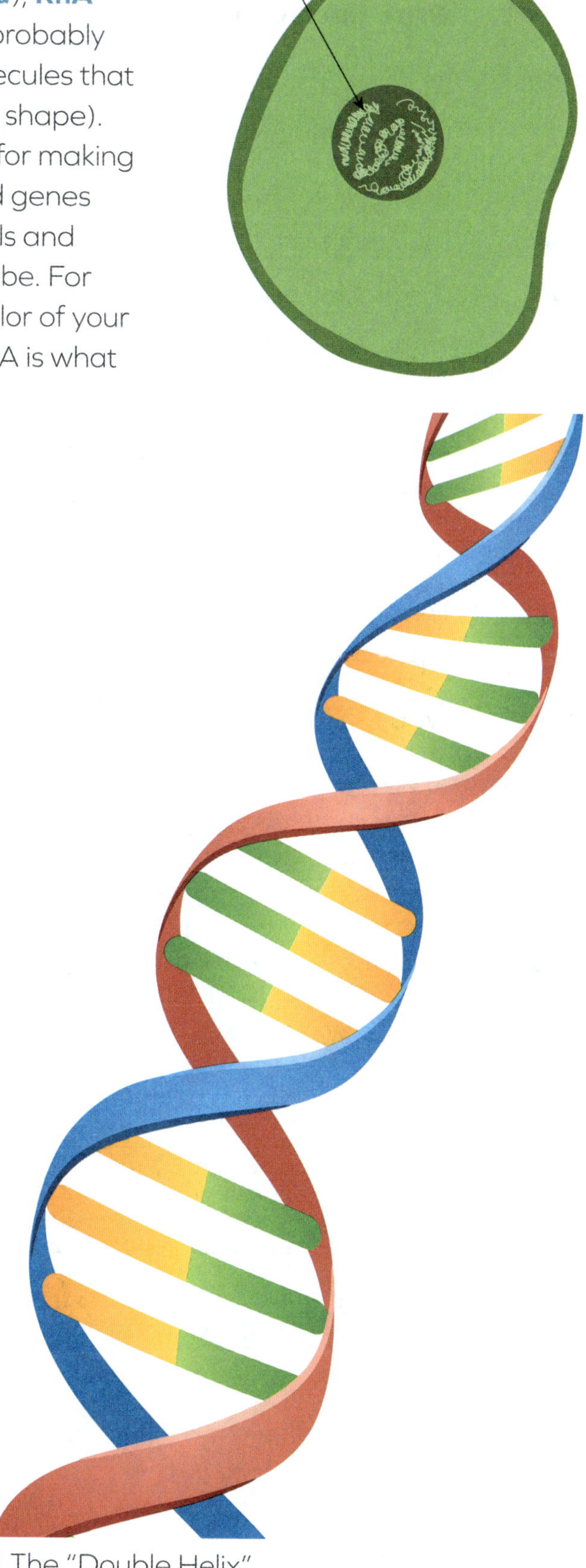

| The "Double Helix".

Write the answers on the lines.

2.1 The ______________________ is the outer structure of each cell.

2.2 The cell membrane consists of two parts: a(n) a. ______________________ double layer and b. ______________________ scattered throughout this double layer.

2.3 The cytoplasm of the cell contains small subparts called ______________________ .

2.4 The outside part of the nucleus is called the ______________________ .

2.5 Within the nucleus are long stands of material called ______________________ .

2.6 ______________________ is a large, complex molecule in a cell that looks like a "twisted ladder" and contains genes.

2.7 When the chromatin inside a nucleus is going to reproduce, it condenses into long strands called ______________________ .

2.8 The ______________________ is very condensed chromatin and is the part of the nucleus that contains mainly RNA and other proteins.

2.9 What are the three main categories of organelles within the cytoplasm?

a. ______________________

b. ______________________

c. ______________________

Answer this question.

2.10 Explain what makes the offspring of a living thing resemble its parent.

____

____

____

____

Plants

Introduction. Now that we have looked at the tiny subparts of the cell, let's consider some special properties of plant cells. We will also do an experiment where we will observe some onion cells.

Cell walls. Cells of plants have some unique characteristics. As mentioned in Section 1, plants have a fourth basic part of the cell called a *cell wall*. The cell wall is usually made of **cellulose**. The cell wall gives support and structure to the plant. Plants are able to "stand up" and remain firm because of the cell walls. Sometimes, the cell within the cell wall of a plant will grow or shrink, depending upon the amount of water the plant is receiving. However, even though the size and the shape of the plant cell may change, the cell wall remains the same and gives support and shape to the overall plant.

The cell wall also contains some very small holes in it. These small holes allow molecules to pass in and out of the cell wall, and thus in and out of the cells.

Chloroplasts. Another unique thing about most green plants is that they contain some special organelles within the cytoplasm. These organelles in plant cells are called **chloroplasts**. These chloroplast organelles in plants are the category that are involved in energy production. They take energy from the sun and produce oxygen and sugars that are used as "food" within the plant. The oxygen is given off from the plant and is later used by animals and human beings to breathe. (We will cover more about this in Section 3.)

| Extra water

| Normal water

| Low on water

Within the chloroplasts is a chemical called **chlorophyll**. The chlorophyll is what gives green plants their "green" color. It is the chlorophyll that combines with the energy from the sun to produce oxygen and sugars from carbon dioxide and water residing in the plant. This process is called **photosynthesis**. This is a very important process in plants. Photosynthesis in plants takes energy from the sun and makes oxygen for you to breathe. (We will look at photosynthesis more in Section 3 of this LIFEPAC.)

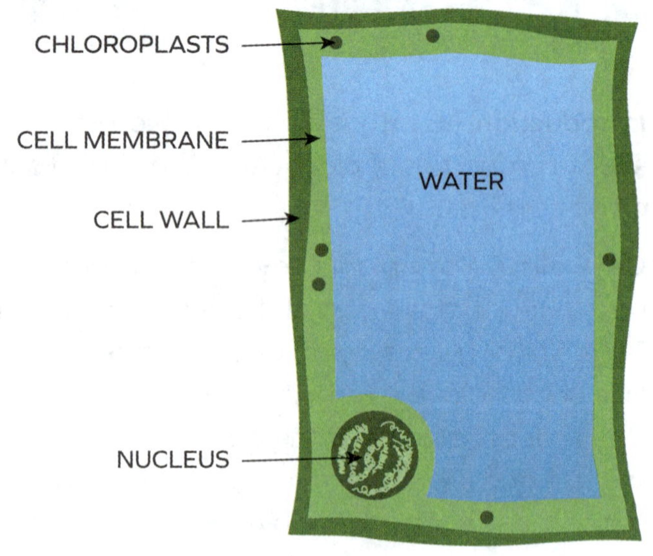

| Plant cell

Answer *true* or *false*.

2.11 __________ The cell wall of a plant is made of chlorophyll.

2.12 __________ The cell wall of a plant gives support and structure to the plant.

2.13 __________ The size of a plant cell may change depending upon the amount of water it receives.

2.14 __________ Chloroplasts are a category of organelles found in the cells of green plants.

2.15 __________ Photosynthesis in plants produces water and carbon dioxide.

2.16 __________ The chlorophyll in plants give them a green color.

501.B ONION CELLS

View 501
Onion Cells: Grade 5 Science experiments video

Overview. You will use an optical microscope to observe cells of an onion bulb. **NOTE:** You may cry during this experiment! (The gases from an onion can make your eyes burn and water.)

These supplies are needed:

- optical microscope
- diluted iodine solution
- slide
- knife
- slide cover
- small eyedropper or toothpick
- tweezers
- onion bulb

Directions. Follows these directions carefully. Place a check mark in the box as you complete each step in these directions.

☐ 1. Cut the onion bulb in half widthwise with the knife.

☐ 2. Cut a slice from one of the halves.

☐ 3. Pull off the outer ring and cut off a small section of the ring.

☐ 4. On the inside of the small section of the ring that you just cut off, you will find a very thin layer (or skin) of material. Take the tweezers and carefully pull off this layer from the small section.

☐ 5. Place the thin layer of onion on the slide.

☐ 6. Use the small eyedropper or a toothpick to place a small drop of diluted iodine solution on the onion layer while it is on the slide. (**NOTE:** This will stain parts of the cells and make them easier to view in the microscope.)

☐ 7. Place the slide cover over the stained onion cells.

☐ 8. Adjust the microscope settings until you can see the onion cells clearly. (**NOTE:** If you have trouble adjusting the microscope to view the slide, have your teacher assist you.)

(continued on the following page)

Record your observations.

2.17 Draw what you see in the microscope in the large circle below.

Label the parts of one cell.

NOTE: You might find some cells without a nucleus. Perhaps the cells were broken open and the nucleus was lost when the thin layer was pulled off the onion.

2.18 Record any other information about this experiment that you found interesting or surprising. ____________________

____

____

____

____

____

____

____

____

____

____

Teacher check:

Initials ____________ Date ____________

Animals

Introduction. God has created billions of animals on the earth. There are many, many varieties of animals, yet all animals are made of the basic unit of living things: cells. Among these animals, we will examine some animals that consist of only one cell! Larger animals and human beings are multicellular. We will examine some of the many types of cells present in multicellular animals, too. You will do an experiment to view some of the one-celled (unicellular) animals in a microscope. You will also have an opportunity to see more of your own cells in a microscope!

CILIA
NUCLEUS
GULLET
CYTOPLASM
CONTRACTILE VACUOLE
FOOD VACUOLES

| Cell

Unicellular animals. God made some animals so tiny that they only consist of one cell. They are called *unicellular animals*. Even though they are microscopic, they still perform many of the functions of larger multicellular animals. These unicellular animals can get food, swim or move about, sense light, and reproduce to form offspring.

Unicellular animals have a great variety of shapes. They can usually be identified by their shapes. Shown below are some unicellular animals from the **protozoan** category of unicellular animals.

In the experiment, you will try to identify some unicellular animals, using these drawings and perhaps some drawings from other books or the internet.

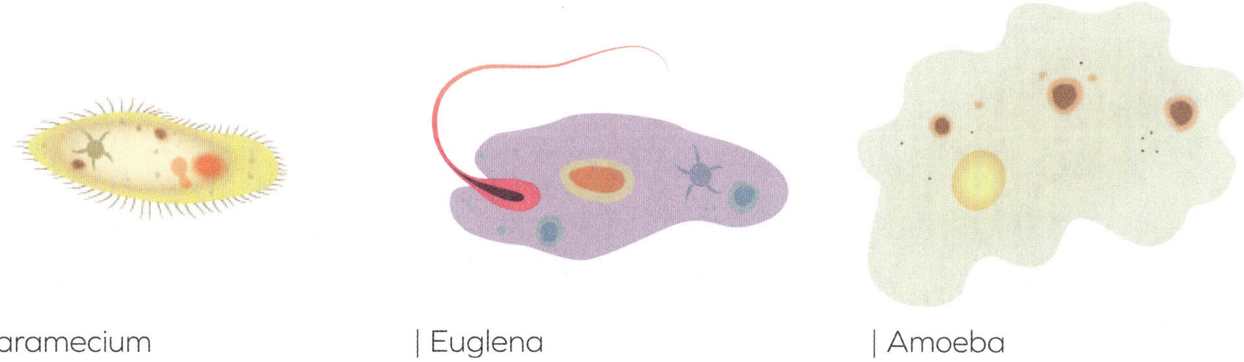

| Paramecium | Euglena | Amoeba

501.C POND WATER EXAMINATION

View 501 Pond Water Examination: Grade 5 Science experiments video

Overview. In this experiment, you will use a microscope to examine pond water for various kinds of unicellular animals.

These supplies are needed:

optical microscope
eyedropper
slide
pond water
slide cover

Follow these directions carefully. Place a check mark in the box as you complete each step.

☐ 1. Go to a farm pond or a small outdoor body of water and collect some pond water in a jar or container.

☐ 2. Using the eyedropper, place one drop of pond water on the slide.

☐ 3. ***Loosely*** place the slide cover over the pond water on the slide. Be careful not to press down on the cover.

☐ 4. Place the slide under the microscope and adjust the microscope until it is focused on the small unicellular animals. **NOTE:** The animals may move very fast!

(continued on next page)

SCIENCE 501

LIFEPAC TEST

NAME ____________________

DATE ____________________

SCORE ____________________

SCIENCE 501: LIFEPAC TEST

Match these items (each answer, 3 points).

1. __________ cells that fight disease
2. __________ contains chlorophyll
3. __________ type of cells in the skin
4. __________ unicellular
5. __________ cytoplasm
6. __________ nucleolus
7. __________ God
8. __________ DNA
9. __________ produced in photosynthesis
10. __________ need energy

a. part of a microscope
b. one-celled living thing
c. fluid material within cell membrane and outside the nucleus
d. white blood cells
e. chloroplasts
f. epithelial
g. contained within the nucleus of a cell
h. created all living things
i. double-helix shape and part of the chromatin
j. oxygen
k. plants and animals
l. cork

Answer *true* or *false* (each answer, 2 points).

11. ______________ Almost all cells are microscopic.
12. ______________ The largest cell is the yolk of an ostrich egg.
13. ______________ The cell wall gives support and structure to the plant.
14. ______________ The chlorophyll in plants gives them a green color.
15. ______________ Chromosomes are a form of blood cells.
16. ______________ Protozoa are a type of unicellular animals.
17. ______________ Nerve cells carry oxygen to the body.
18. ______________ A large cat is larger than a smaller cat because it has larger cells.
19. ______________ Mitosis is the process of one cell splitting apart to form two cells.

20. __________ Male-female reproduction needs two parent cells to begin.

Write the correct letter on each blank (each answer, 3 points).

21. All living things that God has created contain ________ .
a. the nucleus b. chlorophyll c. cells d. a cell wall

22. Eukaryote cells contain (1) a cell membrane, (2) cytoplasm, and (3) ________ .
a. a nucleus b. prokaryote c. protoplasm d. elongated cells

23. In plants, photosynthesis produces ________ .
a. carbon dioxide b. chlorophyll c. oxygen and sugars d. water

24. In the lungs, oxygen is transferred to the ________ .
a. bone b. nerve cells c. chlorophyll d. red blood cells

25. The outside part of the nucleus is called the ________ .
a. cytoplasm b. nuclear membrane
c. jacket d. RNA

Answer these questions (each answer, 3 points).

26. What are two types of microscopes used in viewing cells?
a. ______________________ b. ______________________

27. What are three basic parts of a nucleus?
a. ______________________ b. ______________________
c. ______________________

28. List any four of the six types of body cells covered in this LIFEPAC.
a. ______________________ b. ______________________
c. ______________________ d. ______________________

Write the answer to each question (each answer, 4 points).

29. What is a cell? ______________________________

____

____

____

____

____

30. How does the human body receive the energy it needs?

____

____

____

____

____

____

Record your observations.

2.19 Draw what you see in the microscope in the large circle below. Don't worry if the animals move too fast. Just draw them the best you can as you remember them in the slide.

| Pond Water
First Slide

☐ 5. Prepare two more slides of pond water as you did above.

Record your observations.

2.20 Draw what you see in the second slide in the circle below.

| Pond Water
Second Slide

2.21 Draw what you see in the third slide in the circle below.

| Pond Water
Third Slide

(continued on next page)

2.22 Using the drawings above, the illustrations of the protozoa just before this experiment, and drawings or pictures from any other resources, identify the unicellular animals on your slides. Write their names in the spaces below. If you have some unknown animals, write "unknown" also.

a. Slide one ______________________________

b. Slide two ______________________________

c. Slide three ______________________________

2.23 Record any other information about this experiment that you found interesting or surprising!

____

____

____

____

____

____

____

____

Teacher check:

Initials ____________________ Date ____________________

2.24 This is an activity to help you recognize some of the words you have learned so far in Section 2 of this LIFEPAC. Look at the "jumbled" words. For example, the word "**j**umbled" might be written as "be**j**ldmu." Your task is to write the words below correctly. Notice that the beginning letter of each word is in **boldface** type.

a. reb**m**maen ____________________ b. ne**p**toir ____________________

c. s**c**rhsemoomo ____________________ d. plhlrl**c**ohoy ____________________

e. clrul**u**nlaie ____________________ f. lo**p**hpsdiipho ____________________

g. lulc**n**esou ____________________ h. ls**c**leuole ____________________

i. stho**p**tehsonsiy ____________________ j. ar**p**toozo ____________________

Multicellular animals. Many animals need more than one cell to survive. These are called multicellular animals. You can see many multicelled animals without a microscope. For example, cats, dogs, fish, and birds are all multicellular animals. There are many more besides these examples.

Multicellular animals contain cells with various shapes and sizes. This is because these cells do different things within the multicellular animal. The shape of the cells is different because they perform different functions. The greatest variety of cell shapes occurs in human beings and other multicellular animals. We will now look at some of the various cells within your body, since you also are multicellular!

White blood cells fight infections and harmful substances that invade the body. Although most of them are round and colorless, they vary in size and also the shape of their nucleus. Some of the white blood cells are able to surround and destroy germs and other disease-causing particles. Other white blood cells produce **antibodies**. These antibodies are proteins that destroy bacteria, viruses, and other invaders of the body, or they make them harmless.

Red blood cells carry oxygen to **tissues** of the body (more on tissues later in this section). The red blood cells also remove carbon dioxide from these tissues. The red blood cells are thinner in the middle than at the edges—kind of like a doughnut without a hole!

Nerve cells carry messages throughout the body. They make the body aware of things happening inside and outside the body.

Bone cells provide for the support and protection of the body.

Epithelial *cells* are the cells that form the body's skin, inner linings, and glands. (You saw epithelial cells in the first experiment of this LIFEPAC when you examined your palm cells.)

Muscle cells are elongated and elastic. They help the body's movement. For example, your muscle cells help you walk, breathe, and digest food.

With all of these examples of different body cells, you can see how there are a great variety of cells in multicellular animals. Let's now take a look at some of the cells in your own body in the next experiments.

| White blood cells

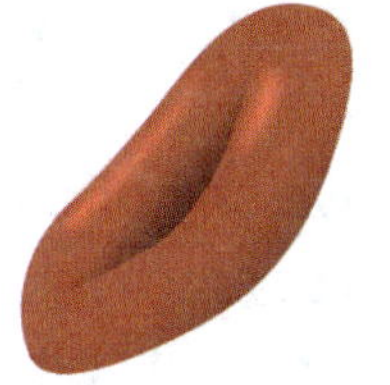
| Red blood cells

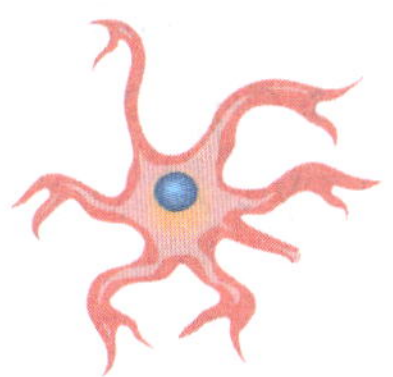
| Nerve cell

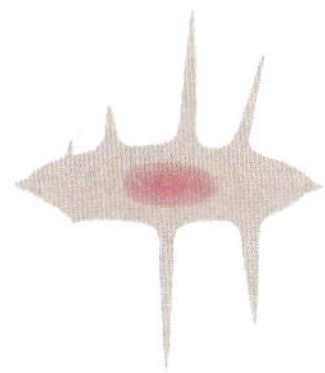
| Bone cells

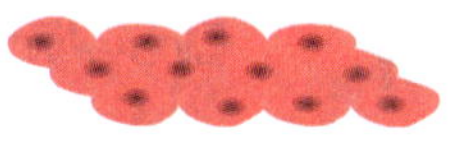
| Epithelial cells

| Muscle cells

501.D CHEEK CELLS

View 501 Cheek Cells: Grade 5 Science experiments video

Overview. In this experiment, you will use a microscope to examine some cells from inside your cheek. These cells are a form of epithelial cells, as were your palm cells.

These supplies are needed:

- optical microscope
- iodine solution
- slide
- toothpick
- slide cover
- eyedropper

Follow these directions carefully. Place a check mark in the box as you complete each step.

☐ 1. With the wide end of the toothpick, gently scrape the inside of your cheek.
☐ 2. Carefully transfer this cheek material to the slide.
☐ 3. Use the eyedropper to stain the material with the iodine solution.
☐ 4. Cover the stained material with the slide cover.
☐ 5. Place the covered slide under the microscope and focus the microscope.

Record your observations.

2.25 Draw what you see in the microscope in the large circle below.

| Cheek Cells

(continued on next page)

2.26 Record any other information about this experiment that you found interesting or surprising! ________________________________

____

____

____

____

____

____

____

Answer these questions. Compare the view of cheek cells with the view of palm cells from Experiment 501.A. Use your observations to answer the following questions..

2.27 What are some similarities? ________________________________

____

2.28 What are some differences? ________________________________

____

2.29 What could be the reasons for the similarities or differences? ________________________________

____

Teacher check:

Initials ________________ Date ________________

501.E BLOOD CELLS

View 501
Blood Cells: Grade 5
Science experiments
video

Overview. In this experiment, you will use a microscope to examine some red blood cells from your finger.

NOTE: The red blood cells must be obtained by drawing a drop of blood from your finger. You may prefer to purchase a prepared human blood smear slide to use for this experiment.

Homeschool Students: **DO NOT** do this experiment unless your parent is present to supervise.

Students in a school: **DO NOT** proceed unless you have submitted a permission slip to your teacher signed by your parent.

These supplies are needed:

- optical microscope
- two slides
- slide cover
- rubbing alcohol
- cotton ball
- needle
- eyedropper
- Methylene blue (ink stain)

Follow these directions CAREFULLY. Place a check mark in the box as you complete each step.

- ☐ 1. Moisten the cotton ball with the alcohol and rub it on your finger where you will draw the blood. Also rub the alcohol on the tip of the needle. (This will sterilize your finger and the needle and prevent infection.) A pin must *not* be used!
- ☐ 2. Carefully prick your finger with the needle.
- ☐ 3. Gently squeeze a drop of blood out on one of the slides.
- ☐ 4. Using the edge of the other slide, spread the drop of blood over the first slide until a very thin level of blood remains.
- ☐ 5. Wash your finger with soap and warm water. You may place a bandage over the needle prick if needed.
- ☐ 6. Cover the blood with Methylene blue (ink stain or Wright's stain). Allow it to dry for a least one minute before going to the next step.
- ☐ 7. Put several drops of water all over the blood and slide. Then allow it to dry for at least three more minutes.

(continued on next page)

☐ 8. Rinse the slide under a tap or faucet in order to move excessive particles from the slide and put the slide cover over the dried sample.

☐ 9. Place the slide under the microscope and adjust it to view the cells.

Record your observations.

2.30 Draw what you see in the microscope in the circle below. Label the parts of one of the cells.

2.31 Record any other information about this experiment that you found interesting or surprising. ______________________________

____

____

____

____

____

____

____

____

Teacher check:

Initials ______________ Date ______________

Write the answers on the lines.

2.32 One-celled animals are called __________________________ .

2.33 Animals with more than one cell are called __________________________ .

2.34 __________________________ blood cells fight infections and harmful substances that invade the body.

2.35 __________________________ blood cells carry oxygen to tissues of the body and remove carbon dioxide from them.

2.36 __________________________ cells carry messages throughout the body.

2.37 __________________________ cells form the body's skin, inner linings, and glands.

2.38 __________________________ cells are elongated and elastic and help the body's movement.

Tissue

Introduction. The cells of multicellular plants and animals are normally grouped together in structures that perform similar functions. These similar groups of cells are called tissues. There are four main types of plant tissues. There are also four main types of animal tissues. We will first examine the types of plant tissues and then explore the types of animal tissues.

Plant tissue. The four main types of plant tissue are (1) **epidermal**, (2) connective, (3) storage, and (4) support.

Epidermal tissues provide the plant cover. This type of plant tissue covers the leaves as well as the roots. The epidermal tissue helps to protect and support the plant. Gases (carbon dioxide and oxygen) are brought in and travel out through the epidermal tissues of leaves. Water and various salt compounds travel through the epidermal tissue of the roots.

| A close-up of a leaf.

The plants need the gases, water, and salts to survive. Once these materials pass through the epidermal tissues they must travel to the other locations in the plant where they are needed. The plant's connective tissues, called the **xylem**, help these materials travel through the plant.

Another type of tissue is located in the leaves. It is used for storage of fat-type material that the plant needs.

Finally, as the xylem in the plant dies, it forms a harder tissue that is used for the support of the plant.

Animal tissue. Cells in multicellular animals form four main types of tissues: (1) epithelial, (2) muscular, (3) nervous, and (4) connective.

You have already observed examples of epithelial tissues in previous experiments in this LIFEPAC. Your palm cells and cheek cells were examples of epithelial tissues. Epithelial tissues act as a protective cover for the body. Epithelial tissues make up the skin. There are glands located inside the epithelial tissues that provide the skin with moisture and lubrication. Epithelial tissues also provide linings for the lungs, stomach, intestines, and other parts in the body.

Muscle tissues make movement of the body possible. The cells in the tissue work together to move the muscles and thus the body. When a few of the cells in muscle tissue contract or expand, there is a small movement in a body part. When many cells in the muscle tissue contract or expand, there is a larger movement! Muscle tissue is also part of the heart. The heart is a large muscle that must keep moving constantly. It never stops. Other muscle tissues are located in the stomach and intestines. These muscle tissues help move and digest food in the body.

Nervous tissues are the body's "message carrying" system. The nerve cells in the nervous tissue are close together and can send signals, or impulses, from one to another very quickly. Nervous tissue is located all through the body. It forms the communication network to and from the brain. Sensory nervous tissue is responsible for sending information to the brain. This sensory information comes from nerve cells and nerve tissues located in the eyes, ears, nose, mouth, and skin. The brain then receives and processes these messages and information. Then, information is sent out from the brain through motor nervous tissues in order to move muscles, activate certain glands, or

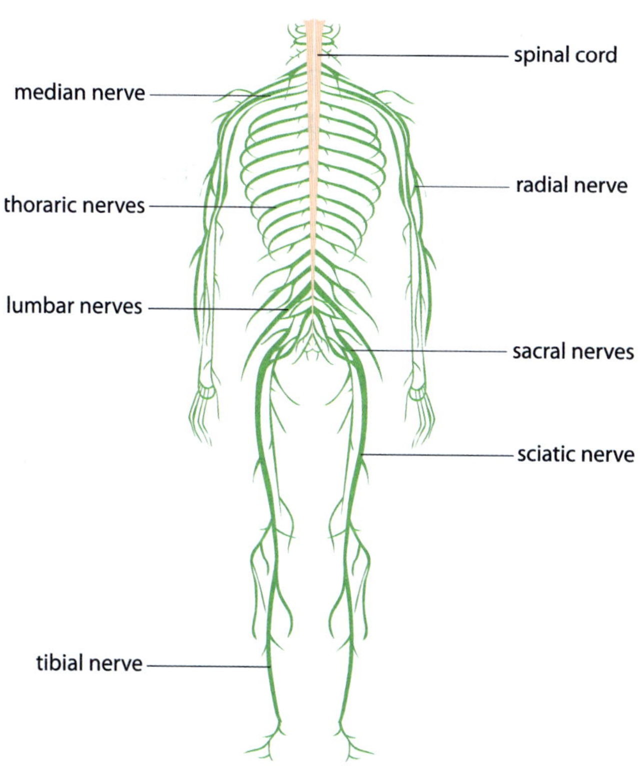

perform other body functions. Connective tissues consist of many different types of cells. These tissues either support or connect the rest of the cells in the body. Some of the different types of connective tissues are bone, blood, fatty tissue, membranes, cartilage, and protective fibers.

Complete these lists.

2.39 What are the four main types of plant tissues?

a. ________________ b. ________________

c. ________________ d. ________________

2.40 What are the four main types of animal tissues?

a. ________________ b. ________________

c. ________________ d. ________________

Answer these questions.

2.41 What is a tissue? ________________

____

____

2.42 How are tissues of plants similar to tissues of animals? ________________

____

____

2.43 How do nervous tissues in animals act as message-carriers in the body? Explain.

____

____

____

Read Psalm 139:14-18.

2.44 How do these verses in the Bible support the information that you have learned about cells in this LIFEPAC? Write your thoughts on this question on the following lines.

____

____

____

____

____

____

____

____

Teacher check:

Initials ____________ Date ____________

Review the material in this section to prepare for the Self Test. The Self Test will check your understanding of this section and will review the other section. Any items you miss on this test will show you what areas you will need to restudy in order to prepare for the unit test.

SELF TEST 2

Write *true* or *false* (each answer, 2 points).

2.01 __________ The cell membrane contains a double layer of phospholipid molecules.

2.02 __________ Almost all cells are microscopic.

2.03 __________ All cells are the same size.

2.04 __________ The cytoplasm of a cell consists mainly of water.

2.05 __________ Chromatin consists of long strands of material located within the nuclear membrane.

2.06 __________ Chromosomes are a form of blood cells.

2.07 __________ God designed the DNA in living things to produce other living things similar to them.

2.08 __________ In plants, the cell wall is usually made up of cellulose.

2.09 __________ Chlorophyll makes some plants look yellow.

2.010 __________ Protozoa are a type of unicellular animals.

2.011 __________ Nerve cells carry oxygen to the body.

Complete these statements (each answer, 4 points).

2.012 A cell is the ________________________ of all living things.

2.013 The nucleus contains a nuclear membrane, chromatin, and the ________________________.

2.014 __________ cells provide for the support and protection of the body.

2.015 The only way to view most cells is to use a(n) ________________________.

2.016 Gases are brought into and out of a plant through its ________________________.

2.017 Animals that contain many cells are called ________________________.

Match these items (each answer, 3 points).

2.018 ________ cytoplasm
2.019 ________ photosynthesis
2.020 ________ prokaryote
2.021 ________ organelles
2.022 ________ DNA
2.023 ________ white blood cells
2.024 ________ epithelial cells
2.025 ________ muscle cells
2.026 ________ God
2.027 ________ multicellular

a. carry messages throughout the body
b. chlorophyll
c. contain many cells
d. created all living things
e. elongated, elastic cells that help the body's movement
f. form the body's skin, inner linings, and glands
g. fight infections and harmful substances that invade the body
h. large, complex molecules that look like a "twisted ladder"
i. tiny subparts of a cell located in the cytoplasm
j. contains only two basic parts of a cell: membrane and protoplasm
k. process in plants that uses energy from the sun
l. inner fluid material within the cell membrane

Answer these questions (each answer, 5 points).

2.028 What are some differences between plant and animal cells? ________________
____
____
____
____

2.029 What happens to cause the body to make large and small movements? ________________
____
____
____
____

2.030 Explain what happens to make the offspring of a parent resemble its parent.

____

____

____

____

2.031 What are tissues and what are the four types of animal tissues? ____________

____

____

____

____

Teacher check: Initials ____________

Score ____________ Date ____________

77/96

3. ENERGY AND GROWTH OF CELLS

Objectives

Review these objectives. When you have completed this section, you should be able to:

8. Define what energy is and explain how plants and animals receive and produce energy.
9. Explain how cells reproduce and grow.

Vocabulary

Study these new words. Learning the meanings of these words is a good study habit and will improve your understanding of this LIFEPAC.

budding (bud' ing). A form of cell reproduction in plants.

energy (en' ər jē). The capacity to do work. Both plants and animals need energy to do their work.

mitosis (mī tō' sis). A process of cell reproduction whereby a single cell splits apart to form two new cells.

reproduction (rē' prə duk' shən). The process by which cells make new cells like themselves.

respiration (res' pə rā' shən). A process by which cells combine oxygen with food and give off carbon dioxide and energy.

Pronunciation Key: h**a**t, **ā**ge, c**ã**re, f**ä**r; l**e**t, **ē**qual, t**ė**rm; **i**t, **ī**ce; h**o**t, **ō**pen, **ô**rder; **oi**l; **ou**t; c**u**p, p**u̇**t, r**ü**le; **ch**ild; lo**ng**; **th**in; /ŦH/ for **th**en; /zh/ for mea**s**ure; /u/ or /ə/ represents /a/ in **a**bout, /e/ in tak**e**n, /i/ in penc**i**l, /o/ in lem**o**n, and /u/ in circ**u**s.

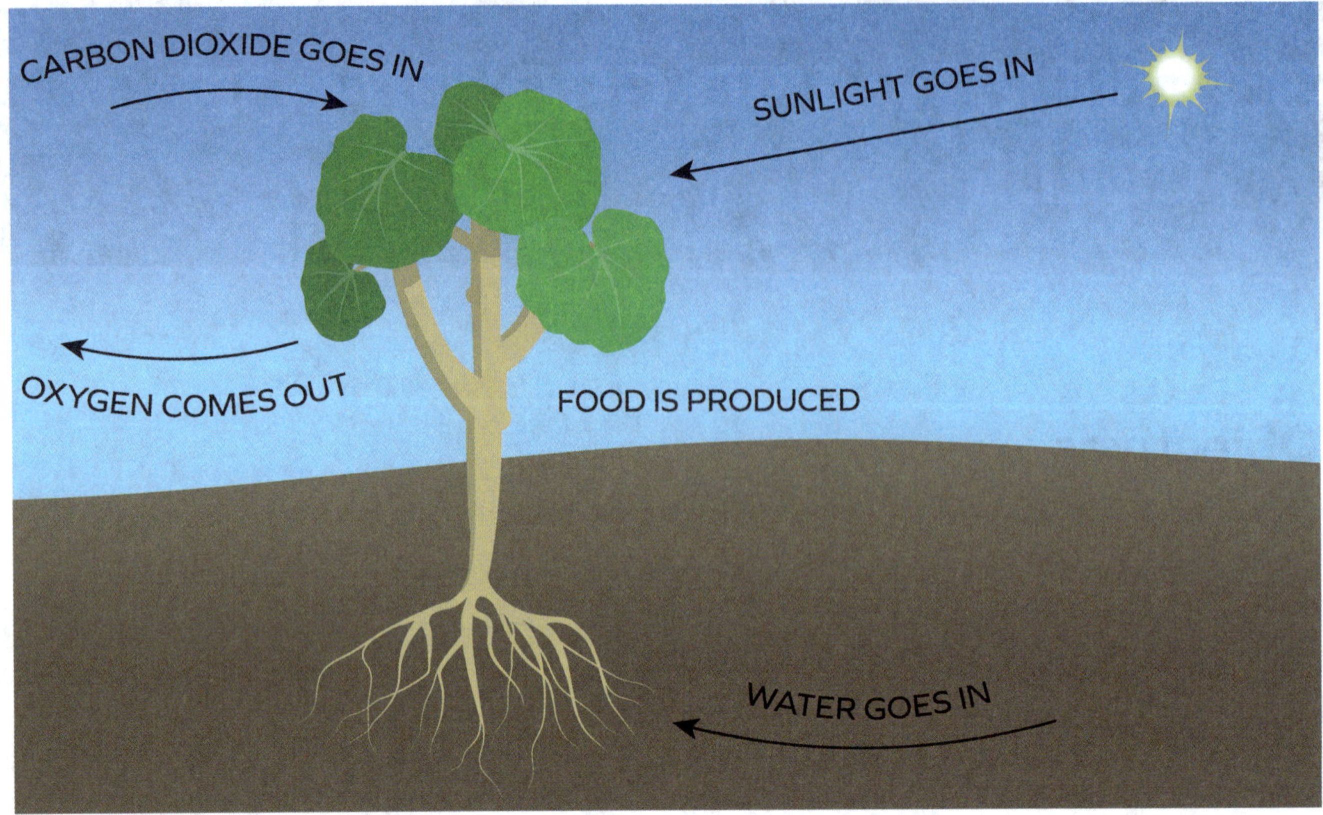

| Photosynthesis

Introduction. In this LIFEPAC, you have learned what cells are. You have examined the make-up and activities of cells. You have also examined various types of cells and tissues. In this last section of this LIFEPAC, you will learn more about the ways plants and animals produce foods and energy. You will also learn about the ways plants and animals grow and reproduce. God has provided a wonderful design for life and for all living things.

Energy

Definition. Energy is the capacity to do work. In order for something to move or grow, energy must be supplied to it. For example, for an automobile to travel on the highway, gasoline must be burned in the engine to provide the energy to move the car. In a similar way, every living thing needs energy to live and perform work. Both plants and animals need energy to do the work needed. We will explore this process of energy and work in plants and animals.

Plants. As we saw in Section 2 of this LIFEPAC, green plants use the energy from sunlight in a chemical process called *photosynthesis*. Green plant cells contain organelles called chloroplasts, which, in turn, contain chlorophyll. Plants take in carbon dioxide gas through their leaves and water from their roots. The carbon dioxide and the water make their way to the leaves of the plant. In photosynthesis, the chlorophyll in the plant receives the energy needed from the sun to cause a chemical reaction with the carbon dioxide and the water in the plant. As a result, oxygen gas is produced, along with sugars and other materials that the plant can then use as food within its cells. The oxygen is given off through the leaves and provides the oxygen in the atmosphere around us. From the sugars produced by photosynthesis—together with nitrogen, sulfur, and phosphorus obtained from the soil through the roots—green plants can make "food." This food consists of starch, fat, protein, vitamins, and other complex compounds that are essential for life.

Through photosynthesis, green plants convert carbon dioxide and water into oxygen and "food." Plants and animals then "burn" this food by combining it with oxygen to release energy for growth and the other activities carried on by the cells. (Plants use some of the oxygen produced by photosynthesis to do this.) This process of combining food with oxygen to give energy for growth and development is called **respiration**. Respiration is the opposite of photosynthesis. In respiration, oxygen is used up and carbon dioxide and water are given off. Plants then use the carbon dioxide and water to produce more food and oxygen. Through this process of photosynthesis and respiration, God brings about the natural balance of carbon dioxide and oxygen in the earth's atmosphere.

Answer these questions.

3.1 What happens in a plant during photosynthesis? ____________________

____

____

____

____

3.2 Can photosynthesis take place at night when it is dark? ____________________

3.3 What happens in a plant during respiration? ____________________

____

____

____

____

Animals. All plants and animals need energy to live and perform work. As we have seen, plants receive energy through both photosynthesis (from the sunlight) and from respiration (from the "burning" of foods combining with oxygen). However, photosynthesis does not take place in animals and human beings. Animals and human beings can only receive energy through respiration. They do this by eating other plants and animals and "burning" these foods with oxygen during respiration.

In animals and human beings, oxygen is brought into the body through the breathing passages and the lungs. In the lungs, the oxygen is transferred to the red blood cells and then taken to every cell of the body through the blood stream. Food is brought into the body through eating and the body's digestive system. The blood stream also carries food particles from the digestive system to each cell in the body. The cell accepts the food and oxygen through the cell membrane. Then, respiration occurs when the food is combined with the oxygen, giving off energy the cell needs to perform its life and work. Respiration also results in carbon dioxide gas, and this carbon dioxide is transferred back through the cell membrane and into the blood stream. It is then carried back to the lungs, where it is exhaled from the body and enters the atmosphere for the plants to use.

Just as plants need energy for each cell, so do animals. The total body of an animal or human being cannot function properly unless each cell in the body is functioning properly. Animals must receive an adequate amount of food and oxygen for each cell of its body in order to produce the energy needed to live and carry on the activities of life.

Carbon cycle. Plants and animals depend on each other to carry on life. Plants must have adequate carbon dioxide given off by animals and human beings in order for the process of photosynthesis to take place. In turn, animals and human beings rely on plants for the oxygen and much of the food they receive. God has arranged this important cycle of energy in the world. This cycle is sometimes called the *carbon cycle*. This carbon cycle has been designed by God so that physical life on the earth may exist and continue.

| Carbon cycle

Write the correct letter and answer on each line.

3.4 In plants, photosynthesis produces ______________________________ .

a. carbon dioxide
b. chlorophyll
c. oxygen and sugars
d. water

3.5 Respiration takes place in ______________________________ .

a. plants only
b. both plants and animals
c. animals only
d. human beings only

3.6 In the lungs, oxygen is transferred to the ______________________ .

a. bone b. nerve cells c. chlorophyll d. red blood cells

3.7 Respiration occurs when oxygen combines with food, giving off ______________ .

a. white blood cells b. chlorophyll c. energy d. sugars

3.8 Plants and animals depend on ______________________ .

a. each other b. chlorophyll c. night d. nothing

Answer these questions.

3.9 How does the human body receive the energy it needs? ______________________

____

____

____

____

3.10 What is the carbon cycle? Explain. ______________________________

____

____

____

____

Cell Reproduction

Introduction. All living things begin as one cell. Some living things always remain as one cell (unicellular). However, for all living things that are multicellular, new cells must be produced from the original single cell. In addition, as some cells in multicellular living things die or are damaged, they have to be replaced. New cells must be produced. In addition, one generation of living things produces another generation. This also means that new cells must be produced. This process of producing new cells is called *cell* ***reproduction***. We will now discuss several ways for cell reproduction to occur in living things.

Mitosis. One of the most common ways that cells reproduce is called **mitosis**. It occurs in eukaryote cells only; that is, cells that have a cell membrane, cytoplasm, and a nucleus. Mitosis is the process of one cell splitting apart to form two new cells. This "splitting apart" of the cell is known as *cell division*. Mitosis brings about cell division and two new cells from one original cell.

Mitosis starts when the chromatin within the cell begins to rearrange and condense into orderly strands called *chromosomes*. The chromosomes then move into pairs. After that, the chromosome pairs begin to pull apart from each other. Eventually, the chromosome pairs split apart.

When they split apart, cell division occurs. Then there are two new cells instead of the original single cell. The two new cells are smaller than the original cell. However, because the DNA of the two new cells is the same as the original cell, the two new cells will be like the original cell,

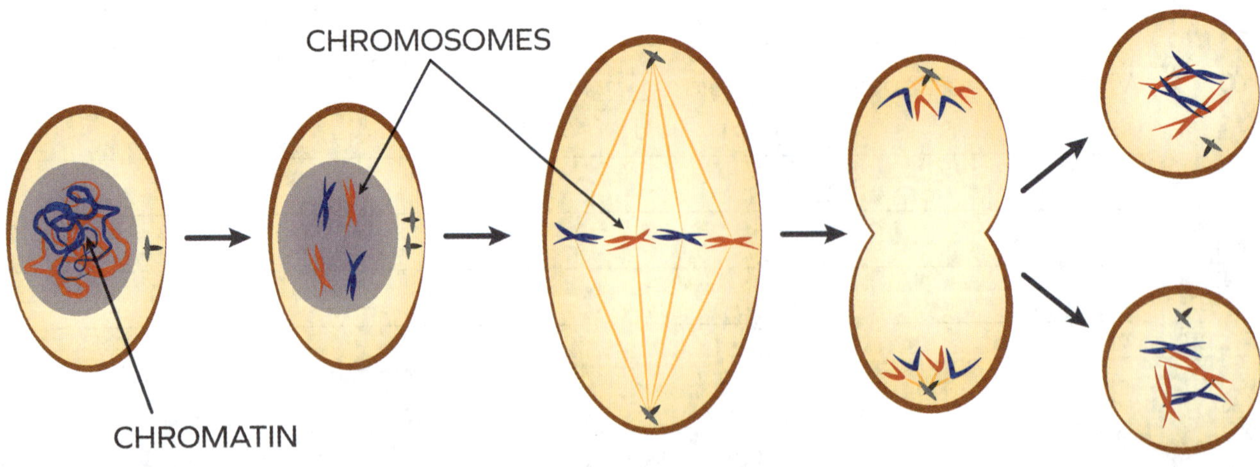

| Mitosis

only smaller. In time, the two new cells will grow larger in size, until they also begin the process of mitosis and split into new cells.

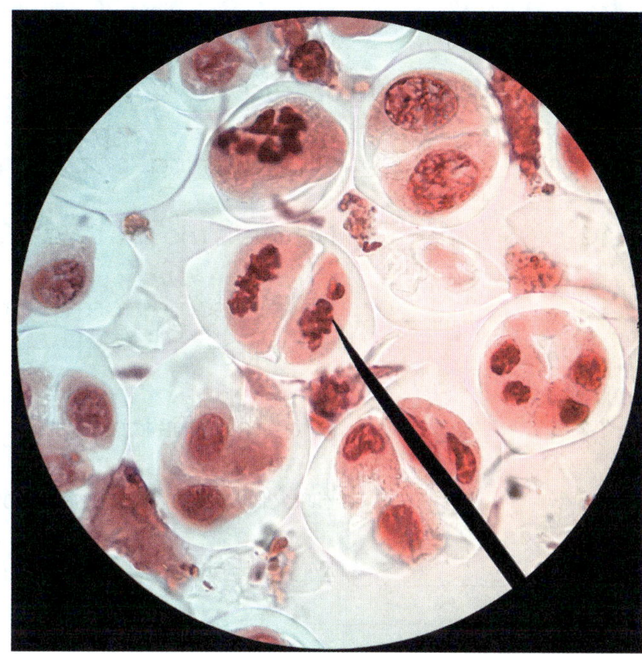
| Cells under a microscope undergoing mitosis

Mitosis is the way that most one-celled living things reproduce. New individual cells are formed whenever an individual cell divides through mitosis. The new cells appear to be just like the former cells, although they may be a bit smaller at first.

Mitosis also happens when cells are worn out, damaged, or need to be replaced. Skin cells and red blood cells are examples of cells that can replace themselves. Nerve cells, however, cannot be replaced when they are damaged. Some animals can replace lost body parts through mitosis!

Multicellular animals can grow by producing more cells than they lose. For example, a small cat grows into a larger cat by producing more cells. The cells of the larger cat are not larger than the cells of a smaller cat. There are just *more* cells in a larger cat than a smaller cat. Therefore, the size of a cat depends upon the number of cells that it has. Mitosis is the process by which a cat gets more cells and thus grows larger.

Budding. A few tiny organisms reproduce themselves through a process known as **budding**. In this process of cell reproduction, a small bud begins to form on the parent cell. The bud grows into a copy of the parent through mitosis. When the growing bud is able to survive, it separates from the parent and breaks away, forming a completely new cell. In the budding process of reproduction, only one parent is needed to form a new cell.

Male-female reproduction. Most of the multicellular plants and animals reproduce themselves by the process known as *male-female reproduction*. A cell from a male parent and a cell from a female parent join together to form a new cell. This process begins a new living thing that has characteristics of both parents. The newly formed cell then begins to reproduce itself through mitosis. This type of male-female reproduction will be covered in more detail in a later science LIFEPAC.

Write *true* or *false*.

3.11 __________ All living things begin as two cells.

3.12 __________ Mitosis is the process of one cell splitting apart to form two cells.

3.13 __________ Chromosomes form from the cell chromatin before the cell begins to divide.

3.14 __________ A large cat is larger than a smaller cat because it has larger cells.

3.15 __________ Budding is a way that some very tiny organisms can reproduce.

3.16 __________ Male-female reproduction needs two parent cells to begin.

Write the answers on the lines.

3.17 For all multicellular living things, ____________________ cells must be produced from the original single cell.

3.18 The most common way that cells reproduce is called ____________________ .

3.19 The "splitting apart" of cells is known as ____________________ .

3.20 Skin cells and ____________________ cells are examples of cells that can replace themselves.

3.21 ____________________ cells cannot be replaced when they are damaged.

Write what you know about cells.

3.22 In this LIFEPAC, you have learned a lot about cells. Imagine that you are going to meet someone who had never heard about cells or what they were. How would you explain cells to this person in a short but clear way?

In this activity, you are asked to write your explanation about cells on a separate piece of paper. Then read over your explanation and see if it is clear. Will the person know what a cell is after reading your explanation? Did you explain what cells are? Did you mention anything about the shape and size of cells? Did you mention tissues, energy, and cell reproduction? Finally, did you say anything about God in your explanation?

After you correct your explanation on the separate piece of paper and check it for correct spelling, write your explanation below in your best handwriting.

____

____

____

____

____

____

____

____

____

____

____

____

____

____

Teacher check:

Initials ____________ Date ____________

Before you take this last Self Test, you may want to do one or more of these self checks.

1. ________ Read the objectives. See if you can do them.
2. ________ Restudy the material related to any objectives that you cannot do.
3. ________ Use the **SQ3R** study procedure to review the material:
   a. **S**can the sections.
   b. **Q**uestion yourself.
   c. **R**ead to answer your questions.
   d. **R**ecite the answers to yourself.
   e. **R**eview areas you did not understand.
4. ________ Review all vocabulary, activities, and Self Tests, writing a correct answer for every wrong answer.

SELF TEST 3

Write *true* or *false* (each answer, 2 points).

3.01 ________ Some animals can replace lost body parts by growing new ones.

3.02 ________ Nerve cells can be replaced after they are damaged.

3.03 ________ A cell is the basic unit of life.

3.04 ________ A cell with a cell membrane, cytoplasm, and nucleus is a prokaryote cell.

3.05 ________ Mitosis is the process of one cell splitting apart to form two cells.

3.06 ________ Chromatin consists of long strands of material located within the nuclear membrane.

3.07 ________ The process of producing new cells is called cell reproduction.

3.08 ________ A cell wall is found only in plants.

3.09 ________ Energy is the capacity to do work.

3.010 ________ Green plants use energy from sunlight in a process called respiration.

3.011 ________ Animals and plants rely on each other in a process called the carbon cycle.

Write the correct letter on each blank space (each answer, 4 points).

3.012 Scientists are still making new ________ today about cells.

a. computer programs
b. textbooks
c. discoveries
d. names

3.013 Some shapes of cells include ________ .

a. round and oval
b. hearts and corkscrews
c. cubed and columnar
d. all of these

3.014 Chloroplasts are a category of ________ found in the cells of green plants.

a. organelles
b. bacteria
c. tissues
d. protozoa

3.015 Photosynthesis in plants produces water and ________ .

a. oxygen
b. carbon dioxide
c. chlorophyll
d. protoplasm

3.016 __________ cells fight infections and harmful substances that invade the body.

a. Unicellular b. Epithelial c. White blood d. Muscle

3.017 The splitting apart of cells is known as __________ .

a. cell division b. kenosis

c. energy production d. fusion

Write the correct answer (each answer, 5 points).

3.018 What cell tissue helps carry messages? ______________________

3.019 What cell tissue helps animals and humans move? ______________________

3.020 What molecules form the double layer of cell membranes?

____

3.021 The chromatin within a nucleus is made up of what three components?

a. ______________________ b. ______________________

c. ______________________

Answer these questions (each answer, 6 points).

3.022 How does mitosis work in reproducing cells? Describe.

____

____

____

____

3.023 How do most multicellular plants and animals reproduce themselves? Briefly describe. ______________________

____

____

____

____

3.024 What is the difference between photosynthesis and respiration?

____

____

____

____

3.025 What is helpful in viewing most cells? ____________________

____

____

____

____

In the Introduction to this LIFEPAC, you asked some questions about cells. Go back and check to see if you learned the answers in this LIFEPAC. You also wrote down some of the things that you knew about cells. Were your ideas correct? ________ (yes/no) Do you have more questions about cells? If you do, write your questions in the following space and discuss them with your teacher.

____

____

____

____

____

____

____

____

____

____

____

____

____

____

Teacher check: Initials ____________

Score ____________ Date ____________

80/100

Before you take the LIFEPAC Test, you may want to do one or more of these self checks.

1. ________ Read the objectives. See if you can do them.
2. ________ Restudy the material related to any objectives that you cannot do.
3. ________ Use the **SQ3R** study procedure to review the material.
4. ________ Review activities, Self Tests, and LIFEPAC vocabulary words.
5. ________ Restudy areas of weakness indicated by the last Self Test.

NOTES

NOTES

NOTES

SCIENCE 502
PLANTS: LIFE CYCLES

Author:
Barry G. Burrus, M.Div, M.A., B.S.

Editor:
Brian Ring

Illustrations:
Brian Ring

Media Credits:
Page 3: © Nancy Kennedy, iStock, Thinkstock; **5:** © Top Photo Corporation, Thinkstock; **9:** © John Seiler, iStock, Thinkstock; **10:** © Daniel Cole, Hemera, Thinkstock; **15:** © Gyro Photography, amanaimages, Thinkstock; **20:** © loveischiangrai, iStock, Thinkstock; **21:** © richterfoto, iStock, Thinkstock; **22:** © Dušan Kostić, iStock, Thinkstock; © tchara, iStock, Thinkstock; © aerogondo, iStock, Thinkstock; **23, 28:** © Dorling Kindersley, Thinkstock; **28:** © Eraxion, iStock, Thinkstock; © Elena Belyakova, iStock, Thinkstock; **30:** © lindavostrovska, iStock, Thinkstock; **35:** © fotosd, iStock, Thinkstock; **41:** © monkeybusinessimages, iStock, Thinkstock; **45:** © Ralph A. Clevenger, Fuse, Thinkstock; **48:** © BIOphotos, iStock, Thinkstock; **49:** © Dorling Kindersley, Thinkstock; **51:** © Photos.com, Thinkstock; **52:** © AnnekeDeBlok, iStock, Thinkstock; **59:** © micro_photo, iStock, Thinkstock; **60:** © Wlad74, iStock, Thinkstock.

804 N. 2nd Ave. E.
Rock Rapids, IA 51246-1759

PLANTS: LIFE CYCLES

Plants are among the living things that God has created upon the earth. In the Book of Genesis, we read: "And God said, Let the earth bring forth grass, the herb yielding seed, and the fruit tree yielding fruit after his kind, whose seed is in itself, upon the earth: and it was so. And the earth brought forth grass, and herb yielding seed after his kind, and the tree yielding fruit, whose seed was in itself, after his kind: and God saw that it was good." (Genesis 1:11-12). All of these living things are the part of God's creation called plants.

In this LIFEPAC® you will learn about various kinds of plants, fungi, and protists. Fungi and protists have some similarity to plants, but they are also different. You will examine aspects of the life cycles of these living things. You will learn about some differences among plants, fungi, and protists. You will also learn about their common structures of and the ways they reproduce. Finally, you will have an opportunity to observe some of these living things close-up during experiments!

Objectives

Read these objectives. The objectives tell you what you will be able to do when you have successfully completed this LIFEPAC. Each section will list according to the numbers below what objectives will be met in that section. When you have finished this LIFEPAC, you should be able to:

1. Classify all living things into one of five kingdoms.
2. Identify the main kinds and parts of plants.
3. Describe the life cycles of plants, fungi, and some protists.
4. Identify the main reproductive parts of seed-bearing and spore-bearing organisms.
5. Classify plants, fungi, and protists you observe.
6. Explain differences between the main categories of plants, fungi, and protists.
7. Relate the structure of plants, fungi, and protists with their reproduction in a life cycle.

1. CLASSIFYING LIVING THINGS AND PLANTS

God has created a great variety of living things on the earth. God has placed these living things throughout the earth in all regions and environments. Many scientists today classify all living things into five main groups. These five groups are sometimes called *kingdoms*. The five kingdoms of living things are (1) animals, (2) plants, (3) fungi, (4) protists, and (5) monerans.

These living things are classified within one of these five kingdoms because they share certain basic characteristics. There are several characteristics that scientists consider when classifying living things. Some of these basic characteristics include the physical structure and make-up, the means of obtaining food, and the means of reproduction. For example, protists and monerans are simple, tiny organisms made up of one cell or only a few types of cells, while plants and animals are complex organisms made up of many types of cells. Fungi can be simple, one-celled organisms, or they may be more complex. But all fungi are organisms that lack chlorophyll, the green coloring that many plants use to make food and oxygen. Therefore, fungi must obtain their food from outside sources. Table 1 shows some characteristics and examples of living things within each of the five kingdoms.

Objectives

Review these objectives. When you have completed this section, you should be able to:

1. Classify all living things into one of five kingdoms.
2. Identify the main kinds and parts of plants.
3. Describe the life cycles of plants, fungi, and some protists.
4. Explain differences between the main categories of plants, fungi, and protists.

Vocabulary

Study these new words. Learning the meanings of these words is a good study habit and will improve your understanding of this LIFEPAC.

adulthood (ə dult′ hůd). The time of life when an organism is grown up enough to reproduce.

algae (al′ jē). A group of water plants. Some have many cells. Others have one cell.

botany (bot′ n ē). The study of plants.

fungi (fun′ jī). One of the five main kingdoms of living things. They do not produce chlorophyll.

monerans (mo ner′ uns). Very tiny and simple organisms that are one of the five main kingdoms of living things.

protists (prō′ tists). One of the five main categories of living things. They are tiny organisms.

spores (spôrz). Spores are tiny, specialized structures that are able to grow into a new organism. Spores help an organism survive and move from place to place.

vegetative (vej′ ə tā′ tiv). The parts of a flowering plant that include the roots, stems, and leaves. It is also another form of reproduction of some plants.

yeast (yēst). A single-celled fungi.

Note: *All vocabulary words in this LIFEPAC appear in* **boldface** *print the first time they are used. If you are unsure of the meaning when you are reading, study the definitions given.*

Pronunciation Key: h**a**t, **ā**ge, c**ã**re, f**ä**r; l**e**t, **ē**qual, t**ė**rm; **i**t, **ī**ce; h**o**t, **ō**pen, **ô**rder; **oi**l; **ou**t; c**u**p, p**ů**t, r**ü**le; **ch**ild; lo**ng**; **th**in; /ŦH/ for **th**en; /zh/ for mea**s**ure; /u/ or /ə/ represents /a/ in **a**bout, /e/ in tak**e**n, /i/ in penc**i**l, /o/ in lem**o**n, and /u/ in circ**u**s.

KINGDOM	CELL TYPE	FOOD	EXAMPLES
Animals	multicellular	obtain from outside sources	worms, insects, birds, fish, mammals
Plants	multicellular	produce their own	moss, trees, flowering plants
Fungi	unicellular or multicellular	obtain from outside sources	mushrooms, **yeast**, mold
Protists	unicellular or multicellular	produce their own and obtain from outside sources	protozoa, paramecium, green **algae**, red algae
Monerans	unicellular or multicellular	engulfed from outside sources	bacteria, blue-green algae

Table 1 | Classifying Living Things

In this LIFEPAC, we will examine some similarities and differences among various types of plants, fungi, protists, and monerans. We will especially focus on plants. In the next LIFEPAC, we will focus on animals.

In this section of the LIFEPAC, we will explore the kinds of plants, the structure of plants, and explain what is meant by the *life cycle* of living things.

Write the answers on the lines.

1.1 ______________ has created a great variety of living things.

1.2 Scientists classify all living things into five ______________________________ .

1.3 The five ______________________________ of all living things are:

a. ______________________________ b. ______________________________

c. ______________________________ d. ______________________________

e. ______________________________

Answer these questions.

1.4 What are some of the basic characteristics that scientists consider when classifying living things?

____

____

____

____

1.5 How do fungi differ from green plants?

____

____

____

____

1.6 What are two examples in each of the five kingdoms of living things?

____

____

____

____

Kinds of Plants

Plants are very important to us. Plants furnish people with the oxygen we breathe. The food we eat comes from plants or animals that eat plants. Plants also supply us with clothing from the fibers of plants such as cotton. Much of our shelter comes from plants, such as the lumber from trees used in building our homes. God has given us plants to support our life on earth.

Plants are one of the most common of the living things that you see every day. Grass, trees, flowers, and shrubs are some of the types of plants that are around you. There are probably over 260,000 kinds of plants on the earth! They vary greatly in size. Some plants that grow on forest floors are so tiny that they can barely be seen. Others, such as the giant sequoia trees growing in California are among the largest of all living things. These trees can grow to over 290 feet high and measure over 30 feet wide!

The study of plants is called **botany**, and the people who study plants are called botanists. Botanists classify plants into five basic groups. You will learn more about two of these plant groups in this LIFEPAC. One of these groups is seed-bearing plants. You will learn more about seed-bearing plants in Section 2 of this LIFEPAC. Ferns are another important group of plants. You will learn more about ferns in Section 3 of this LIFEPAC.

| Giant Sequoia tree

Activity 502.A Observing Plants

1.7 Go outside to your yard or to a park and observe the different kinds of plants that you see. Make a list of as many types of plants as you can identify and share this list with your teacher.

Teacher check:

Initials ____________________ Date ____________________

Parts of Plants

All living things, including plants, are made up of cells. All plants are multicellular; that is, they have many cells. The cells are organized in each plant to perform different functions. Each group of cells with a similar function is called a *tissue*. Plants have several types of tissues. As you learned in a previous LIFEPAC on cells, there are four main types of plant tissues: (1) epidermal, (2) connective, (3) storage, and (4) support. The epidermal tissues provide plant cover in the leaves as well as the roots. The connective tissues help the water, gases, and food compounds to travel to various parts of the plant. Storage tissues are contained in the leaves to store fat-type materials for the plant. Some plants, such as beets, carrots, radishes, and sweet potatoes, also have storage tissues in the roots to help store food for the plant. Finally, the support tissues help support the plant and keep it stable.

Plants also have different *parts*. Flowering plants, the most common type of plants, have four main parts: (1) roots, (2) leaves, (3) stems, and (4) flowers. The roots , stems, and leaves are called the **vegetative** parts of a plant. The flowers, fruits, and seeds are known as the reproductive parts of the plant. We will learn more about the reproductive parts of flowering plants in Section 2 of this LIFEPAC.

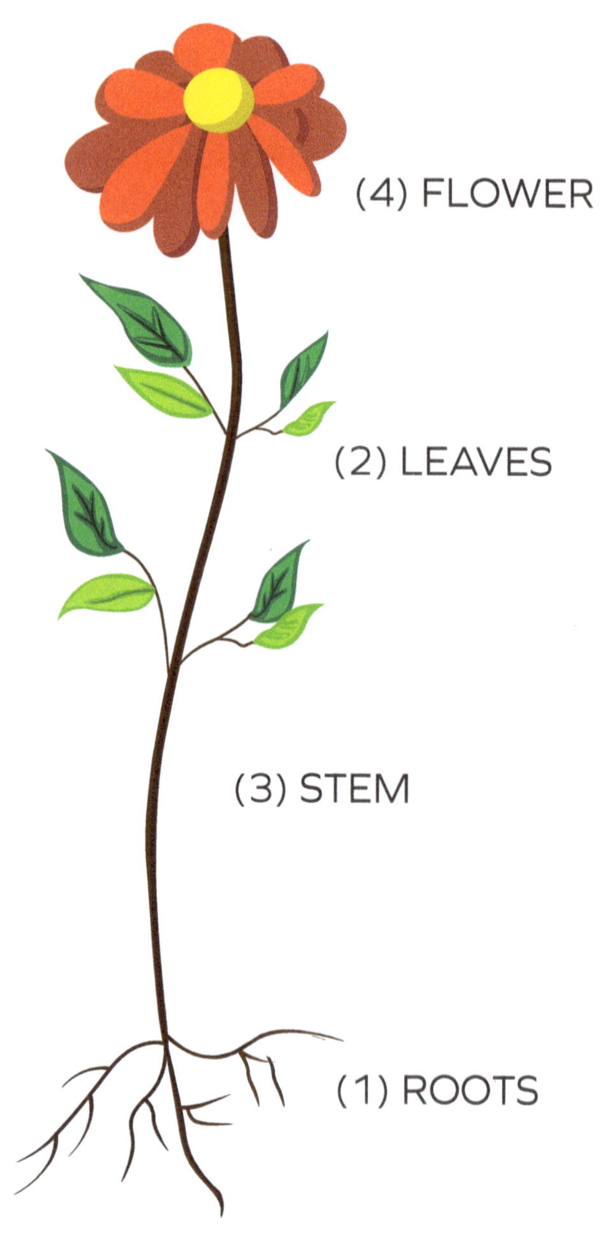

| Four parts of a flowering plant

Life Cycles

All living things go through *life stages*. For example, they all have a beginning life stage and an ending life stage. Most living things also have a growth stage and a stage for **adulthood**. All of these stages for a living thing are called a *life cycle*. Similarity in life cycles is also one way we can classify or categorize living things. Many types of plants have similar life cycles. Some plants also have a similar life cycle to types of fungi and protists. Therefore, in this LIFEPAC, we will focus on similarities in life cycles among various types of plants, fungi, and protists.

The stages of life are important in the life cycle of any living thing. For example, consider the life cycle of a typical corn plant. The four stages of the life cycle of a corn plant are (1) beginning, (2) growth, (3) adulthood, and (4) death — or end. The beginning stage of a corn plant starts when a new seed is made. After the seed is planted and receives proper nourishment of water and minerals, it enters the growth stage. The seed begins to develop into a mature plant. The mature plant occurs when the plant reaches adulthood and begins to produce ears of corn and many new seeds. Finally, the last stage is when the corn plant comes to an end and dies. These four stages in the lifetime of a corn plant are the life cycle of the corn plant.

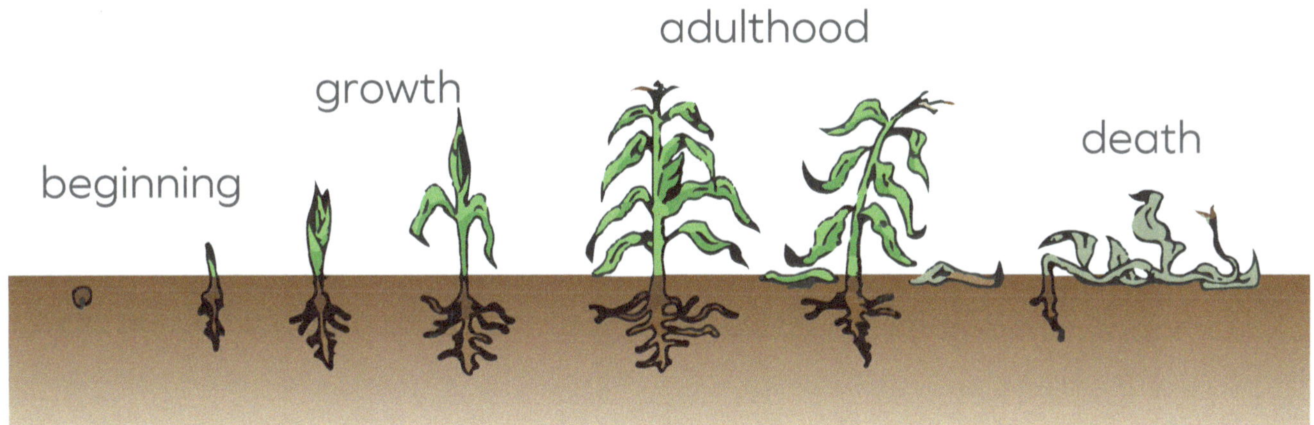

| Life cycle of a corn plant

In the remaining sections of this LIFEPAC, we will explore the similar life cycles of 3 categories of living things: (1) seed-bearing plants, (2) **spore**-bearing plants and fungi, and (3) one-celled fungi and protists.

Answer *true* or *false*.

1.8 __________ Plants furnish people with oxygen.

1.9 __________ Plants do not vary greatly in size.

1.10 __________ Plants are both unicellular and multicellular.

1.11 __________ Cells that perform similar functions in a plant are called tissue.

1.12 __________ The roots, stems, and leaves of flowering plants are called the vegetative parts.

1.13 __________ All living things have a life cycle.

1.14 __________ The last life stage of a corn plant occurs when the seed begins to grow.

Answer these questions.

1.15 What are the four types of tissues in a plant?

a. ____________________

b. ____________________

c. ____________________

d. ____________________

1.16 What are the four main parts of flowering plants?

a. ____________________

b. ____________________

c. ____________________

d. ____________________

1.17 What are the four life stages of a corn plant?

a. ____________________

b. ____________________

c. ____________________

d. ____________________

Review the material in this section to prepare for the Self Test. The Self Test will check your understanding of this section. Any items you miss on this test will show you what areas you will need to restudy in order to prepare for the unit test.

SELF TEST 1

Match these items (each answer, 2 points).

1.01 __________ animals
1.02 __________ plants
1.03 __________ fungi
1.04 __________ protists
1.05 __________ monerans
1.06 __________ kingdoms
1.07 __________ botany
1.08 __________ reproductive parts
1.09 __________ vegetative parts
1.010 __________ epidermis

a. the study of plants
b. flowers, fruits, and seeds
c. roots, stems, and leaves
d. provides plant cover on leaves and roots
e. storage tissue
f. over 290 feet high
g. five main groups of all living things
h. bacteria, blue-green algae
i. protozoa, red algae
j. yeast, molds
k. moss, trees
l. insects, birds

Complete these statements (each answer, 4 points).

1.011 ________________ has created a great variety of living things.

1.012 Some of the basic characteristics of all living things include the physical structure and make-up, the means of obtaining ________________, and the means of reproduction.

1.013 Fungi can be unicellular or ____________________________.

1.014 There are probably over ________________________ kinds of plants on earth.

1.015 All living things go through ________________ stages.

Write the life stages of a corn plant in the proper order (each answer, 5 points).

1.016 ________________________________

1.017 ________________________________

1.018 ________________________________

1.019 ________________________________

Write the correct letter and answer on the blank (each answer, 4 points).

1.020 All fungi lack ______________________ .

a. roots b. stems c. chlorophyll

1.021 People who study plants are called ______________________ .

a. botanists b. chemists c. physicians

1.022 A mature corn plant occurs when the plant reaches ______________________ .

a. five feet b. old age c. adulthood

1.023 The total number of life stages for a living thing is called a ______________________ .

a. growth period b. life cycle c. tissue

1.024 Some plants have a similar life cycle to ______________________ .

a. fungi b. protists c. both a and b

Answer this question (each answer, 5 points).

1.025 What are the four main parts of a flowering plant?

a. ______________________

b. ______________________

c. ______________________

d. ______________________

Teacher check: Initials ____________

Score ______________________ Date ____________

80
100

2. SEED-BEARING PLANTS

You have probably seen many kinds of seeds. Apple seeds, corn seeds, and flower seeds are some common ones. All of the plants that produce seeds are called *seed-bearing plants*. God has created many different varieties of seed-bearing plants. In this section, you will learn about the two major types of seed-bearing plants: (1) flowering plants called angiosperms, and (2) cone-bearing plants called gymnosperms. You will learn about the main parts of these seed-bearing plants. You will also learn something about the life stages and life cycle of seed-bearing plants.

Objectives

Review these objectives. When you have completed this section, you should be able to:

3. Describe the life cycles of plants, fungi, and some protists.
4. Identify the main reproductive parts of seed-bearing and spore-bearing organism.
5. Classify plants, fungi, and protists you observe.
6. Explain differences between the main categories of plants, fungi, and protists.
7. Relate the structure of plants, fungi, and protists with their reproduction in a life cycle.

Vocabulary

Study these new words. Learning the meanings of these words is a good study habit and will improve your understanding of this LIFEPAC.

angiosperms (an′ jē ō spurmz). A name given to flowering plants.
anther (an′ thər). The part of a plant where pollen is made.
delicate (del′ ə kit). Easily hurt or broken.
digestion (də jes′ chən). The act of changing food into a form that cells use for energy.
embryo (em′ brē ō). The little plant inside a seed.
fertilization (fėr′ tl ə zā′ shən). When a sperm cell joins an egg cell, a new life is started.
filament (fil′ ə mənt). One of the male parts of a flowering plant that connects to the anther.

gymnosperms (jim′ nuh spurmz). A name given to nonflowering plants that produce seeds. They are cone-bearers.

offspring (ôf′ spring). The result of reproduction. A new organism that will grow up to be similar to the parent.

ovary (ō′ vər ē). The part of the plant that makes and holds the egg cells.

petal (pet′ l). The brightly colored part of the flower that is easiest to see.

pistil (pis′ tl). The part of a flower where seeds form and that is made up of the ovary, style, and stigma.

pollen (pol′ ən). Grains of dusty powder formed by flowers to carry sperm cells.

sacs (saks). Little bags on certain plant parts that hold something.

sperm (spėrm). The male cell that must join the female cell to begin new life.

stamen (stā′ mən). The part of the flower where pollen is stored. It is made up of the anther and the filament.

stigma (stig′mə). The part of the flower that takes in pollen.

style (stīl). The tube that connects the stigma to the ovary.

Pronunciation Key: hat, āge, cãre, fär; let, ēqual, tėrm; it, īce; hot, ōpen, ôrder; oil; out; cup, pu̇t, rüle; child; long; thin; /ŦH/ for then; /zh/ for measure; /u/ or /ə/ represents /a/ in about, /e/ in taken, /i/ in pencil, /o/ in lemon, and /u/ in circus.

Life Stages

Seed-bearing plants have a life cycle similar to the corn plant that you examined in Section 1 of this LIFEPAC. In fact, corn is a seed-bearing plant. There are four main life stages in the life cycle of these seed-bearing plants. They are (1) beginning stage, (2) growth stage, (3) adult stage, and (4) death stage. Let us examine in more detail each of these stages in the life of seed-bearing plants.

Beginning stage. The first stage in seed-bearing plants begins with reproduction. Most of these plants begin life when a single cell called the *egg cell* is joined with another single cell called the **sperm** cell. The process of joining the egg and sperm cells is called **fertilization**. Without fertilization, neither the sperm cell nor the egg cell could continue to live. Once the sperm cell and egg cell join together in fertilization, they combine to form a single new cell called the *fertilized egg*. It is from the fertilized egg cell that the new plant begins to grow.

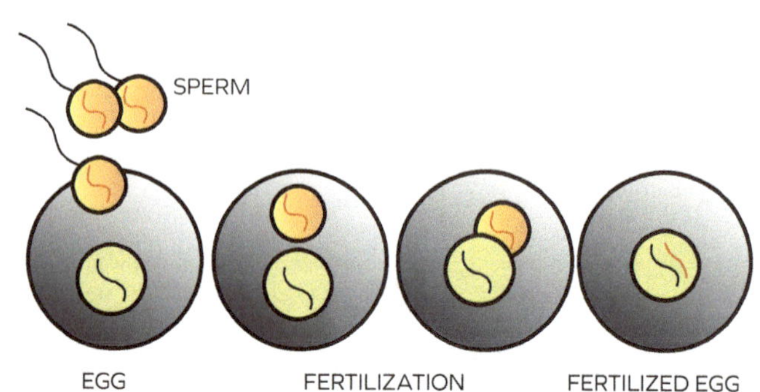

| Fertilization process

Egg cells and sperm cells are located in different parts of seed-bearing plants. You will learn more about their locations later in this section of this LIFEPAC. However, in order for the sperm to fertilize the egg, the sperm must move from its location on the plant to an egg cell located on another part of that plant or even another plant. Sperm cells move in the form of **pollen**. Often, the pollen must travel through the air to reach an egg cell in another location. When the sperm does reach the egg cell and fertilization takes place, a new plant begins.

Complete these statements.

2.1 Plants that produce seeds are called ______________________________ .

2.2 Angiosperms are commonly known as ______________________ plants.

2.3 Cone-bearing plants are also called ___________________________ .

2.4 The process of the joining of sperm and egg cells is known as

________________________ .

2.5 Sperm cells move in the form of ______________________ .

Growth stage. A new plant begins with fertilization. The new fertilized egg cell of the plant will eventually divide into two new cells. These two cells will then divide again, forming four new cells. From the previous LIFEPAC in this Science series, you might remember that this process of cell division is called *mitosis*. The new plant cells will continue to divide until eventually a *seed* is formed. This formation of a seed through the process of mitosis is the first part of the *growth stage* of the plant. For flowering plants (angiosperms), the seed will be contained in part of the flower or the fruit of the plant. For cone-bearing plants (gymnosperms), the seed grows in a cone.

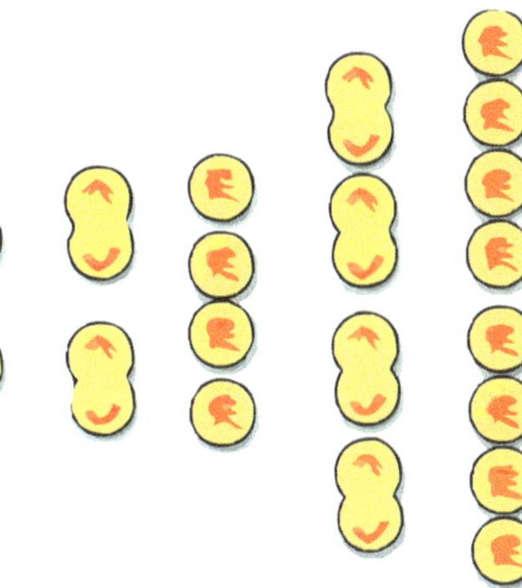

| Mitosis: The Process of Cell Division

The second part of the growth stage of a seed-bearing plant comes after the seed is planted and watered. The food from the seed and the water from the soil help the new plant begin to grow from the seed. After leaves are formed on the plant, the young plant begins to make its own food and grows until it begins the adult stage of the plant.

Review.

2.6 You studied the term mitosis in the first LIFEPAC of this series (Science LIFEPAC 501). A good understanding of mitosis is very important as you study the life cycles of plants and other living things. In the space below, write what you remember about mitosis and the process that occurs during mitosis.

____

____

____

____

____

____

____

____

2.7 Now refer to the Science LIFEPAC 501 to check yourself and your answers. Please correct any mistakes and add any missing information. Write your corrected statements on mitosis here.

____

____

____

____

____

____

____

____

Adult stage. The plant reaches the adult stage (adulthood) when it is ready to reproduce. Some adult plants are fully grown and do not continue to grow. Others continue to grow each year, even though they are in the adult stage. Trees are an example of this yearly growth. Even though adult trees reproduce each year, they also continue to grow each year.

Each adult plant may make many egg cells during reproduction. These egg cells can then be fertilized by sperm cells and form new seeds and, ultimately, new plants. The new plants — the **offspring** — are formed just like the parent plant was when it began its life cycle. The new seeds grow, and life for this species of plant continues. We will examine the reproductive parts of the adult plants and other living things in more detail later in this LIFEPAC.

Death stage. Eventually, every adult plant will enter old age and begin to die. Some seed-producing plants in adulthood may be able to reproduce only one time, and they usually die within a short time. Others may have many more periods of reproduction and produce new seeds during each of these periods. Whatever the case, old age causes some parts of the plant to become weaker, and eventually, the plant will die.

Match these items.

2.8	________ forms a seed through mitosis	a. beginning stage
2.9	________ sperm cell and egg cell join	b. growth stage
2.10	________ leaves are formed	c. adult stage
2.11	________ plant begins to make its own food	d. death stage
2.12	________ plant is ready to reproduce	
2.13	________ plant makes many egg cells	
2.14	________ old age brings final changes in plant	

Flowering Plants

Flowering plants are the most common type of seed-bearing plants. They make up about 90 percent of the more than 260,000 kinds of plants! Flowering plants are also called **angiosperms**. This name comes from two Greek words meaning "enclosed seed." All plants that produce flowers and fruits are called angiosperms.

Since flowering plants are the most common type of plants, you have probably seen many kinds of flowering plants. For example, wild flowers, garden plants, and most trees are flowering plants. In fact, most of the plants that produce the fruits, grains, and vegetables that you and your family eat are flowering plants.

Many flowering plants are grown for their flowers. Tulips, roses, pansies, and lilacs are examples. They are beautiful when their flowers appear, and they also smell very good. God has given us many pleasing things to see, touch, and smell. Flowering plants are some of the most beautiful things God has created. In fact, Jesus referred to the beauty of the flowers of the field when he said, "Consider the lilies of the field, how they grow; they toil not, neither do they spin: And yet I say unto you, That even Solomon in all his glory was not arrayed like one of these." (Matthew 6:28-29)

| Tulips

Other flowering plants are grown for their fruit or vegetables that they provide as food. Watermelons, cucumbers, cherries, and tomatoes are all examples of these types of flowering plants. Where are the flowers on these plants? The flowers appear during a life stage of the plant before the fruit or vegetable appears! (We will examine this in more detail later in this section.) God is so good to give us such a great variety of flowering plants as food.

| Orange trees blossom flowers before they produce fruit.

Activity 502.B Flowering Plant Poster

2.15 Make a poster from pictures or drawings in magazines, newspapers, printouts from Internet sites, etc. showing different types of flowering plants. Try to find a variety of flowering plants for your poster. Find one flowering plant that is very unusual, and find out more about that plant and where it grows. Then write a one-half page report on that plant.

Teacher check:

Initials ________________ Date ________________

| Flowering plants grown for their fruit

Structure of flowering plants. The main purpose of the flower in a flowering plant is to accomplish reproduction. Each part of the flowers structure is designed by God so that reproduction of the plant can occur. However, even if reproduction in the flower does not occur, the flower is still a flower, and it can still be pleasing to see and smell.

Most of the common flowering plants have a structure that contains both male and female parts. However, there are other flowering plants that produce flowers with separate male and female parts. For reproduction to take place in plants, both male and female parts must be present, but the parts do not need to be present in the same flower or even on the same plant.

The tulip is a flower that contains within itself both male and female parts. The outer part of the flower is called the **petal**. Some flowers have petals of different colors. Petals protect the tiny, more **delicate** parts of the flower located inside the petal. The petals also help the flower to collect pollen so that the sperm may fertilize the egg cells of the plant.

To observe the other parts of a flower, it is helpful to look at a cross-section of the flower. We will look now at a cross-section of a flower that contains both male and female parts. After examining this drawing of the cross-section of the flower, you will have the opportunity to do an experiment where you will examine these parts of a flower.

Let us first consider the female part of the flower. The female part is called the **pistil**. The pistil consists of three smaller parts, all of which make up the female reproductive parts of the flower. Looking at the cross-section of a flower, you will see the **ovary** located at the base of the flower below the petals. The ovary contains the egg cell (or egg cells if there are more than one) of the plant. Growing up from the ovary is a stalk-like tube called the **style**. The style serves as a connecting tube to allow the egg cells in the ovary to be fertilized. At the end of each style is a **stigma**. The stigma contains a sticky substance which allows pollen containing the sperm cells to be captured. Once the pollen is captured by the stigma, the sperm cells in the pollen can travel down the style to the ovary.

The male parts of the flower are contained in the **stamen**. The stamen consists of two important parts: the **filament** and the **anther**. The filament grows out of the center section of the flower, and the anther is located at the end of the filament. Pollen is made and stored in the anther. Each grain of pollen holds a sperm cell. The process of reproduction can occur when pollen from the anther (a male part) travels to the stigma (a female part).

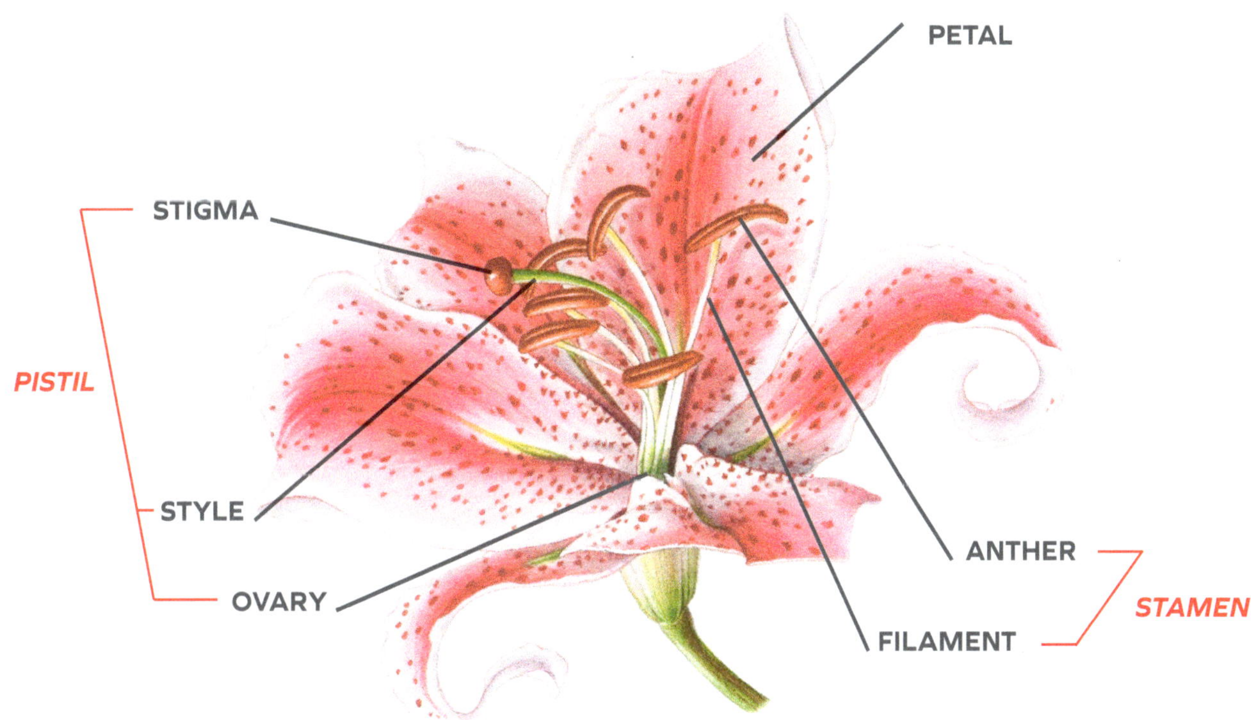

| Male and female parts of a flower

Activity 502.C Labeling Two Flowers

2.16 Select two different types of flowers from two different types of flowering plants. On a separate sheet of paper, draw each of the flowers. Label the parts you can see. (You can use the drawing from the cross-section of a flower above to help you identify the parts that you can see.)

Teacher check:

Initials ______________ Date ______________

Answer *true* or *false*.

2.17 __________ Flowering plants are the most common type of seed-bearing plants.

2.18 __________ Flowering plants are also called gymnosperms.

2.19 __________ The plants that produce most of the fruits, grains, and vegetables that people eat come from flowering plants.

2.20 __________ The pistil is the female part of a flowering plant.

2.21 __________ The petal is the male part of a flowing plant.

2.22 __________ Reproduction of a flowering plant can occur when the pollen from the anther reaches the stigma of the flower.

Answer this question.

2.23 In Matthew 6:28-29, what did Jesus mean when he compared the lilies of the field to Solomon?

____

____

____

____

____

____

EXPERIMENT 502.A FLOWER DISSECTION

View 502
FLOWER DISSECTION:
Grade 5 Science experiments video

You will dissect some flowers and look at their parts by using magnifying equipment.

These supplies are needed:

- 2 flowers
- straight pins
- microscope
- paper
- 2 microscope slides
- dropper
- 2 slide covers
- sharp knife
- magnifying glass or dissection scope

Follow these directions carefully. Select two different types of flowers. If possible, it would help to make one of your flowers a member of the lily family.

Call one of your flowers **Flower A** and the other one **Flower B**.
Complete the steps for **Flower A** first, and then complete the same steps for **Flower B**.
Place a check mark in the box as you complete each step for **Flower A**, and then place a check mark in the circle as you complete each step for **Flower B**.

A	B	
☐	○	1. Put the knife at the spot where the petals come together near the base of the flower.
☐	○	2. Slice the petals apart, moving toward the flower stem. Do not cut all the way through the flower.
☐	○	3. Pull back the petals and pin them down with the straight pins.

☐ ○ 4. Look closely at the flower with a magnifying glass or a dissection scope. Try to identify the different parts of the flower. (Use the cross-section drawing of the flower in this section of the LIFEPAC to help identify the parts. If needed, you may also consult an encyclopedia, the Internet, or a book on flowers to help you identify the parts of some flowers.)

☐ ○ 5. Make a drawing of each flower in the space below, showing the different parts of the flower. Label the parts.

Flower A **Flower B**

☐ ○ 6. Remove the stamens from the flower and tap some pollen from the stamens onto the microscope slide.

☐ ○ 7. Put a drop of water on the pollen that is on the slide and put a slide over the pollen on the slide.

☐ ○ 8. Place the slide under the microscope and focus until you observe the grains of pollen.

☐ ○ 9. Draw in the circles below what the pollen looks like in the microscope.

Flower A **Flower B**

☐ ○ 10. CAREFULLY cut the ovary in half by slicing it open toward the stem.

☐ ○ 11. Use the magnifying glass or dissection scope to help you see what the ovary looks like.

☐ ○ 12. Draw in the circles below what the sliced ovaries look life under magnification.

Flower A **Flower B**

Answer these questions.

2.24 In what ways were the flowers similar?

____

____

____

____

2.25 In what ways were the flowers different?

____

____

____

____

Teacher check:

Initials ______________ Date ______________

Fertilization. In order for fertilization to take place in a flowering plant, the flower has to grow sufficiently so that two things happen: (1) egg cells are produced in the ovary, and (2) pollen (and sperm cells) have been formed in the anther. When these things occur, the reproduction of the flowering plant can happen. It reproduces through the fertilization of the sperm cells with the egg cells of the plant.

The first step towards fertilization must be the movement of the pollen from the anther to the stigma. God has provided several ways for the movement of the pollen to occur. One way is for bees or insects to carry the pollen. They do this when they move inside the flower and touch the anther, rubbing off some of the pollen on their bodies. Then the bees or insects must touch the stigma and transfer some of the pollen from their bodies to the stigma.

Another way that the pollen can travel from the anther to the stigma is to be carried by the wind. The wind can blow the pollen from the anther to the stigma. Fortunately, God designed the stamen to produce much more pollen than is needed, so that even though some of the pollen is lost through the air by the wind, enough pollen is produced so that some of it lands on the stigma.

When the pollen reaches the stigma, it is held there for a time by the sticky surface of the stigma. Then a tube is formed by the pollen that leads down the style to the ovary. The sperm cell then moves down this tube to the ovary and egg cell. When the sperm cell reaches the egg cell in the ovary, fertilization occurs. A new plant life begins!

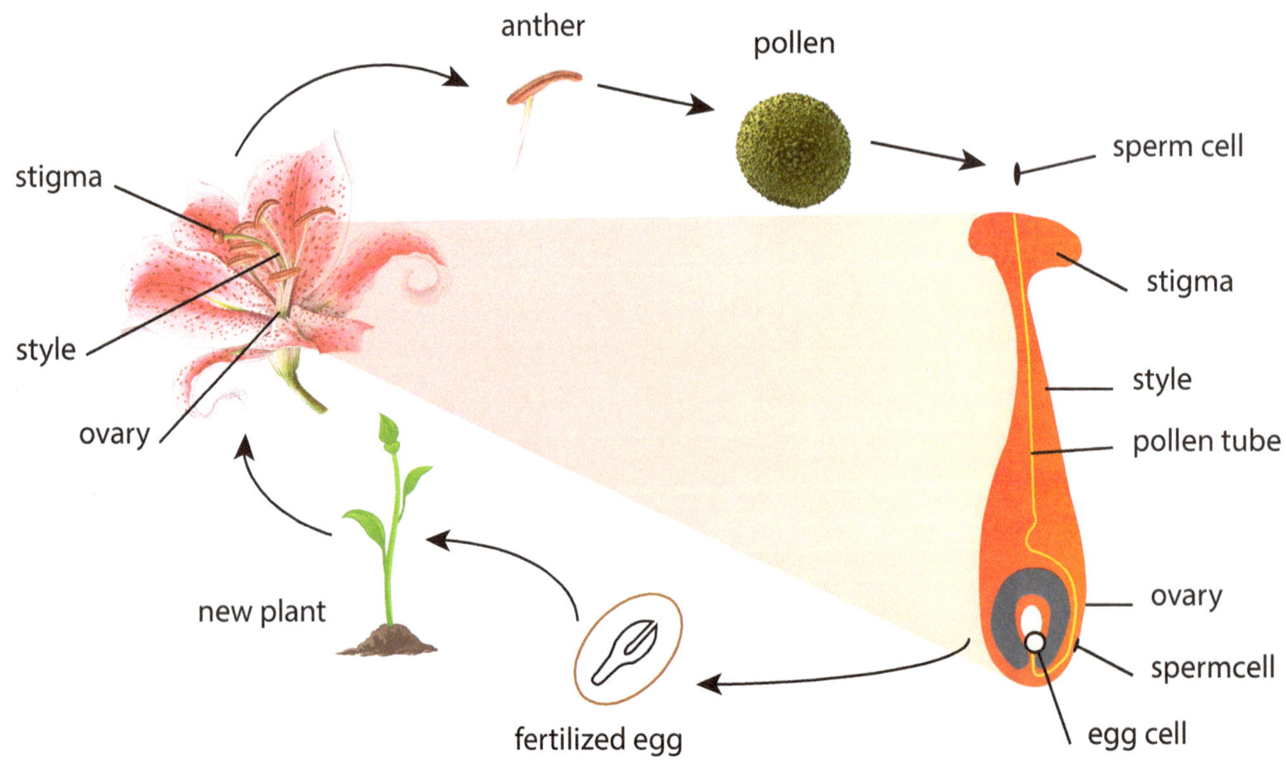

| Plant cycle

Complete these activities.

2.26 List the three female parts of a flower.

a. ______________________________

b. ______________________________

c. ______________________________

2.27 List the two male parts of a flower.

a. ______________________________

b. ______________________________

Write the correct answers. Use complete sentences.

2.28 What part of the flower makes pollen?

____

____

____

____

2.29 Describe how pollen gets to the stigma.

____

____

____

____

2.30 What happens to the pollen after it reaches the stigma?

____

____

____

____

Seeds and fruit. When the egg cell is fertilized by a sperm cell, a new cell is formed called the fertilized egg. This new cell then begins to grow into new cells through the process of mitosis. This continues until a seed is formed. A seed is really an **embryo** inside a seed coat. A supply of food is also stored around the embryo inside the seed.

As the seed develops, the flower's style and stamen dry up. The ovary begins to grow around the seed or seeds until it becomes fruit. You have probably seen such fruits as oranges, cherries, and apples that contain the fruit around the inner seeds. However, such flowering plants as squash, walnut, peas, and corn kernels are also considered "fruit."

God provided an amazing variety in the fruits of flowering plants. He made each fruit to serve several purposes. One purpose of the fruit is to carry the seeds and protect them. Another purpose of fruit is to help the seeds to get moved from one place to another. For example, dandelions have a very light seed container that allows easy movement in the wind. Cherries are eaten by birds, and the seeds pass through the birds' **digestion** without being damaged. When the birds' droppings containing the seeds fall to the ground, the seeds can begin to grow in the soil. Acorns and nuts can be moved from one location to another by squirrels. Some seeds are caught in animal fur because they contain hook-like structures on the seeds. These seeds are then transferred by the animal's movement from one place to another. Finally, people enjoy eating some fruits and throw away the seeds, which sometimes fall to the ground and begin to grow!

A third purpose of fruit is to provide an important food source for animals and people. Finally, God has given us many fruits that are very colorful — providing for beauty and enjoyment in nature.

Sometimes the fruit only contains one seed. Some fruits have many seeds. When more than one seed develops in a fruit, the flower's ovary contained several eggs that were fertilized.

| Fruit with seeds

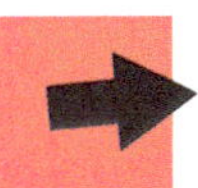

Activity 502.D Compare Some Fruits and Seeds

Select three different ripe fruits. (Remember that the dandelion, tomato, and pepper are also considered to be "fruit.")

Record the name of the three fruits that you use.

Fruit A ______________ Fruit B ______________ Fruit C ______________

Remove the seeds from the fruits. (If any of the fruits are food, you may eat the fruit!

2.31 How many seeds did each fruit have?

Fruit A ______________ Fruit B ______________ Fruit C ______________

2.32 Draw the shape of each seed in the space below.

Fruit A

Fruit B

Fruit C

2.33 Measure a seed from each fruit and record its length below.

Fruit A ______________ Fruit B ______________ Fruit C ______________

2.34 Describe how the seeds of each fruit could be moved from one place to another.

Fruit A ____

____

____

Fruit B ____

____

____

Fruit C ____

____

____

2.35 Make a chart from the information you gathered in this activity.

Give your chart a title. An example of your chart might look like the following.

TITLE OF CHART			
	A	**B**	**C**
Name of fruit			
# of seeds			
Shape of seeds			
Measurement (mm)			
How seed is moved			

Teacher check:

Initials ______________ Date ______________

EXPERIMENT 502.B SEED DISSECTION

View 502
SEED DISSECTION:
Grade 5 Science experiments video

You will observe the internal parts of a lima bean and a corn seed.

These supplies are needed:

lima bean seed
small glass of water
knife
tweezers
corn seed
magnifying glass or dissecting scope

Follow these directions carefully. Put a check mark in the box after completing each step.

☐ 1. Place the lima bean seed and the corn seed in the glass of water and let them soak overnight.

☐ 2. Remove the seeds from the water and CAREFULLY use the knife and tweezers to open each seed.

☐ 3. Observe each seed closely using a magnifying glass or a dissecting scope. (You should find two different sections inside each seed and the seed cover on the outside.)

☐ 4. Identify the food and embryo of each seed.

2.36 Record what you observe in the space below.

LIMA BEAN	CORN SEED

Teacher check:

Initials ____________ Date ____________

Vegetative reproduction. Many flowering plants can reproduce without having to grow from seeds. They do this by using a part of the plant to grow into an entirely new plant. This process is called *vegetative reproduction*. It is called this because the new plant does not come from the reproductive part or seeds of the old plant. Rather, it comes from the *vegetative* part of a parent plant, such as the root, stem, or leaf.

In addition to growing a plant from a seed, bulb, or spore, a plant can be grown from a cutting taken from the parent plant.

| Vegetative reproduction

Perhaps you have seen someone cut a stem from a plant and put the stem in soil. Eventually, the stem will produce the other parts of the plant such as the roots, leaves, and reproductive parts. Roses, fruit trees, and raspberries are usually reproduced in this way by people using the process of vegetative reproduction.

SCIENCE 502

LIFEPAC TEST

NAME ____________________

DATE ____________________

SCORE ____________________

80
100

SCIENCE 502: LIFEPAC TEST

Match these items (each answer, 2 points).

1. __________ pollen
2. __________ budding
3. __________ anther
4. __________ spore cases
5. __________ fungus
6. __________ petal
7. __________ cone
8. __________ mold
9. __________ hyphae
10. __________ pistil
11. __________ yeast
12. __________ fruit
13. __________ fern
14. __________ stamen
15. __________ pine

a. one-celled living thing

b. seed-bearing plant

c. spore-bearing living thing

Complete these statements (each answer, 4 points).

16. When a broken stem grows roots, ________________________ reproduction takes place.
17. An acorn is considered to be a ________________________ .
18. A fungi spore grows at the end of a ________________________ .

Write the correct letter and answer on the blank (each answer, 4 points).

19. When a sperm cell joins an egg cell, ______________________ occurs.
a. osmosis b. photosynthesis c. fertilization

20. Cell division is called ______________________ .
a. mitosis b. budding c. hyphae

21. Sperm can be carried by ______________________ grains.
a. spore b. stamen c. pollen

22. Some plants can grow from both a ______________________ .
a. seed and spore b. cutting and seed c. spore and cutting

23. The ______________________ is the time when reproduction takes place.
a. beginning stage b. growth stage c. adult stage

Put these life-cycle events in the proper order. Start with a growing plant (each event, 4 points).

fruit is formed	flower matures	seed moves
bees help	petals dry up	fertilization
pollen makes tube form in the style		

24. ______________________

25. ______________________

26. ______________________

27. ______________________

28. ______________________

29. ______________________

30. ______________________

Answer these questions (each answer, 5 points).

31. What are the functions of fruit?

____

____

____

____

____

32. How do yeast cells reproduce?

____

____

____

____

____

Vegetative reproduction occurs most frequently in plants with stems that run horizontally just above or below the ground. As the stems of the plants grow horizontally just above or below the surface, they eventually form other roots that attach to the soil and form entirely new plants distinct from the parent plant. Strawberries, blueberries, irises, and many kinds of grasses grow by this type of vegetative reproduction.

| Potatoes

Farmers normally use vegetative reproduction to raise many food crops such as apples, bananas, oranges, and white potatoes. The white potatoes, for example, are cut into many parts, making sure that each part has at least one "eye" (bud). Each piece of potato will grow from this part into an entirely new potato plant. Using this means of vegetative reproduction will produce new potatoes much more quickly than by trying to use seeds of the potato plant.

Many plants that are weeds also use vegetative reproduction to spread. They are sometimes difficult to eliminate because they can often re-grow their lost parts by vegetative reproduction. For example, even though people might pull off the flowers, leaves, and stems of a dandelion, the plant will regrow new stems, leaves, and flowers if even only a part of its roots are left in the soil.

God has provided many abundant ways for flowering plants to reproduce and grow in His creation. We should thank God for providing flowering plants for our food and oxygen. We should also thank Him for the beauty He created in so many of the flowering plants.

Match these items.

2.37 ________ seed
2.38 ________ fruit
2.39 ________ vegetative reproduction
2.40 ________ grown from stem
2.41 ________ mitosis

a. carries seed and protects it
b. an embryo inside a seed coat
c. roses and raspberries
d. new plant comes from vegetative part of parent plant
e. digestion
f. process of growth of fertilized egg
g. potato eye

Complete this activity.

2.42 List four purposes of fruit.

a. ________________________________
b. ________________________________
c. ________________________________
d. ________________________________

Answer these questions.

2.43 How do farmers use vegetative reproduction to grow white potatoes?

____
____
____
____

2.44 What are some ways that fruits help seeds to move from one place to another?

____
____
____
____
____
____

Cone-Bearing Plants

The first category of seed-bearing plants that you have just studied is flowering plants, or angiosperms. The second category of seed-bearing plants is cone-bearing plants, or **gymnosperms**. The word *gymnosperm* comes from two Greek words meaning "naked seed." Gymnosperms have naked or uncovered seeds that they bear in their cones. They do not have any fruit surrounding the seeds. They do not produce flowers. Some examples of these cone-bearing plants are pine, cedar, and spruce trees.

| Male cone

| Female cone

Structure of cone-bearing plants. Cone-bearing plants have two types of cones on the same plant — male cones and female cones. The male cones are smaller than the female cones and grow near the top of the plant. The sperm cells are formed in these smaller male cones. The larger female cones are located lower on the plant. The egg cells are formed in the female cones.

Both male and female cones are made with scales that are connected to a central part of the cone. These scales are soft when the cone is growing. The scales of the female cone become very hard after fertilization takes place. Under each scale of the male cone, two pollen **sacs** are located. On the upper side of the female cone scales there are two parts which contain the egg cells.

Fertilization. Cones grow during the adult stage of the cone-bearing plants life cycle. This time is similar to the stage in flowering plants when the flowers grow. When the cones are mature, pollen grains drop from the male cones located higher up in the plant. These pollen grains usually land on the upper side of the female cones located below the male cones on the same plant. Wind can carry some of the pollen from the male cones to the female cones of other plants, too. As in the case of flowering plants, God has designed the cone-bearing plants to produce much more pollen than needed since some of it gets lost as it travels through the air. However, some of the pollen eventually reaches the tops of the female cones.

When the pollen from the male cones reaches the female cones, a sticky fluid holds the pollen onto the female cones. Then the female cone opens to allow the male sperm cells contained in the pollen to get inside it. The sperm cells grow tubes that lead to the egg cells in the female cone. The sperm cells follow the tubes to the egg cells. When the sperm cells join with the egg cells, fertilization takes place. New lives have begun! New seeds start developing.

Activity 502.E Examining Cones

If you can obtain some male and female cones from a cone-bearing plant, take some time to examine them. Use the following ideas to help guide your examination of the cones.

a. Compare the size of the male and female cones.
b. Look for the pollen sacs in the male cone.
c. Look for the ovaries in the female cone.
d. Check the hardness of the scales of each cone.
e. Find the sticky parts.
f. Try to determine if the female cone has been fertilized.

Can you see seeds?

yes (Good!)

no (Ask a helper to assist you.)

Teacher check:

Initials ______________ Date ______________

Complete these statements.

2.45 The a. ______________ cone is larger than the b. ______________ cone.

2.46 Pollen is held in the female cone by a ______________ .

2.47 Cones are made of ______________ around a central part.

2.48 As it moves through the air, much ______________ is lost.

2.49 Fertilization takes place when the a. ______________ joins with the b. ______________ .

Answer *true* or *false*.

2.50 __________ Cone-bearing trees grow flowers.

2.51 __________ Pollen grains drop from male cones.

2.52 __________ Egg cells are found on the bottom side of a cone.

2.53 __________ Both male and female cones may be found on some plants.

2.54 __________ A pine tree is a cone-bearing plant.

Seeds. Just as in flowering plants, the fertilized egg cell of cone-bearing plants grows through the process of mitosis. Food from the female cone helps the embryo grow and develop. It may look like a tiny plant. Many seeds are developed inside each female cone. During the warm part of the year, the female cone opens up. The seeds then drop to the ground and begin to grow. This process of reproduction and seed development could last as long as two years in some cone-bearing plants.

The cone is not considered a fruit. It does not grow from a flower like a fruit does. However, in some ways, the cone functions as a fruit for the plant.

Make comparisons.

2.55 Review the paragraphs on seeds and fruits of flowering plants.
The fruits have several purposes. Which purposes might be similar to those of a cone?

____

____

____

____

____

2.56 In what ways are cones different from flowers?

____

____

____

____

____

Activity 502.F Go On A Seed Hunt

This activity will allow you to discover some of the kinds of seeds that are present in your area of the country.

These supplies are needed:

poster board
glue
container for seed collecting

Follow these directions. Place a check mark in the box after completing each step.

☐ 1. Decide on a location where you will hunt for seeds (kitchen, school yard, house yard, park, garden, etc.)

☐ 2. Decide when you will go on the hunt.

☐ 3. Go to your teacher and discuss your plans.

☐ 4. Write the plans that you agree on in the spaces below.

My plans are to go to the ______________________________ .
(where)

I will hunt for seeds ______________________________ .
(when)

☐ 5. Hunt for as many *different* kinds of seed as you can find and store them in your container.

2.57 Make a poster with the seed you collected.
Glue the seeds to the poster.
Name as many seeds as you can and label them on your poster.
If you have trouble naming them, ask someone else to help you.
You may need to consult some books or some people who sell seeds to identify some of your seeds.
Find a place to display your poster.

Teacher check:

Initials ____________________ Date ____________________

Review the material in this section to prepare for the Self Test. The Self Test will check your understanding of this section and will review the previous section. Any items you miss on this test will show you what areas you will need to restudy in order to prepare for the unit test.

SELF TEST 2

Match these items (each answer, 2 points).

2.01 ________ pistil

2.02 ________ petal

2.03 ________ stamen

2.04 ________ stigma

2.05 ________ egg

2.06 ________ ovary

2.07 ________ anther

2.08 ________ stem

2.09 ________ fruit

2.010 ________ pollen

a. male part

b. female part

c. neither male nor female part

Answer *true* or *false* (each answer, 2 points).

2.011 ________ Male and female parts must be present for flowering plants to reproduce.

2.012 ________ *Life cycle* means the life stages of any group of plants.

2.013 ________ Some flowering plants can reproduce without seeds.

2.014 ________ All plants stop growing during a certain stage of the life cycle.

2.015 ________ Each seed contains many cells when it is mature.

2.016 ________ Only the female cones have scales.

2.017 ________ Flower petals protect tiny, more delicate parts.

2.018 ________ Flowering plants are the most common type of seed-bearing plants.

2.019 ________ Flowering plants are also called gymnosperms.

2.020 ________ Egg cells are found on the bottom side of a cone.

Write the four main stages of a flowering plant like the corn plant (each answer, 5 points).

2.021 ______________________________

2.022 ______________________________

2.023 ______________________________

2.024 ______________________________

Write the letter of the correct answer on the blank (each answer, 3 points).

2.025 Cell division is called __________ .

a. vegetative b. mitosis c. sacs

2.026 There are probably over __________ kinds of plants on earth.

a. 50,000 b. 150,000 c. 260,000

2.027 The female cone is __________ the male cone.

a. smaller than b. larger than c. the same size as

2.028 Reproduction of a flowering plant occurs when the __________ from the anther reaches the stigma of the flower.

a. egg b. pollen c. ovary

2.029 Another way that some flowering plants can grow is by __________ .

a. vegetative reproduction
b. chlorophyll
c. cool temperatures

Complete these statements (each answer, 4 points).

2.030 Angiosperms are commonly known as __________________ plants.

2.031 The process of the joining of sperm and egg cells is known as __________________ .

2.032 Cones are made of __________________ around a central part.

2.033 A __________________ is an embryo inside a seed coat.

2.034 The __________________ is the female part of a flowering plant.

Answer this question (this answer, 5 points).

2.035 In what ways are cones different from flowers?

____

____

____

____

____

Teacher check: Initials ____________

Score ____________ Date ____________

80 / 100

3. SPORE-BEARING PLANTS AND FUNGI

Some living things do not grow flowers or cones where seeds are produced. However, they are still able to reproduce. God has designed these living things to reproduce by means of spores. Spores are tiny, specialized structures that are able to grow into a new organism. Spores help an organism survive and move from place to place.

Many of the living things that produce spores are as familiar to you as flowering plants. You have probably observed mosses and ferns growing in the woods. You may have also seen toadstools or mushrooms, too. Perhaps you have observed mold on cheese or bread. All of these living things produce spores during the reproductive part of their life cycles. Many kinds of plants, plus certain kinds of fungi, algae, bacteria, and protozoans form spores.

In this section of the LIFEPAC, we will examine the life cycles of living things that produce spores. Then we will specifically examine how plants called ferns produce spores and also how fungi produce spores.

Objectives

Review these objectives. When you have completed this section, you should be able to:

3. Describe the life cycles of plants, fungi, and some protists.
4. Identify the main reproductive parts of seed-bearing and spore-bearing organisms.
5. Classify plants, fungi, and protists you observe.
6. Explain differences between the main categories of plants, fungi, and protists.
7. Relate the structure of plants, fungi, and protists with their reproduction in a life cycle.

Vocabulary

Study these new words. Learning the meanings of these words is a good study habit and will improve your understanding of this LIFEPAC.

exposed (ek spōzd'). Uncovered or opened up.

hyphae (hi' fe). Plural of *hypha*. The thread-like bodies of certain fungi.

Pronunciation Key: h**a**t, **ā**ge, c**ã**re, f**ä**r; l**e**t, **ē**qual, t**ė**rm; **i**t, **ī**ce; h**o**t, **ō**pen, **ô**rder; **oi**l; **ou**t; c**u**p, p**u̇**t, r**ü**le; **ch**ild; lo**ng**; **th**in; /ŦH/ for **th**en; /zh/ for mea**s**ure; /u/ or /ə/ represents /a/ in **a**bout, /e/ in tak**e**n, /i/ in penc**i**l, /o/ in lem**o**n, and /u/ in circ**u**s.

Life Stages

Just as flowering plants go through special stages, so do living things that produce spores. The life stages of beginning, growth, adulthood, and death are similar. The events of each stage are somewhat different.

Beginning stage. Life for these living things begins as a spore. The parent plant releases the spore into the air. The spore can begin growing as soon as it settles on something moist. It needs a small amount of water on something to begin its life. Warmth also helps spores to grow.

Most spores are able to remain alive in difficult situations. Heat, cold, or dryness will not kill many spores unless they are **exposed** to these conditions for long periods of time.

Spores vary greatly in size and shape. To help them survive, some spores are protected by tough coats. Others may have hair-like covers so that they become attached to other organisms. Many spores are light and feathery — they may stay in the air for long periods of time.

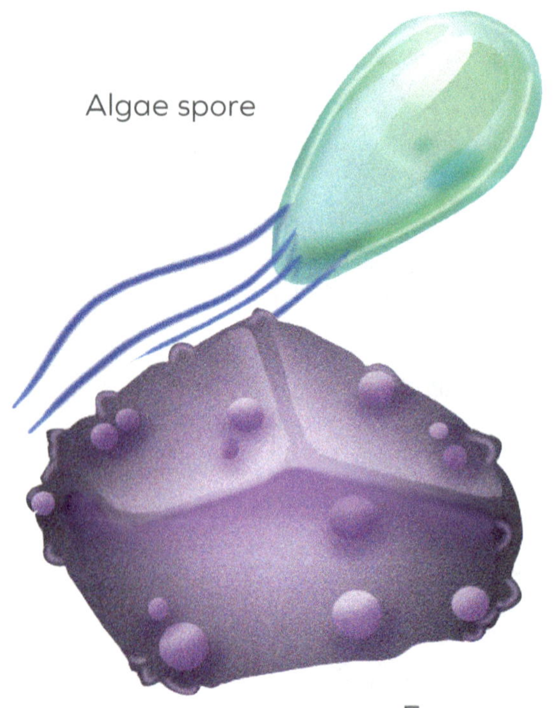

Growth stage. Growth of the organism happens by mitosis. Moisture helps the cells divide. However, the spores must also be attached to something that will provide food for them. They cannot produce their own food. When the spore has enough moisture and food provided for it, mitosis continues and the spore grows into an adult organism. The growth stage of the organism can be either in two parts or one part, depending upon the type of parent organism.

Fungal spores

Growth happens very quickly for some living things that have spores. Adulthood can be reached in less than a day! Other organisms take much longer to reach adulthood as spore-producers. Ferns and mosses may take several years before they reach adulthood.

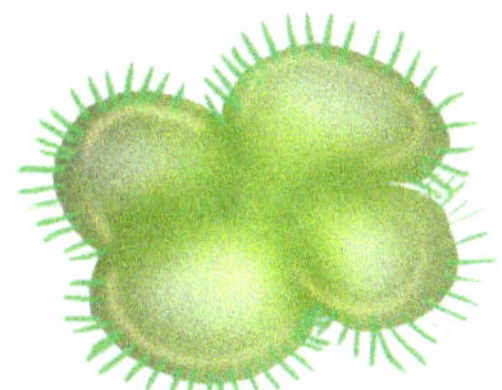
Fungal spores

Adult stage. The spore organism becomes an adult when it is ready to reproduce. The adult organism produces spores. When the spores are fully developed, they are released into the air. As adults, some spore-bearing organisms live many years. Others may complete a life cycle within months. Most adult organisms in this group can reproduce more than once in a lifetime.

Old age and death. When old age comes to these spore-producing organisms, they stop reproducing. The organism does not function well enough. It then dries up and dies. Yet, millions of spores from the parent remain after the organism dies. Given the right conditions, these spores could easily replace the parent.

Spiral shaped fungal spore

Complete this activity.

3.1 List five examples of living things that produce spores.

a. ______________________________

b. ______________________________

c. ______________________________

d. ______________________________

e. ______________________________

3.2 List the four life stages of spore-producing organisms.

a. ______________________________

b. ______________________________

c. ______________________________

d. ______________________________

3.3 Briefly explain the growth stage of spore-producing organisms.

____

____

____

____

____

Fern Plants

A *fern* is a green, nonflowering plant that grows in most parts of the world. There are over 10,000 varieties of ferns on the earth. Ferns vary widely in size and shape. Some ferns are about one inch long, while others can grow to more than 65 feet tall! Ferns have some of the most varied and beautiful leaves in the world. Some are long, lacy, and have many smaller leaflets. Other ferns have simple and rounded leaves. The leaves of ferns are sometimes called *fronds*. All ferns produce spores as a means of reproducing.

| A spiral fern

Structure of ferns. A fern is similar to seed-bearing plants in some ways. The fern has roots, stems, and leaves. It is also a green plant. Being green means that it contains chlorophyll in its leaves and undergoes photosynthesis. Through this process, the plant can make its own food and produce oxygen.

Since the fern is spore-bearing, it has no flowers, fruits, or seeds. Most ferns have leaves that branch into many sections. On the underside of the fern's leaves are tiny casings. The spores grow inside these tiny casings on the underside of the fern's leaves. The casings look like little brown spots on the leaves. The casings protect the spores from weather until they are ready to be released.

Fertilization. The spore can mature as any single cell matures. The young spore remains one cell until the parent fern releases it. Until the time of release, the spore would not be ready to grow into a new plant.

Spores are usually formed during the fall of the year. During the fall, the spore cases dry up. Then they open to release the spores. When the spores reach the ground, they will begin to grow if there is adequate moisture present.

The fern is an example of a spore-producing plant that goes through two parts of the growth stage, since the initial new plant does not resemble the parent plant. The spores grow into very tiny green plants through mitosis. However, the tiny new fern plants do not look like the parent fern. Instead, they are small and flat. At this point, the new plant is called a *prothallus*. After a few weeks, the prothallus produces sperm and egg cells. These male and female cells grow in different parts of the same plant.

The sperm cells swim along the plant to the eggs and fertilize them. Dew or water must be on the plant for the sperm to swim to the egg.

After fertilization, an embryo is formed. The embryo grows through mitosis. It receives its food from the little plant. After it grows its own leaves, the new fern, like the parent plant, can produce its own food. The little flat prothallus is no longer needed. It dries up and dies.

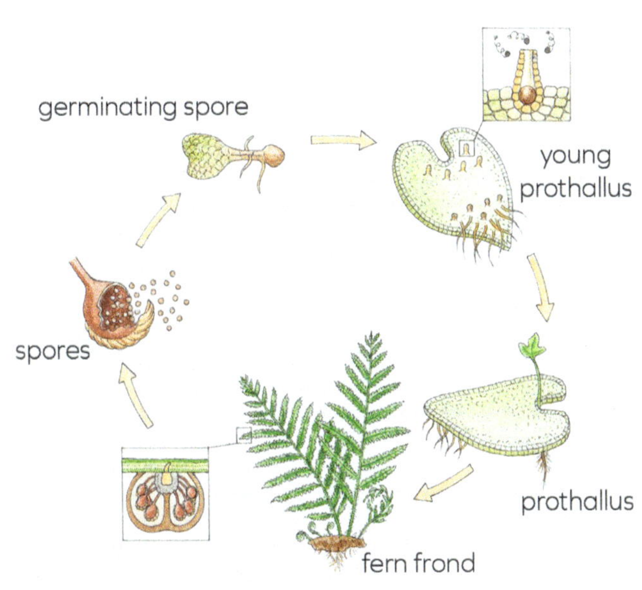

| Fern life cycle

The new fern will grow into an adult plant. It will produce spores by itself. The fern life cycle — called *alternation of generations* — continues in this way. In one generation, the spores are produced that grow into the tiny, heart-shaped prothallus plant. This tiny plant produces sperm cells and egg cells. The sperm and egg cells join in fertilization and form the embryo of the second generation fern plant. The second generation embryo grows into a fern leaf (frond) resembling the original parent that produced the spores.

God has provided an amazing example of his creativity in producing ferns through this life cycle process called alternation of generations!

Write the correct letter and answer on the blank.

3.4 Fern life begins as ______________________________ .

a. an egg b. a spore c. a sperm

3.5 Spores are formed in ______________________________ .

a. spore cases b. ovaries c. anthers

3.6 Ferns grow by ______________________________ .

a. photosynthesis b. mitosis c. reproduction

3.7 Sperm and egg cells are formed in ______________________________ .

a. fern leaves b. spore cases c. the prothallus

3.8 The sperm cells get to the egg by ______________________________ .

a. bees moving them b. wind blowing them c. swimming through water

Answer *true* or *false*.

3.9 __________ Most spores are easily killed.

3.10 __________ Spores need moisture to begin growing.

3.11 __________ Spore cases are found under fern leaves.

3.12 __________ Spore cases are hard to see because they are green.

3.13 __________ Spores need to be fertilized.

3.14 __________ The tiny plant called the prothallus grows from a spore that looks just like the parent plant.

Vegetative reproduction. The reproduction of ferns by bearing spores is common. Some ferns may reproduce another way, however, similar to the vegetative reproduction of flowering plants.

The leaves of the fern grow old. They bend down and touch the ground. Root-like parts of the fern begin to grow. A new stem may develop. When this happens, a new plant is born.

LOOK IT UP!

One of the more common ferns that has vegetative reproduction is the *walking fern*. Search the Internet, read library books, or use an encyclopedia to answer these questions.

3.15 In what part of the world does the walking fern grow?

____

3.16 In what kind of setting would you find the walking fern?

____

3.17 Does the walking fern produce spores?

____

Fungi

In the first section of this LIFEPAC, you learned that fungi were one of the five kingdoms of living things in the world. Even though some fungi might look like a type of plant, they are in a category of their own. Fungi do not have chlorophyll in their cells. They cannot produce food, so they must depend upon other living or dead things for food. Fungi cannot survive alone.

| Mushrooms are a common fungi.

There are over 100,000 species of fungi. Their size varies considerably. Yeasts and other one-celled fungi are too small to be seen without a microscope. But most types of fungi can be seen with our unaided eye. Some of the most common fungi are mushrooms, mildews, molds, and plant rusts.

Structure of fungi. Fungi have no roots or stems. Instead, their bodies are made up of tangled masses of tiny threads called **hyphae**. When the fungi are ready to reproduce, they grow a stalk that can hold spores. Mushrooms and toadstools may have a wide stalk with a cap-like crown. Spores develop in little casings under the cap. Mold has thin stalks. Spore cases grow on the end of these mold stalks. Hundreds of spores are inside each of these cases.

The growth stage of fungi can happen quickly. Sometimes a mushroom seems to appear overnight. Maybe you have also noticed that foods can become moldy in less than a week. How do these fungi get started? We will now explain the fertilization process of fungi.

| Puffball mushrooms giving off spores

Fertilization. Ordinarily, millions of microscopic fungi spores are floating in the air. These fungi spores may settle on furniture and look like dust. We usually do not even think about their presence among us.

When a fungi spore settles on something warm and damp, it can begin to grow. However, some objects are a better home for fungi than others! Products made from plants or animals are good places for molds to grow. Old logs or leaves are places where mushrooms or toadstools grow.

The spores of fungi grow into adults through mitosis. When in the adult stage, new spore casings grow on the ends of the stalk. When the casings break open, the spores are carried to new locations. Fungi continue to survive through this cycle.

Complete these activities.

3.18 Define *hyphae* ______________________________

____

3.19 Where do fungi get their food supply?

____

3.20 Where are spores grown in fungi?

____

3.21 Explain how ferns and fungi are different.

____

____

____

EXPERIMENT 502.C MOLD

View 502
MOLD: Grade 5 Science experiments video

In this experiment, you will grow some mold on bread and then observe its appearance over several days

These supplies are needed:

slice of bread
large jar with lid
microscope
magnifying glass or dissection scope
microscope slide
tweezers
slide cover
dropper

Follow these directions carefully. It would be good to read all of the steps in this experiment before proceeding so that you will better understand the activities suggested. Place a check in the box as you complete each step of the experiment.

☐ 1. Place the bread on a shelf and leave it uncovered overnight. ______________
Today's date

☐ 2. Take the bread from the shelf and dampen it with a small amount of water.

☐ 3. Put the dampened bread inside the large jar. Replace the lid.

☐ 4. Label the jar with your name and the date.

☐ 5. Place the jar in a warm spot.

☐ 6. Let the jar sit in a warm spot for two days.

☐ 7. After two days, remove the bread from the jar and observe it with a magnifying glass or a dissection scope.

☐ 8. Record your observation of the mold in the following "Daily Observation Chart" for ***Day 1***.

3.22

DAILY OBSERVATION CHART

	COLOR	AMOUNT OF MOLD	LOCATION OF MOLD ON BREAD
Day 1			
Day 2			
Day 3			
Day 4			
Day 5			

- ☐ 9. Return the bread to the jar, replace the lid, and store the bread for another day.
- ☐ 10. Remove the bread from the jar on the next day and examine it with a microscope or dissection scope. Record your observations in the "Daily Observation Chart" for the next day.
- ☐ 11. Repeat steps 7-10 for five days. You may check off the boxes below after you have completed the observation and recording for each day.

  ☐ Day 2 ☐ Day 3 ☐ Day 4 ☐ Day 5

3.23 After 5 days, explain the parts of the life cycle you observed.

____

____

____

3.24 Draw the life cycle of mold. Use the diagram of the fern life cycle as an example.

- ☐ 12. After the fifth day of observation, place the moldy bread carefully near you.
- ☐ 13. Carefully lift off some of the mold with the tweezers.
- ☐ 14. Place the mold on a microscope side.
- ☐ 15. Put a drop of water in the mold. Cover it with a slide cover.
- ☐ 16. Place the slide under a microscope and focus it.

3.25 Record what you see under the microscope.
Label the parts of the mold that you can see.

- ☐ 17. Wrap the moldy bread in a paper towel and throw it in the waste basket.

Teacher check:

Initials ____________ Date ____________

Write a Report.

3.26 Fungi are useful to human beings. Use the library and/or the Internet to find information about the uses of fungi. After you have completed your research, write a report about the good things that fungi do for us. When the report is finished, take it to be checked.

Teacher check:

Initials ____________________ Date ____________________

Review the material in this section to prepare for the Self Test. The Self Test will check your understanding of this section and will review the previous sections. Any items you miss on this test will show you what areas you will need to restudy in order to prepare for the unit test.

SELF TEST 3

Answer *true* or *false* (each answer, 3 points).

3.01 __________ Fungi have chlorophyll.

3.02 __________ Ferns grow seeds in little cases.

3.03 __________ Ferns have hyphae.

3.04 __________ Ferns make their own food.

3.05 __________ Fungi grow spores inside their stalks.

3.06 __________ The air usually has fungi spores in it.

3.07 __________ Both fungi and ferns grow through mitosis.

3.08 __________ Ferns grow flowers.

3.09 __________ Sperms swim to the eggs on fungi plants.

3.010 __________ Molds grow best where it is cool.

Match these items (each answer, 2 points).

3.011 __________ flower parts

3.012 __________ cone parts

3.013 __________ fungi parts

3.014 __________ fern parts

3.015 __________ vegetative reproduction

3.016 __________ cell division

3.017 __________ male cell

3.018 __________ female cell

3.019 __________ flowering plant

3.020 __________ fungi

a. without seeds
b. egg
c. pistil and stamen
d. photosynthesis
e. mold
f. scales
g. mitosis
h. sperm
i. hyphae
j. pine tree
k. leaf and spore case
l. cherry tree

Place these events of a fern life cycle in correct order (each answer, 4 points).

adulthood	spore	fertilization	prothallus

3.021 ____________________

3.022 ____________________

3.023 ____________________

3.024 ____________________

Answer these questions (each answer, 4 points).

3.025 Where do eggs grow?

____

3.026 In what containers do spores grow?

____

3.027 What carries sperm in flowering plants?

____

3.028 How do certain fern plants reproduce without growing from a spore?

____

3.029 Which living thing is just a body without roots or leaves?

____

Complete this item (this item, 4 points).

3.030 Explain what the term *life cycle* means.

____

____

____

____

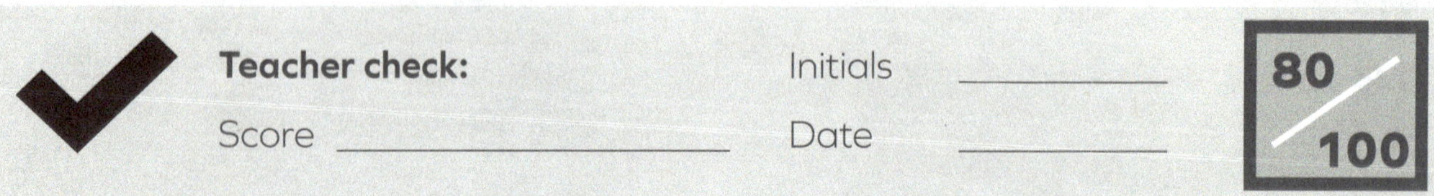

Teacher check: Initials ____________

Score ____________ Date ____________

80/100

4. ONE-CELLED LIVING THINGS

God has made many one-celled organisms to dwell on the earth. As you learned in Section 1 of this LIFEPAC, these living things may be fungi, protists, or monerans. In this section, we will examine the life cycles of one-celled organisms. We will also specifically look at algae and yeast. Algae may be either from the protist or moneran kingdoms. Yeasts are in the fungi kingdom.

Objectives

Review these objectives. When you have completed this section, you should be able to:

3. Describe the life cycles of plants, fungi, and some protists.
6. Explain differences between the main categories of plants, fungi, and protists.
7. Relate the structure of plants, fungi, and protists with their reproduction in a life cycle.

Vocabulary

Study this new word. Learning the meanings of these words is a good study habit and will improve your understanding of this LIFEPAC.

absorbs (ab sôrbz'). A body takes some liquid into itself by osmosis and holds it in.

Pronunciation Key: h**a**t, **ā**ge, c**ã**re, f**ä**r; l**e**t, **ē**qual, t**ė**rm; **i**t, **ī**ce; h**o**t, **ō**pen, **ô**rder; **oi**l; **ou**t; c**u**p, p**u̇**t, r**ü**le; **ch**ild; lo**ng**; **th**in; /ŦH/ for **th**en; /zh/ for mea**s**ure; /u/ or /ə/ represents /a/ in **a**bout, /e/ in tak**e**n, /i/ in penc**i**l, /o/ in lem**o**n, and /u/ in circ**u**s.

Life Stages

One-celled organisms have interesting life stages. They take some of the material present in the parent to begin life. Then they grow into adults. To reproduce, one-celled organisms give up part of themselves.

Beginning stage. Life for a one-celled organism begins when the parent cell starts to divide into two cells. This division may be accomplished by either mitosis or budding. For a time, the two new cells remain attached to each other. During this time, both new cells are able to perform the functions necessary for them to survive. When each cell is able to live by itself, the cells break away from each other.

Growth stage. The two new cells are smaller than the original parent cell; however, they are now ready for growth. By taking in food and water the new cells add to their size. Eventually, the cells become large enough to reproduce.

Adult stage. The adult stage for one-celled organisms is usually not very long. When the cell is large enough to reproduce, it splits. This splitting occurs through the process of mitosis.

| One-celled algae come in many types and shapes.

Algae

Algae can be either protists or monerans. They can be unicellular or multicellular. Even if they are multicellular, the cells are usually very similar, and they are still very tiny. Most algae live in water. We will study the one-celled algae in this section.

Structure of algae. Algae do not have leaves, flowers, roots, or stems! Yet, they have features similar to other living things. Each cell has a cell wall. Each cell has chloroplasts with chlorophyll. With chlorophyll, algae can make their own food.

One-celled algae come in many sizes and shapes. Some algae are formed around a piece of sand or other mineral.

| Algae can grow to look like grass. It adds oxygen to the water. In the ocean it can grow very large and we call it 'seaweed'.

Reproduction. Algae are reproduced through the process of mitosis. The parent cell splits into two new cells. The two new cells grow to adulthood, and they, in turn, split to form four new cells. Growth and reproduction of algae happen quickly, and it doesn't take long for many algae to be formed in this way.

Quick growth and reproduction are very important for algae. They are small and nearly helpless. Other organisms use algae for food and eat them!

God also designed algae to provide oxygen to the earth. Since algae can undergo photosynthesis, they can produce oxygen in this way. You might think that tiny algae would not make much oxygen for the earth. Yet, if all the single-celled algae could be weighed together, they would weigh more than all the plants on earth! God certainly can use small things for important purposes.

Complete these statements.

4.1 Algae can make their own food because they have ______________________________ .

4.2 Algae reproduce through ____________________________ .

4.3 Algae provide a. ______________________ and b. ______________________ for animals.

4.4 New algae cells are ___________________________ than the parent cell.

4.5 If all the algae on earth were weighed together, they ____________________________ than all of the other plants on earth.

Yeast

Yeast is a single-celled organism that bakers use to make bread dough rise. Cakes of yeast can be bought at a grocery store. Some types of yeast help produce beer, wine, and other alcoholic beverages. There are about 600 species of yeast, but only a few are used commercially.

Yeast belongs to the fungi kingdom. Yeasts reproduce rapidly, and they grow especially well in substances containing sugar. Yeast cells contain cytoplasm and a nucleus. They are covered by a cell membrane and a cell wall. A yeast cell does not move by itself, it must be carried by another organism, air currents, or water.

Structure. The oval-shaped yeast cell is not green. The yeast cell cannot make its own food, and needs to get food from other sources. When the yeast cell **absorbs** water and sugar, it is able to live, grow, and produce offspring.

Yeast does not have a special structure for producing offspring. God has designed the yeast plants to reproduce through budding.

Reproduction. You have learned that in budding, the parent cell develops a bump on itself. Some cytoplasm and parts of the nucleus move into the lump or bud. The cell membrane will soon pinch away from the bud. Two yeast cells are produced.

Sometimes both cells remain attached even if both have their own separate nuclei. A colony of yeast plants can grow in this way. Yet, each yeast cell remains an individual. Each yeast cell performs all functions to keep alive, even when it is attached to other cells. If any yeast cell would separate from the others, it could live without the other cells. Reproduction happens very fast in yeast cells. If conditions are favorable, new cells can be formed in hours. During this rapid growth, carbon dioxide gas is given off. The gas is what makes dough rise. (Little bubbles are formed in the dough.)

| Yeast reproduces by budding.

Write the correct answers. Use complete sentences.

4.6 Describe budding in yeast plants.

____

____

____

____

4.7 Compare the structure of yeast and algae.

____

____

____

____

4.8 Explain how yeast cells can be considered single-celled organisms when they are still connected together.

____

____

____

____

Before you take this last Self Test, you may want to do one or more of these self checks.

1. ________ Read the objectives. See if you can do them.

2. ________ Restudy the material related to any objectives that you cannot do.

3. ________ Use the **SQ3R** study procedure to review the material:

a. **S**can the sections.

b. **Q**uestion yourself.

c. **R**ead to answer your questions.

d. **R**ecite the answers to yourself.

e. **R**eview areas you did not understand.

4. ________ Review all vocabulary, activities, and Self Tests, writing a correct answer for every wrong answer.

SELF TEST 4

Answer *true or false* (each answer, 3 points).

4.01 __________ Yeast cells move by themselves.

4.02 __________ There are male and female algae.

4.03 __________ Yeast produces spores.

4.04 __________ Mold is a one-celled plant.

4.05 __________ Many flowers have anthers.

4.06 __________ Yeast uses photosynthesis to provide its own energy.

4.07 __________ There are male and female cones.

4.08 __________ Spores are in the air much of the time.

4.09 __________ There are more yeast organisms than algae organisms.

4.010 __________ Yeast has chlorophyll.

4.011 __________ Mold has roots.

4.012 __________ Algae have cell walls.

4.013 __________ There are some many-celled algae.

4.014 __________ Yeast plants can produce very quickly.

4.015 __________ Mushrooms grow seeds under their cap-like crowns.

Write the correct letter and answer on the blank (each answer, 5 points).

4.016 Yeast reproduces by ______________________________ .

a. mitosis b. spores c. budding

4.017 __________________ produces its own food through photosynthesis.

a. Yeast b. Fungi c. Algae

4.018 ______________________________ is produced as yeast reproduces.

a. Carbon dioxide gas b. Water c. A mineral

4.019 Algae is important to the earth's ________________ supply.

a. nitrogen b. oxygen c. hydrogen

4.020 Yeast and fungi are not ________________ .

a. green b. large c. living things

4.021 Yeast and algae grow by adding ________________ .

a. chlorophyll b. seeds c. cytoplasm

Write the correct answers (each item 5 points).

4.022 What are hyphae?

____

____

4.023 Explain how budding works.

____

____

____

____

4.024 How did Jesus use the example of a lily in Matthew chapter 6?

____

____

____

____

____

4.025 What is unusual about the fern's life cycle?

____

____

____

____

____

4.026 Name five parts of a plant where vegetative reproduction can take place.

a. ______________________________

b. ______________________________

c. ______________________________

d. ______________________________

e. ______________________________

Teacher check: Initials ____________

Score ____________ Date ____________

80/100

Before you take the LIFEPAC Test, you may want to do one or more of these self checks.

1. ________ Read the objectives. See if you can do them.
2. ________ Restudy the material related to any objectives that you cannot do.
3. ________ Use the **SQ3R** study procedure to review the material.
4. ________ Review activities, Self Tests, and LIFEPAC vocabulary words.
5. ________ Restudy areas of weakness indicated by the last Self Test.

NOTES

SCIENCE 503
ANIMALS: LIFE CYCLES

Author:
Barry G. Burrus, M.Div, M.A., B.S.

Editor:
Brian Ring

Illustrations:
Brian Ring

Media Credits:
Page 3: © Lenorlux, iStock, Thinkstock; **5:** © Bussarakam, iStock, Thinkstock; **7:** © ALesik, iStock, Thinkstock; © Ameng Wu, iStock, Thinkstock; **9:** © Coprid, iStock, Thinkstock; **13:** © PlazaCameman, iStock, Thinkstock; **18:** © Comstock, Stockbyte, Thinkstock; **26:** © Dorling Kindersley, Thinkstock; **32:** © Saddako, iStock, Thinkstock; **33:** © therry, iStock, Thinkstock; **34:** © idizimage, iStock, Thinkstock; **35:** © sekarb, iStock, Thinkstock; **36:** © randimal, iStock,Thinkstock; **39:** © italiansight, iStock,Thinkstock; **40:** © Comstock, Thinkstock; **45:** © MR1805, iStock, Thinkstock; **47:** © Purestock, Thinkstock.

804 N. 2nd Ave. E.
Rock Rapids, IA 51246-1759

ANIMALS: LIFE CYCLES

God has created a rich variety of animals. In the Book of Genesis, we read: "And God said, Let the waters bring forth abundantly the moving creature that hath life, and fowl that may fly above the earth in the open firmament of heaven. And God created great whales, and every living creature that moveth, which the waters brought forth abundantly, after their kind, and every winged fowl after his kind: and God saw that it was good. And God blessed them, saying, be fruitful, and multiply, and fill the waters in the seas, and let fowl multiply in the earth. And the evening and the morning were the fifth day. And God said, Let the earth bring forth the living creature after his kind, cattle, and creeping thing, and beast of the earth after his kind: and it was so. And God made the beast of the earth after his kind, and cattle after their kind, and every thing that creepeth upon the earth after his kind: and God saw that it was good." (Genesis 1:20-25)

Fish, birds, insects, lizards, cattle, and bears are all examples of the animals that God has created. In this LIFEPAC®, you will explore the rich variety of animals found in the waters and on the earth. You will also learn about some one-celled, animal-like protists such as amoeba and paramecium. You will examine aspects of the life cycles of these living things. You will learn about some similarities and differences among various animals and protists. You will also learn about their common structures and the ways they reproduce. Finally, you will have an opportunity to observe some of these living things close-up during experiments!

Objectives

Read these objectives. These objectives tell what you will be able to do when you have successfully completed this LIFEPAC. Each section will list according to the numbers below what objectives will be met in that section. When you have finished this LIFEPAC, you should be able to:

1. Describe the life cycles of invertebrates.
2. Explain the differences between the life cycles of invertebrates.
3. Describe the life cycles of vertebrates.
4. Explain the differences between the life cycles of vertebrates.
5. Name the groups to which the animals belong.
6. Show the relationship of the structures of animals to their reproduction in a life cycle.

1. INVERTEBRATES

In the previous LIFEPAC, Science 502, you learned that God has created a great variety of living things. You learned that scientists classify all living things into 5 kingdoms: animals, plants, fungi, protists, and monerans. In the previous LIFEPAC, you studied the life cycles of plants, fungi, protists, and monerans. In this LIFEPAC, you will learn about the life cycles, structures, and reproduction of animals. We will also cover a couple of examples of one-celled, animal-like protists in this LIFEPAC. We will cover these protists because, like almost all animals, they are able to move about in their environments.

God has created such a rich variety of animals that no one knows for sure how many kinds of animals there are! Scientists have classified and named over one and a half million different kinds of animals. However, many scientists believe that there may be from two million to as many as fifty million different kinds of animals. Many new kinds of animals are discovered, named, and classified each year. The world of animals is exciting! The study of animals is called zoology, and scientists who study animals are called *zoologists*.

Objectives

Review these objectives. When you have completed this section, you should be able to:

1. Describe the life cycles of invertebrates.
2. Explain the differences between the life cycles of invertebrates.
5. Name the groups to which the animals belong.
6. Show the relationship of the structures of animals to their reproduction in a life cycle.

Vocabulary

Study these new words. Learning the meanings of these words is a good study habit and will improve your understanding of this LIFEPAC.

amoeba (ə mē' bə). A microscopic, one-celled protist.

carnivores (kär' nə vorz). Animals that eat only other animals. They are also called meat-eaters.

extends (ek stendz'). Stretches out or reaches out.

flukes (flüks). Flatworms of a certain type.

fragmentation (frag' mən tā' shən). A method of asexual reproduction in animals by the division of the body into two or more pieces.

gills (gilz). The parts of a fish body that take oxygen from the water.

herbivores (her' bə vorz). Animals that eat only plants.

host (hōst). An animal that has another animal living in or on it.

invertebrates (in ver' tə brəts). Animals that do not have backbones. Insects, jellyfish, snails, spiders, and worms are examples of invertebrates.

larva (lär' və). The worm-like form of an early stage in the life cycle of some insects.

larvae (lär' vē). Plural form of larva.

maggot (mag' ət). The larva of a fly.

mollusks (mol' əsks). Animals with soft bodies. Adults often grow hard shells. A snail is an example of a mollusk.

nymph (nimf). The part of certain insect life cycles where the young animal has no wings or reproductive organs.

octopus (ok' tə pəs). A mollusk with a soft body and eight long arms.

omnivores (om' nə vorz). Animals that eat both plants and animals.

paramecium (par' ə mē' see um). A one-celled, animal-like protist that has a special shape.

parasites (par' ə sīts). Animals that live on or in other animals. They get their food from the hosts.

protozoans (prō' tə zō ənz). A large group of one-celled protists.

pupa (pyü' pə). The form of certain insects between the time they are larvae and adults.

pupae (pyü' pē). Plural for pupa.

squid (skwid). A mollusk that lives in the sea.

testes (tes' tēz). The body parts of male animals where sperm is formed.

variety (və rī' ə tē). Different kinds or types.

vertebrates (vėr' tə brits). Animals that have backbones. Birds, fish, reptiles, and mammals are examples of vertebrates.

zoology (zō ol' ə gē). The science of the study of animals.

Note: *All vocabulary words in this LIFEPAC appear in* **boldface** *print the first time they are used. If you are unsure of the meaning when you are reading, study the definitions given.*

Pronunciation Key: h**a**t, **ā**ge, c**ã**re, f**ä**r; l**e**t, **ē**qual, t**ė**rm; **i**t, **ī**ce; h**o**t, **ō**pen, **ô**rder; **oi**l; **ou**t; c**u**p, p**u̇**t, r**ü**le; **ch**ild; lo**ng**; **th**in; /ŦH/ for **th**en; /zh/ for mea**s**ure; /u/ or /ə/ represents /a/ in **a**bout, /e/ in tak**e**n, /i/ in penc**i**l, /o/ in lem**o**n, and /u/ in circ**u**s.

Like plants, animals come in many shapes and sizes. Most kinds of animals are less than an inch long. Some are so tiny that they can only be seen with a microscope. Other animals are very large, like the elephant, the giraffe, and the blue whale.

As you learned in previous LIFEPACs in this series, animals and plants are dependent on one another. Plants depend on the carbon dioxide given off by animals and human beings. In turn, animals and human beings depend upon plants for oxygen and food. As you learned, this cycle of life is called the *carbon cycle*. In addition, some plants depend upon animals to reproduce. For example, bees and birds carry pollen from plant to plant so that the plants might be fertilized.

Animals differ from plants in their ability to move around in their environment. Most plants are fixed on one place by roots or root-like structures. However, almost all animals can move around from one location to another.

| Reptiles, like snakes, are cold-blooded; their body temperature is based on their surroundings. The sidewinder snake (above) moves sideways in order to move forward.

There are many ways to classify the different kinds of animals. For example, some animals live on the land, while others live in water. Some animals are *cold-blooded*, while others are *warm-blooded*. Cold-blooded animals are warm when their surroundings are warm or cool when their surroundings are cool. Warm-blooded animals, however, almost always have the same body temperature regardless of the temperature of their surroundings.

| Dolphins are warm-blooded mammals. They require air to breathe, unlike fish.

Animals can be classified according to what they eat. Animals that only eat plants are called **herbivores**. Cows and giraffes are examples of herbivores. Animals that eat only other animals are called **carnivores** or *meat-eaters*. Lions, sharks, and dogs are carnivores. Animals that eat both plants and animals are called **omnivores**. Bears are omnivores.

Animals can also be classified according to whether or not they have backbones. Animals that do not have backbones are called **invertebrates**. The vast majority of animals are invertebrates. Insects, jellyfish, snails, spiders, and worms are examples of invertebrates. Animals that do have a backbone are called vertebrates. Birds, fish, reptiles, and mammals are examples of **vertebrates**.

In this LIFEPAC, we will study animals by classifying them as either invertebrates or vertebrates. In this section of the LIFEPAC, you will learn about invertebrates. In the next section, you will explore vertebrates.

Complete these statements.

1.1 Scientists classify all living things into ________________ kingdoms.

1.2 The study of animals is called ______________________ .

1.3 Scientists have named and classified over _______________________ different kinds of animals.

1.4 ______________________________ animals are warm when their surroundings are warm and cool when their surroundings are cool.

1.5 Animals that eat both plants and other animals are called ___________________________ .

1.6 Animals that do not have backbones are called ____________________________ .

1.7 Animals differ from plants in their ability to ____________________________ in their environments.

What is your favorite animal? Why? Look up some information on this animal in a book or encyclopedia, the library, or the Internet. Then, write a short paper (less than one page) about your favorite animal. Include some information about where the animal lives, what it eats, how it breathes, and any other things that you find interesting about your favorite animal. Let your teacher read about your favorite animal when you have finished.

Teacher check:

Initials _____________________ Date ____________________

Life Cycles of Invertebrates

In the previous LIFEPAC Science 502, you learned that living things go through *life cycles*. There are various *life stages* in a life cycle of living things; for example, beginning, growth, adulthood, and end. Animals go through life stages, too. They also begin, grow, and become adults. For example, consider the earthworm. The earthworm has no backbone, so it is an invertebrate. The earthworm begins life as a tiny, fertilized egg. After hatching from the egg, it grows into a mature worm. When it reaches maturity, it mates with another earthworm and lays many new eggs. Finally, the earthworm gets old and dies. The earthworm is just one of many types of worms. Worms have soft, slender bodies and no backbones or legs. Other examples of worms besides the earthworm are flatworms, roundworms, and leeches. Other worms may have life cycles like the earthworm. They may differ, however, in the number of offspring that they produce. Other worms may reproduce more times or fewer times. All worms are invertebrates. Yet, not all invertebrates have life stages like those of the earthworm. You will now learn some things about the various life stages of invertebrates.

Answer these questions.

1.8 What is a *life cycle* of a living thing? (You may need to refer to the Science 502 LIFEPAC, Section I to help you answer this question.)

____

____

____

1.9 Why is an earthworm an invertebrate?

____

____

Beginning stage. Like almost all living things, the first stage in the life cycle of invertebrates begins with reproduction. Invertebrates can reproduce in one of two ways: (1) *asexual reproduction*, and (2) *sexual reproduction*. In asexual reproduction, only one parent is needed to produce an offspring. In sexual reproduction, two parents—one male and one female—are needed to produce offspring. Most animals and invertebrates reproduce through sexual reproduction.

Asexual reproduction only takes one parent to produce an offspring. This happens in two ways: (1) **fragmentation**, or (2) budding. Fragmentation is used by invertebrates such as planarians and some other flatworms. In this method of reproduction, a single parent usually divides into two pieces, one with the head and the other with the tail! Each section then grows the parts that are missing and becomes a completely new individual animal. Budding occurs when the animal produces small projections, called *buds*, from its side. (You learned about this process for cells and plants in previous LIFEPACs in this series.) Invertebrates known as hydras and some sea anemones reproduce by budding. The buds develop into tiny copies of the parent. Eventually, the buds grow large enough to detach from the parent and become a new individual animal.

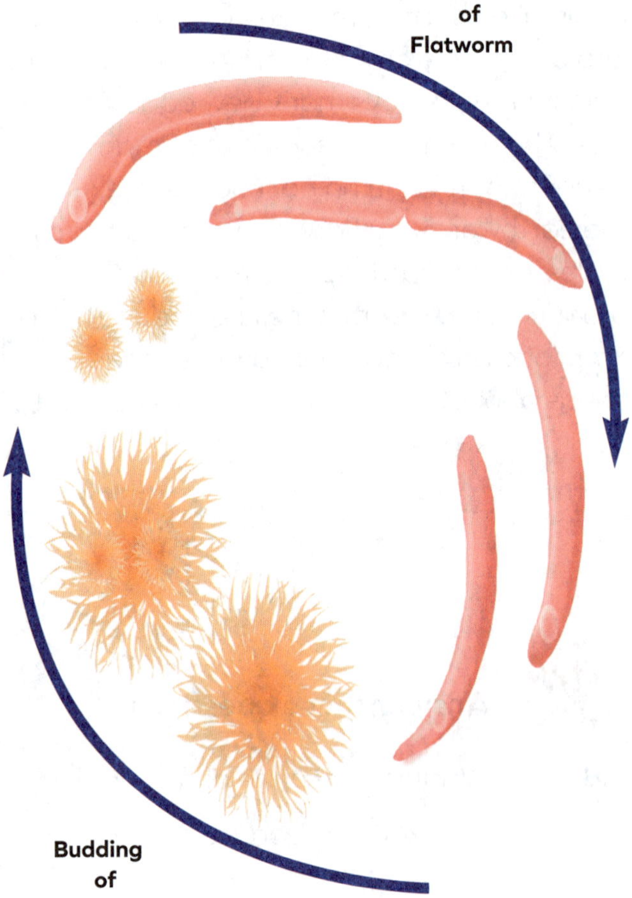

Fragmentation of Flatworm

Budding of Sea Anemone

| Asexual reproduction

Sexual reproduction is used by most animals and invertebrates. In this method, a male sperm unites with a female egg cell to produce a fertilized egg. It is at this point that a new animal life begins. The means of fertilization can either occur outside the female body or within the female body.

In sexual reproduction, the beginning stage of the life cycle starts with a single cell. This cell is produced through fertilization of a female egg cell with a male sperm cell. After it is fertilized, the egg cell begins growing and reproducing. This is the next stage in the life cycle of the invertebrate: the growth stage.

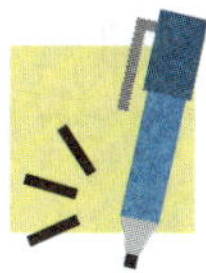

Match these items.

1.10 __________ asexual reproduction
1.11 __________ sexual reproduction
1.12 __________ fragmentation
1.13 __________ budding
1.14 __________ fertilization

a. the result of a male sperm combining with a female egg
b. a single parent divides into two or more pieces
c. only one parent needed to produce offspring
d. two parents, male and female, needed to produce offspring
e. produces small projections from one parent which split off to form offspring
f. the process of cell division

Growth stage. Sexual reproduction can occur either within or without the female body; that is, the sperm may either reach the egg inside the female body or outside the female body. If fertilization of the egg occurs within the female body, the fertilized egg is then laid outside the female body. If the fertilization took place outside the body, the fertilized egg remains outside the female's body. Now an embryo begins to form within the fertilized egg. This occurs through the process of *mitosis*, the division of cells. (Recall that you learned about mitosis in previous LIFEPACs in this series.)

Each fertilized egg contains some food for the growing embryo. Growth of the embryo inside the egg is the first part of the growth stage. As soon as the new animal can live outside the egg, it hatches from the egg.

| Growth stages of silverfish

Other invertebrates go through a different process of growth after hatching from an egg. They are hatched in **larva** form. (You will learn more about this later in this section.) **Larvae** do not look like their parents. They turn into **pupa** form before becoming adults. Larvae and some **pupae** get their own food as they grow.

Some other invertebrates have an even different process occur during their growth stage. After hatching from an egg, the new invertebrate is called a **nymph**. (You will learn more about this later in this section.) The nymph looks somewhat like the parent invertebrate, but some parts are missing. Nymphs are able to get their own food for continued growth. As they grow, they begin to form the missing parts of their bodies that will allow them to become adult invertebrates.

Answer *true* or *false*.

1.15 __________ An embryo forms inside a fertilized female egg of invertebrates.

1.16 __________ Embryos must search for their own food outside the egg.

1.17 __________ After hatching, the "baby" of some invertebrates looks like a miniature adult.

1.18 __________ Some invertebrates hatch in larva form and become a pupa before becoming an adult.

1.19 __________ A nymph looks somewhat like a parent invertebrate, but some body parts are missing.

Adult stage. The adult stage of an invertebrate is reached when it grows to full size and is able to reproduce. It looks very much like its parents. Its form will change very little during the adult stage. It can begin to reproduce. Some invertebrates will reproduce many times during their adult stage.

The egg-laying female invertebrate may produce many eggs at one time. Most of these eggs may be fertilized by sperm from the male invertebrate. The new fertilized eggs are then deposited outside the body of the female if they were not already outside the body. New animals are formed just like the parent began. These hatch into babies. The babies grow. Life for that species continues.

Old age and death. Some invertebrates live to an old age. For a few invertebrates, old age arrives soon after they reproduce one time. Death will follow soon after. Other invertebrates may live to reproduce many times before old age begins. In each invertebrate, old age causes some parts of the body to stop working as they did before. The invertebrate gets weaker. Its life comes to an end, and it dies.

Most invertebrates do not reach old age. They die at an earlier stage in the life cycle. The harsh conditions of changing weather can cause the death of invertebrates. Larger animals feed on invertebrates. Other reasons may cause an early death. Yet, enough of these animals survive so that life can continue as they grow to adulthood and reproduce. They usually lay many more fertilized eggs than needed so that life can continue for each kind of invertebrate. God continues the cycle of life for His creatures.

| A wolf spider carries her egg sac. Once the babies hatch, she carries them on her body.

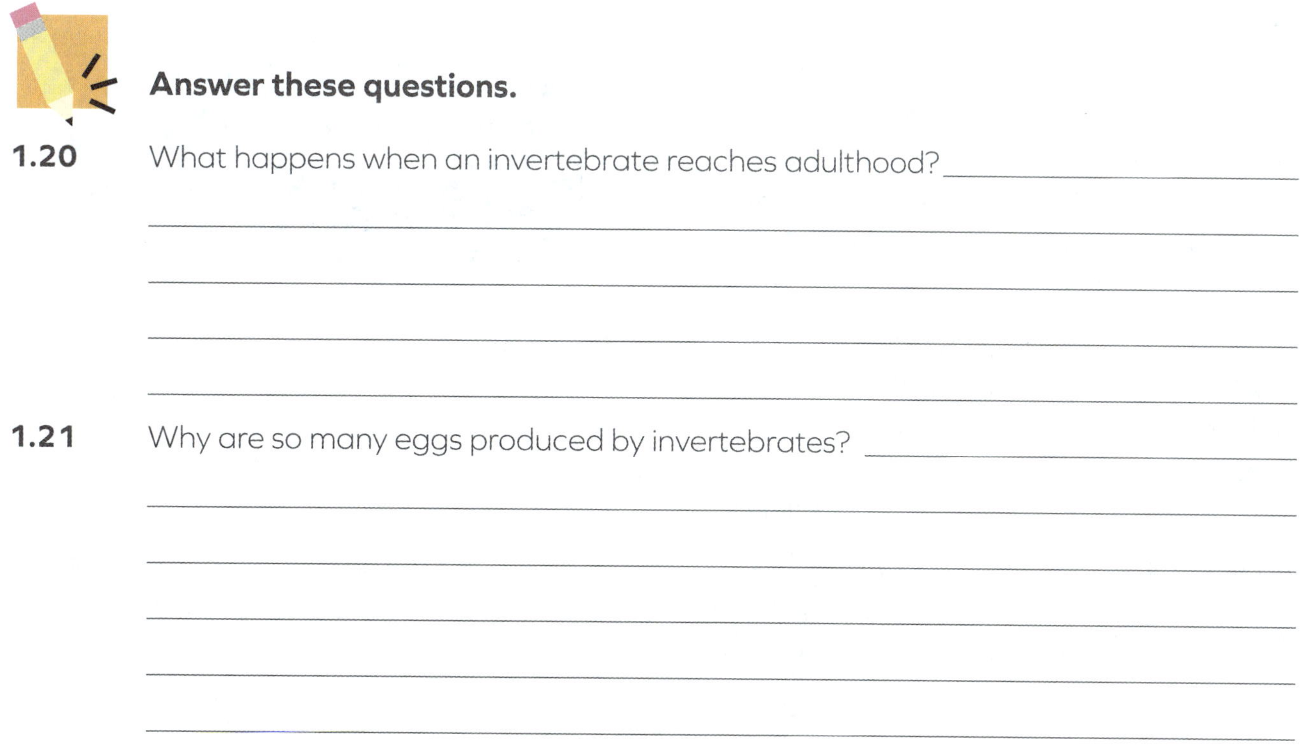

Answer these questions.

1.20 What happens when an invertebrate reaches adulthood? ______________________

____

____

____

____

1.21 Why are so many eggs produced by invertebrates? ______________________

____

____

____

____

____

One-Celled, Animal-Like Protists

As you learned in the Science 502 LIFEPAC, protists are one of the five kingdoms of living things. They can be unicellular (one-celled) or multicellular (many-celled). Some protists have characteristics similar to plants, such as green algae and red algae. Other protists have characteristics similar to animals, such as **protozoans**. In fact, in the past, many people included these animal-like protists into the animal kingdom. Because these animal-like protists are able to move around like animals and have no backbones like invertebrates, we will briefly discuss them in this section.

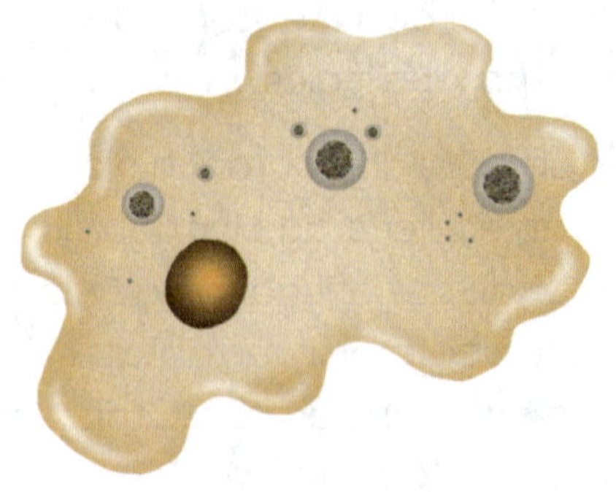

| Amoeba

Protozoans are one-celled, animal-like protists. There are more than 30,000 different kinds of protozoans. They like to live in moist places. Some of them live in the sea, others in fresh water. They also live in soil, plants, and animals. Some even live within your mouth and intestines!

The **amoeba** and the **paramecium** are two of the more common kinds of protozoans. They have similar life cycles. Their life cycles compare closely to other protozoans, too. By examining the amoeba and the paramecium, we can learn a lot about the whole group of protozoans.

Structure. The amoeba and the paramecium are both *eukaryote*, one-celled organisms; that is, they both contain a cell membrane, cytoplasm, and a nucleus. Amoeba and paramecium do not have legs, arms, eyes, or hearts. Neither do they have places for sperm or eggs to grow.

| Paramecium

The amoeba is one of the simplest protozoans. The single cell that makes up the body of the amoeba carries on all the necessary functions for life. The amoeba eats, breathes, moves, and responds to its surroundings. In these ways, it is animal-like.

The amoeba does not have a basic shape. It changes shape often. The nucleus in the amoeba moves around within the cell to different positions. When the amoeba wants to move, a "false foot" extends out from the cell body and makes it move.

The paramecium has a stiffer cell membrane than the amoeba. This membrane helps give the paramecium a definite shape. The membrane has many tiny openings. Some of the cytoplasm within the cell **extends** through the openings to form small "hairs." These hairs move or "wave" in the surrounding water. This allows the paramecium to move about in the water.

Food is taken in by protozoans through the cell membrane. The paramecium has a definite groove on one side of its cell membrane that serves as a mouth. Food taken in by the protozoans is dissolved in the cytoplasm. To stay alive and to grow larger, the protozoan needs the food. Waste is also removed back through the cell membrane to the surroundings.

The protozoans breathe by taking in oxygen through the cell membrane. This is accomplished by a process known as *osmosis*. The oxygen is used by the protozoan to burn up the foods for energy. As a result, carbon dioxide is produced and is passed out of the cell membrane through osmosis.

Reproduction. Reproduction in most protozoans occurs through mitosis. Soon after the parent protist becomes full-sized, the nucleus divides. Part of the cytoplasm surrounds each new nucleus. The two new cells then split apart, forming two new offspring. Each of the new protozoans has a nucleus and half of the parent's cytoplasm.

After splitting apart, the two new protozoans are able to live apart. They each get more food. They breathe. Growth takes place. They become adults and then reproduce through mitosis.

Protozoans reproduce in other ways, too. Some protozoans reproduce through *budding*. The parent cell suddenly swells in one direction. The swollen part (the *bud*) breaks off and forms a new protozoan. Certain protozoans reproduce by dividing into many cells called *spores*. In this way, they reproduce like some plants and fungi. Other protozoans show the beginnings of *sexual reproduction*, where male and female parents with sperm and egg are required. In all the forms of protozoan reproduction, the cell's nucleus is divided among the new individuals. God has provided an amazing variety of reproduction in these tiny creatures.

Some protozoans are able to complete a life cycle in a very short time. Some paramecium can divide two or three times in a day. Many new living organisms are produced in this way.

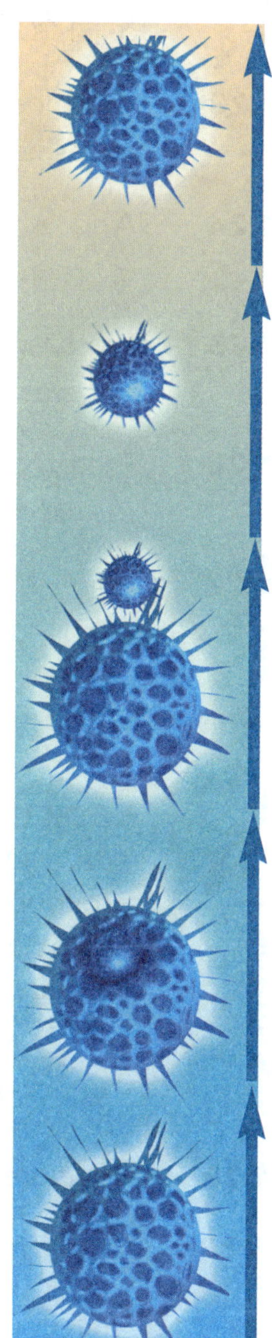

| A protozoan "budding"

Write the correct letter and answer on the blank.

1.22 There are more than ____________ different kinds of protozoans.
a. 1,000 b. 10,000 c. 30,000

1.23 An amoeba moves by means of ____________________ .
a. osmosis b. tiny hairs c. a "false foot"

1.24 A paramecium moves by means of ____________________ .
a. reproduction b. tiny hairs c. feet

1.25 Protozoans take in food through their ____________________ .
a. eyes b. cell membrane c. nucleus

1.26 Protozoans breathe by taking in ____________________ .
a. oxygen b. carbon dioxide c. air

1.27 Reproduction occurs in most protozoans through ____________________ .
a. budding b. sexual reproduction c. mitosis

LOOK IT UP: God has made a great variety of protozoans. Use the library or the Internet to find information about a protozoan type other than the amoeba or paramecium. Find out about the structure and the means of reproduction of the protozoan that you choose. Write your findings on the following lines:

PROTOZOAN NAME: ________________________

1.28 Structure:

____

____

____

____

____

1.29 Reproduction:

____

____

____

____

Teacher check:

Initials ____________________ Date ____________________

Egg-Laying Invertebrates

Invertebrates are animals that do not have a backbone. Many kinds of invertebrates lay eggs outside the female's body during part of the life cycle. Among these are insects, worms, and **mollusks**. However, all of these invertebrates are different in many ways. Their structures are very different, and sometimes their means of reproduction differ. Their life cycles may be different in some ways. In the remainder of this section, we will examine each of these three types of egg-laying invertebrates: insects, worms, and mollusks.

Insects. Insects can be found all over the world. Some insects live in the cold Arctic regions. Other insects can be found in the hot desert places. Many insects make their homes near the water. Still others travel from one place to another during their lifetimes.

God has created a great variety of insects. Yet they are all small, six-legged creatures. Of the total one and a half million kinds of animals that scientists have named and classified, about one million are insects. Even within insect groups that have similar characteristics, there are many varieties. For instance, if you see two differently colored butterflies, you are probably seeing members of two different butterfly species.

Color, shape, and size are often differences among the various insect species; however, insects are alike in some ways. All adult insects have six legs. Most adult insects have three body sections. Insect bodies are covered with a hard skeleton.

The life cycle of insects begins with eggs. Most insects need to have the female's eggs fertilized by sperm from the male insect. The female forms eggs in the ovaries. The sperm is produced in **testes** at the rear of the male's body. As the male and female mate, sperm is left in a special part of the female body. The eggs are fertilized by the stored sperm at the time the female begins to lay eggs outside her body.

Female insects lay their fertilized eggs in different places. Some female insects place their eggs on leaves. Others lay their eggs in the ground. Certain female wasps lay eggs in other animals. Bees and other insects build cases for their eggs. The egg sizes and shapes vary as much as the parent insects do.

The growth stage of the insect life cycle varies from one insect species to another. The silverfish, cricket, and housefly all come through their growth stages in different ways. We will describe the growth stages of each one of these three insects as examples of the main ways that insects grow during the growth stage of the life cycle.

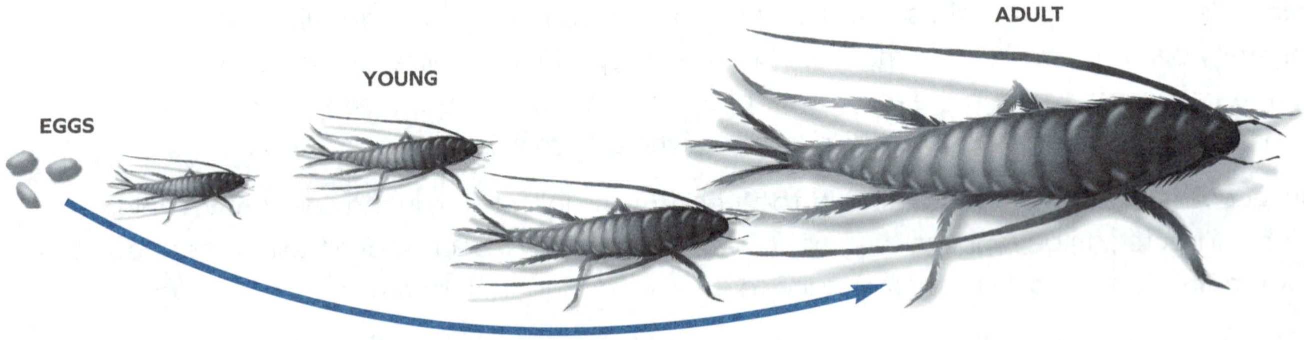

After a queen bee lays eggs in the empty cells, the worker bees cap and feed the babies until they hatch

EGGS

YOUNG

ADULT

GROWTH STAGE OF THE SILVERFISH

EGG

NYMPHS

ADULT

GROWTH STAGE OF THE CRIKET

A few types of insects hatch from an egg into a tiny copy of the parent. The main change during the growth stage is the change in size. The silverfish is one insect that develops during the growth stage in this way.

Many insects go through the *nymph* form in the growth stage. Crickets are examples of insects that use this form of growth. The newly hatched cricket looks nearly like its parent. However, it does not have wings. The young cricket also does not have reproductive organs at first. It is called a *nymph* at this growth stage. As the cricket nymph grows, it gets larger. Wings begin growing. Reproductive organs develop. Finally, at the end of the growth stage, its wings and reproductive organs are fully developed, and it enters adulthood.

The housefly is an example of a complex insect growth stage. The fly hatches into a worm-like creature called a larva. The fly larva is also called a **maggot**. The larva (or maggot) begins to eat soon after hatching. As the larva grows, its hard skin becomes too small. The larva sheds the skin and continues to grow. When the fly larva is developed fully, it changes into a pupa. The pupa moves very little. After several days, the pupa changes into an adult housefly.

The larva of each insect that goes through a complex growth stage can be identified. Color, size, and shape are ways that you can tell a difference between larvae. Some larvae are known as caterpillars. Grubs and maggots are other types of larvae.

When an insect reaches the adult stage, it is fully developed and ready to reproduce. Male and female adult insects mate. Eggs are fertilized and laid. The life cycle continues.

HOUSEFLY

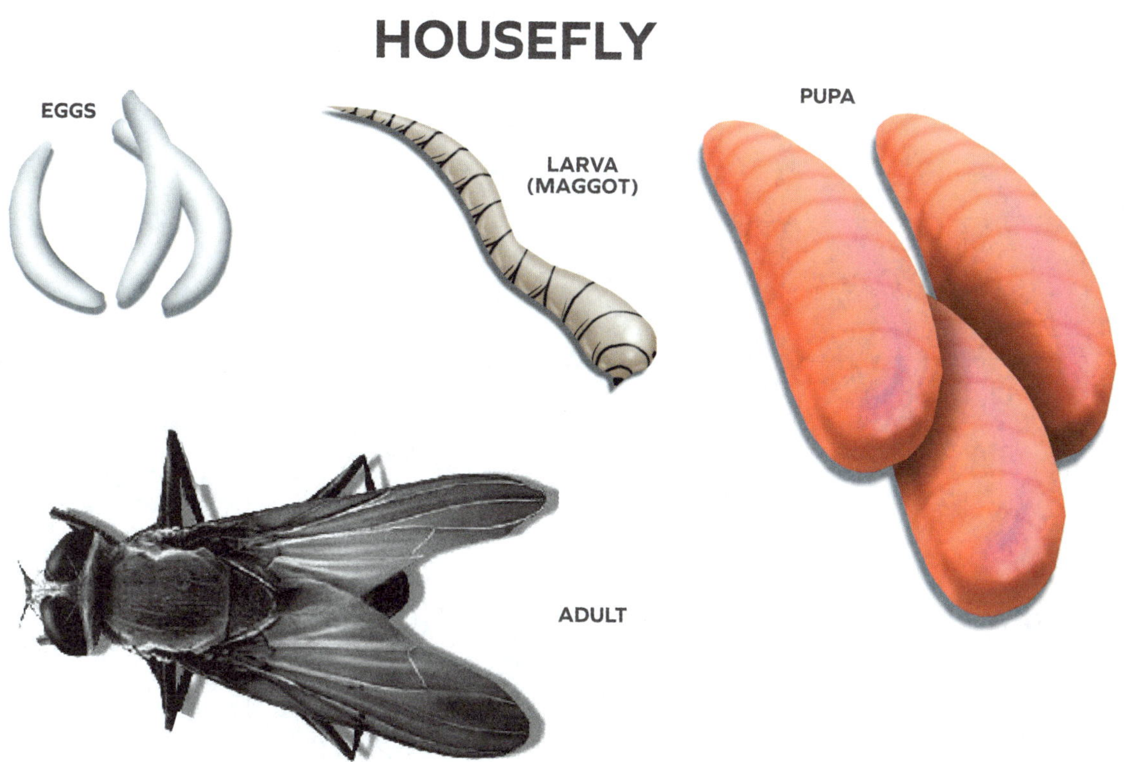

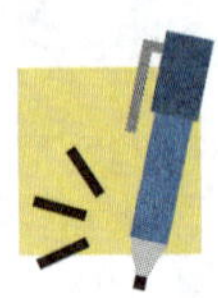

Match these items.

1.30 __________ It goes through a pupa form.

1.31 __________ When it is hatched, it looks like a tiny copy of the parent.

1.32 __________ It has a larva form.

1.33 __________ When it is hatched, it doesn't look like the parent.

1.34 __________ It goes through a nymph form.

1.35 __________ When it is hatched, it looks like a copy of the parent without wings.

a. housefly
b. silverfish
c. cricket

Complete these statements.

1.36 Scientists have named and classified about ______________________ different kinds of insects.

1.37 The sperm is produced in the ______________________ of male insects.

1.38 The eggs are produced in the ______________________ of female insects.

1.39 A maggot is a fly ______________________ .

EXPERIMENT 503.A MEALWORM OBSERVATION

View 503 Mealworm Observation: Grade 5 Science experiments video

You will observe the development of a small larva called a mealworm into an adult grain beetle over several weeks. As the animal grows and develops, you will observe and record what you see.

These supplies are needed:

- baby food jar or canning jar
- magnifying glass
- bran flakes or oatmeal
- mealworm
- potato
- knife

Follow these directions carefully. Place a check mark in the box as you complete each step.

☐ 1. Obtain a healthy mealworm. These can normally be bought at local pet stores.

☐ 2. Pour some bran flakes or oatmeal into a jar. (Less than half a jar of flakes is enough.)

☐ 3. Cut a small piece off the potato. Place it in the jar for dampness. *You will need to replace the piece of potato each week so that it doesn't rot or get dry.*

☐ 4. Place the mealworm inside the jar. It will be the mealworm's home for several weeks!

☐ 5. Have your teacher help you make a small hole in the jar lid so that the mealworm can breathe. Loosely place the lid on the jar.

☐ 6. Write your name on the jar.

☐ 7. Put the mealworm jar in a warm, dark, and safe place. Bring it out only when you are observing the mealworm.

1.40 Draw a picture of the mealworm in the space below. Use the magnifying glass to help you see the features of the mealworm.

1.41 Keep a diary of the mealworm's growth stage. Each day observe the mealworm and record your observations in your diary. Write about the changes the mealworm is going through. This observation and recording should only take you a few minutes each day. You should continue working in this LIFEPAC after each day's observation.

1.42 When a big change occurs in your mealworm, draw it in this space below. Be sure to record the date. There may be several drawings recorded here, so be sure to leave room for several drawings or you may use a separate sheet of paper.

Answer these questions after the insect becomes an adult.

1.43 What life stages did you observe? ______________________________

____

____

1.44 What do you expect to happen next in the life of the insect? ______________________

____

____

____

____

Teacher check:

Initials ____________________ Date ____________________

LOOK IT UP: Use the library or the Internet to help you answer the following questions and complete this activity.

1.45 Why is a spider not considered an insect? ______________________

____

____

____

____

1.46 Explain the stages of a spider life cycle. ______________________

____

____

1.47 How does the spider life cycle compare with the insect life cycles? ____________

____

____

1.48 Choose an unusual insect to study. Write a report about it on a separate piece of paper. Include information about the insect's life cycle. When finished share your report with a friend and with your teacher or parent.

Friend's name: ____

Teacher check:

Initials ____________________ Date ____________________

Worms. Worms are animals that have soft, slender bodies and no backbone or legs. There are thousands of different kinds of worms. The largest worms are several feet long, and the smallest ones cannot be seen without a microscope.

Worms have no outside covers or bones to give them protection. Since worms have no protective structures, they live in places that are safer for them. Most of their lives are spent under the ground, in water, or inside other animals.

The larvae of some insects sometimes look like worms, but they are not really worms. There are big differences in the life cycles of real worms and the larvae of insects. Larvae will change into adult insects sometime during the life cycle. The adult insects no longer look like worms. Worms will stay worms all their lives. The adult worms can reproduce. Insect larvae cannot reproduce.

The most commonly known worm is the earthworm. **Flukes**, flatworms, roundworms, tapeworms, and leeches are other types of worms. Most of these worms have similar types of life cycles. However, some life cycles of worms cannot be completed unless the worms are located in the right place. The need for the right place to live is especially important to worms who live in other animals. These worms that live in other animals are known as **parasites**. The animal where the parasite lives is called the **host**.

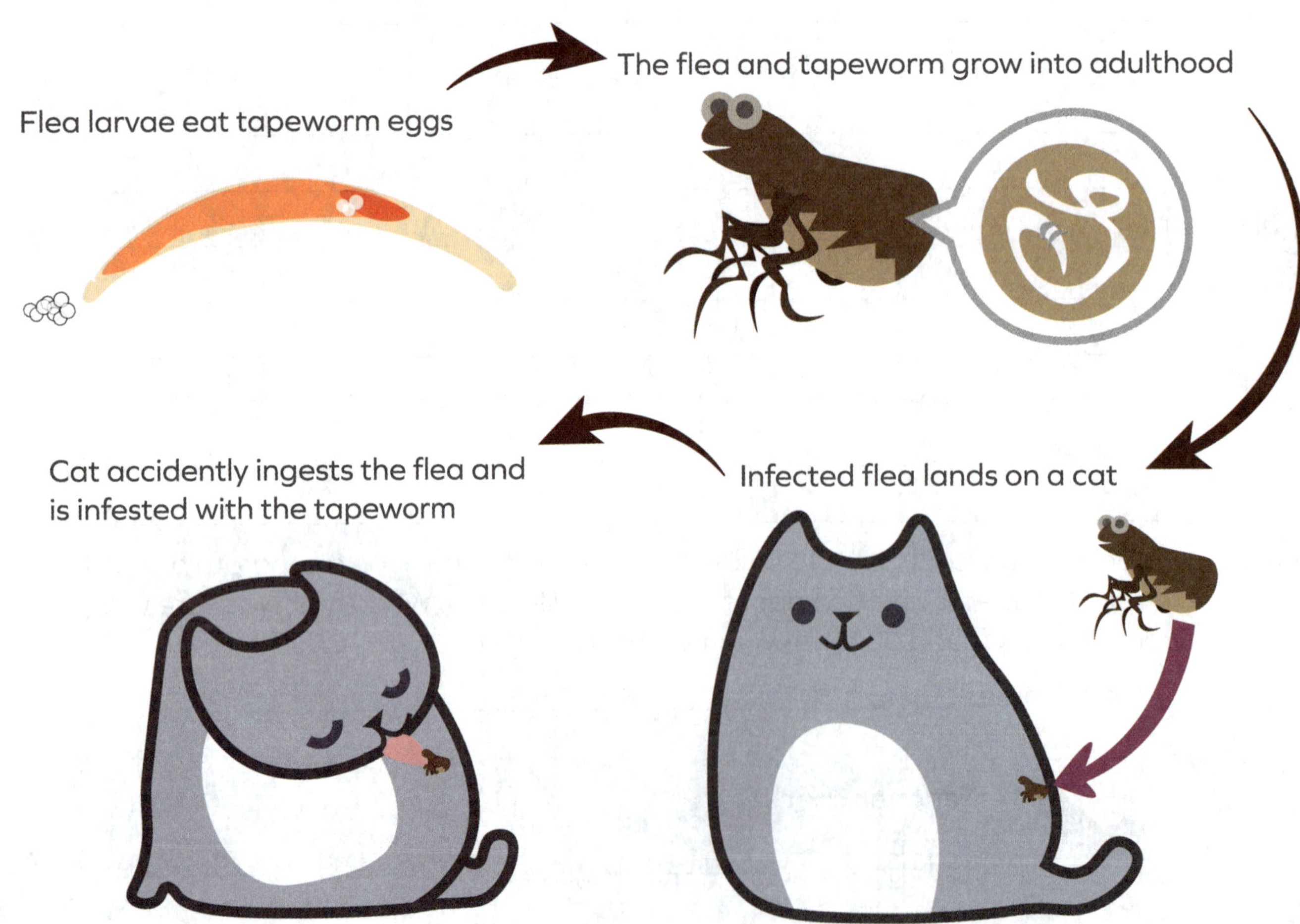

The worm life cycle is fairly simple. It begins when the egg is fertilized by the sperm. Most species have male worms and female worms. They must mate for fertilization to take place.

Some kinds of worms have both male and female parts rather than being either male or female worms. The earthworm has this kind of structure. Yet, two earthworms are needed for mating. One worm's male part releases sperm into another worm's female part. Soon afterward, the egg case is released. Fertilization occurs in the case.

During the growth stage, some worms appear very much like the parent worms. However, some worms are hatched as larvae that do not look much like the parent worms. Most of these larvae need to find the right host or they will quickly die.

An example of a parasite worm life cycle involves the common house cat. Perhaps you have heard of a pet cat that has had worms. The cat is likely a host for parasite tapeworms. The cat did not get the worms by eating them directly. The hosts for the tapeworm larvae are usually fleas. The host fleas are infested with the tapeworm larvae.

When the cat cleans itself, it swallows the fleas. The tapeworm larvae on the fleas change into tiny tapeworms. They then live and grow as parasites in the intestines of the cat. The tapeworms produce eggs and fertilize them with sperm. The fertilized eggs are carried out of the cat's body as waste.

How do the fleas get the tapeworm larvae? Fleas feed on animal waste. If tapeworm eggs are in the waste, the eggs are brought into the fleas where they hatch into larvae. When the cat swallows the larvae-infested fleas, the tapeworm life cycle continues.

Answer these questions.

1.49 What are worms? ______________________________

____

____

____

____

1.50 What are some differences between insect larvae and worms? ______________

____

____

____

____

1.51 What is a parasite?____

____

____

1.52 Explain how common house cats get "worms." ____________________________

____

____

____

____

Examples of Mollusks

Snail Squid Clam

Mollusks. A *mollusk* is a soft-bodied invertebrate animal that has no bones. Most species of mollusks grow hard shells to protect themselves. Snails, clams, and oysters are examples of hard-shelled mollusks. **Squid** and **octopus** are examples of mollusks that do not have hard, outer shells for protection, although a squid does have a soft, inner shell in its body called a *pen*.

Mollusks live in most parts of the world. Wherever they live—in the water, the forests, or even the desert—they must keep their bodies moist to remain alive. Mollusks make up the largest group of water animals. Mollusks that live mostly in the water breathe through **gills**. They also move by means of a foot. There are about 50,000 kinds of living mollusks, with about 1,000 new kinds being discovered every year.

Most mollusks have similar life cycles. The cycle begins when the female's eggs are fertilized by the male's sperm. In some mollusks, fertilization takes place inside the female's body. Other mollusks lay eggs first, and then the eggs are fertilized by the sperm outside the female's body.

Mollusk eggs are in small cases when they are laid. Most eggs hatch into larvae while they are still inside the cases. This stage has two types of larvae. Some types of larvae come out of the cases and find a plant or animal host. Other mollusk larvae stay in the cases and come out as young adults. Shells are sometimes grown by mollusk larvae, but mollusks grow their main shells during their adult stage.

SCIENCE 503

LIFEPAC TEST

NAME ____________________

DATE ____________________

SCORE ____________________

80
100

SCIENCE 503: LIFEPAC TEST

Match these items (each answer, 3 points).

1. __________ zoology
2. __________ vertebrates
3. __________ invertebrates
4. __________ omnivores
5. __________ herbivores
6. __________ fragmentation
7. __________ protozoans
8. __________ gills
9. __________ mammals
10. __________ fish

a. a method of asexual reproduction
b. one-celled, animal-like protists
c. used for breathing
d. only animals that nurse their babies with milk
e. move with the aid of tail and fins
f. process of cell division
g. the study of animals
h. contain a backbone
i. insects, worms, and mollusks
j. eat only plants
k. eat only animals
l. eat both plants and animals

Complete these sentences (each answer, 3 points).

11. Scientists classify all living things into ________________ kingdoms.
12. Animals differ from plants in their ability to ____________________________ in their environments.
13. All animal species have a life _______________ .
14. After the eggs are fertilized, a(n) ______________________ develops.
15. A(n) _____________________________ is an animal that lives off other animals.

Write the correct letter and answer on each blank (each answer, 3 points).

16. Examples of reptiles are ______________________________ .
a. toads and lizards b. lizards and snakes c. toads and snakes

17. Some Pacific Ocean salmon may journey ______________________________ to reproduce.
a. two or three miles b. 100 miles c. 2,000 miles

18. A maggot is another name for ______________________ .
a. a fly larva b. nymph c. pupa

19. The sperm is produced in the __________________ of the male animal.
a. ovaries b. egg sac c. testes

20. The amoeba and the _______________________ are two common types of protozoans.
a. mitosis b. paramecium c. lizard

Put these life-cycle events in the correct order (each answer, 3 points).

becomes adult	egg hatches	larva grows	egg is fertilized	pupa forms

21. ____

22. ____

23. ____

24. ____

25. ____

Answer this question (this answer, 5 points).

26. Explain how a common house cat gets "worms." ______________________________

____

____

____

____

____

____

Answer *true* or *false* (each answer, 2 points).

27. __________ An octopus is a mollusk that does not have a hard shell.

28. __________ Budding produces small projections from one parent which split off to form offspring.

29. __________ Embryos must search for their own food outside the egg.

30. __________ A nymph looks somewhat like a parent invertebrate but is missing some body parts.

31. __________ Of the total one and a half million animals that scientists have named, about one million are insects.

32. __________ A spider is an insect.

33. __________ Most mammals lay eggs.

34. __________ Most adult mammals reproduce for several years.

35. __________ Birds are cold-blooded animals.

36. __________ An earthworm contains both male and female parts in its body.

Answer these questions.

1.53 What are mollusks? ____________________

____

____

1.54 How are the life cycles of mollusks and insects alike? ____________________

____

____

1.55 How are the life cycles of mollusks and insects different? ____________________

____

____

1.56 At what point during the life cycle could some mollusks be considered parasites?

____

____

____

Complete this crossword puzzle.

1.57 **Across**

b. A group of soft-bodied animals. Most have shells.

e. An animal that lives on or in other animals.

i. The part of the male animal that produces sperm.

k. All animal species have a life ___________ .

m. The form some insects go through during which there is not much movement.

Down

a. A long, thin, soft-bodied animal.

c. The form some insects go through when they look like worms.

d. The unit of life for all living things.

f. A simple, single-celled protozoan.

g. The housefly and crickets are members of this animal group.

h. What some animals do so that the sperm will reach the egg.

j. A mollusk without a hard, outer shell.

l. The female produces this in her ovaries.

Review the material in this section to prepare for the Self Test. The Self Test will check your understanding of this section. Any items you miss on this test will show you what areas you will need to restudy in order to prepare for the unit test.

SELF TEST 1

Match these items (each answer, 3 points).

1.01 __________ The body has no regular shape.
1.02 __________ Adult grows a hard shell.
1.03 __________ Adult is long, thin, and soft.
1.04 __________ Adult has six legs.
1.05 __________ Some have a pupa form.
1.06 __________ One cell. Adult has a regular shape.
1.07 __________ Many are parasites during growth and adult stages.
1.08 __________ Adult has gills.
1.09 __________ A nymph grows wings.
1.010 __________ About one million different kinds.

a. mollusk
b. worm
c. insect
d. amoeba
e. paramecium

Answer *true* or *false* (each answer, 3 points).

1.011 __________ Amoebas grow from eggs.
1.012 __________ Embryos must search for their own food outside the egg.
1.013 __________ A tapeworm is a parasite.
1.014 __________ Some worms grow from larvae.
1.015 __________ Some insects do not go through the pupa and larva forms.
1.016 __________ Sperm is produced in the testes of an animal.
1.017 __________ Eggs must be fertilized inside the female's body.
1.018 __________ A paramecium grows from a nymph.
1.019 __________ A spider is an insect.
1.020 __________ A larva sheds its skin as it grows.

Write the correct letter and answer in each blank (each answer, 2 points).

1.021 The study of animals is called ______________________________.

a. botany b. zoology c. microbiology

1.022 Animals that eat only plants are called ______________________________.

a. carnivores b. herbivores c. omnivores

1.023 A life cycle can be completed in less than a day by ______________________________.

a. worms b. mollusks c. parameciums

1.024 A ____________________ looks like the parent, but doesn't have wings or reproductive organs.

a. nymph b. larva c. pupa

1.025 A parasite ______________________________.

a. lives alone
b. eats mostly blood
c. lives in or on other animals

1.026 An animal without a backbone is called ______________________________.

a. a weak animal b. a vertebrate c. an invertebrate

1.027 An egg cell is made fertile by ______________________________.

a. mitosis b. a sperm cell c. an amoeba

1.028 Maggot is another name for ______________________________.

a. a fly larva b. nymph c. pupa

1.029 An invertebrate that has both male and female parts is the ______________________________.

a. larva b. paramecium c. earthworm

1.030 Animals that have six legs are ______________________________.

a. spiders b. vertebrates c. insects

Put these events of a life cycle in proper order (each event, 3 points).

wings grow	egg is laid	an egg cell is fertilized
adulthood	nymph is hatched from egg	

1.031 ______________________________

1.032 ______________________________

1.033 ______________________________

1.034 ______________________________

1.035 ______________________________

Complete this activity (this answer, 5 points).

1.036 Describe the life cycle of a mollusk.

____

____

____

____

____

Teacher check: Initials ____________

Score ____________ Date ____________

80/100

2. VERTEBRATES

Animals that have backbones are called vertebrates. The backbones of vertebrates are connected to other bones that protect the organs of the animal's body. The bones also help to give the vertebrates shape.

There are about 40,000 different kinds of vertebrates in the world. Salmon, frogs, box turtles, robins, and wolves are examples of vertebrates. The five animals are each representative of five of the eight major classifications of vertebrates: bony fish, amphibians, reptiles, birds, and mammals. In this section of the LIFEPAC, you will examine each of these five types of animals in more detail in order to learn more about vertebrates. You will also explore the life cycles of vertebrates.

Objectives

Review these objectives. When you have completed this section, you should be able to:

3. Describe the life cycles of vertebrates.
4. Explain the differences between the life cycles of vertebrates.
5. Name the groups to which the animals belong.
6. Show the relationship of the structures of animals to their reproduction in a life cycle.

Vocabulary

Study these new words. Learning the meanings of these words is a good study habit and will improve your understanding of this LIFEPAC.

amphibians (am fib′ ē əns). Animals that live part of their lives as water animals and part as land animals.

chemical (kem′ ə kəl). A material that may be found in nature or produced by man. Iron, oxygen, carbon dioxide, tin, and plastics are examples of chemicals.

mammal (mam′ əl). Vertebrate animal that bears its young alive and can produce milk with which to feed them.

metamorphosis (met′ ə môr′ fə sis). The process by which a young larva (such as a tadpole) changes into the adult animal (a frog).

migrate (mī grāt). To move from one place to another.

reptile (rep′ tīl). An animal that crawls or creeps. Some have shells. Others have scales. Turtles, snakes, and lizards are examples of reptiles.

salmon (sam′ ən). A large fish found in the Atlantic or Pacific Oceans. They return to their home river or streams to reproduce.

tadpole (tad′ pōl). The form of a frog immediately after hatching from an egg. It has gills and a tail.

Pronunciation Key: hat, āge, cãre, fär; let, ēqual, tėrm; it, īce; hot, ōpen, ôrder; oil; out; cup, pu̇t, rüle; child; long; thin; /ŦH/ for then; /zh/ for measure; /u/ or /ə/ represents /a/ in about, /e/ in taken, /i/ in pencil, /o/ in lemon, and /u/ in circus.

Life Cycles of Vertebrates

Vertebrates go through special stages of life just as invertebrates do. Those stages are a beginning, growth, adulthood, and old age and death. The events in each stage may be different for different types of vertebrates.

Beginning Stage. All vertebrates begin their lives as fertilized egg cells. Many of these fertilized eggs develop covers. The covered eggs are laid and hatched outside the body of the female. Some eggs need to be protected and warmed by the parents. Other types of vertebrate eggs are placed by the parents in a safe location.

Chickens lay eggs and sit on them to provide warmth while the chick develops inside.

A large group of vertebrates does not lay fertilized eggs. Among these animals, the new life is developed inside the female's body. When the baby is ready, it leaves the female's body. This part of the beginning stage is called *being born* rather than being hatched. Reptiles such as a skink, common lizard, boa constrictor, and green anaconda are vertebrates that bear live young in this manner. There are some aquarium fish and also some sharks that are considered as live bearing vertebrates.

Growth stage. After the egg cell is fertilized, it develops through mitosis into an embryo. For some vertebrates, the embryo develops inside an egg cover. If the embryo is inside an egg cover, some of the cells have developed into a yolk. The embryo uses the yolk as its food. Other vertebrates develop inside the mother's body. The embryo that develops inside the mother's body gets its food from the mother's blood stream. After the new vertebrate is hatched or born, it takes food by mouth. Some baby vertebrates are able to get their own food. Others need to have the adults feed them.

Vertebrates do not go through a nymph or pupa form. Only a few species have a larva. Most vertebrates are not exact copies of the parents at birth. The new offspring may be similar to the parents, and then they make small changes as they grow to adulthood.

Large vertebrates often take several years to get through the growth stage. Smaller vertebrates normally take less than a year to reach adulthood. For many vertebrates, the growth stage is also a time of learning. During the growth stage, many animals learn how to find the right food, protect themselves, and how to function as adults with other members of their species.

Adult stage. Vertebrates are considered adults when they can reproduce. Often, vertebrates can produce offspring before they are fully grown. When their reproductive organs mature, mating can take place between the male and female vertebrates.

Most adult vertebrates are able to reproduce many times during their adulthood. Some vertebrates reproduce only once before they die. God has arranged for some vertebrates to produce thousands of eggs during each reproduction. Other vertebrates may only lay a few eggs or give birth to only a few— even only one — offspring during reproduction. God is glorious in the wonderful variety he has given to all his creatures!

| Kangaroos carry their babies in stomach pouches. Baby kangaroos are called 'joeys'.

Old age and death. At the end of their adult life, most vertebrates grow weak in their bodies. Eventually, their bodies develop too many problems or cannot fight off disease as well, and the animal dies. Some vertebrates die shortly after they reproduce. As in most living things, the life cycle comes to an end with old age and death.

Complete these statements.

2.1 Vertebrates are animals that have ______________________________.

2.2 Some vertebrate offspring develop inside the mother's ______________________________.

2.3 After the eggs are fertilized, a(n) ______________________ develops.

2.4 Vertebrates are considered adults when they ______________________ .

2.5 For some vertebrates, the life cycle is nearly finished after they ______________ once.

Egg-Laying Vertebrates

Many types of vertebrates lay eggs. From these eggs, the offspring will hatch and continue their growth stage. In this section, we will consider four major types of vertebrates that are egg-layers: fish, amphibians, reptiles, and birds. You will learn about specific characteristics of a species in each of these four groups of vertebrates. For fish, we will look at the life of a Pacific Ocean salmon. In the amphibian category, you will learn about the interesting life cycle of the common frog. For a reptile, you will examine the life of a box turtle. Finally, in the bird category, we will look at the robin. Hopefully, these examples will help you understand more about the life cycles of other vertebrates in each of these four groups.

Fish. Fish are vertebrates that live in the water. Some fish live in salt water (like the oceans) and others live in fresh water. Some can live in both salt water and fresh water. There are more kinds of fish than all the other kinds of land and water vertebrates put together. Scientists have named and classified about 22,000 kinds of fish.

Fish are not only vertebrates, but they also use *gills* to breathe. Their gills remove oxygen from the surrounding water. Most fish are covered with scales on the outside of their bodies. They also move through the water with the aid of a tail and fins. Most fish lay eggs, but a few species develop eggs inside the body. To help examine the life cycle of fish, let's take a look at the Pacific Ocean salmon. God has given it a very interesting life cycle. We can learn about other fish life cycles by comparing them with this salmon.

| Salmon return to the river they were born in to reproduce.

Pacific Ocean salmon live most of their lives in the ocean. However, when it is time for them to reproduce, they return to the fresh water streams where they were born. It is truly amazing that these fish can find their home streams! Some of these salmon must swim nearly 2,000 miles to get there. Their journey may take several months.

To find their homes, Pacific salmon navigate in the ocean by sensing the magnetic field of the earth, the ocean currents, and the position of the sun. When they reach the coast, they remember the "odor" of their old home and follow the smell of certain **chemicals** in the water of their home streams! Salmon become strong swimmers as they travel upstream to their homes. Sometimes they swim against strong currents and jump up waterfalls as high as ten feet. They do not eat during this time, but live off the fat stored in their bodies.

When the salmon reach their birth place, the males pair off with females. The female digs a hole for the eggs in the pebbles of the stream bed. She turns on her side and beats the stream floor, forming a hole in which the eggs can be deposited. Then the female swims over the hole and releases some eggs down into the hole. The male salmon follows and sprays the eggs with sperm. The female then beats the stream bed again to cover the fertilized eggs in the hole with pebbles. The salmon repeat this process for several holes in the stream bed until anywhere from 2,000 to 17,000 eggs have been laid and sprayed with sperm. At the end of this journey, the bodies of the parent salmon are so worn out that they drift downstream and die.

The salmon embryos that remain covered on the stream bed slowly develop in the fertilized eggs through the winter. By spring, the embryos have grown into little salmon, and they are ready to hatch. The baby salmon then break through the egg covering. The yolk sacs are still attached to the baby salmon to supply them with food. The babies remain hidden in the gravel of the stream for up to several more months. As they grow, they begin to get their own food. Some of them immediately leave for the ocean, while other species of salmon might remain for up to three years in the fresh water. Eventually, they leave to go to their permanent home in the ocean.

| Once back in their birthing waters, salmon fertilize eggs and then slowly die.

Only a small percentage of the salmon that leave the fresh waters for the ocean will survive. Other fish and birds will eat many of them along the way, and polluted waters will cause many to die. Fortunately, some do make it to the ocean, where they will spend from six months to seven years. Then they will come back to their fresh water home to reproduce and end their life cycle.

Unlike the salmon, many other types of fish remain alive to reproduce several times. Most of these other fish do not have to travel as far as the salmon to lay their eggs. However, the basic life cycles of the fish are the same. Eggs are laid and fertilized. The parents go elsewhere. The eggs hatch into tiny fish. These tiny fish grow into adults. The adult fish reproduce.

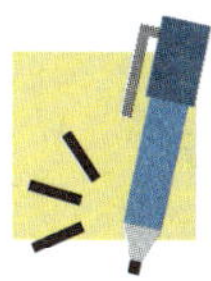

Answer *true* or *false*.

2.6 __________ There are about 22,000 kinds of fish.

2.7 __________ Most fish lay eggs.

2.8 __________ Pacific Ocean salmon fertilize eggs outside the female body.

2.9 __________ Pacific Ocean salmon reproduce several times in a life cycle.

2.10 __________ Newly hatched salmon still have yolk sacs attached to their bodies.

2.11 __________ Most of the new salmon survive to return to the ocean.

2.12 __________ The Pacific Ocean salmon life cycle events are similar to many other fish.

2.13 __________ All fish are vertebrates.

Draw a diagram.

2.14 On a separate sheet of paper, draw pictures to show the life cycle of the Pacific Ocean salmon.

Teacher check:

Initials __________________ Date __________________

Amphibians. Amphibians are vertebrates that have scaleless skin and live part of their lives in water and part of their lives on land. (There are a few exceptions to this among amphibians.) There are about 4,000 kinds of amphibians. Frogs and toads are among them.

To help us understand the life cycle of amphibians, let us take a look at the common frog. Frogs live mostly on land. They also spend time in water, but they cannot breathe under water. When it is time for them to reproduce, they go to the water. The male will give out a "mating call" in order to attract a female frog mate.

When the female has responded to the male's call and is ready to reproduce, she releases her eggs into the water. The male frog then releases his sperm over them. As the eggs are fertilized, a tough coating forms over them. The eggs may gather in clumps around plants or may be in flat bunches near the water surface. After the eggs are laid and fertilized, the parent frogs return to the land.

The frog embryos grow inside the eggs. They hatch, but the new animal looks more like a fish than a frog! It has gills like a fish and a long tail. This baby "frog" is called a tadpole. It will dwell solely in the water as it begins to grow and develop. The process by which the **tadpole** changes into a frog is called **metamorphosis**. During the tadpole's metamorphosis, its lungs develop so that it can breathe out of water. Legs begin to grow. The tail shrinks and disappears. The mouth gets much larger. Eventually, the tadpole becomes a small frog and is ready to live on the land.

The frog will grow into an adult as it continues to eat. It has a long, sticky tongue that it snaps out to catch insects for food. After the frog becomes an adult, it can reproduce.

Answer these questions.

2.15 What is an amphibian? ____________________

____

2.16 How many kinds of amphibians are there? ____________________

2.17 When is a frog like a fish? ____________________

2.18 How are male and female frogs attracted to each other to mate? ____________________

____

2.19 What is *metamorphosis* in the life cycle of a frog? ____________________

____

____

____

____

Reptiles. Reptiles are vertebrates that have a dry, scaly skin and breathe by means of lungs. There are about 6,500 species of reptiles. Reptiles include alligators, crocodiles, lizards, snakes, and turtles.

A big difference between amphibians and reptiles is in the life cycle. Reptiles do not go into the water to reproduce. Their offspring are hatched from eggs on the ground. The young look very much like their parents. Although reptiles also go to the water, they must come to the surface to breathe because they have lungs, not gills. Reptiles are covered with scales or shells (called plates). Some reptiles have both scales and plates.

| Newborn turtles

The box turtle is an example of a reptile. It is an egg-laying reptile. After mating with a male, the female digs a hole in a sandy place. She usually lays 3 to 8 eggs into the hole, and then covers them with sand. Then the female leaves the nest. Sun shining on the nest keeps the eggs warm.

The turtle embryo within the egg gets food that is stored in the egg. After two months, it is ready to live outside the egg. It hatches. The newly hatched turtle looks somewhat like its parents. Yet the shell is not fully hard. Because it is still soft, the little turtle could make a good meal for a larger animal! Within a year of growing, the new turtle's shell will become very hard and difficult to eat.

Box turtles take several years to become adults. Then they can reproduce. They are able to reproduce many times during their lifetimes. Box turtles have been known to live as long as 100 years. They have a long life cycle.

Write the correct letter and answer in the blank.

2.20 A(n) ______________________ does not have scales.
a. fish b. amphibian c. reptile

2.21 The vertebrate that has lungs all its life is a(n) ______________________.
a. fish b. amphibian c. reptile

2.22 A turtle embryo gets its food from ______________________.
a. inside the egg b. outside the egg c. its mother

2.23 Examples of reptiles are ______________________.
a. toads and lizards b. lizards and snakes c. toads and snakes

Birds. Birds are the only animals that have feathers. All birds have wings, and almost all of them can fly. (The ostrich and penguin cannot fly.) They are the fastest animals on earth, with some of them able to reach speeds of 100 miles per hour. There are about 9,700 kinds of birds, and God has created a great variety in types, colors, and shapes of birds.

| A robin feeds the chicks

Birds have feathers, wings, two legs, and lungs. They lay hard-shelled eggs. Many birds **migrate** from one part of the earth to another. Some of them fly many thousands of miles to seek warmer climates during the winter. The Arctic terns are the champion birds among those that migrate. They fly 11,000 miles from their nesting grounds in the Arctic to their winter homes in the Antarctic and then return in the spring. That's a round trip of about 22,000 miles each year!

Some birds have down or feathers when they are hatched. These young birds can do some things for themselves after they hatch. Other kinds of birds have no feathers when hatched and have their eyes closed. They are helpless and cannot do anything for themselves. Adults must be nearby to help feed these young birds and to give them protection.

The robin is a good example of a typical bird. Its feathers and coloring are beautiful. It flies and runs, but it seldom swims. It does, however, take "baths" in the water. Perhaps you have seen one in a birdbath.

In the spring, robins travel north and mate. Much chirping and singing goes on among the robins before they mate. The eggs are fertilized inside the female's body.

Both the male and female robin work to build the nest for the fertilized eggs that will be laid. The nests are made mainly of mud and grass. When the nest is finished, the female lays three to six blue eggs in it. The parents warm the eggs by sitting on them. They also turn the eggs often. In about two weeks, the eggs hatch.

Newborn robins are nearly helpless. Their eyes are closed. They cannot feed themselves, so their parents get insects and bring them to the young. When another animal or bird gets near the nest, the parents protect the young robins. After the little robins grow enough to survive on their own, they are pushed from the nest by the parents. New eggs are laid two or three times during the summer. Young robins stay near the nest for the first summer.

At the end of the summer, robins gather to migrate south for the winter. In the spring, they will return to the north to reproduce. Even the year-old robins will mate and reproduce.

Complete these activities.

2.24 Define *migrate* as it applies to birds. ____________________

____

____

2.25 Make a "lifeline" of a robin over the first year of its life. Include important events.

EXPERIMENT 503.B
EXAMINING A CHICKEN EGG

You will use a magnifying glass to observe some details of a chicken egg. You may also need to do some additional research at the library or on the Internet to answer some questions about parts of the chicken egg.

These supplies are needed:

chicken egg
small dish
magnifying glass
dropper
tissue paper
food coloring

Follow these directions. Check the box at the left of each step when it is completed.

- ☐ 1. Use the magnifying glass to look at the eggshell. Record what you see in 2.26.
- ☐ 2. Use the dropper to put some food coloring on the eggshell. Wipe the shell dry with the tissue. Record what you see in 2.27.
- ☐ 3. Gently crack the egg on one end. Remove a piece of the shell. Record what you see in 2.28.
- ☐ 4. Crack the egg open. Put the contents within the eggshell in the dish. Record what you see in 2.29.

2.26 Record the eggshell observation in this circle.

(Continued on next page)

2.27 Use the magnifying glass to view the *pores* of the colored shell. Record your observation.

2.28 Use the magnifying glass to view the *membrane* of the cracked shell. Record your observation.

2.29 Use the magnifying glass to observe the *egg white*, *yolk*, and the tiny *white dot* in the yolk. Record your observations.

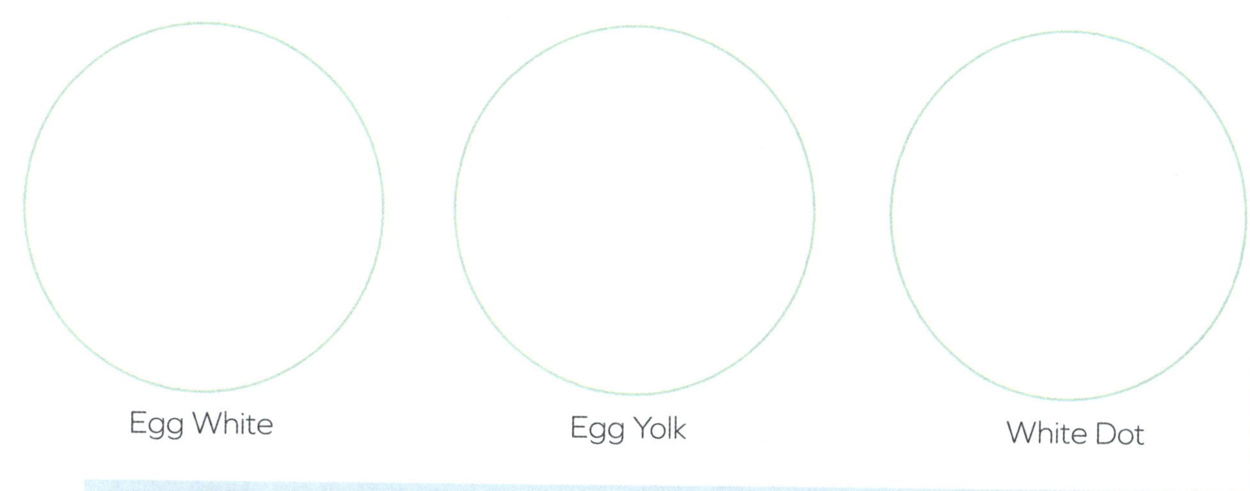

Egg White | Egg Yolk | White Dot

Teacher check:

Initials ____________________ Date ____________________

Answer these questions. Use the egg observation to help you answer these questions. You may also need to go to the library or check the Internet to help you find some of the answers.

2.30 Why does an egg need pores? ______________________________

____

____

2.31 What does a membrane do? ______________________________

____

____

2.32 What is the purpose of the egg white, the yolk, and the tiny white dot?

a. egg white ______________________________

____

b. yolk ______________________________

____

c. tiny white dot ______________________________

____

Live-Bearing Vertebrates

Mammals are the last important group of vertebrates that we will examine. A mammal is an animal that feeds its young on the mother's milk. The offspring are born live rather than hatched from eggs. Mammals differ from almost all other animals in five major ways. (1) Only mammals nurse their babies on the mother's milk. (2) Only mammals have hair. (3) Mammals are warm-blooded. Birds are warm-blooded, too, but nearly all other animals are cold-blooded. (4) Mammals have a larger, more well-developed brain than other animals. (5) Most mammals give their young offspring more protection and training than other animals.

There are over 4,500 kinds of mammals. Some of them are among the most familiar animals to us: cats, dogs, cattle. The largest animal of all is a mammal: the blue whale. It can be more than 100 feet long and weigh more than 150 tons! Mammals live almost everywhere on earth.

| Blue whale

Structure. Mammals are alike in several ways. They have hair or fur. They have lungs for breathing. The mothers feed their newborn babies with milk. Embryos develop inside the mother's body instead of within an egg shell.

The embryo is much safer within the body of the mother. This means that fewer offspring are needed to continue the species. A live baby mammal also takes longer to produce than most other animals.

Baby mammals are very weak at birth. They must be given their food supply by the parents. Initially, this food is supplied by the mother's milk. Babies will then learn what other foods may be eaten. The parents must also protect the baby during its young life.

All mammals have structures of their bodies that help them survive. The color of fur is helpful to some animals so that they hide in their environment or frighten off other animals. Claws and sharp teeth protect some mammals. Mammals usually have keen senses of hearing, sight, and smell to help avoid danger or to obtain food. Most of the young mammals need to be taught how to use their structures well by their parents.

LOOK IT UP: God has created many kinds of mammals.

Choose one of them to study. When you have chosen it, write its name here:

____

(name of mammal chosen)

Use a library or the Internet to help you answer the following questions about the mammal that you have chosen to study.

2.33 On a separate piece of paper, draw a picture of the mammal you are studying.

2.34 How many legs does it use? _______________

2.35 Where does it live? _______________

2.36 What size is it? _______________

2.37 What does it eat? _______________

2.38 How many young does it produce at one time? _______________

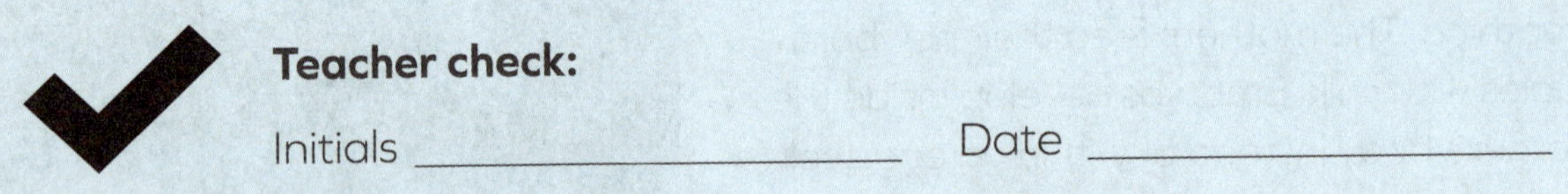

Teacher check:

Initials _______________ Date _______________

Write *true* or *false*.

2.39 __________ Mammals lay eggs.

2.40 __________ Mammal babies are strong at birth.

2.41 __________ The color of a mammal's fur helps some of them survive.

2.42 __________ Mammals have lungs.

2.43 __________ Female mammals nurse their offspring with milk.

Answer this question.

2.44 What are five major ways that mammals differ from almost all other animals?

a. ______________________________

b. ______________________________

c. ______________________________

d. ______________________________

e. ______________________________

Reproduction. All mammals reproduce through sexual reproduction. The female mammals produce egg cells in the ovaries within their bodies. The males produce sperm in testes. The sperm is placed within the female's body during mating. The egg cells are fertilized by the sperm, and the fertilized egg begins to grow through mitosis. The embryo then grows.

Each mammal has a certain period of time before the baby is born. This is called the *gestation* period. Cats develop for about two months before being born. Cattle have a gestation period of more than nine months. Elephant embryos develop for more than twenty months before being born. The "Gestation Chart" on the next page shows typical gestation periods for various mammals.

Once the baby is born, it drinks its mother's milk for some time. In time, the young mammal begins to learn how to find its own food. During this time, it is protected by the adult mammals. The young mammals are also taught by the adults how to live on their own.

| Zebras

Some smaller mammals become adults within a year after their birth. Larger mammals take longer to reach adulthood. Some of them are not adults before they are ten years old or older.

Most adult mammals reproduce for several years. Much of the adults' time is spent feeding the young, protecting them, and training them to become adults. If the adults did not provide for their young in these ways, the species would soon die out. Fortunately, God watches over all of His creatures to give them His loving care and provision.

Gestation Chart

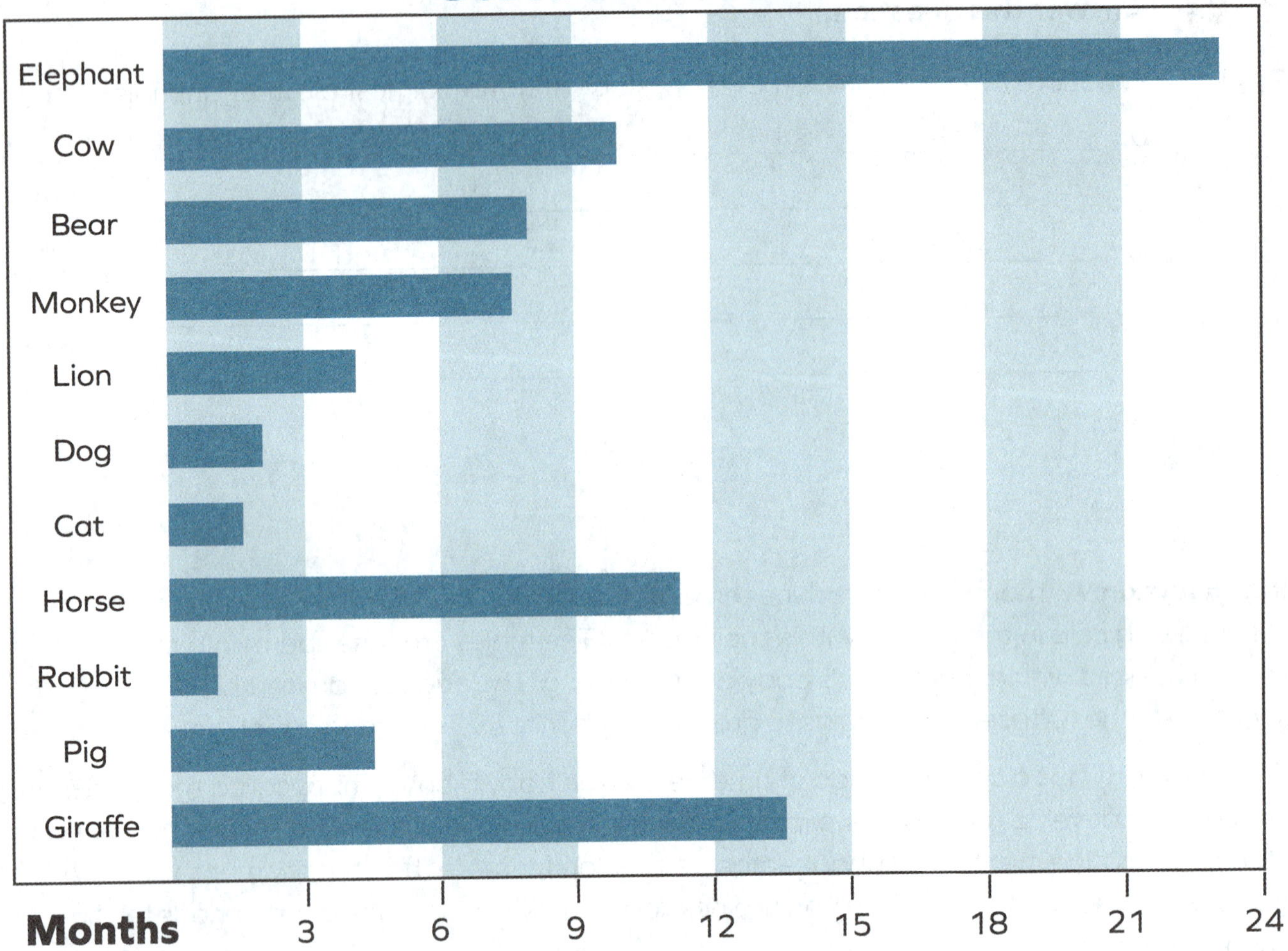

Elephant
Cow
Bear
Monkey
Lion
Dog
Cat
Horse
Rabbit
Pig
Giraffe

Months 3 6 9 12 15 18 21 24

| Length of time for development before birth

Write a report.

2.45 Use the library or the Internet to help you write a report about the mammal you chose to study. Include information about its life cycle. Tell how it feeds, protects, and trains its young.

Teacher check:

Initials __________________ Date __________________

Use your Bible. In Psalm 104:10-30, the writer praises God for many things. The psalmist is thankful for the animals that God has created. Read these verses with another family member. Talk over the meaning of the passage.

2.46 In this space, write what you think the psalm writer was telling you about God and animals. ____

____

____

____

____

____

____

____

____

____

____

____

Teacher check:

Initials ____________________ Date ____________________

Before you take this last Self Test, you may want to do one or more of these self checks.

1. ________ Read the objectives. See if you can do them.

2. ________ Restudy the material related to any objectives that you cannot do.

3. ________ Use the **SQ3R** study procedure to review the material:

a. **S**can the sections.

b. **Q**uestion yourself.

c. **R**ead to answer your questions.

d. **R**ecite the answers to yourself.

e. **R**eview areas you did not understand.

4. ________ Review all vocabulary, activities, and Self Tests, writing a correct answer for every wrong answer.

SELF TEST 2

Write *true* or *false* (each answer, 2 points).

2.01 __________ Frog eggs are fertilized outside the female body.

2.02 __________ A robin is a parasite.

2.03 __________ Birds give birth to live babies.

2.04 __________ There are over 4,500 kinds of mammals.

2.05 __________ Box turtles bury their eggs in sand.

2.06 __________ Salmon lay thousands of eggs.

2.07 __________ Nymphs reproduce themselves.

2.08 __________ Vertebrates are animals with backbones.

2.09 __________ Carnivores are animals that eat other animals.

2.010 __________ All fish reproduce only once.

Match these items (each answer, 3 points).

2.011 __________ Feed milk to their young.

2.012 __________ Live all their lives under water.

2.013 __________ Tadpoles.

2.014 __________ Adults have plates or scales.

2.015 __________ Creep or crawl most of their lives.

2.016 __________ Adults are covered with feathers.

2.017 __________ Snakes.

2.018 __________ Adults have gills to breathe.

2.019 __________ Undergo metamorphosis.

2.020 __________ Adults have hair or fur.

a. fish
b. amphibians
c. reptiles
d. birds
e. mammals

Write the correct letter and answer in the blank (each answer, 2 points).

2.021 Examples of warm-blooded animals are ______________________.
a. mammals and reptiles b. fish and birds c. mammals and birds

2.022 ______________________ can reproduce.
a. Earthworms b. Larvae c. Pupae

2.023 Sperm is produced in the ______________________ of male animals.
a. testes b. ovaries c. gills

2.024 Some adult ______________________ have scales.
a. fish and mollusks b. mollusks and reptiles c. reptiles and fish

2.025 The largest animal of all is a(n) ______________________, the blue whale.
a. fish b. mammal c. amphibian

2.026 Fish remove oxygen from the water through their ______________________.
a. lungs b. gills c. mouths

2.027 During its lifetime a Pacific Ocean salmon reproduces ______________________.
a. only once b. every year c. twice each year

2.028 The fastest animals on earth are from the ______________________ species.
a. fish b. bird c. mammal

2.029 Box turtles become adults after ______________________.
a. six months b. many years c. one year

2.030 Bird eggs are fertilized ______________________.
a. inside the mother's body
b. outside the mother's body
c. by the mother

2.031 Most adult mammals must provide ______________________ for their young.
a. food, protection, and training
b. food only
c. shelter only

Answer the following question (each answer, 2 points).

2.032 List five major ways that mammals differ from almost all other animals.
a. ______________________
b. ______________________
c. ______________________
d. ______________________
e. ______________________

Complete this activity (each life cycle stage, 2 points).

2.033 Describe the first three life cycle stages of a frog.

____

____

____

____

____

____

____

____

Answer this question (each part, 4 points).

2.034 In a chicken egg, what is the purpose for the egg white, yolk, and tiny white dot?

a. egg white ____

____

b. yolk ____

____

c. tiny white dot ____

____

Teacher check: Initials ________

Score ______________ Date ________

80/100

Before you take the LIFEPAC Test, you may want to do one or more of these self checks.

1. ________ Read the objectives. See if you can do them.
2. ________ Restudy the material related to any objectives that you cannot do.
3. ________ Use the **SQ3R** study procedure to review the material.
4. ________ Review activities, Self Tests, and LIFEPAC vocabulary words.
5. ________ Restudy areas of weakness indicated by the last Self Test.

SCIENCE 504
BALANCE IN NATURE

Author:
Barry G. Burrus, M.Div, M.A., B.S.

Editor:
Alan Christopherson, M.S.

Editor:
Brian Ring

Illustrations:
Brian Ring

Media Credits:
Page 3: © Givga, iStock, Thinkstock; **5:** © somchaij, iStock, Thinkstock; **11:** © snapgalleria, iStock, Thinkstock; **15:** © pigphoto, iStock, Thinkstock; **16:** © Maxim Kulko, iStock, Thinkstock; © Eric Isselee, iStock, Thinkstock; © Eriklam, iStock, Thinkstock; © Jezperklauzen, iStock, Thinkstock; **20:** © GlobalIP, iStock, Thinkstock; © antpkr, iStock, Thinkstock, © Eric Isselee, iStock, Thinkstock; © Melinda Fawver, iStock, Thinkstock; © PicturePartners, iStock, Thinkstock; © a-poselenov, iStock, Thinkstock; **22:** ©armckw, iStock, Thinkstock; **28:** © mike proto, iStock, Thinkstock; 30: © Ten03, iStock, Thinkstock; **33:** © jesiotr9, iStock, Thinkstock; **34:** © m_grageda, iStock, Thinkstock; © PaulReevesPhotography, iStock, Thinkstock; **37:** © lukaves, istock, Thinkstock; © mart_m, iStock, Thinkstock; **39:** © ekina, iStock, Thinkstock; **41:** © Natalia Bratslavsky, iStock, Thinkstock; **46:** © Fuse, Thinkstock; **47:** © Ingram Publishing, Thinkstock; **48:** © michal kodym, iStock, Thinkstock; **49:** © Hung_Chung_Chih, iStock, Thinkstock; © Dmitry Berkut, iStock, Thinkstock; **50:** © michaeljung, iStock, Thinkstock.

804 N. 2nd Ave. E.
Rock Rapids, IA 51246-1759

BALANCE IN NATURE

In the first three LIFEPACs of this series, you learned about cells, the basic unit of life. All living things are made of cells. You also learned about the life cycles of many living things, especially plants and animals. God has created all these living things. He has given a wonderful variety to all living things.

God has also planned that all living things depend upon one another. You have learned how animals depend upon plants for oxygen and food. Plants, in turn, depend upon animals for carbon dioxide and nutrients. Some plants also depend upon animals to help them reproduce. For example, flowering plants depend upon bees and other insects to help in the process of fertilization. In some way, all living things are connected to other living things and depend upon them.

Have you ever seen a spider's web? The threads of the web are connected to each other so that it forms one whole web. The different parts of the web support one another because they are connected. In a similar way, all living things are "connected" to one another and to the air, water, and earth. We call this great system of the connection among all living things *the web of life*.

In this LIFEPAC® you will learn more about the web of life that God has established among all living things. You will learn how God has planned a *balance of nature* in His creation on earth. You will examine the web of life in one particular type of region on earth—*the prairie*. You will also learn how God has placed human beings on the earth to help care for His creation and to be good stewards of the web of life. Finally, for an experiment, you will have the opportunity to build a small, living model of the web of life—*a terrarium!*

Objectives

Read these objectives. The objectives tell you what you will be able to do when you have successfully completed this LIFEPAC. Each section will list according to the numbers below what objectives will be met in that section. When you have finished this LIFEPAC, you should be able to:

1. Describe three cycles in the physical environment.
2. Explain the balance of nature in the web of life.
3. Explain what is meant by a food chain and to give examples.
4. Know some details about the web of life in a prairie ecosystem.
5. Name two problems that human beings have made for God's web of life.
6. Name at least five things that you can do for plants and animals that will help care for the web of life that God has created.

1. THE BALANCE OF NATURE

God has created everything that exists. God planned for a great variety of things in His Creation. In previous LIFEPACs, you have learned something about the great variety of living things that God has created. There is also a great variety of nonliving things that God has created such as the water, air, soil, rocks, minerals, and chemicals. We often refer to all these things in our world that God has created—both living and nonliving—as nature.

Objectives

Review these objectives. When you have completed this section, you should be able to:

1. Describe three cycles in the physical environment.
2. Explain the balance of nature in the web of life.
3. Explain what is meant by a food chain and to give examples.

Vocabulary

Study these new words. Learning the meanings of these words is a good study habit and will improve your understanding of this LIFEPAC.

affected (ə fekt′ ed). To have had an effect on someone or something.

consumers (kən süm′ urz). Someone or something that uses up or destroys things.

decomposers (dē′ kəm pōz′ ərz). Tiny organisms that eat the dead remains of former living things.

dew (dü). Moisture from the air that settles on cool surfaces during the night.

drought (drout). A long time without rain. Plants begin to dry up during a drought.

ecology (ē kol′ ə jē). The scientific study of the relationships of living things to one another and to their environment.

ecosystem (e ko′ sis təm). The complex level of organization within nature consisting of both the physical and biological environments.

environment (en vī ′ rən mənt). Everything around a living thing—such as the earth, air, water—that helps to determine how it develops.

evaporates (i vap′ ə rātz′). The natural process that occurs when a liquid changes to a gas or vapor.

nature (na′ chər). All of the living and nonliving external things in our world that God has created.

nitrogen (nī ′ trə jən). A very important gas that makes up most of the air. It is colorless, tasteless, and odorless. It is part of the chemical cycle in nature.

population (pop′ yə lā′ shən). The members of one species of living things within a given area.

precipitation (pri sip′ ə tā ′ shən). Water that falls to the earth such as rain, snow, sleet, hail, mist, dew, or some other form of water.

producers (prə dü′ sərz). Green plants that grow and are partly or fully eaten by animals.

rodents (rōd′ ntz). A member of a group of animals with teeth that are especially good for chewing wood, woody plants, or seeds.

terrarium (tə rer′ ē əm). A transparent container (plastic or glass) in which small plants or animals are kept. It reproduces as closely as possible a natural setting or environment.

Note: *All vocabulary words in this LIFEPAC appear in* **boldface** *print the first time they are used. If you are unsure of the meaning when you are reading, study the definitions given.*

Pronunciation Key: h**a**t, **ā**ge, c**ã**re, f**ä**r; l**e**t, **ē**qual, t**ė**rm; **i**t, **ī**ce; h**o**t, **ō**pen, **ô**rder; **oi**l; **ou**t; c**u**p, p**u̇**t, r**ü**le; **ch**ild; lo**ng**; **th**in; /ŦH/ for **th**en; /zh/ for mea**s**ure; /u/ or /ə/ represents /a/ in **a**bout, /e/ in tak**e**n, /i/ in penc**i**l, /o/ in lem**o**n, and /u/ in circ**u**s.

God has so arranged nature that living things are able to exist by depending on other living and nonliving things for food and energy. For example, green plants receive energy from the sun. The plants receive minerals, nutrients, and water from the soil. Plants also receive carbon dioxide from the air. The plants give off oxygen to the air.

Rabbits feed on the plants. The rabbits also receive oxygen from the air and water to drink. Rabbits give off carbon dioxide as they breathe and add chemicals to the soil through their wastes.

Foxes sometimes eat rabbits for food. The foxes also receive oxygen from the air and water to drink. The foxes, like other animals, give off carbon dioxide to the air and add minerals to the soil through wastes. Eventually, the foxes will die and their dead bodies will provide food for other organisms. Their dead bodies will also be turned into minerals and nutrients for the soil which will, in turn, be used by new plants.

In this example, we see how the life needs of living things are met. When the life needs of all the living things in an area of the earth are met, we say that there is a *balance of nature*. When there is a balance of nature, the **population** of one species of living things stays fairly stable. For example, the population of rabbits and the population of foxes would be stable over time when there is a balance of nature. Enough of these animals would receive adequate food, oxygen, and water in order to survive, grow, and reproduce.

If something happened so that adequate water, food, or air was not received by the rabbits or foxes, the balance of nature would be upset, and the populations of rabbits and foxes would begin to change. However, in time, the balance of nature could be restored as the living things adjust to the changes. God also wants human beings to help keep or restore the balance of nature. The balance of nature has been provided by God so that the life needs of all living things are met. Through the balance of nature, the web of life continues.

There is a name for the scientific study of the balance of nature and the relationships of living things to one another and to their **environment**. This science is called **ecology**. The scientists who study these relationships are called *ecologists*.

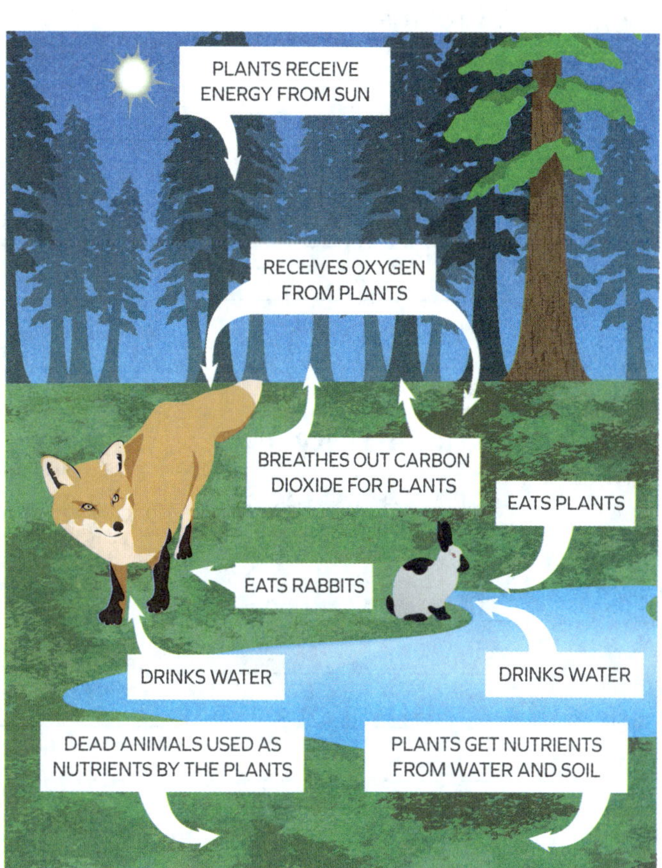

In this first section of the LIFEPAC, you will learn more about the balance of nature. You will learn how nonliving things help meet the life needs of living organisms. These are such things as water, the air, the soil, and the weather. This can be called the *physical environment*. You will also learn in this section about the way living things within the environment depend on one another, especially for food. The living things make up what can be called the *biological environment*. Finally, you will have an opportunity to build a small, living model of the web of life—a **terrarium**.

Answer these questions.

1.1 What are some of the nonliving things that God has created?

____

____

____

____

1.2 What is *the balance of nature*?

____

____

____

1.3 What is the difference between the physical environment and the biological environment?

____

____

____

____

____

Do this activity.

1.4 Look up Psalm 104: 24-30 in the Bible. Explain how this passage relates to *the balance of nature*.

____

____

____

____

The Physical Environment

The physical environment includes such nonliving things as water, the air, the soil, and the weather. These things help support life on the earth. They help supply the life needs of living things. Some parts of the physical environment go through *cycles* as they help support living things and the balance of nature. We will consider three of these cycles: the *water cycle*, the *carbon cycle*, and the *chemical cycle*.

Water cycle. Water is the most common substance that God has put on the earth. Water covers more than 70 percent of the earth's surface. Water is in the oceans, rivers, lakes, and other streams of the earth. It is also in the ground and in the air.

Without water, there would be no life on the earth. Every living thing consists mostly of water. In fact, the cells in all living things are mostly water. Your body is about 65 percent water. An elephant is about 70 percent water. A potato is about 80 percent water. So, all living things need water to support life.

Water helps living things grow and survive. It helps the cells do their work. Water helps the nutrients dissolve and flow to the different parts of plants and animals. Water is also used to transport wastes out of plants and animals. The water that is lost by the plants and animals must be replaced or they will die.

Organisms that live in the sea, lakes, or rivers can easily receive water. Plants and animals that live on the land receive water through the rain or **dew** that falls on the earth. The plants absorb this water, primarily through their roots. This water is collected into lakes, rivers, and streams from which the animals can drink. Animals also receive water through the food they eat. God has provided a way for all living things to receive water.

All of the water on the earth continually goes through a *water cycle*. In the water cycle, the waters of the earth move continuously from the oceans, lakes, rivers, and streams to the air. It does this when the sun's heat **evaporates** the water so that it enters the air. Actually, some of the water on the earth also evaporates into the air. The water that evaporates becomes water vapor. The water vapor mixes with the cool air in the atmosphere and forms clouds. Eventually, enough water vapor collects so that it produces rain, snow, dew, or some other form of **precipitation**. The precipitation falls from the clouds to the earth and to the bodies of water on the earth. This precipitation not only supplies the water needed to "make up" for the water that has evaporated, but it also supplies the water needed to support the living things on earth and in the waters.

Eventually, much of the water that falls on the earth collects into streams and rivers and makes its way back to the ocean. Then the water evaporates again, and the water cycle continues over and over. In the process, God provides water to support the web of life.

The balance of nature is supported by the water cycle. It is also **affected** by the water cycle. For example, if there is not enough rain or precipitation in an area or region of the earth, **drought** occurs. The soil then dries up. Water levels in lakes, rivers, and streams go down. Some of the plants and animals that depend on the soil or these bodies of water may die. The balance of nature changes.

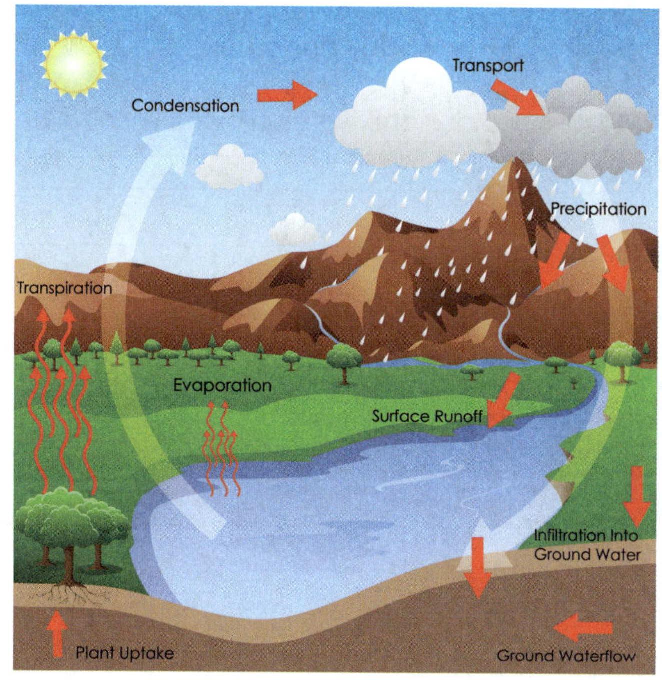

| The water cycle

Too much water in an area or region of the earth may also cause a problem. Floods may occur, causing drowning of plant and animal life. Snow may cover the earth too long, making it difficult for animals to get adequate food. Again, the balance of nature changes, depending upon the way the water cycle is working.

Fortunately, God is watching over His creation. The water cycle eventually returns to favorable conditions. The balance of nature is restored. The web of life adjusts and continues.

Write the correct word in the blank space.

1.5 The most common substance on earth is ______________________ .

1.6 The cells in all living things are mostly ______________________ .

1.7 The heat from the sun ______________________ water so that it enters the air.

1.8 Rain, snow, dew, and hail are all forms of ______________________ .

1.9 If there is not enough rain or precipitation in an area, ______________________ occurs.

1.10 The ____________________ of nature is supported by the water cycle.

Answer this question.

1.11 What is the water cycle? Describe what happens.

____

____

____

____

____

____

____

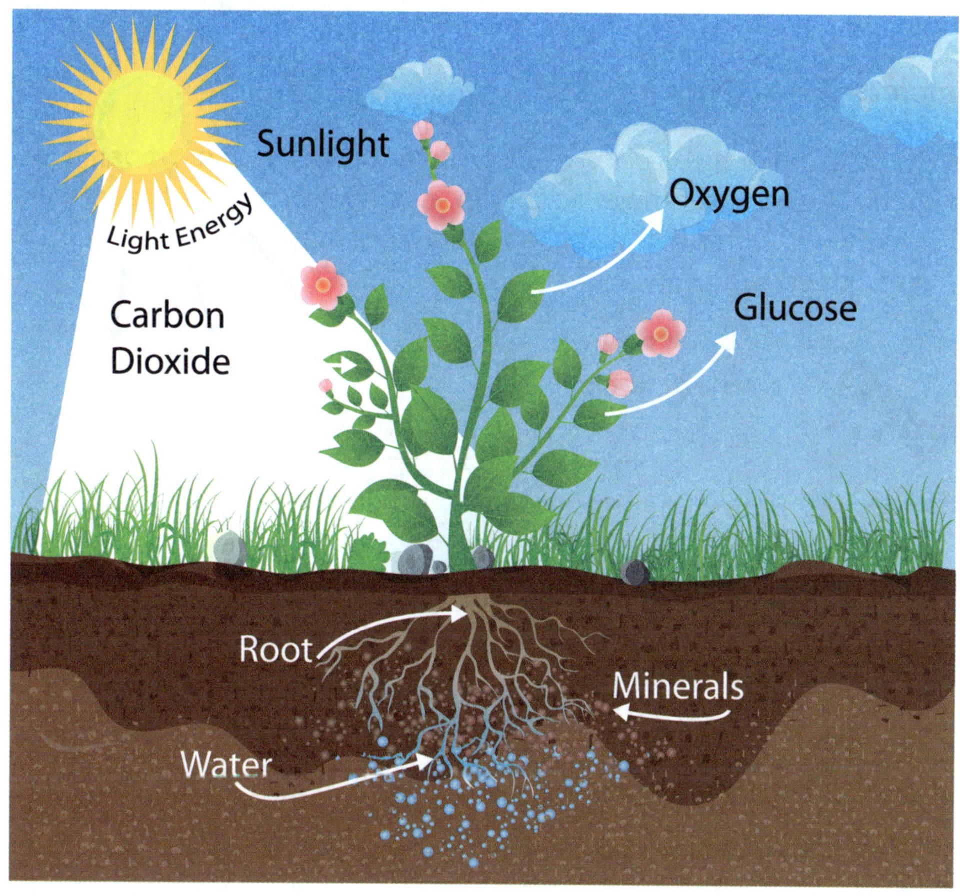

| Photosynthesis

Carbon cycle. There is another "cycle" in the physical environment that helps support living things and the balance of nature. Green plants use energy from the sun to convert carbon dioxide and water into food and oxygen. As you learned in LIFEPAC Science 501, this process is called *photosynthesis*. Plants and animals, in turn, "burn" food by combining it with the oxygen produced by photosynthesis to release energy for growth. Carbon dioxide and water are given off in this process, which is called *respiration*. Respiration is the reverse of photosynthesis. Plants then use the carbon dioxide produced by respiration to produce more oxygen. Thus, there is a cycle of carbon dioxide and oxygen being used and produced by plants and animals. This cycle is called the *carbon cycle*. The oxygen and carbon dioxide produced in the carbon cycle are part of the physical environment that supports life.

The balance of nature also depends on this carbon cycle of oxygen and carbon dioxide. For example, consider what would happen in a small pond if all the plants died. If the plants died, there would not be any more oxygen produced by the plants for the water. Soon, the fish and other microscopic organisms would not have enough oxygen to survive. Other animals that feed on the fish and the microscopic organisms in the pond would not have adequate food supplies, and they, too, would die. The balance of nature would be upset by the death of the plants, and, eventually, the other living things would die. The web of life would be broken.

Complete this activity.

1.12 Draw a diagram of the carbon cycle on a separate piece of paper. (Use a cow, some grass, and the sun as some examples in your diagram. Use other plants and animals, too, if you wish.) Refer to the carbon cycle diagram in Section 3 of LIFEPAC Science 501 if you need to.

Teacher check:

Initials ________________ Date ________________

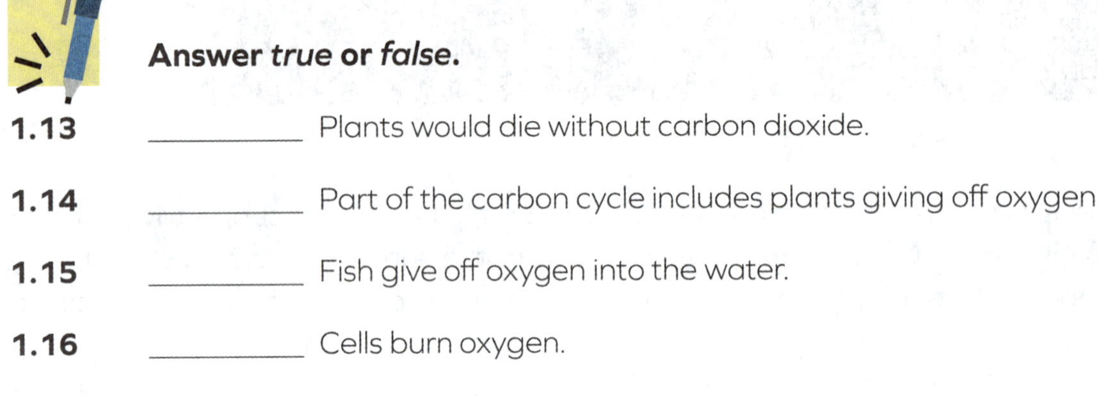

Answer *true* or *false*.

1.13 __________ Plants would die without carbon dioxide.

1.14 __________ Part of the carbon cycle includes plants giving off oxygen.

1.15 __________ Fish give off oxygen into the water.

1.16 __________ Cells burn oxygen.

1.17 __________ The balance of nature needs carbon dioxide.

The Chemical Cycle

Chemical cycle. The final cycle in the physical environment is called the *chemical cycle*. Besides water, carbon dioxide, and oxygen, there are other chemicals that are important to the web of life and the balance of nature. Plants need bacteria and other micro-organisms to break down dead things. Animals need the chemicals in plants. These chemicals include hydrogen, **nitrogen**, phosphorus, and sulfur.

These chemicals come into plants through their roots. From the sugars produced by photosynthesis— together with nitrogen, sulfur, and phosphorus obtained from the soil through the roots—green plants can make "food." This food consists of starch, fat, protein, vitamins, and other complex compounds that are essential for life. Animals get these chemicals when they eat the plants.

The next step is when the plants or animals make waste products or die. Bacteria help dead plants and animals to decay. The chemicals then return to the ground. These chemicals go into new plants and begin the chemical cycle again.

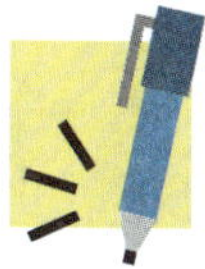

Write the letter of the correct answer in the blank.

1.18 Some chemicals that cycle through the environment are ________ .

a. hydrogen and nitrogen b. phosphorus and sulfur c. all of these

1.19 These chemicals are brought into plants mainly through their ________ .

a. leaves b. stems c. roots

1.20 These chemicals are needed by plants to make ________ and other food essential for life.

a. protein b. chlorophyll c. energy

1.21 Waste products and dead organisms return to the soil with the help of ______ .
a. sunlight b. bacteria c. predators

1.22 Chemicals are provided to support life through the ______ .
a. chemical cycle b. air c. offspring of animals

Read Genesis 3:19 and answer these questions.

1.23 In Genesis 3:19, God is speaking. With whom is He talking? ______

1.24 In Genesis 3:19, what is God speaking about? ______

1.25 God says something will happen to the body. What will happen? ______

______

1.26 What have you learned in this LIFEPAC that God created to help this process take place? ______

______

Complete this activity.

1.27 In the space below, draw a diagram that includes the water cycle, carbon cycle, and chemical cycle. You may use pictures to illustrate your diagram.

Teacher check:

Initials ______ Date ______

Ecosystems

God made the physical environment that consists of nonliving things such as the water, soil, air, weather, nutrients, and energy. He also made the biological environment that consists of all living things. God planned that the physical and biological environments depend on one another to support life and maintain a balance of nature.

There are many activities that take place within nature, both in the physical environment and the biological environment. Ecologists, the scientists who study ecology and the environment, try to understand how all these activities interact within nature. They call this complex level of organization within nature an **ecosystem**.

To better understand an ecosystem, ecologists have given names to various things that make up the ecosystem. They also study the way energy and food move through the ecosystem. They call this the *food chain*. Ecologists follow the movement of energy and food through the ecosystem by identifying parts of the food chain. We will first examine the ecological names for things in the ecosystem. Then we will look more closely at how they are part of the food chain.

Producers. Green plants use the energy from the sun, carbon dioxide from the air, and chemicals and water from the soil to produce food. They are the main living things that produce food. Animals, fungi, and some other plants cannot make their own food. They must receive it from green plants. Since green plants are the only food makers in the ecosystem, they are called **producers**. Examples of producers are grass and trees.

| Wild grass is a producer.

Consumers. Living things that must get their food from green plants are called **consumers**.

There are two types of consumers:
(1) *primary* consumers and
(2) *secondary* consumers.

Primary consumers get their food directly by eating green plants. They are able to digest the plants and receive energy from the food stored in the plants. Examples of primary consumers are grasshoppers, mice, rabbits, sheep, and goats. Birds are primary consumers when they eat the seeds of plants.

Secondary consumers are animals that eat other animals for food. They eat the primary consumers. In this way, the secondary consumers receive the necessary food and energy stored in the primary consumers who have eaten plants. Foxes, dogs, lions, and wolves are examples of secondary consumers. Birds are secondary consumers when they eat insects, **rodents**, or other birds that have eaten plants.

Lambs and birds are primary consumers. The wolf eats birds and lambs, making it a secondary consumer.

Decomposers. There are other living things in the ecosystem that are called **decomposers**. Bacteria and fungi are examples of decomposers. They feed on the waste products or dead bodies of plants or animals. You learned that these organisms are an important part of the chemical cycle. When bacteria or fungi use the food stored in the wastes or dead remains of plants or animals, they break them down into chemicals that go back into the soil. These chemicals and nutrients in the soil can then be used again by the producers: the green plants.

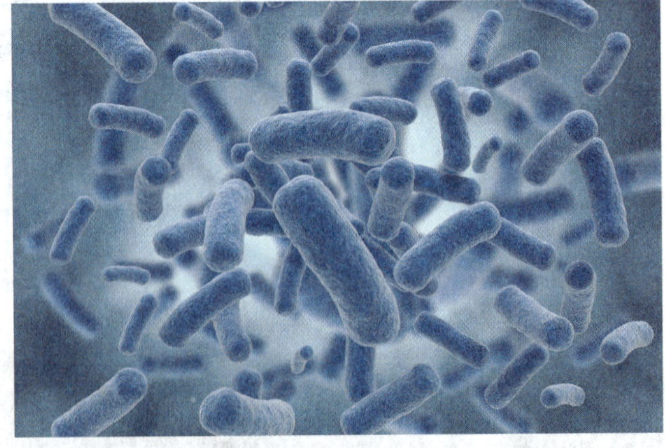

Bacteria is a decomposer of dead animals, plants, or other wastes. The bacteria decomposes the bodies of the animals.

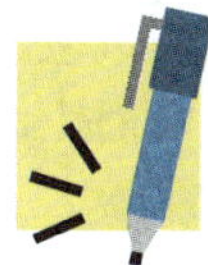

Write the correct letter and answer in the blank.

1.28 The complex level of organization within nature is called a(n) ______________________ .
a. physical environment b. ecosystem c. chemical cycle

1.29 A living thing that makes its own food is called a ______________________ .
a. producer b. consumer c. decomposer

1.30 Some ______________________ are both primary consumers and secondary consumers.
a. sheep b. bacteria c. birds

1.31 A primary consumer can ______________________ .
a. digest green plants b. make its own food c. decompose animals

1.32 An example of a producer is ______________________ .
a. a grasshopper b. a pine tree c. a mushroom

Complete this activity.

1.33 Fill in this chart. Each of the organisms can be put in one or more groups. Put a check mark in the column of the ecological name or names where you think it belongs. You may use library or Internet resources to help you.

ORGANISM	PRODUCER	PRIMARY CONSUMER	SECONDARY CONSUMER	DECOMPOSER
chicken				
lettuce				
tiger				
monkey				
cow				
mouse				
mushroom				
bull snake				
silverfish				
salmon				

Teacher check:

Initials ______________________ Date ______________________

The food chain. In an ecosystem, the series of stages that energy goes through in the form of food is called a *food chain*. Producers, consumers, and decomposers all have a role in the food chain.

Many food chains are found in nature. Some of them are long and complex. Some of them are short and simple. For example, one simple food chain is shown in the "Introduction" to this section of the LIFEPAC. In this example of a food chain, grass is the producer. The primary consumer, a rabbit, eats the grass. The rabbit, in turn, is eaten by the secondary consumer, a fox. The decomposer, bacteria, breaks down the dead body of the fox when it dies. Energy, in the form of food, moves along this simple food chain from producer to primary consumer to secondary consumer to decomposer.

| Nature's food chain

The kind of food chain that exists depends upon the particular ecosystem where the organisms live. For example, a food chain in a wetland area might be very different from the food chain in a desert region. Climate and land features are also important factors in determining food chains. You will examine some food chains in a specific ecosystem in the next section of this LIFEPAC.

| Woodland food chain

Often, many food chains exist in a particular type of ecosystem. For example, in a woodland area, robins may be part of a food chain. Another food chain might exist in the same woodland that involved deer. The robin and the deer exist side by side in the same woodland, but one is not part of the other's food chain.

The balance of nature depends on the food chain. For example, if a secondary consumer in a food chain were removed, problems would result. Other primary consumer animal groups could grow too large. These larger groups of primary consumers could destroy the population of some green plants. Then, other smaller primary consumer groups would begin starving. This process would, in turn, cause other secondary consumers to starve. The balance of nature would be upset.

Food webs. Most ecosystems have a great variety of producers, consumers, and decomposers. These form an overlapping network of food chains called a *food web*. Usually, primary consumers eat a variety of producer plants. Secondary consumers usually prey on different kinds of primary consumer animals. Also, some animals, like the birds we have already seen, eat both plants and animals. In all of this variety, interconnected food chains called food webs are established. Once again, we learn that God has provided a rich variety of things that make up the web of life.

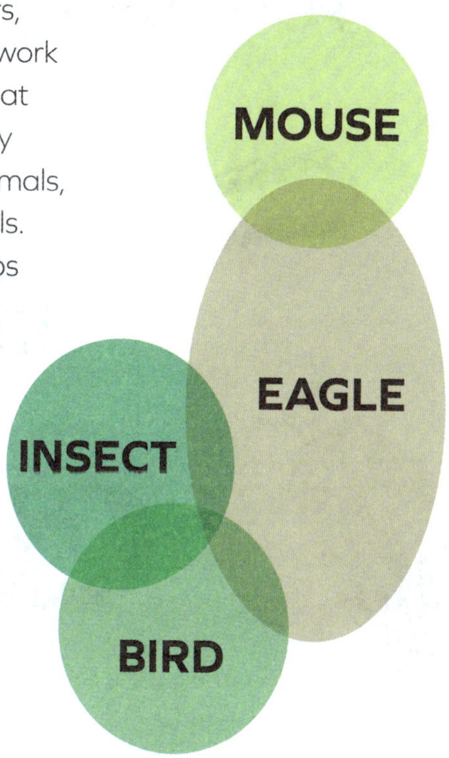

MOUSE

EAGLE

INSECT

BIRD

| Food web

Complete these activities.

1.34 What is the correct order of these food chains? Draw arrows to show the order. Draw arrows from the organism to the organisms it is eaten by (eaten by = →).

Teacher check:

Initials ______________________ Date ______________________

Draw a picture of a food chain.

1.35 Follow these directions:

a. Think of some food chains that might be in the ecosystem where you live. Choose one of these food chains to draw. (If you need some ideas, go to a friend, parent, or teacher.)

b. Find a large piece of drawing paper for your drawing.

c. Draw pictures of your producers, consumers, and decomposers.

d. Label each picture using one of these terms: producer, primary consumer, secondary consumer, decomposer.

e. Take the drawing to your teacher for display.

Teacher check:

Initials ________________ Date ________________

Answer these questions.

1.36 What is a food web?

____

____

____

____

____

1.37 How is the food chain related to the web of life?

____

____

____

____

____

EXPERIMENT 504 BUILD A TERRARIUM

Overview: A terrarium is the name for a plastic or glass container in which small land animals and/or plants are kept. The container is usually covered to prevent the loss of moisture. The terrarium is really a model of a natural life system or ecosystem.

In this experiment, you will build a terrarium if conditions permit. You will be gathering examples of living things from a certain place. These living things will be placed inside the terrarium container so you may observe them. You will record your observations over a period of time. Hopefully, you will be able to see how living things depend on each other.

If you are having winter now, you may have difficulty finding an adequate number of living things to establish your terrarium. Three ways to solve this problem are suggested:

1. Use an aquarium as an example of a life system. Do the activities suggested.
2. Ask a friend, parent, or teacher about where you could look for plant or animal life. A hobby store or pet shop may also be of help. If your problem is solved, build the terrarium by following the directions in this experiment.
3. Wait until spring to do this experiment.

After you have discussed your ideas on this experiment, write your plans here and share them with your teacher or parent. ______________________________

____

____

____

These supplies are needed:

Large container (glass or clear plastic)—at least 2-liter capacity container
cover or lid
gravel
several cans or small jars
small sprinkling can
something to punch holes in lid
potting soil
bottle cap
sand
small shovel
water

Follow these directions carefully. Place a check in the box when each step is completed.

- ☐ 1. Place the gravel in the bottom of the large container until it is about 3 cm deep.
- ☐ 2. Cover the gravel with sand.
- ☐ 3. Put a 5 cm layer of potting soil over the sand. Make some hills and valleys in the soil by making the soil thicker in some places.
- ☐ 4. Position the bottle cap in a lower place and fill it with water. Also sprinkle some water over the soil.
- ☐ 5. Go to an area near your home or school to gather small plants. Choose several kinds of plants. Use the shovel to dig them up. Roots and soil should be kept on the plants. (Be sure to obtain permission before digging plants on private property.)
- ☐ 6. Bring the plants back to your terrarium in the small cans. Gently place them in the terrarium soil. Water them lightly.
- ☐ 7. Use the cans and jars to bring in a few small animals from the outside. Insects, frogs, worms, or lizards are best. Birds or kittens are too large.
- ☐ 8. Place the cover over the terrarium container opening. You will need to water the plants regularly. Some of the creatures may need food. Use the library or Internet to research how to properly feed the creatures you selected for your terrarium. Remove the lid for a short time each day or make small holes in the lid.
- ☐ 9. Place the terrarium where it can get some sunlight each day.

Teacher check:

Initials ____________________ Date ____________________

Answer these questions.

1.38 Why is water necessary for the terrarium? ____________________

____

____

1.39 Why should you feed some of the creatures? ____________________

____

____

1.40 Why should you allow outside air to come inside the terrarium?

____

____

____

1.41 Why should you place the terrarium where the sun reaches it?

____

Keep a daily record.

1.42 Each day you will spend some time recording information about your terrarium.
A small notebook might help keep your records organized.
After each daily observation and recording, you should continue to work in this LIFEPAC.
Several times as you work in this LIFEPAC, you will be directed to take your terrarium records to the teacher for a teacher check.

The following example of a daily terrarium log shows how one student recorded his observations. His ideas may help you plan your observations. Be sure to discuss your recording plans with your teacher.

DATE	WHAT I DID	DESCRIPTION, CHANGES, BEHAVIOR, PROBLEMS
10/7	I watered the plants. I fed an ant to the spider. I will put the jar in a dark place before I go home.	The spider has begun to spin a web. Small drops of water are on the side of the jar. Everything is still alive.
10/8	I put a fly in the jar	I saw the worm today when I came to school. It went into the ground when I put the jar in the sunlight. The spider web is larger.

Teacher check:

Initials ______________ Date ______________

Review the material in this section to prepare for the Self Test. The Self Test will check your understanding of this section. Any items you miss on this test will show you what areas you will need to restudy in order to prepare for the unit test.

SELF TEST 1

Match these items (each answer, 3 points).

1.01 __________ nature
1.02 __________ ecology
1.03 __________ water cycle
1.04 __________ carbon cycle
1.05 __________ chemical cycle
1.06 __________ ecosystem
1.07 __________ food chain
1.08 __________ producers
1.09 __________ consumers
1.010 __________ decomposers

a. movement of hydrogen, nitrogen, phosphorus, and sulfur
b. the complex level of organization within nature
c. all living and nonliving things in our world
d. the study of the relationships of living things to their environment
e. get their food from producers
f. bacteria and fungi
g. movement from oceans to air to earth
h. oxygen and carbon dioxide are used and produced
i. transparent containers
j. a mixture of air and water
k. the way energy and food move through the ecosystem
l. green plants like grass and trees

Answer *true* or *false* (each answer, 3 points).

1.011 __________ The most common substance on earth is water.
1.012 __________ Carbon dioxide is used by plants.
1.013 __________ Some animals produce their own food.
1.014 __________ A bird could be both a consumer and a producer.
1.015 __________ Some animals can be part of several food chains.
1.016 __________ The balance of nature depends on the food chain.
1.017 __________ A food web is an overlapping network of food chains.

1.018 __________ Bacteria are used in photosynthesis.

1.019 __________ The connection among all living things is called the web of life.

1.020 __________ A mushroom is a decomposer.

Write the letter for the correct answer on the blank (each answer, 4 points).

1.021 The heat from the sun ________ water so that it enters the air.
a. cools b. evaporates c. illuminates

1.022 Rain, snow, dew, and hail are forms of ________ .
a. producers b. consumers c. precipitation

1.023 Green plants use energy from the sun during ________ .
a. photosynthesis b. drying c. evaporation

1.024 Chemicals are needed by plants to make ________ and other food essential for life.
a. protein b. chlorophyll c. energy

1.025 Some ________ are both primary consumers and secondary consumers.
a. sheep b. bacteria c. birds

Put these items in order (each correctly placed item, 2 points).

1.026 Here is a list of organisms in a food chain. Put them in order starting with the producer.

cat	bird	bacteria	leaf	caterpillar

a. ______________________________

b. ______________________________

c. ______________________________

d. ______________________________

e. ______________________________

Answer this question (this answer, 10 points).

1.027 What is *the balance of nature*? (Use examples if you wish.)

____

____

____

____

____

____

____

____

Teacher check: Initials ____________

Score ____________ Date ____________

80/100

2. THE PRAIRIE WEB OF LIFE

We can learn some more about the web of life everywhere by studying a specific ecosystem. In this section, we will look at the prairie ecosystem.

Many people think of the central North American plains when they hear the word *prairie*. That area is where much of the prairie ecosystem remains today; however, it is different from what it was before settlers started farming the land in the 19th century. It was a huge region of grassland. Few trees were there except near rivers and streams. It was an area that covered more than the Midwestern United States.

In this section, you will learn about the web of life on the prairie of the past. You will examine the physical environment. You will learn about the food chains that existed there. You will then compare the prairie before the settlers came with the prairie as it is today. From this study, you should be able to understand more about God's design for life.

Objectives

Review these objectives. When you have completed this section, you should be able to:

3. Explain what is meant by a food chain and to give examples.
4. Know some details about the web of life in a prairie ecosystem

Vocabulary

Study these new words. Learning the meanings of these words is a good study habit and will improve your understanding of this LIFEPAC.

numerous (nü′ mər əs). Many.

prairie (prer′ ē). A large grassland area with rolling hills and few trees.

predators (pred′ ə tərz). Animals that hunt and kill other animals.

scavengers (skav′ ən jərz). Animals that feed on dead or rotting animals. They seldom kill the other animals.

thrive (thrīv). To be successful or grow strong.

Pronunciation Key: h**a**t, **ā**ge, c**ã**re, f**ä**r; l**e**t, **ē**qual, t**ė**rm; **i**t, **ī**ce; h**o**t, **ō**pen, **ô**rder; **oi**l; **ou**t; c**u**p, p**u̇**t, r**ü**le; **ch**ild; lo**ng**; **th**in; /ŦH/ for **th**en; /zh/ for mea**s**ure; /u/ or /ə/ represents /a/ in **a**bout, /e/ in tak**e**n, /i/ in penc**i**l, /o/ in lem**o**n, and /u/ in circ**u**s.

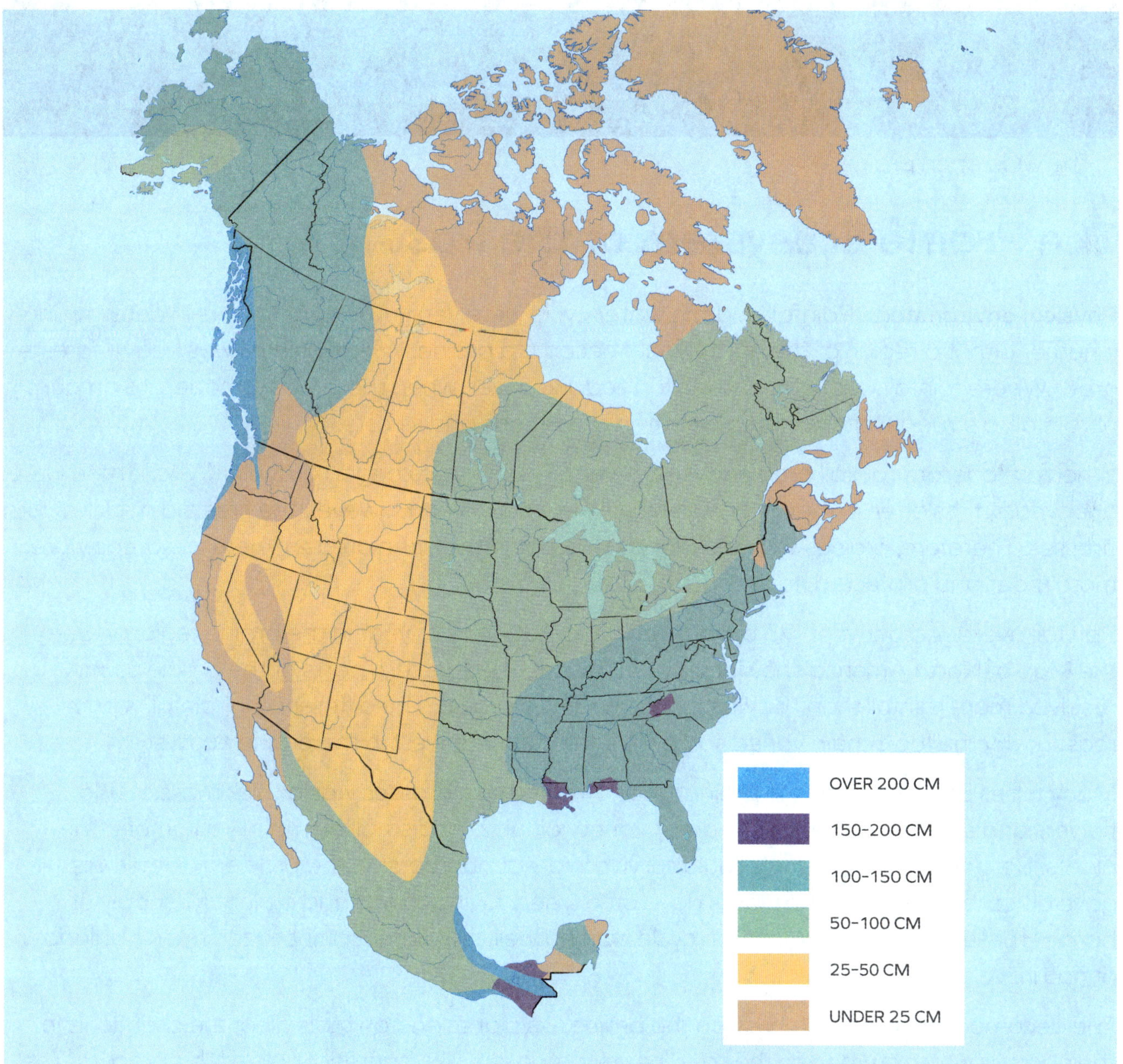

| Map of North America showing annual rainfall / 1 cm = 0.39 inch

| The wide open prairie

The Prairie Ecosystem of the Past

Physical environment. Rainfall and the water cycle were very important factors in determining whether or not a region of the earth would become a prairie. Where rainfall was heavy, forests grew. Where rainfall was light, deserts formed. However, when there was a moderate amount of rainfall, a struggle often existed between grasslands and forests.

When a moderate rainfall area had wetter years, many trees began growing. When there were drier years, fires often occurred and killed off the small trees. However, the fires did not kill most grasses. Therefore, prairies with grasslands won out in the open areas. Where the areas were more moist and protected, forests grew.

Rainfall averaged between 25 cm per year and 100 cm per year in the prairie regions. (See the Map of North America showing annual rainfall.) The eastern parts of the prairie usually received more rainfall than the western parts of the prairie. The difference in rainfall is one reason why the food chain varied somewhat from east to west in the prairie ecosystem.

Many types of grasses grew in prairie lands. Under these grasses was a thick mass of wild flowers and small woody plants. A great variety of large and small animals lived among the plants. Both plants and animals could survive in great numbers on the prairie. The animals gave off carbon dioxide. The plants gave off oxygen. Living things had a plentiful supply of both of these life needs. The carbon cycle worked well. It was important to the prairie balance of nature.

The decomposers were also busy on the prairie. As plants and animals died, the chemicals in their bodies were returned to the soil. The decomposers, like bacteria, helped this process. The prairie land was a rich source of these chemicals and minerals. Plants such as clover provided much nitrogen to the soil. The chemical cycle worked well on the prairie.

SCIENCE 504

LIFEPAC TEST

SCI 504 LIFEPAC TEST

NAME ______________________

DATE ______________________

SCORE ______________________

SCIENCE 504: LIFEPAC TEST

Match these items (each answer, 3 points).

1. __________ takes energy from the sun
2. __________ helps dead organisms decay
3. __________ food is mostly animals
4. __________ takes water in mainly through its roots
5. __________ plant eater
6. __________ fungus
7. __________ predator
8. __________ rabbit
9. __________ helps return chemicals to the earth
10. __________ tall grass

a. producer
b. primary consumer
c. secondary consumer
d. decomposer

Answer *true* or *false* (each answer, 2 points).

11. __________ The most common substance on earth is water.
12. __________ The balance of nature depends on the food chain.
13. __________ Water evaporates during the food cycle.
14. __________ Humans can be predators.
15. __________ Bacteria are used in photosynthesis.
16. __________ Bison and grasshoppers are both secondary consumers.
17. __________ The study of the relationships of living things to their environment is called ecology.
18. __________ Water pollution is no longer a problem.
19. __________ Carbon dioxide is used by plants.
20. __________ A food web is made up of many connecting food chains.

Write the letter for the correct answer on the blank (each answer, 5 points).

21. Chemicals in the chemical cycle are brought into plants mainly through their ________ .
a. leaves b. stems c. roots

22. The complex level of organization within nature is called a(n) ________ .
a. physical environment b. ecosystem
c. chemical cycle

23. Taking good care of plants and animals is called good ________ .
a. business b. health c. stewardship

24. Two problems created by humans to the balance of nature are loss of life and ________ .
a. disease b. poverty c. pollution

25. A clear container in which small land animals and plants are kept is called a ________ .
a. terrarium b. aquarium c. web of life

26. In the past, the prairie had more ________ than it does today.
a. bison b. cattle c. grasshoppers

Draw this diagram (this drawing, 10 points).

27. Draw a food chain. Label at least five animals, plants, or decomposers in the chain.

Answer these questions (each answer, 5 points).

28. What is *the balance of nature*?

____

____

____

____

____

____

29. How do you compare in importance to God with the importance of a sparrow?

____

____

____

____

Answer these questions.

2.1 From the map showing average rainfall per year, what states in the United States and what provinces in Canada might be considered part of the prairie? Use an atlas to help you name these areas if needed.

____

____

____

____

____

2.2 How did the amount of rainfall help determine the formation of the prairie?

____

____

____

____

____

____

____

2.3 What was the carbon cycle on the prairie like?

____

____

____

____

____

2.4 What was the chemical cycle on the prairie like?

____

____

____

____

____

____

Producers. A great variety of grasses grew in the prairie. Several types of tall grass grew where the rainfall was heavier. Adult tall grasses often grew higher than a person, reaching to more than seven and a half feet tall (2.3 meters). Their roots reached into the soil nearly thirteen feet deep (4 meters). The roots of these grasses grew together underground. This tangled mass of roots helped the plants form a thick cover for the soil.

| Short Grasses

| Mid Grasses

| Tall Grasses

| Forest

Mid grasses were only half the height of the tall grasses; that is, they were three to four feet tall (1 to 1.2 meters). They grew in clumps, and their roots were not tangled. These grasses grew more in upland areas and needed less rain.

The short grasses were able to survive where very little rain fell. Their roots were heavily tangled, but they did not grow deep. Short grasses seldom grew taller than ten inches (25 cm). These grasses covered the western prairie.

What determined which grasses would grow in a certain area? Rainfall was one factor. When more rain fell, taller grasses took over. With drought, shorter grasses would be stronger. In some areas, tall and short grasses survived together.

The grasses on the prairie provided food for a great number of animals. The root system allowed the grasses to continue growing after the animals ate other parts of the grass. The life cycles of the grasses could continue even when the animals ate the leaves and seeds. All of these grasses had life cycles which continued from year to year. With each year, young grasses would gain stronger root systems.

Other plants, too, were growing on the prairie. These plants were wild flowers, weeds, vines, and mosses. Some of these plants were eaten by animals. God provided protection for those plants with less hardy life cycles. Thorns, woody stems, and sharp leaves protected some plants from the animals. Yet, they added to the prairie balance of nature. Insects and worms may have received food from them. Bees also made honey from some of these plants.

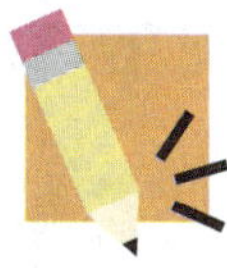

Complete these statements.

2.5 Tall grasses grow best in areas with more ________________ .

2.6 Because of the ________________ systems, grasses can keep growing after animals eat part of them.

2.7 Less hardy plants are protected from being destroyed by grazing through growing a. ________________ stems, b. ________________ leaves, and c. ________________ .

2.8 More often than not, ________________________ determines which grass is to grow in a land area.

2.9 Plants are important to the balance of nature because they provide a. ________________ for animals and give off b. ________________ .

Consumers. The prairie was able to support many consumers. Consumers on the prairie were both large and small. These consumers were worms, insects, birds, reptiles, and mammals. These animals could all be classed in the primary or secondary consumer groups.

The grasshoppers were the most **numerous** primary consumers. Some of them ate grasses. The rest fed on other types of plants. A great many other insects were primary consumers, too. Included were the larva of butterflies and moths.

Grazers were also primary consumers. Bison were the largest animals on the prairie. They roamed in great herds in search of food. Bison were so large that they were difficult prey. For this reason, the food chain seldom went beyond the healthy bison. Decomposers and **scavengers** (like vultures) fed on the bodies of dead bison. Deer, another primary consumer and grazer, relied on speed to get away from their **predators**.

| Bison

Small **rodents** were mostly primary consumers. Among these were ground squirrels, gophers, prairie dogs, rats, and mice. They mainly lived in underground nests. They ate mostly tender young plants, roots, and seeds. These animals sometimes fed on small animals or grasshoppers, but they relied on plants for most of their food.

| Prairie dog

Among primary consumers that stayed near the wooded areas of the prairie were rabbits. They needed tall grass and bushes for protection. Speed also helped them get away from their predators. Yet, they were a great source of food for secondary consumers. Rabbits were able to produce a great number of offspring in their lifetimes. This large number of offspring helped the rabbit population to survive while providing food for other species.

Prairie chickens, meadowlarks, red-winged blackbirds, cowbirds, killdeer, larks, and pheasants are only a few of the birds that made the prairie their home. Some of them ate mostly seeds and plant parts.
They were primary consumers. In the winter, the prairie could not support all of the birds. The secondary consumers needed to fly south for the winter in search of more food.
Most seed eaters stayed on the prairie during the winter.

| Killdeer

Some hunting birds also lived on the prairie. They were secondary consumers. Included were hawks, golden eagles, owls, and falcons. Small animals, snakes, and insects were their food. On occasion, large predatory birds would swoop down and snatch a baby deer or a jackrabbit for a meal.

The predators, who were secondary consumers, were important to the balance of nature on the prairie. Ants, beetles, and wasps ate smaller insects. Badgers, skunks, and snakes ate small animals. Foxes, wolves, and prairie grizzly bears fed on other animals they could catch, including other predators. These predator groups had smaller populations than the primary consumers. They did not produce offspring as often.

Decomposers. The decomposer group was at work on dead prairie organisms. Bacteria and fungi were present in great amounts. Animal wastes and organism wastes, in addition to dead bodies, were returned to the earth by the decomposers.

Answer *true* or *false*.

2.10 __________ Bison and grasshoppers were both primary consumers.

2.11 __________ Some prairie birds were primary consumers, and others were secondary consumers.

2.12 __________ Rabbits need speed to catch their prey.

2.13 __________ Foxes sometimes ate other secondary consumers.

2.14 __________ Weasels and skunks often preyed on bison.

2.15 __________ Seed-eating birds need to migrate south in winter.

Complete this activity.

2.16 God created some very interesting prairie birds. Some of them were named in this section under the heading *consumers*. Choose one of them to learn more about.

Write its name here: ______________________________ .

Use library books or the Internet to find out more information about your chosen bird. Write a report using the following outline to organize your ideas:

I. Bird's description

II. Bird's life cycle

III. Bird's place in food chain

Teacher check:

Initials ____________________ Date ____________________

Food chains. How did all these plants and animals fit together in food chains? Did plant eaters consume any plant they found? Did predators catch all kinds of animals for food? Perhaps these questions can be answered by reviewing certain animals found on the prairie.

Bison liked to eat the tender leaves of grass. Insects lived on less hardy plants. Rodents and birds ate seeds. So, you see that plant eaters, or the primary consumers, selected their food. The animal's size and structure were important in deciding what it would eat.

The size and structure of predator animals were important factors, too, in deciding what they ate. Hawks could catch rabbits, but not weasels. The weasels were able to keep away from the hawks. Foxes could catch prairie chickens, but they could not catch hawks. Beetles caught other insects, but they could not catch rabbits. Some of the predators did eat a wide variety of other animals, but even the best hunters of the predators probably did not feed on every other type of animal.

Some animals were eaten by many different predators. Grasshoppers, mice, and rabbits were links in many food chains. Among other things, these animals were probably placed on Earth to help provide food for others.

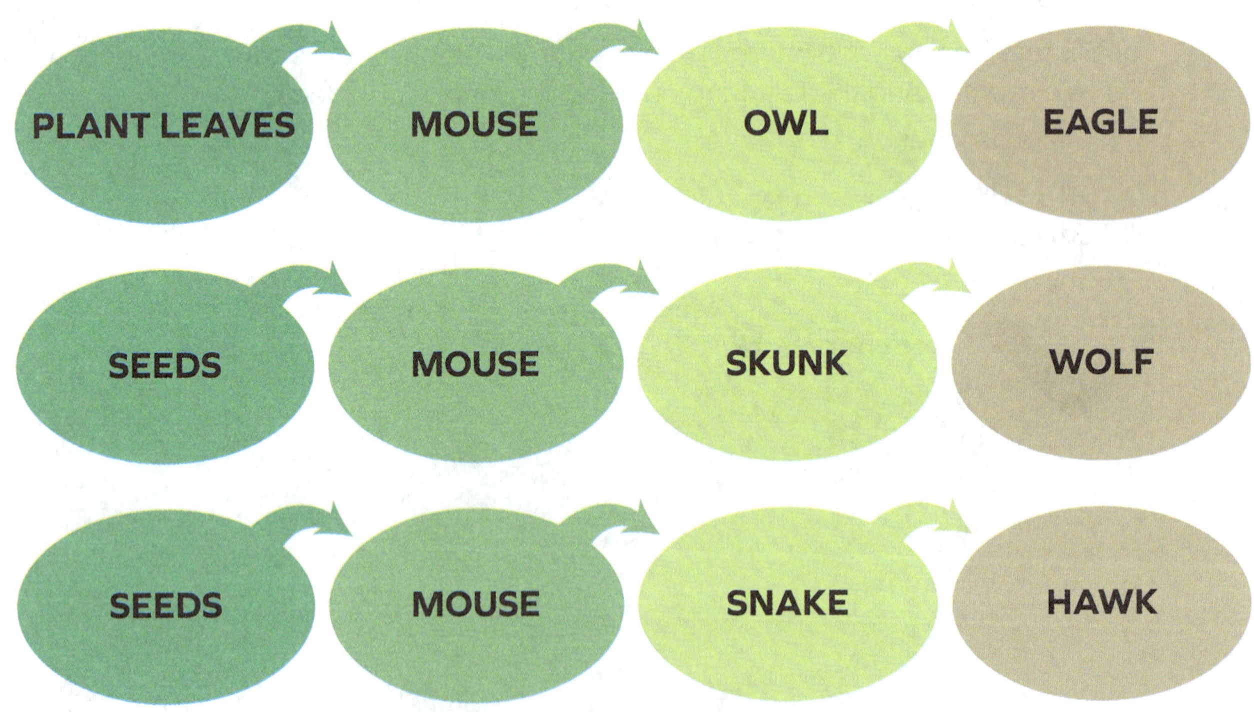

| Food chains

Food web. When several food chains on the prairie are brought together, they appear interconnected like a web. Therefore, we call it a *food web*. An example of a food web on the prairie is shown by the illustration below.

Complete this activity.

2.17 Select a special ecosystem to learn about. It could be your region or one that is new to you. Other ecosystems include coniferous forests, deciduous forests, tropical rain forests, ponds, swamps, Arctic, savannas, deserts, and grasslands. Find several of the food chains in your selected ecosystem. On another piece of paper, place these chains in a web-like design. (Use pictures instead of words if you wish.). Share your food web with your teacher or parent.

Teacher check:

Initials ____________________ Date ____________________

Look at your terrarium and answer these questions. You may use your daily observation notes and your terrarium to help answer these questions.

2.18 What are some changes you have observed since the first day?

____

____

____

2.19 Why have these changes taken place?

____

____

____

2.20 What have you learned from your terrarium so far?

____

____

____

Teacher check:

Initials ____________________ Date ____________________

Changes in the Prairie Balance of Nature

| Dried grass prairie

Changes occurred in the prairie balance of nature over time. Some of these changes were from *natural* causes. All ecosystems undergo changes from time to time due to changes in the weather, the water cycle, floods, drought, disease, or other causes that can occur in nature. Changes also occur when a new species of animals or plants is introduced to an ecosystem from outside. This is particularly true when human beings settle into an ecosystem in a new way. Changes in the balance of nature might then have *human* causes.

In the remaining part of this section of the LIFEPAC, we will look at natural changes and human changes that occurred in the prairie balance of nature.

Natural changes. The prairie plant and animal groups depended on each other for survival. They needed each other in good times and bad.

Think of what happened when drought came to the prairie. Grasses could not get enough water or moisture. Some of the taller grasses did not grow fast. Shorter grasses took over. The grasshoppers that lived in the area produced their usual number of offspring. More grasshoppers survived in dry years. Soon, the smaller amount of grass could not support all the grasshoppers. So the grasshoppers moved on, joining others in great numbers.

Soon, not enough grass was left to feed all the grasshoppers and other plant eaters. Some of these primary consumer populations grew larger. As the secondary consumers ate the weakened grasshoppers, their source of food supply went down. They, too, became weak. Finally, the highest-order secondary consumers—wolves, eagles, bears—had a large supply of weakened animals to eat. Their numbers grew large until the food ran out. Then these higher-order animals became weak.

The weak and unhealthy animals slowly died off until just enough of each kind of animal remained for the dry prairie to support.

Wet years on the prairie caused the plant and animal populations to increase. The population would decrease as the rainfall returned to normal.

Wet years and dry years were important factors in how the prairie changed. Seasons caused great changes, too. Spring and summer brought the growing season for plants. This season was also reproduction time for most animals. When the animal population was highest, the plant food was most plentiful. By fall, many younger or weaker animals had become prey to others. Plant food became scarce. It was harder to find good hiding places. Winter weakened some animals. By springtime, only enough of the strong animals had survived to keep life going on the prairie.

Complete these items.

2.21 Name three natural causes of change in the prairie balance of nature.

a. ______________________

b. ______________________

c. ______________________

2.22 What type of animal was usually eaten first when an animal group became too large for the food supply?

____

2.23 Why were the populations of animals larger in spring and summer?

____

____

Use your Bible.

The balance of nature is just one of the many patterns of life prepared by God. One might think that God created the prairie, then let it develop its own system without His concern. That idea is not true. The Bible tells us that He cares about animals.

Read Matthew 10:28-31, and complete these statements.
(Jesus was talking to His disciples in these verses.)

2.24 Verse 29 tells us that God knows when each bird ______________________ .

2.25 Jesus' purpose in giving these ideas is to let us know that each of us is

______________________ .

2.26 In these verses, we learn that God knows a. ______________________ , and He cares about His creation — especially b. ______________________ .

Human changes. Native American Peoples lived on the prairie for many years. They were part of the balance of nature. They consumed plants. They hunted animals. However, they respected nature, and their numbers were few. Therefore, they did not cause large changes in the balance of nature.

Then, in the settlement of the West in the 19th century, many pioneers came to the prairie region. They made much larger changes to the prairie than the Native Americans. They plowed land for growing crops. They put up fences to keep in sheep and cattle. Hunters shot down many of the bison. Many predators were frightened away to more protected areas where there were fewer people.

Today, the prairie is covered by many farms and ranches. Natural grasses have been replaced by great fields of wheat, corn, and other planted crops. Nearly all the bison are gone. Deer seek cover in wooded areas. Eagles and other birds are protected from hunters by law. Pigs, sheep, dairy cattle, beef cattle, chickens, and turkeys are raised in great numbers. The prairie water, carbon, and chemical cycles help farmers grow crops. The balance of nature has been changed in many ways by the increase in the human population and human activities on the prairie.

Yet, humans have not changed the prairie ecosystem completely. Rodents live well among the new types of plants. Birds **thrive**. Chemicals used for farming have not gotten rid of insects. Weeds still grow along roads, near creeks, and in farmer's fields. Food chains may have changed, but they continue to be important to the prairie web of life.

| Prairie farm

Complete these activities.

2.27 A present-day food chain may look like this:

On a separate sheet of paper, list several food chains using plants and animals found in the prairie today.

2.28 Why is the prairie a good place to raise crops?

____

____

2.29 Why are some animals protected by law?

____

____

Terrarium check.

2.30 You should be continuing to keep your daily terrarium record. Take your record to your teacher or parent to be checked.

Teacher check:

Initials ______________ Date ______________

Review the material in this section to prepare for the Self Test. The Self Test will check your understanding of this section and will review the other section. Any items you miss on this test will show you what areas you will need to restudy in order to prepare for the unit test.

SELF TEST 2

Match these items (each answer, 3 points).

2.01	__________ land covered with grass	a.	past prairie
2.02	__________ sheep	b.	present prairie
2.03	__________ weeds	c.	both past and present prairies
2.04	__________ carbon cycle		
2.05	__________ many people		
2.06	__________ wheat		
2.07	__________ many bison		
2.08	__________ predators		
2.09	__________ fences		
2.010	__________ balance of nature		

Write the correct letter and answer on the blank (each answer, 5 points).

2.011 The grasses that need the most moisture are ______________________________ .
a. tall grasses   b. mid grasses   c. short grasses

2.012 Wolves are ____ .
a. primary consumers   b. secondary consumers   c. decomposers

2.013 Changes in the amount of __________________________ caused big changes in the prairie balance of nature.
a. carbon dioxide   b. rainfall   c. chemicals

2.014 Bison and grasshoppers are both ____________________________________ .
a. gone today   b. primary consumers   c. secondary consumers

2.015 A big change occurred in the prairie balance of nature when ___________________ came.
a. settlers   b. Native Americans   c. wolves

2.016 Some plants were protected from grazers by ___________________ .
a. thorns   b. eagles   c. roots

2.017 Grasses were not killed off by ______________________, but small trees were killed.

a. water b. insects c. fire

2.018 The roots of the ______________________ reach deep into the ground.

a. short grass b. mid grass c. tall grass

2.019 Part of an eagle food chain might be a ______________________.

a. bison b. bear c. snake

2.020 Decomposers eat ______________________.

a. only plants b. only animals c. both plants and animals

Complete these items (each item, 5 points).

2.021 Compare your importance to God with the importance of a sparrow.

____

____

____

____

____

2.022 Define the word *scavenger*.

____

____

____

____

____

2.023 Explain how the prairie is different now from how it was in the past.

____

____

____

____

____

2.024 How did the amount of rainfall help determine the formation of the prairie?

____

____

____

____

____

____

____

____

Teacher check: Initials ____________

Score ____________ Date ____________

3. HUMANS AND THE WEB OF LIFE

Humans are part of the web of life. We breathe oxygen and give off carbon dioxide. Our cells need food for energy. Therefore, we are part of the balance of nature wherever we live. God has given us special abilities to make decisions. He created us to be responsible for other living things (Genesis 1:26).

You have seen what an influence humans have on the balance of nature. When settlers came to the prairie, changes to the balance of nature came with them. Some changes were good. Other changes were harmful. In this section of the LIFEPAC, you will consider how some of these changes caused problems in nature.

Objectives

Review these objectives. When you have completed this section, you should be able to:

5. Name two problems that human beings have made for God's web of life.
6. Name at least five things that you can do for plants and animals that will help care for the web of life that God has created.

Vocabulary

Study these new words. Learning the meanings of these words is a good study habit and will improve your understanding of this LIFEPAC.

exposed (ek spōzd'). Open, uncovered.

influence (in' flü əns). To have an effect on someone or something.

pollution (pə lü' shən). Substances that make an environment dirty or not clean.

stewardship (stü' ərd ship). The duty of taking care of things for someone else.

Pronunciation Key: hat, āge, cãre, fär; let, ēqual, tėrm; it, īce; hot, ōpen, ôrder; oil; out; cup, pu̇t, rüle; child; long; thin; /ŦH/ for then; /zh/ for measure; /u/ or /ə/ represents /a/ in about, /e/ in taken, /i/ in pencil, /o/ in lemon, and /u/ in circus.

Problems

There are two main problems that humans have caused in the balance of nature. The first is *loss of life*. The second is **pollution**. We will now discuss each of these problems in this section.

Loss of life. When people move into an area, loss of plant and animal life usually occurs. Land is taken over for buildings. Farmers clear land for their crops. As cities begin to develop, large areas of land are covered with concrete. Hunters kill animals for food. They also kill dangerous predators.

Trees are large plants that mature slowly. They provide homes and food for animals, especially in forests. However, people have many uses for the wood of trees. Sometimes, trees stand in the way of roads, farms, or buildings. People remove the trees, and this action causes a change for some animals.

As a result of these human activities, the balance of nature changes. The consumers have less plant life. The population of some animals goes down. Other animals must change their eating habits. Some animals must even begin to depend upon humans to supply much of their food.

The killing of too many predators causes problems. Animals that were once the prey of predators begin to increase. Sickly animals live longer. They all need food. Either starvation begins to come, or they begin raiding farm crops and animals. The humans begin to take the place of natural predators. Chemical sprays may be used to kill insects and some birds. Traps may be set for animal pests.

Hunting is a sport many people enjoy. It is very closely managed. Does this sport hurt the balance of nature? Not if the hunters know what animals to shoot and how many they should take. The hunter becomes just another predator. Hunters can be helpful in keeping a balance of nature, especially if other predators are scarce.

| A lumberjack

Answer these questions.

3.1 What are some of the ways that loss of life occurs when humans move into an area?

____

____

____

____

3.2 How can hunting by human beings be harmful to the balance of nature?

____

____

____

____

3.3 How can hunting by human beings be helpful to the balance of nature?

____

____

____

____

Pollution. Most of our cities have grown larger. More factories are built. Cars, buses, airplanes, and other machines are increasingly used. All of these developments produce waste products. Some of their wastes enter the air. Other wastes enter the water in lakes, streams, rivers, and seas. This waste is often harmful to plants and animals. Then it is called *pollution*.

What is *air* pollution? Sometimes people see clouds of smoke coming from factories. It looks like terrible pollution. But it actually may be harmless water vapor or steam. Some of the smoke clouds, however, may contain chemicals that are harmful to plants and animals.

| Air pollution

In addition, cars can put out a colorless pollution in the air. Many larger cities seem to have a cloud of pollution over them because of all the waste products entering the air from cars and factories. Waste gases have joined together above the city. Sometimes the wastes react with other chemicals in the atmosphere to cause more air pollution.

| Parts of the world have so much air pollution that people wear masks to protect themselves.

Air pollution can damage plants. When plants are **exposed** to air pollution for years at a time, growth may be slowed. Sometimes photosynthesis is slowed or stopped. The plant life cannot go on.

Similar problems face animals and humans from air pollution. Studies have shown that much air pollution can shorten lives. Lungs are harmed. The body can become more open to disease. Oxygen supplies may be lowered.

| Water pollution

What is water pollution? Water pollution takes many forms. Garbage gets into rivers and streams. Chemical wastes from factories may be dumped into rivers. Farmers use chemicals to control insects and pests. Rain may wash these chemicals into nearby streams or ground water. Sometimes oil tankers have been damaged or sunk in the ocean, spreading a harmful layer of oil on the water surface.

Plants can be affected by polluted water. Some of the chemicals may stop photosynthesis. Carbon dioxide needed by water plants is suffocated out of the water by pollutants. Plant growth is slowed or stopped.

Water pollution causes problems for animals, too. Some chemicals poison the fish. Animals that drink polluted water may be slowly poisoned. Oil is also dangerous to waterfowl and insects. It can cover their bodies and make it impossible for them to fly. They cannot get food. Drowning may occur.

The pollution problem caused by humans is a threat to the web of life. Many people are concerned. They are trying to find ways to reduce or stop pollution. Answers are not easy to find, but there has been progress. God is able to give us wisdom to manage His creation better.

Complete these statements.

3.4 Air pollution can affect plant life by slowing or stopping ______________________ .

3.5 Air pollution can affect animal life by weakening the body and by reducing the ______________________ supply through the lungs.

3.6 Pollution has become a big problem because more people are dumping wastes in the a. ______________________ and b. ______________________ .

3.7 Farmers may cause pollution when they use ______________________ to control insects.

Stewardship

As part of His plan, God made human beings *responsible* for taking care of the rest of His creation (Genesis 1:26). Each person is only as responsible as the *choices* that he or she makes.

Being responsible. In Genesis 1:26, you can read where God made humans responsible over all other living things. God had an important reason why He wanted someone to care for the plants and animals. *He liked His creation!* Several times in the first chapter of Genesis, we read that God looked at His creation and saw that "it was good." The earth is full of the goodness of the Lord as shown by His creation (Psalm 33:5-7).

The Lord wants people to have **stewardship** over His creation. Stewardship means that we do more than live with other living things. We need to care about life and to take care of life. Our decisions and choices must show concern for life.

Making choices. People with governmental power can make choices that cause changes. Laws and regulations can force others to work on problems of pollution. We cannot force them to care. God asks us for that concern. Each person, young or old, has an influence on the care of God's creation by the choices that are made.

| Be socially responsible, help clean up the Earth!

The decision that each person must make is whether to be careful or careless. Good stewardship of plants and animals would involve being careful. A careful person will work to use God's creation wisely. If you are a careful person, consider the following ideas. Walk or take your bicycle instead of taking a car. Place litter in containers, and recycle or reuse items rather than throwing them in the trash. Do not bother animals or their nests. Hunt or fish within the law. Wisely use needed water. Pray that God will show you other ways to be a good steward of His creation.

Complete these activities.

Write your answers in complete sentences. This section gave several suggestions for being careful stewards of God's creation. In the following spaces, tell why the suggestions would be helpful.

3.8 Walking or riding a bike:

____

____

3.9 Putting litter in containers:

____

____

3.10 Not bothering nests:

____

____

3.11 Hunting or fishing within the law:

____

____

3.12 Using small amounts of water:

____

____

3.13 Praying:

____

____

Use the Bible.

3.14 How many times in the first chapter of Genesis can you find these words: "...and God saw that it was good"? ________

3.15 Explain what Psalm 33:5-7 says about the creation.

____
____
____
____
____
____
____
____
____
____

Check your terrarium.

3.16 Write a summary of what you learned about your terrarium.
The following questions may help guide your writing:

a. What growth have you observed?

b. What have you done to keep life going?

c. What problems did you face? What did you do to solve them?

d. How has the terrarium helped you to understand the web of life?

Have your teacher or parent review your record and written summary.

Teacher check:

Initials ____________________ Date ____________________

Before you take this last Self Test, you may want to do one or more of these self checks.

1. ________ Read the objectives. See if you can do them.
2. ________ Restudy the material related to any objectives that you cannot do.
3. ________ Use the **SQ3R** study procedure to review the material:
   a. **S**can the sections.
   b. **Q**uestion yourself.
   c. **R**ead to answer your questions.
   d. **R**ecite the answers to yourself.
   e. **R**eview areas you did not understand.
4. ________ Review all vocabulary, activities, and Self Tests, writing a correct answer for every wrong answer.

SELF TEST 3

Answer *true or false* (each answer, 3 points).

3.01 ________ Hunting animals usually destroys the balance of nature.

3.02 ________ Laws have been passed that encourage people to reduce pollution.

3.03 ________ Humans have changed the balance of nature in some places.

3.04 ________ Cars produce air pollution.

3.05 ________ If one person chooses to litter, it does not really matter.

3.06 ________ We can find easy answers to pollution problems.

3.07 ________ Many plants have been destroyed by people building roads and cities.

3.08 ________ The early prairie had mostly trees and some grass.

3.09 ________ Bison were predators of the prairie.

3.010 ________ One function of grasshoppers is to provide food for other animals.

Label this food chain (each organism, 2 points).
Use the terms *decomposer, producer, primary consumer, secondary consumer*.

3.011 seed a. ________________________

mouse b. ________________________

snake c. ________________________

eagle d. ________________________

bacteria e. ________________________

Make a list of ideas (each item, 2 points).

3.012 List five of the ways suggested in this LIFEPAC for being careful stewards of God's creation.

a. ______________________________

b. ______________________________

c. ______________________________

d. ______________________________

e. ______________________________

Write the correct letter and answer in the blank (each answer, 5 points).

3.013 Stewardship involves being ______________ living things.

a. careless with b. careful with c. afraid of

3.014 Rain, snow, and hail are forms of ______________ .

a. producers b. consumers c. precipitation

3.015 Some ______________ are both primary consumers and secondary consumers.

a. sheep b. bacteria c. birds

3.016 The grasses that need the most moisture are ______________ .

a. tall grasses b. mid grasses c. short grasses

3.017 Hunting can be ______________ to the balance of nature.

a. harmful b. helpful c. both harmful and helpful

3.018 Photosynthesis can be ______________ by air pollution.

a. slowed or stopped b. helped c. increased

Answer these questions (each answer, 10 points).

3.019 How does stewardship fit into the study of the web of life?

____

____

____

____

____

____

3.020 What are some of the ways that loss of life occurs when humans move into an area?

____

____

____

____

____

____

____

Teacher check: Initials ____________

Score ____________ Date ____________

80 / 100

Before you take the LIFEPAC Test, you may want to do one or more of these self checks.

1. ________ Read the objectives. See if you can do them.
2. ________ Restudy the material related to any objectives that you cannot do.
3. ________ Use the **SQ3R** study procedure to review the material.
4. ________ Review activities, Self Tests, and LIFEPAC vocabulary words.
5. ________ Restudy areas of weakness indicated by the last Self Test.

NOTES

NOTES

NOTES

SCIENCE 505
TRANSFORMATION OF ENERGY

Author:
Barry G. Burrus, M.Div, M.A., B.S.

Editor:
Brian Ring

Illustrations:
Brian Ring

Media Credits:
Page 3: © Sergey Nivens, iStock, Thinkstock; **4:** © witoldkr1, iStock, Thinkstock; **8:** © Dmitry Kalinovsky, iStock, Thinkstock; © KatePhoto, iStock, Thinkstock; © Daniel Hurst, iStock, Thinkstock; **13:** © Ingram Publishing, Thinkstock; **20:** © hxdyl, iStock, Thinkstock; **21:** © Victor Borisov, Stockbyte, Thinkstock; **24:** © daseugen, iStock, Thinkstock; **27:** © Andrei Krauchuk, iStock, Thinkstock; © danilo sanino, iStock, Thinkstock; **30:** © Peter Hermes Furian, iStock, Thinkstock; **33:** © matheesaengkaew, iStock,Thinkstock; **39:** © 123ArtistImages, iStock, Thinkstock; **41:** © Zelfit, iStock, Thinkstock; **42:** © Tyler Oliver, iStock, Thinkstock; **44:** © sv-time, iStock, Thinkstock; **46:** © hansenn, iStock, Thinkstock; **54:** © aurin, iStock, Thinkstock.

804 N. 2nd Ave. E.
Rock Rapids, IA 51246-1759

TRANSFORMATION OF ENERGY

God designed all living things so that they need energy to survive, grow, and perform the activities of life. You learned in previous LIFEPACs that the sun provides energy for green plants. The green plants use the sun's energy for photosynthesis. During photosynthesis, the green plants produce oxygen and food. This food is used by plants, animals, and other living things to produce the energy that they need to survive. But, what is *energy*?

In this LIFEPAC®, you will learn more about energy and how energy is transformed into several different forms. We call this the transformation of energy. You will also learn how energy is used to do work. You will learn about some of the sources of energy that God has provided for the earth. You will examine some of the concerns that we have about present sources of energy. Finally, you will consider how other energy sources may be used in the future.

Objectives

Read these objectives. These objectives tell what you will be able to do when you have successfully completed this LIFEPAC. Each section will list according to the numbers below what objectives will be met in that section. When you have finished this LIFEPAC, you should be able to:

1. Describe energy.
2. Identify forms of energy.
3. Describe work.
4. Explain the relationship between work and energy.
5. Identify energy concerns of today that may be problems of the future.
6. Describe several possible energy sources of the future.

1. ENERGY AND WORK

Energy is one of the most basic parts of God's creation. Whenever anything moves or grows, energy is used. We use energy to do work. Energy lights our homes and cities at night. Our cars, buses, trains, and airplanes all use energy. In our modern world, we have learned to use and control energy to bring about great changes in the way we live. Energy is very important to human beings and to all living things.

Energy is very closely related to work. As stated above, we use energy to do work. Whenever anything moves due to a force applied to it, energy is being used.

In this section of the LIFEPAC, you will learn more about energy and the various forms of energy. You will also learn more about the term "work" and how energy is related to work.

Objectives

Review these objectives. When you have completed this section, you should be able to:

1. Describe energy.
2. Identify forms of energy.
3. Describe work.

Vocabulary

Study these new words. Learning the meanings of these words is a good study habit and will improve your understanding of this LIFEPAC.

explosion (ek splō′ zhən). A blowing up with a loud noise.

fuel (fyü′ əl). Something that can be burned to get fire and energy.

kinetic (kin et′ ik). Of or relating to the motion of objects.

matter (mat′ər). The material that makes up things.

mechanical (mə kan′ə kəl). Of machines; a form of energy that is of motion or movement.

nuclear (nü′ klē ər). Having to do with the center of atoms.

particles (pär′ tə kəlz). Tiny parts of a material or substance.

potential (pə ten′ shəl). Something possible; the ability to go into action or to produce movement.

radiates (rā′ dē ātz). Gives out rays.

solar (sō′ lər). Having to do with the sun.

transformation (tran′ sfər mā′ shən). Change in form or condition.

Note: *All vocabulary words in this LIFEPAC appear in* **boldface** *print the first time they are used. If you are unsure of the meaning when you are reading, study the definitions given.*

Pronunciation Key: h**a**t, **ā**ge, c**ã**re, f**ä**r; l**e**t, **ē**qual, t**ė**rm; **i**t, **ī**ce; h**o**t, **ō**pen, **ô**rder; **oi**l; **ou**t; c**u**p, p**ů**t, r**ü**le; **ch**ild; lo**ng**; **th**in; /ŦH/ for **th**en; /zh/ for mea**s**ure; /u/ or /ə/ represents /a/ in **a**bout, /e/ in tak**e**n, /i/ in penc**i**l, /o/ in lem**o**n, and /u/ in circ**u**s.

Energy

Energy makes things happen. If you look around you right now, you can probably see energy being used. If it is daytime, the sun is giving off heat energy and light energy. If it is night, the light bulbs are using electrical energy to give off light energy.

Definition. Energy is commonly defined as *the ability to do work*. Notice carefully this definition. Energy and work are very closely related. When energy is used, work is done. For example, when you run or play, your body uses energy to help you move. When energy is stored, work *can be* done. For example, when you are at rest, the energy stored in your body's fat and muscle tissues will allow you to start running when you are ready. So, the *ability* to do work, either actually being done or ready to be done, is called energy.

Types of energy. This leads us to the two basic types of energy. Energy that is stored is called **potential** energy. In this case, no work is being done. However, the energy is ready and available to do work. Therefore, it is called *potential energy*. The other basic type of energy occurs when a body or material thing is moving or in motion. Energy that is moving is called **kinetic** energy. Any **matter** that is moving has *kinetic energy*.

Let's consider an example. Do you have a pencil (or pen) on your desk or table? If it is at rest, it has *potential* energy. If you shove the pencil over the side of your desk or table, it will fall to the floor. When this happens, the pencil is moving as it falls to the floor.

| The pencil at rest has *potential* energy.

As it is falling it has kinetic energy.

Now consider what happens as you pick the pencil off the floor and put it back on your desk. You use your own energy to lift and move the pencil. Moving the pencil to a higher position from the floor *adds energy* to the pencil. If you place the pencil on the table, it again has potential energy. Placing the pencil at a higher position, such as a door frame, *adds potential energy* to the pencil. If it falls to the floor again, it would have a greater distance to fall, creating more energy.

| The falling pencil has *kinetic* energy.

If the pencil drops from the door frame, the kinetic energy created would be *greater* than the kinetic energy created when it fell from the table.

Remember:
resting at greater height = more potential energy
resting at less height = less potential energy
falling from greater height = more kinetic energy
falling from lesser height = less kinetic energy

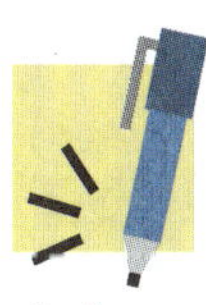

Write the correct words in the blank spaces.

1.1 Whenever anything moves or grows, ____________________ is used.

1.2 Energy is the a. ____________________ to do b. ____________________ .

1.3 Energy that is stored is called ______________________________ energy.

1.4 Energy that is moving is called ______________________________ energy.

Label these pictures. Use the words *potential energy* and *kinetic energy* to label the pictures.

1.5 ____

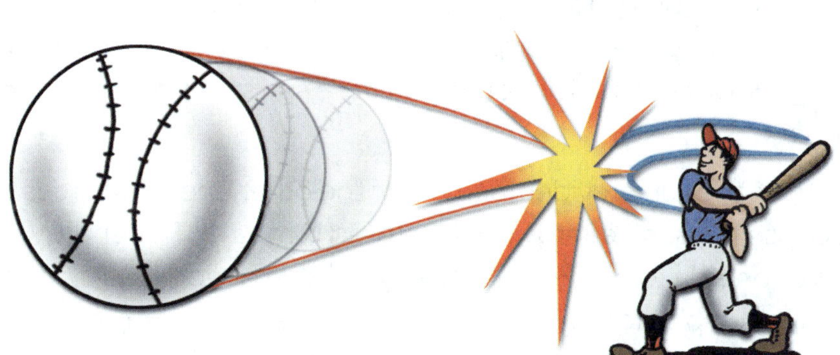

1.6 ____

| Energy from the sun is stored in food.

| Animals benefit from this stored energy.

| The stored energy in food also gives us energy.

Sources of energy. God has provided us with many sources of energy. Our main source of energy is the sun. Each day, a great amount of energy is released from the sun. The sun's energy comes to us in the forms of heat energy and light energy. Only a small portion of the sun's energy falls on the earth. However, this small amount of the sun's energy is more than enough to support life on our planet.

Energy from the sun provides for most of the other energy sources that we have on earth. It does this because the sun's energy can be stored in matter. This energy in matter can be used as other sources of energy for us. For example, you have already learned that part of the sun's energy is stored in green plants as food. This food can be used as an energy source for other living things. The food is eaten and the cells of living things *burn* it for energy. The cells in your body burn food and provide the energy you need to move, grow, and do all of your activities.

One of the first sources of energy that human beings used was wood from trees. The wood can be burned in fire. When wood burns, the energy stored in the wood is given off as heat energy and light energy.

When living things die, there is still energy stored in the matter of the dead bodies. Over time, this dead matter can be turned into other substances like coal, oil, and natural gas. These materials contain great amounts of stored energy. We call these materials "fossil **fuels**." These materials can be burned and give off heat and light energy. Thus, coal, oil, and natural gas are important sources of energy for human beings today.

As you learned in a previous LIFEPAC, the sun causes water in the oceans and lakes to evaporate. This water vapor eventually forms rain upon the earth, producing rivers and streams. Eventually, human beings learned to use the energy of the flowing rivers and streams to turn waterwheels. Waterwheels, in turn, provided energy to turn large millstones to crush wheat and other grains for food. Thus, water became an important source of energy for people. Flowing water is still used today in many dams to produce electrical energy to supply our energy needs.

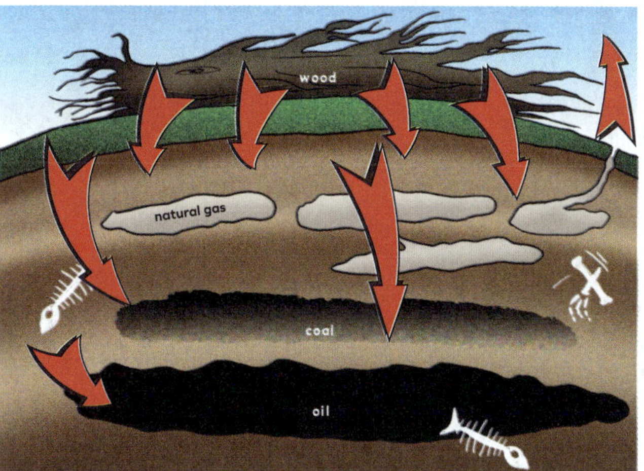

| Wood, coal, oil, and natural gas are sources of energy.

The wind was also used by human beings many years ago to turn windmills and move sailing ships. The sun's energy, combined with temperature differences on the earth and in the atmosphere, helps the wind to move. This energy in the wind is also a source of energy that can still be used today.

God has provided many other sources of energy. For example, **nuclear** energy, chemical energy, and solar energy are also sources of energy being used today. You will learn more about some of these sources of energy later in this LIFEPAC.

Complete this activity.

1.7 Do a word search for *sources of energy* in the puzzle below. There are eleven sources of energy that have been mentioned so far in this LIFEPAC.
All eleven words are in the puzzle. The words are either listed across or down.
None of the words are listed backwards or diagonally.
When you find the words, circle them and write them in the spaces below.

Word Search

C	N	O	P	W	O	O	D	C
L	A	E	D	I	X	I	F	H
M	Z	C	N	N	P	L	Q	E
R	F	O	O	D	S	W	L	M
B	W	A	T	C	G	A	S	I
S	O	L	A	R	Z	T	N	C
U	F	M	A	L	M	E	P	A
N	U	C	L	E	A	R	A	L

Across	Down
a. ______________	g. ______________
b. ______________	h. ______________
c. ______________	i. ______________
d. ______________	j. ______________
e. ______________	k. ______________
f. ______________	

Forms of energy. Energy can take many forms. It is constantly changing from one form to another. We call this changing from one form of energy to another the **transformation** of energy. When energy is transformed from one form to another, no energy is lost. The total sum of energy always remains the same.

You learned that energy comes to us from the sun in two forms: *light* energy and *heat* energy. These are two of the forms of energy. When energy from the sun is stored in matter such as wood, coal, oil, and gas, the energy becomes *chemical* energy. Chemical energy is another form of energy.

When matter is burned, the chemical energy in the matter is changed into heat energy. There is a transformation of energy from chemical energy to heat energy. Heat energy, in turn, can cause other matter to get warmer. Heat energy warms things by causing the smallest **particles** in matter to move faster.

Heat energy can also be generated by another form of energy—**mechanical** energy. Mechanical energy is the energy of moving things. It is one form of kinetic energy. Mechanical energy can be transformed into heat energy.

You can observe this happening. Rub your hands together. Do they feel warmer when you rub them? The rubbing of your hands together is mechanical action. It is mechanical energy. Heat is generated on the surface of your hands by the rubbing action. The heat is from the heat energy produced by the mechanical action. This is another example of the transformation of energy. In this case, some of the mechanical energy is transformed into heat energy. That is why your hands feel warmer when you rub them together.

| Results of mechanical energy

Mechanical energy can produce other results besides heat. For example, if you dropped an egg on the floor, the shell might break. The mechanical energy of the falling egg would be enough to break open the eggshell. Another example of mechanical energy is represented by a baseball moving through the air. If the baseball hit a window, the mechanical energy in the baseball could cause the window to break.

Of course, mechanical energy is not always a problem. Mechanical energy can be useful, too. For example, a nail can be driven into wood as a result of the mechanical energy contained in a moving hammer head. Therefore, mechanical energy was probably used to build your home.

Heat energy can be changed into light energy as it **radiates** off matter that is hot. For example, a piece of metal that is heated to a high temperature will glow as it gives off light energy. In the same way, the heat from the high temperatures on the sun gives off light energy. **Solar** energy is a common term for the light energy received from the sun.

Whenever you turn on a light, use a flashlight, or hear a radio, you are using *electrical* energy. Electrical energy is one of the most important forms of energy in our modern world. The source of the electrical energy might be a battery, or it might come into your home through power lines from an electrical power company. Lightning in the sky is another type of electrical energy.

Another form of energy is *sound*. The sound of an **explosion** can shake a house or break its windows. Some dentists use drills that use high-pitched sound to drill teeth. Such use of sound energy is one of the more recent developments in our use of energy.

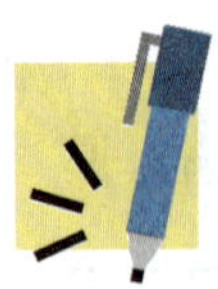

Match these energy forms.

1.8 __________ solar energy

1.9 __________ a falling apple

1.10 __________ burning causes it

1.11 __________ batteries are sources

1.12 __________ an explosion may rock a house

1.13 __________ energy of movement

1.14 __________ burning changes this form to heat

1.15 __________ oil stores it

a. chemical energy

b. heat energy

c. mechanical energy

d. light energy

e. electrical energy

f. sound energy

Work

| Example of work

We have defined energy as the ability to do work. But what is *work*? The word *work* has several different meanings as people commonly use it. For example, you may have to *work* on some math problems for school. Or, you might discover that your clock does not *work*. Sometimes, your relatives may go to *work*, meaning that they are going to the place where they are employed. However, when we use the word work as we talk about energy, work has a special meaning.

Definition. Work is done when a force moves an object by a distance. Energy supplies the force needed to move objects through a distance. If you move your chair to another place, you do work. Anytime an object is moved by a force, work is done. If the object does not move, no work is done, even though a force may be applied to it. For example, if you push on your chair, but it does not move, no work is done.

Work is also done when matter changes shape or form. For example, if you change the shape of a glass by breaking it, then work is done. Energy is also used in this process. The same would be true when a lump of clay is molded by a potter into the form of a bowl. The clay changes its shape and form. Work is done by the potter on the clay.

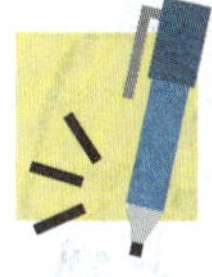

Try these activities. Using the special definition of work as it applies to energy, complete these exercises.

1.16 Blink your eyes.

a. Was work done? Yes No (circle one)

b. Explain your answer. ____________________

____

1.17 Pick up your book.

a. Was work done? Yes No

b. Explain your answer. ______________________________

____

1.18 Hold your book steady in the air without moving it for 3 seconds.

a. Was work done? Yes No

b. Explain your answer. ______________________________

____

1.19 Write your name here. ______________________________

a. Was work done? Yes No

b. Explain your answer. ______________________________

____

1.20 Crumple a piece of paper.

a. Was work done? Yes No

b. Explain your answer. ______________________________

____

Can play really be work? Often when you play, work is being done at the same time. Beside each picture is a space. Explain what work is being done in each of these pictures.

1.21 ______________________________

____

____

____

____

____

1.22 ____
____
____
____
____
____

1.23 ____
____
____
____
____
____

Measurement of work. When something moves, the work that is done can be measured. The amount of work that is done is equal to the force applied to an object multiplied by the distance that the object moves. The amount of work can be shown this way:

WORK = FORCE X DISTANCE

Scientists and engineers measure work in units that represent both force and distance. In the United States, the *foot-pound* is the most commonly used unit of work. One foot-pound equals the work done when a force of 1 pound moves something a distance of 1 foot. Therefore, if a 50 pound weight is lifted 3 feet off the ground, the amount of work done is:
50 pounds X 3 feet = 150 foot-pounds.

In the metric system of measurement, the unit of work is the *joule*. One joule is the amount of work done when a force of 1 *newton* moves something a distance of 1 meter. Therefore, 1 joule equals 1 *newton-meter*. For example, if a 2 newton force moves an object a distance of 5 meters, then the amount of work done is 2 newtons X 5 meters = 10 newton-meters = 10 joules.

Calculate the measurement of some work.

1.24 If a 100 pound weight is lifted 5 feet off the ground, how much work is done?

____

1.25 A force of 10 newtons moves a box 5 meters. How much work is done?

____

1.26 Jim pushes hard on a rock that weighs 500 pounds. He pushes with a force of 50 pounds, but the rock doesn't move. How much work did Jim do? _______________

Explain. _______________

Use your Bible. The definition that we used for work in this LIFEPAC differs from the meaning of the word in most of the Bible. For example, an important use of the word *work* was used by Jesus in John 6:26-35. Read this passage from the Bible and answer the following questions.

1.27 How does Jesus explain work in John 6:29? _______________

1.28 Why do you think that God's work is important? _______________

1.29 How is Jesus' meaning of work different from the definition that we have been using in this LIFEPAC? _______________

Review the material in this section to prepare for the Self Test. The Self Test will check your understanding of this section. Any items you miss on this test will show you what areas you will need to restudy in order to prepare for the unit test.

SELF TEST 1

Answer *true* or *false* (each answer, 2 points).

1.01 ________ The sun is the main source of energy on earth.

1.02 ________ Energy is never lost.

1.03 ________ Play cannot be work.

1.04 ________ Whenever anything moves or grows, energy is used.

1.05 ________ Energy is very closely related to work.

1.06 ________ A pencil at rest on a table has potential energy.

1.07 ________ Any matter that is moving has kinetic energy.

1.08 ________ Food is used as an energy source for living things.

1.09 ________ Wood is one of the newest sources of energy that people have used.

1.010 ________ Wind and water cannot provide energy.

1.011 ________ Energy cannot change from one form to another.

1.012 ________ Mechanical energy is the energy of moving things.

1.013 ________ Chemical energy is stored in coal, oil, and natural gas.

1.014 ________ An explosion is an example of sound energy.

1.015 ________ Work has the same meaning in all common uses of the word.

Match these items (each answer, 3 points).

1.016	________ energy		a.	coal, gas, and oil
1.017	________ work		b.	causes particles in matter to move faster
1.018	________ fossil fuels		c.	stored energy in matter
1.019	________ heat energy		d.	ability to do work
1.020	________ electrical energy		e.	force times distance
1.021	________ chemical energy		f.	supplied by a battery
			g.	energy of moving things
			h.	explosion is a form

Write the letter for the correct answer in the blank (each answer, 3 points).

1.022 The mechanical action of rubbing causes __________ energy.
a. chemical b. heat c. potential

1.023 When a 5 pound weight is lifted 10 feet, __________ of work is done.
a. 15 foot-pounds b. 50 foot-pounds c. 50 newton-meters

1.024 Wood burning gives off __________ energy.
a. heat b. mechanical c. potential

1.025 A falling pencil has __________ energy.
a. electrical b. chemical c. kinetic

1.026 Energy changing into different forms is called __________ of energy.
a. multiplication b. reduction c. transformation

1.027 Jesus described work in John, chapter 6 as __________ .
a. hard b. force moving an object c. having faith in Him

Complete these sentences (each answer, 4 points).

1.028 When energy is used, __________ is done.

1.029 Energy that is stored is called __________ energy.

1.030 Energy that is moving is called __________ energy.

1.031 __________ has provided us with many sources of energy.

1.032 A common term for the light energy received from the sun is __________ energy.

1.033 The energy stored in oil is called __________ energy.

Define and explain these words (each answer, 5 points).

1.034 energy: ______________________________

____

____

____

____

1.035 work: ______________________________

____

____

____

____

Teacher check: Initials ______

Score ______ Date ______

80 / 100

2. WORK FROM ENERGY

Work results from the transformation of one energy form into another energy form. Heat energy can do work and chemical energy can do work. Other forms of energy can also do work. In this section of the LIFEPAC, you will learn more about the way energy can do work. Specifically, you will explore how work can be done from heat energy and chemical energy. You will see that as the transformation of energy takes place in heat energy and chemical energy, work is done.

Objectives

Review these objectives. When you have completed this section, you should be able to:

1. Describe energy.
2. Identify forms of energy.
3. Describe work.
4. Explain the relationship between work and energy.

Vocabulary

Study these new words. Learning the meanings of these words is a good study habit and will improve your understanding of this LIFEPAC.

acids (as′ idz). Chemical compounds containing hydrogen that cause heat when mixed with water.

chamber (chām′ bər). An enclosed space. It is a tube-like space in an engine.

collision (kə lizh′ ən). Rushing against strongly; very strong crash.

flint (flint). A very hard stone.

friction (frik′ shən). Resistance caused when two objects rub together.

ignite (ig nīt′). To set on fire; start burning.

piston (pis′ tən). A piece of solid material that moves back and forth within a tube or chamber. Pistons are used in engines to help supply power to machinery.

reactor (rē ak' tər). A device used to control release of energy from atoms.

renewed (ri nüd'). Made like new again.

Pronunciation Key: hat, āge, cãre, fär; let, ēqual, tėrm; it, īce; hot, ōpen, ôrder; oil; out; cup, pu̇t, rüle; child; long; thin; /ŦH/ for then; /zh/ for measure; /u/ or /ə/ represents /a/ in about, /e/ in taken, /i/ in pencil, /o/ in lemon, and /u/ in circus.

Heat Energy

Heat is one of the most important forms of energy. We use heat in many ways. It warms our homes and cooks our food. Heat also provides our homes with hot water. Heat dries our laundry and makes electric light bulbs give off light.

Thousands of mirrors focus the sun's light into a very small spot, creating extremely high heat on solar panels.

All matter has heat. Some matter has more heat energy than other matter. For instance, if you boil water, you can easily feel the heat that is in the boiling water. But what about ice? Does it have heat? The answer is yes. It has heat, but it has much less heat than boiling water. It also has less heat than your body. That is why ice feels "cold" to you. However, ice still has heat energy.

Sources of heat. Where does heat energy come from? For something to have an increase in heat energy, it must receive energy from another source. There are six main sources of heat that we experience on earth. They are (1) the sun, (2) the earth, (3) mechanical energy, (4) chemical reactions, (5) electricity, and (6) nuclear energy. We will discuss each one of these sources of heat energy and describe how they generate heat.

The sun. The sun is our main and most important source of heat. As you have already learned, the sun provides heat energy and light energy to the earth to support life on our planet. Sunlight can be turned into heat energy. When the light energy from sunlight hits matter, heat energy is formed. The sun's light and heat are absorbed by the seas, the ground, the atmosphere, and the plants on earth. Work is done as the sun's energy is absorbed by matter of the earth.

Sunlight can also be reflected from one object to another to form heat energy. Matter that is not in direct sunlight can still receive light energy indirectly and form heat. For example, large amounts of the sun's energy can be collected by using devices known as *solar furnaces*. These furnaces have mirrors that reflect the sun's light from a large area onto one small spot. Whatever is located at this spot is heated by the sun's rays collected there. Some solar furnaces can generate enough heat to melt steel! Small solar furnaces are sometimes used outdoors by hikers and campers to cook food.

EXPERIMENT 505.A HEAT FROM THE SUN

You will use a thermometer to observe the effect of direct and indirect sunlight on the heat energy of matter. NOTE: This experiment should be conducted on a sunny day.

These supplies are needed:

yellow construction paper
a thermometer (Fahrenheit or Celsius)

Follow these directions carefully. Place a check mark in the box as you complete each step. All steps should be completed indoors.

- ☐ 1. Place the thermometer inside a dark drawer for five minutes.
- ☐ 2. Remove the thermometer. Record the temperature. ____________ degrees.
- ☐ 3. Place the thermometer in direct sunlight that is coming in a window for five minutes.
- ☐ 4. Record the temperature. ____________ degrees.
- ☐ 5. Place the thermometer out of direct sunlight but near the window.
- ☐ 6. Focus the construction paper so that the sun's rays coming in the window are reflected on the bulb of the thermometer. Leave it for five minutes.
- ☐ 7. Record the temperature. ____________ degrees.

Teacher check:

Initials ____________________ Date ____________________

Answer these questions.

2.1 Why was heat measured by the thermometer in the drawer?

____

____

2.2 What was the difference between the thermometer readings in the drawer and in direct sunlight? ____________ degrees.

2.3 What accounts for this difference in temperatures?

____

____

2.4 How could you tell that heat energy could be transferred from the reflected rays of sunlight?

____

____

____

The earth. The earth contains much heat below its surface. Perhaps you have seen a picture or video of an erupting volcano. The lava from a volcano is molten rock. It has been melted by heat deep within the earth. When a volcano erupts, some of this heat escapes to the surface. Some of the heat below the earth's surface also escapes to the surface in *geysers*. These are springs of water that have been heated to boiling by the hot rocks within the earth. Today, some people have begun to use this heat below the earth's surface to generate electricity, heat homes and buildings, and do other work. This source of heat energy is sometimes called *geothermal energy*.

Do some research.

2.5 Using the library or Internet, do some research on geysers and how they work. Write a short paper about geysers based upon your research. Share your findings with your teacher.

Teacher check:
Initials ____________________ Date ____________________

Mechanical energy. As you learned in the first section of this LIFEPAC, mechanical energy can be transformed into heat energy. Recall that when you rubbed your hands together, you felt heat. When objects rub together, they cause **friction**. This friction between objects generates heat energy. Thus, friction is a common source of heat.

Long ago, people learned to use friction to start fires. They struck two pieces of **flint** rock together to produce sparks. The mechanical energy caused the two moving stones to touch each other. This caused friction. Friction changed the mechanical energy into heat energy. Work was done when the sparks flew and started a fire.

| Long ago, people started fires by using friction between rocks.

Today, machines can change mechanical motion to heat energy. Parts that slide against each other cause friction. Heat results. Sometimes this heat is useful. Sometimes it is not. Sometimes friction may actually cause damage to a machine or cause parts to wear out or break down. For this reason, oil or grease is often used between parts of a machine or metal surfaces that move against each other. The oil reduces friction and thus reduces the amount of heat generated.

Friction is not the only way that mechanical energy can be turned into heat energy. Bending or changing the shape of objects can also generate heat. This occurs today in machines that shape or bend objects.

EXPERIMENT 505.B
HEAT FROM BENDING

You or a partner will bend some metal paper clips and observe any changes in heat energy.

These supplies are needed:
two paper clips

Follow these directions carefully. Place a check mark in the box as you complete each step.

- ☐ 1. Select a partner for this activity. ______________________
  Partner's name
- ☐ 2. Open one of the paper clips.
- ☐ 3. Have your partner rapidly bend the paper clip back and forth.
- ☐ 4. Lightly touch the paper clip at the bending point.
- ☐ 5. Touch the other paper clip and compare the temperature of the two paper clips.

Teacher check:
Initials ______________ Date ______________

Answer these questions.

2.6 How did the bent paper clip feel? ____________________

____

2.7 How did the unbent paper clip feel? ____________________

____

2.8 What would happen if you rapidly bent back and forth the second paper clip?

____

____

2.9 What was the source of mechanical energy in this experiment?

____

____

Mechanical energy can also transform into heat energy through a **collision**. Whenever one object collides with another, heat is generated. Heat energy is formed when you hammer a nail or when you bump into someone. Heat energy is formed even by such a small collision as the pencil dropping on your desk. Most of the time we do not feel the heat energy when we bump things, but we can often feel heat after repeated collision between objects.

Write *true* or *false*.

2.10 __________ Heat energy can come from friction.

2.11 __________ Heat energy may not be useful.

2.12 __________ Breaking a window causes heat energy.

2.13 __________ Some matter does not have heat energy.

2.14 __________ Changing the shapes of objects will cause heat energy.

Chemical reactions. Another source of heat energy comes from chemical reactions. The chemical energy in matter is transformed in chemical reactions to produce heat energy. When the chemicals in matter start to burn, heat energy is given off. When food is used as the matter, heat energy is given off as the food is "burned." When some chemicals are mixed, a chemical reaction occurs that results in heat being given off. In other chemical reactions, heat energy is absorbed from the materials or the surroundings.

How can matter burn? Fuel, oxygen, and heat are needed. Some fuel burns easier than other fuel. Not as much heat is needed to start easier-burning fuels. Gasoline is one of these easy burning fuels. Just a tiny spark can **ignite** gasoline. A great amount of heat energy is produced by the burning of gasoline.

The food you eat is transformed into heat energy through chemical reactions. It is also changed into other types of energy to help you move and grow and build new tissues in your body. The heat energy generated by food in your body comes from a complicated series of chemical reactions carried out by the living cells.

God created you so that the heat energy produced in your body is just the right amount. This heat energy helps keep your body normally at a constant temperature—98.6 degrees Fahrenheit. Your body controls the amount of chemical energy that can be changed into heat energy at one time. Therefore, your body temperature stays the same. Your body could not survive if it had too much or too little heat energy.

| Your body is normally a constant 98.6 degrees Fahrenheit.

By mixing certain chemicals, heat energy is formed. Sometimes the mixture heats up. Sometimes it cools. In either case, heat energy is transferred between the chemical mixture and the surroundings. Sometimes the chemical reaction can be so violent that the mixture explodes. Batteries contain a mixture of chemicals. They can not only generate electrical energy, but they can also generate heat energy.

EXPERIMENT 505.C
HEAT ENERGY IN A CHEMICAL REACTION

View 505
Heat Energy:
Grade 5 Science experiments video

You will conduct a safe chemical reaction with simple kitchen materials and observe the change in heat energy from the reaction.

These supplies are needed:

3 liquid ounces of vinegar
1 tablespoon of baking soda
1 glass jar
1 thermometer (Fahrenheit or Celsius)

Follow these directions carefully. Place a check mark in the box as you complete each step.

- ☐ 1. Pour the vinegar into the jar and let it stand for 5 minutes.
- ☐ 2. Record the temperature of the vinegar in the jar. ______________ degrees.
- ☐ 3. Pour the baking soda into the jar and mix it with the vinegar.
- ☐ 4. Record the temperature of the mixture. ______________ degrees.

Teacher check:

Initials ________________________ Date ________________________

Answer these questions.

2.15 What did you see when you mixed the vinegar and the baking soda?

____

____

2.16 What caused the temperature change of the mixture?

____

____

2.17 Which types of chemical energy were shown in this experiment—burning, food use, or mixing chemicals?

____

____

____

Write the correct letter and answer in the blank.

2.18 Ice has ____________________ energy.

a. mechanical b. cold c. heat

2.19 Rubbing two objects together creates ____________________ .

a. collision b. friction c. mixing

2.20 People of long ago used ____________________ to start fires.

a. collision b. friction c. mixing

2.21 When matter burns, ____________________ energy is changed to heat energy.

a. light b. chemical c. mechanical

2.22 Sunlight can transform into heat energy even when it ____________________ matter.

a. reflects off b. mixes with c. cannot reach

2.23 In the process of eating, ____________________ energy in food is transformed into heat energy by your body.

a. light b. chemical c. mechanical

Electricity. The flow of electricity through some materials (called *conductors*) generates heat. Therefore, electricity is a source of heat energy. Many appliances in your home use electricity to generate heat. For example, ovens, ranges, dryers, toasters, and irons are all common appliances that produce useful heat energy from electricity.

Nuclear energy. Nuclear energy is a modern source of heat energy. It can generate great quantities of heat. Nuclear bombs release so much heat energy that they destroy large areas around them. However, nuclear reactions can be controlled in a device called a nuclear **reactor**. In a nuclear reactor, the release of heat energy is controlled and made slow enough so that the heat can be used to produce electricity and to do other useful jobs.

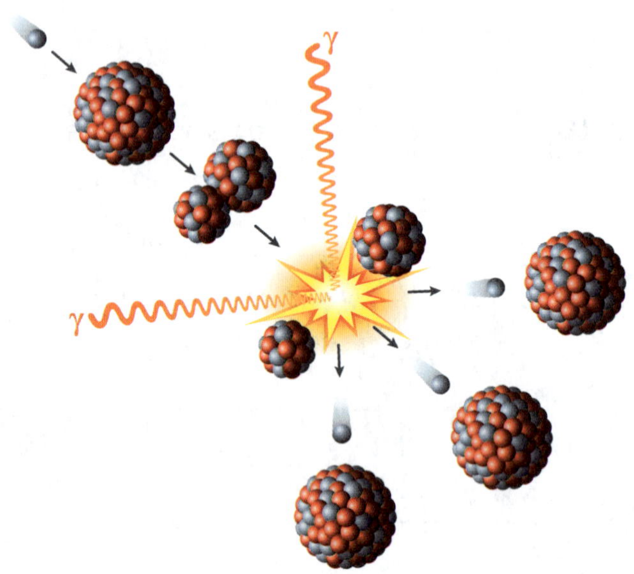

| In nuclear fission, a uranium atom is split, creating tremendous energy which heats water, which creates steam, which turns turbines, which creates electricity.

Work from heat energy. As you have learned, work is the result of energy transformation. Work is done when light, mechanical, chemical, electrical, or nuclear energy is transformed into heat energy. Work involves movement or change in matter. For example, work is done when a piece of paper burns or rubbing creates heat.

You might think that rubbing your hands together or burning paper is useless and is not work. However, remember the special meaning of work in this LIFEPAC. Since there is movement or change of a material, work is done. Of course, the work could be wasted and no useful outcome could take place. However, work is still done. Sometimes, heat energy from a fire is allowed to be lost into the air. At times, heat energy from friction is wasted. In fact, friction can produce heat energy that destroys things.

However, people have learned how to make heat energy do very useful work. In order to make heat useful, it is captured, controlled, and changed into another energy form. For example, the heat from burning fuel in a furnace is useful. The heat warms the air in the furnace. The warmed air rises. The warmed air is replaced by cooler air, which is then warmed. The heat causes the air to move. The moving air has mechanical energy. Heat energy has been transformed into mechanical energy.

Heat is used in engines to do work. Fuel that is burned in engines produces heat energy. In gasoline engines, the gasoline burns quickly and produces gases. The heated gases cause great pressure. These gases are located inside a **chamber**. Connected to the other end of the chamber is a **piston**. The high pressure created by the hot gases makes the piston move in the chamber. The moving piston also moves other parts in the engine. By this process, heat energy

SCIENCE 505

LIFEPAC TEST

NAME ______________________

DATE ______________________

SCORE ______________________

SCIENCE 505: LIFEPAC TEST

Match these items (each answer, 3 points).

1. __________ energy
2. __________ work
3. __________ fossil fuels
4. __________ potential energy
5. __________ kinetic energy
6. __________ heat energy
7. __________ joule
8. __________ solar energy
9. __________ biomass
10. __________ stewardship

a. caused by friction
b. unit of work
c. contained in sun's rays
d. caring for earth's creatures and resources
e. explosion
f. machinery
g. ability to do work
h. force times distance
i. coal, gas, and oil
j. energy that is stored
k. energy that is moving
l. garbage and scrap paper

Answer *true* or *false* (each answer, 2 points).

11. __________ Water and wind are two sources of energy.
12. __________ A falling apple is an example of mechanical energy.
13. __________ The sun is the main source of energy on earth.
14. __________ Energy is never lost.
15. __________ Energy cannot change from one form to another.
16. __________ Chemical energy is stored in coal, gas, and oil.
17. __________ An explosion is an example of sound energy.
18. __________ Heat energy can be received from reflected sunlight.
19. __________ Solar energy is not difficult to store.
20. __________ Oil and coal supplies can be renewed.

Write the correct answer on the blank (each answer, 3 points).

21. Batteries contain ________________ energy.
a. heat b. chemical c. mechanical

22. When a 5 pound weight is lifted 10 feet, ________________ of work is done.
a. 50 foot-pounds b. 50 joules c. 15 foot-pounds

23. Energy changing into different forms is called ________________ of energy.
a. multiplication b. frequency c. transformation

24. Jesus described work in John, chapter 6 as ________________ .
a. hard
b. force moving an object
c. having faith in Him

25. Solar energy does not give off ________________ .
a. pollution b. rays c. light

26. The energy produced by the sun and stars comes from ________________ .
a. mechanical energy
b. nuclear fission
c. nuclear fusion

27. Geothermal energy is produced when water touches ________________ .
a. biomass b. oil c. hot rocks

28. Oil is used for ________________ in some countries.
a. communication b. political power c. cleaning

Complete these sentences (each answer, 4 points).

29. Whenever anything moves or grows, ________________________ is used.

30. Work is done when a ________________________ moves an object some distance.

31. Mixing chemicals together can produce ________________________ .

32. A good ________________________ cares for our energy supplies and uses them wisely.

Answer these questions (each answer, 5 points).

33. What is meant by *transformation of energy*? Give two examples.

____

____

____

____

____

____

34. What are the advantages of using solar energy instead of coal and oil for energy?

____

____

____

____

____

is changed to mechanical energy in an engine. The engine can do much work as a result of the heat energy.

Heat energy can also be used to change the shape of matter. People have learned how to melt metal with heat so that the metal can be formed into useful objects after it has been cooled. The heated metal has heat energy. As it melts, it flows together. The moving metal has mechanical energy. Work has been done. The changed metal is useful to us.

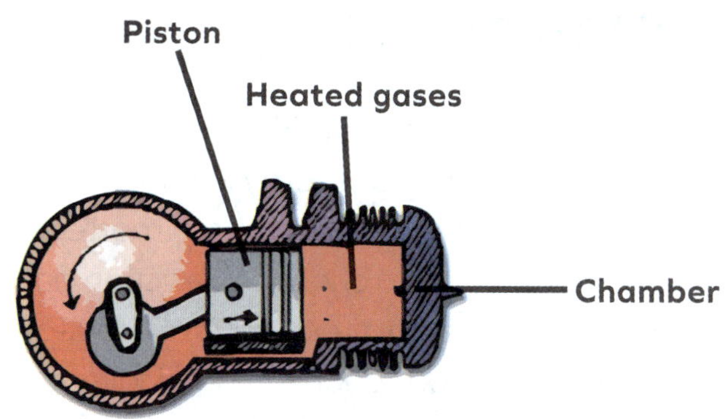

| An engine converts heat to mechanical energy.

Answer *true* or *false*.

2.24 __________ Heat energy can be wasted.

2.25 __________ Heat energy can be transformed into mechanical energy.

2.26 __________ Mechanical energy can be transformed into heat energy.

2.27 __________ Moving air is an example of heat energy.

2.28 __________ Work is done when heat energy is changed into another form of energy.

2.29 __________ Heat energy is useful in changing metals.

Chemical Energy

You learned earlier in this LIFEPAC that another source of heat energy comes from chemical reactions. The chemical energy in matter is transformed in chemical reactions to produce heat energy. When the chemicals in matter start to burn, heat energy is given off. When some chemicals are mixed, a chemical reaction occurs that results in heat being given off. In other chemical reactions, heat energy is absorbed from the materials or the surroundings. Work is a result of the transformation of chemical energy into heat energy.

Chemicals have stored (potential) energy. How did chemicals get this stored energy? Can chemical energy be used up? Can new chemical energy be made as heat energy can be made? We will examine these questions in the rest of this section of the LIFEPAC.

Sources of chemical energy. Fuels have chemical energy. They can burn. Some of the fuels come from oil, coal, and wood. Fuels do not make energy. They already have it. Burning or mixing chemicals can change the form of the energy in fuels.

Wood comes from plants, especially trees. Through photosynthesis, trees take light energy from the sun to make food. The food has chemical energy stored in it. The trees use the food made from photosynthesis for survival. Trees also store the sun's energy in wood. This stored energy is not used up until an animal eats it or it is burned. At that time, the stored chemical energy in the wood is changed into another form of energy.

Both plants and animals have chemical energy. Plants get chemical energy from the food made by photosynthesis. Animals get chemical energy when they eat plants or plant-eating animals. As you will see, this stored chemical energy in plants and animals can be used long after they die.

Coal is material under the earth that has been formed from the remains of plants. Trees and plants that lived long ago were covered and weighed down by sand and mud. The weight of the sand and mud provide great pressure on the plant remains. This great pressure, combined with the passage of time, caused the coal to be formed from the plant remains. The chemical energy that was stored in the plants becomes chemical energy now stored in the coal. It is interesting to note that this chemical energy in coal actually came from the energy of the sun, too, since the coal was once living plants that received their energy from the sun!

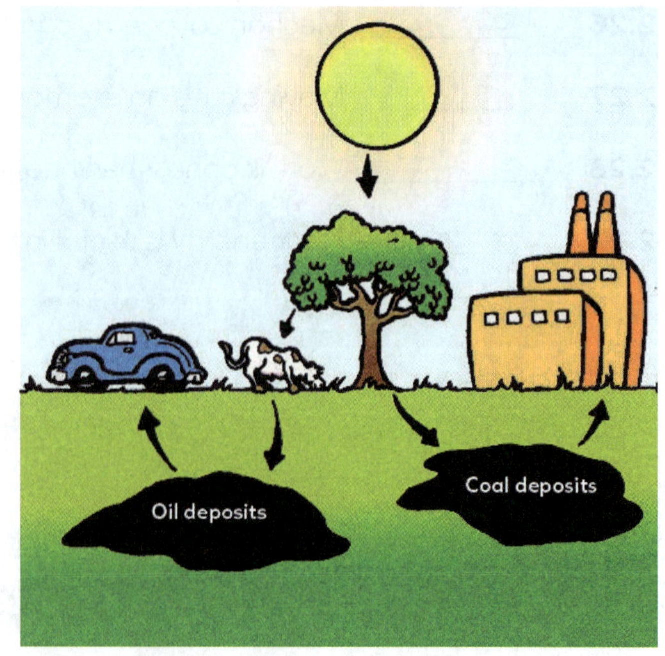

The chemical energy stored in the coal can be transformed into heat energy and other forms of energy when the coal is burned. In fact, coal is burned in many power plants to produce electricity. The chemical energy in coal is eventually transformed into electrical energy.

Oil products are thought to come from the remains of tiny organisms and animal bodies. These remains eventually fell to the sea floor. The pressure of sand and mud caused oil to be formed over a long period of time. Natural gas was often formed along with the oil deposits. Since the animals and organisms got energy from plants, which got energy from the sun, oil has received its stored energy from the sun, too.

The chemical energy stored in oil is used in many ways today. One of the most important uses is to make gasoline, which powers our automobiles. The stored chemical energy in gasoline is used to make heat energy, which is changed into mechanical energy. Work is done from the chemical energy stored in oil.

| Coal and gas are limited and someday will no longer be available.

Chemical energy is constantly being made from light energy and is being stored in plants. Trees may be replaced and new ones grown to take the place of the ones we use. However, coal and gas take a very long time to be formed. The chemical energy of coal and gas is being used up at a great rate by the people who live on earth today. Since the coal and gas take too long to be formed, these sources of chemical energy *cannot* be **renewed**. Therefore, our supply of chemical energy in coal and gas is limited and will no longer be available someday.

Look It Up! Coal and oil deposits are not found everywhere in the world. These sources of chemical energy can only be found in certain locations. Use an atlas, encyclopedia, library books, or the Internet to help you answer these questions about coal and oil deposits.

2.30 Where are the largest coal deposits in the world? (Name at least two countries.)

____

2.31 Where are the largest oil deposits in the world? (Name at least four countries.)

____

____

2.32 Which countries have large deposits of both coal and oil? (Name at least two countries.) ____

____

2.33 What are the advantages for countries to have deposits of coal or oil?

____

____

____

____

In addition to fuels such as wood, coal, or oil, other chemicals have stored chemical energy. However, some of these chemicals do not burn. Yet their chemical energy can be changed to heat energy in other ways.

Mixing chemicals together can produce heat. Water does not burn, but if you mix certain **acids** with water, heat will result. Sometimes the heat will be so great when chemicals are mixed that the mixture will explode! In these cases, the reaction of chemicals in the explosion transforms the chemical energy into mechanical energy and sound energy. Since the exploding particles are moving very fast, there is a lot of mechanical energy being produced. Work is done.

Complete these sentences.

2.34 Fuels can change chemical energy to ______________________ by burning.

2.35 Matter is made up of ______________________ .

2.36 Chemicals can cause reactions when ______________________ .

2.37 Changing light energy into chemical energy in plants is called

______________________ .

2.38 The chemical energy of a. ______________ and b. ______________ is being used up and cannot be renewed.

Work from chemical energy. When chemical energy is changed to another form of energy, work results. Like heat energy, not all work from chemical energy is useful. However, people have learned to control some chemical energy to perform useful work.

WIRE

BATTERY

|A battery contains chemical energy.

Burning chemicals can produce some useful work. As you have learned, gasoline engines have been developed to use this work. Ovens, stoves, and furnaces that use gas, oil, and coal control burning to provide useful work from chemical energy.

When the chemical energy stored in food is transformed in your body, useful work can be done. The heat produced maintains your body temperature. Breathing and heartbeats continue. You can move your body to play and do other activities. Work is done.

Batteries have chemicals inside. The chemicals have stored chemical energy. When the battery is connected from one end to the other by a wire, the chemicals react inside the battery. Heat energy and electrical energy are formed. This transformed energy can be used to light bulbs or operate toys. The large batteries in your car help start the engine. Work is done when the chemical energy stored in batteries is transformed.

Write the correct letter and answer in the blank.

2.39 Engines do work when chemical energy is changed to ________________ energy.

a. heat b. light c. potential

2.40 Sometimes when transforming chemical energy to other forms of energy ________________ can be wasted.

a. acids b. fuel c. work

2.41 The control of ________________ is a useful chemical energy transformation.

a. burning b. heating c. working

2.42 When chemicals in ________________ are connected by wire, work results.

a. batteries b. engines c. bodies

Review the material in this section to prepare for the Self Test. The Self Test will check your understanding of this section and will review the other section. Any items you miss on this test will show you what areas you will need to restudy in order to prepare for the unit test.

SELF TEST 2

Match these items (each answer, 3 points).

2.01 __________ friction causes it
2.02 __________ fuel stores it
2.03 __________ change
2.04 __________ movement or change of shape
2.05 __________ changes light energy to chemical energy
2.06 __________ changes chemical energy to heat energy
2.07 __________ use heat
2.08 __________ reaction
2.09 __________ begin burning
2.010 __________ bumping together

a. food
b. did again
c. photosynthesis
d. ignite
e. heat energy
f. collision
g. forms hot gases and pressure
h. engines
i. chemical energy
j. work
k. caused by mixture of chemicals
l. transformation

Complete these statements (each answer, 4 points).

2.011 Matter is made up of ______________________________ .
2.012 Matter has ______________________________ even when it seems cold.
2.013 Batteries contain ______________________________ energy.
2.014 Mechanical energy is the energy of ______________________________ .
2.015 Mechanical energy can be changed into ______________________________ energy.
2.016 Long ago, people started fires by ______________________________ .
2.017 When light energy hits matter, ______________________________ energy is formed.

Answer *true or false* (each answer, 2 points).

2.018 __________ Breaking a cup causes heat energy.

2.019 __________ Bending a paper clip causes heat energy.

2.020 __________ Rubbing hands together causes heat energy.

2.021 __________ Boiling water causes chemical energy.

2.022 __________ Coal received its chemical energy from energy stored in plants.

2.023 __________ Heat energy can be received from reflected sunlight.

2.024 __________ Some fuels burn easier than other fuels.

2.025 __________ Work is done when heat energy is changed into another form of energy.

2.026 __________ Energy is never lost.

2.027 __________ Heated gases can cause great pressure.

Write the correct answer in the blank (each answer, 3 points).

2.028 Stored energy is ____________________ energy.
a. kinetic b. potential c. old

2.029 In the metric system, the unit of work is the ____________________.
a. joule b. foot-pound c. meter-pound

2.030 Energy changing into different forms is called ____________________ of energy.
a. multiplication b. reduction c. transformation

2.031 Your body controls the amount of ____________________ that can be changed into heat energy at one time.
a. work b. chemical energy c. mechanical energy

Complete these activities (each answer, 5 points).

2.032 Describe how work is done in a gasoline engine.

____

____

____

____

2.033 Explain what is meant by *transformation of energy*. Give two examples.

____

____

____

____

Teacher check: Initials ____________

Score ____________ Date ____________

80/100

3. ENERGY IN THE FUTURE

God has provided our earth with many sources of energy. In the past 100 years, people have used energy in greater and greater amounts to try to make life easier and better. During this time, the use of automobiles has grown. Airplanes have made travel over long distances possible for more people. Rockets have been invented and used to put many satellites in orbit around the earth.

These satellites have helped us communicate around the world through telephone, television, and the Internet. Computers have been invented to help us do many physical and mental tasks.

We are able to move faster, to have more comfort, to do things easier, and to save time because God has provided us with energy supplies. People have learned how to use energy. The work done through the transformation of energy has been put to use in many new ways. However, most of these improvements are using up our supplies of energy. Many of these energy supplies cannot be renewed or replaced. We must think about what will be needed in the years to come.

In this section of the LIFEPAC, you will consider some of the present concerns we face in the use of energy. You will also study some new ways that people are exploring to help meet our energy needs in the future.

Objectives

Review these objectives. When you have completed this section, you should be able to:

4. Explain the relationship between work and energy.
5. Identify energy concerns of today that may be problems of the future.
6. Describe several possible energy sources of the future.

Vocabulary

Study these new words. Learning the meanings of these words is a good study habit and will improve your understanding of this LIFEPAC.

advantage (ad van' tij). To the good; better position.

biomass (bi' ō mas). Any organic material that can be converted into energy or a source of energy. Examples are garbage, liquid wastes, and manure.

efficient (ə fish' ənt). Able to produce with little or no waste.

fission (fish' ən). The splitting of the atomic nucleus of certain elements, especially uranium. It releases a large amount of energy.

fusion (fyü' zhən). The combining of atomic nuclei to form heavier nuclei. It releases an enormous quantity of energy.

hazards (haz' ərdz). Things that are dangerous.

intelligence (in tel' ə jən). The ability to learn and understand.

machinery (mə shē' nər ē). A machine or group of machines; equipment used to do work.

mental (men' tl). Of the mind or done by the mind.

political (pə lit' ə kəl). Concerned with politics; having to do with governing.

Pronunciation Key: hat, āge, cãre, fär; let, ēqual, tėrm; it, īce; hot, ōpen, ôrder; oil; out; cup, pu̇t, rüle; child; long; thin; /ŦH/ for then; /zh/ for measure; /u/ or /ə/ represents /a/ in about, /e/ in taken, /i/ in pencil, /o/ in lemon, and /u/ in circus.

Present Concerns

Although people continue to use energy to improve the quality of life, there are concerns we face in our use of energy. We face some problems that will have to be solved in the future. Perhaps the problems we face today will cause us to search out new answers for tomorrow. With God's help and the efforts of many people, we will be able to supply our energy needs in the future.

Problems. We are using large quantities of fossil fuels today. Since 1900, the amount of fossil fuels burned by people to produce energy has doubled every 20 years. As you learned in the last section, these coal and oil fossil fuels cannot be renewed. At our present rate of use, the supplies of these fossil fuels will run out.

Today, oil furnishes about 40 percent of the energy supply used both in the world and in the United States. Facing the problem of no more oil is a serious problem. Why is oil so important? Surely we can find other good fuels. Coal and wood *could* be used. However, oil is less expensive and is easier to get and to put to use. Since it is a liquid, oil is easier to transport over long distances, especially by pipeline. We have been able to develop the use of oil much better than other energy sources in our modern world because it was easier and cheaper.

Coal cannot permanently replace oil as an energy source because the supplies of coal also cannot be renewed. Although the reserve supplies of coal are greater than those for oil, they are not unlimited. Coal supplies will also run out someday. When it is gone, new coal supplies cannot be created by people.

Wood is an energy source that *can* be replaced, but it does take a long time to grow. Wood is not as good a fuel as oil. It is not as easy to burn, nor does it burn as hot or as quickly as some components of oil like gasoline. Wood is more important for uses other than fuel. For instance, it is used to make paper and to supply lumber as a building material.

Oil is becoming more costly because it is not as easy to get as it once was. Oil-producing facilities must now go deeper into the earth. Often they must be located offshore in the oceans.

Another problem today with oil is that it is not always easy to get supplies from some countries. Some countries use their oil deposits as a form of power over other countries. A country with large supplies of oil can make demands of other countries. In this way a country could use oil for **political** power.

| Countries that sell oil can often charge unreasonable prices to buyers.

Even though supplies of oil are decreasing, the use of oil keeps increasing. Automobiles and power plants are two of the biggest users of oil. More cars are being driven now than ever before. Since cars use a major oil component—gasoline—for fuel, the use of oil for cars keeps increasing. Power plants that use oil supply electricity for people. Because more people are in the world, more electricity is being used each year.

Another major problem with the use of fossil fuels like oil is *pollution*. The burning of these fuels gives off harmful chemicals that cause pollution in the atmosphere. For example, cars pollute through the exhaust of the engines as waste gases enter the atmosphere. Power plants also give off harmful chemical products to the atmosphere in the exhaust from burning fuel for power.

Although some improvements have been made to help prevent pollution from cars and power plants in recent years, the problem has not been solved. Cars and power plants still pollute the atmosphere. Air pollution causes health **hazards**. Therefore, the use of fossil fuels to supply our energy needs creates pollution problems that concern us today.

Air pollution produces harmful smog that hangs over our cities. (Los Angeles pictured)

Answer *true* or *false*.

3.1 ________ In the past 100 years, people have decreased their need for energy.

3.2 ________ Many of our energy supplies cannot be renewed or replaced.

3.3 ________ Coal supplies can be renewed by making new coal quickly.

3.4 ________ Wood is easier to use as a fuel than oil.

3.5 ________ Automobiles and electrical power plants are two of the biggest users of oil.

3.6 ________ Oil is used for political power by some countries.

3.7 ____________ Air pollution problems from cars and power plants have been solved.

3.8 ____________ The growth in the use of electricity is partly due to the increase in the world's population.

Review an idea. In Science LIFEPAC 504, you learned about *stewardship*. Stewardship is an important solution to some of our energy problems. Review the material on stewardship in the previous LIFEPAC if you need to in order to answer the following questions.

3.9 Define *stewardship*.

____

____

____

____

____

3.10 Review Genesis 1:26. How did God expect human beings to show stewardship?

____

____

____

3.11 Read Genesis 3:23. God sent Adam out of the Garden of Eden and told him to do something. What was Adam's responsibility?

____

____

____

____

Stewardship and energy. God created people to be in charge of the earth. He wanted them to take care of all living things on the earth. One way to care for the earth is to be responsible stewards of all things that are part of the earth. Energy should be included in our stewardship of the earth.

Did you ever wonder why God chose humans to be in charge of the earth? Humans are weaker than many of the animals that God created. We are also slower than many of the animals on Earth. We cannot run faster than many animals nor can we fly by ourselves. Our teeth and claws are not dangerous weapons. Yet, we have learned how to use energy to become the strongest and fastest creatures in God's creation on earth.

God gave humans **intelligence** above and beyond what He gave to animals. We are able to think of ways to make and use tools. Some of these tools can be very complex, like computers. Tools allow us to make better use of God's creation. We can be good stewards of what we have been given by God.

We have the ability to invent new things. Therefore, we can make even better use of what God has given us. Unfortunately, we can also make bad use of what He has given us. In fact, we can waste it. Using what God has given us is not bad. We are doing what God asked us to do when we make good use of things. However, when we waste things like energy, we are not doing what God asked us to do.

Good stewards are concerned about energy problems. They do not need to stop using oil or coal, but they do need to try cutting down waste of these fuels. To conserve electricity and fuel, perhaps the house temperature could be lowered in the winter and raised in the summer. This is especially good to do when no one is home. Combining several short errands with the car into one longer trip might save gasoline and time. Working at saving energy can be fun and can help us better organize our time to do other activities. It also makes us good stewards of God's creation.

Many scientists and engineers are working on energy problems today in order to conserve energy and help solve our energy problems. These men and women need encouragement to continue working toward development of new energy sources. We can pray that God will help people find new ways to use energy transformation to do our work in the future.

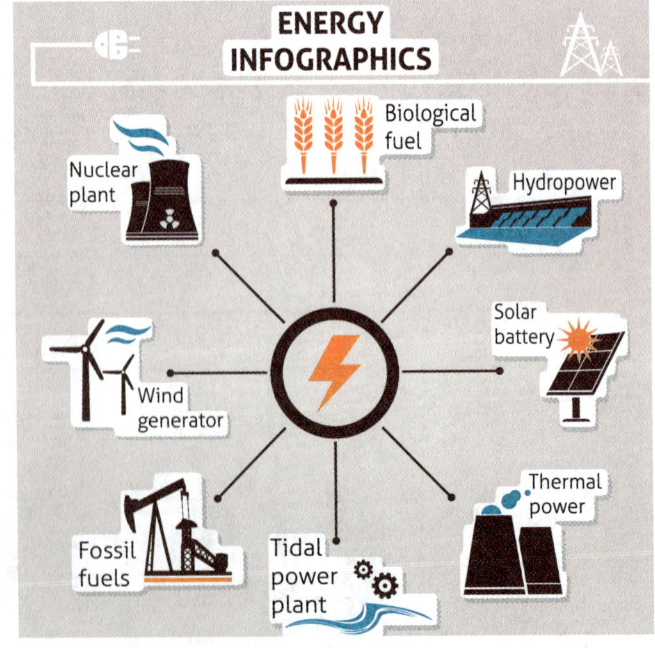

| It's important that we conserve energy and find new sources of energy for the future.

Take a survey. Many people are concerned about our energy problems. Some people are taking steps to deal with the problems. Take a survey to find out what some people are doing to help solve the energy problems. Follow these directions:

- ☐ 1. Write down three questions that you want to ask.

  ____

  ____

  ____

  ____

  ____

- ☐ 2. Select three adults to interview. Write their names here.

  ____
  Name

  ____
  Name

  ____
  Name

- ☐ 3. Go to the people and ask them your questions.
- ☐ 4. Compare their answers and the results of your survey.
- ☐ 5. Write a short report summarizing the results of your survey.
- ☐ 6. Take the report and this LIFEPAC to your teacher for a teacher check.

Teacher check:

Initials ____________ Date ____________

Future Sources of Energy

The chemical energy found in oil, coal, and natural gas has been important for many years. Many people have spent their lives developing new ways to transform these energy sources into other useful forms of energy. They have done very well. Hopefully, new studies will provide a better understanding of the ways oil, coal, and natural gas may be used. Perhaps they will discover ways that our use of these limited resources may be more **efficient**.

Many scientists are directing their abilities toward improving or utilizing other energy resources. These men and women must be able to find ways to make these energy sources easy to use, efficient, and affordable. Perhaps new discoveries will allow the use of new energy sources in the future.

A number of energy sources are being considered for more use in the future. Among these are solar energy, nuclear energy, geothermal energy, and energy from **biomass**. In the remainder of this LIFEPAC, we will explore aspects of these energy sources that may be used more in the future.

Solar energy. Already, solar energy is used throughout the world to do work and perform various small jobs. People collect the sun's light energy with various devices that change the sun's light energy into heat energy or electrical energy. For example, *flatplate solar collectors* change solar energy into heat energy that is used to heat water and the air inside buildings. *Solar cells* convert solar energy into electrical energy. You may have seen small solar cells used to power electronic calculators. *Solar cells* are also used as an electrical energy source for many satellites in space and the International Space Station.

Solar energy seems to be such a good choice for supplying energy needs of the future. The sun's light rays are free, and they are a clean energy source that does not produce pollution. However, some major problems with solar energy need to be overcome if it is to be used on a wide scale in the future. For one thing, sunlight on earth is thinly distributed over a wide area and must be collected and concentrated to produce significant amounts of energy. Buildings, solar collectors, and **machinery** equipped to use solar energy are all expensive and can be very large. Until the costs associated with solar energy can be brought nearer to the costs of coal and oil, solar energy will not be a widely-used source of our energy needs. In addition, another problem with solar energy is that nighttime and bad weather interrupt the supply of sunlight. Since direct sunlight cannot reach the solar collectors at night or on cloudy days, the heat provided from solar energy must be stored. Heat is difficult to

| Solar panels on a house

store for very long. Storage surfaces around the heat "soak up" the stored heat. This heat is then "wasted" to the surrounding air from the storage surfaces. So, unlike the potential energy of oil and coal that can be stored for long periods of time, the potential energy from sunlight is very difficult to store for very long.

EXPERIMENT 505.D
SOLAR ENERGY FOR HEAT

This experiment will show you how the sun's rays can warm water and how soon the water cools off after being taken out of sunlight. NOTE: You will need a sunny day for this experiment.

These supplies are needed:

small jar (like a baby-food jar) filled with water
a thermometer (Fahrenheit or Celsius)

Follow these directions carefully. Read all of the directions before starting this experiment. Place a check mark in the box as you complete each step.

- ☐ 1. Place the jar filled with water in a place where either direct or indirect sunlight will not reach it. Set it aside in this place at least half an hour before using it in the next step.
- ☐ 2. Place the thermometer in the water. Record the temperature in the chart below.
- ☐ 3. Put the jar in direct sunlight.
  (Do not leave the thermometer in the jar or in sunlight.)
- ☐ 4. Measure the temperature of the water every 5 minutes while it is in the sunlight. Record these temperatures on the chart below.
- ☐ 5. After 20 minutes, remove the water from the sunlight.
- ☐ 6. Continue to record the temperature of the water every 5 minutes on the chart.
- ☐ 7. You may go to the next part of this LIFEPAC as you wait between the readings.

IN SUNLIGHT			OUT OF SUNLIGHT		
Beginning	________	degrees	After 20 minutes	________	degrees
After 5 minutes	________	degrees	After 25 minutes	________	degrees
After 10 minutes	________	degrees	After 30 minutes	________	degrees
After 15 minutes	________	degrees	After 35 minutes	________	degrees
After 20 minutes	________	degrees	After 40 minutes	________	degrees

3.12 How does water respond to sunlight?

____

____

____

____

3.13 What happens to the stored heat after water is removed from the sun?

____

____

____

____

3.14 How might you keep the water warm longer after you remove it from sunlight?

____

____

____

____

Teacher check:

Initials ________________ Date ________________

To make partial use of solar energy, some new homes and other buildings are being built to take **advantage** of the sun's light. They also use normal electrical supplies, but use solar panels to help warm and cool the buildings. Less outside electricity is used in these homes than would be used without the solar energy. The building owners can save some money, because the sunlight is free.

Combining solar energy with other forms of energy appears to be one good answer for the energy needs of the future. By doing this, big and expensive changes may not be needed in buildings and equipment. Engineers and scientists continue to research the development of more efficient systems using solar energy.

Write the correct answer in the blank.

3.15 Light rays from the sun are called ______________________.

a. solar energy b. heat energy c. chemical energy

3.16 One of the major problems in using solar energy has been ______________________.

a. heat b. cost c. speed

3.17 Another problem with solar energy is that nighttime and cloudy days ______________________ the sunlight.

a. increase b. collect c. interrupt

3.18 Combining solar energy with ______________________ appears to be promising for the future.

a. other forms of energy b. explosions c. darkness

Be creative! The following activities will challenge your imagination. Choose at least one of these to do. Put a check mark in the box next to the activity you choose. After you make your choice, take this page to your teacher. Discuss your decision before starting to work. After you complete the activity, take it to your teacher or parent for review and check.

- ☐ a. Design and construct a poster showing how energy is used. Compare good uses with wasteful uses.
- ☐ b. Make a design for a future car that uses solar energy.
- ☐ c. Write a short story about the use of solar energy in the future. Include the way people use it after dark.
- ☐ d. Write a poem about the sun. Perhaps Psalm 19 can give you ideas.

Adult check:

Initials ____________________ Date ____________________

Nuclear energy. Nuclear energy is already one of the main sources of energy in our world today. It provides about 6 percent of the energy used in the world and 8 percent of the energy used in the United States. However, because nuclear energy produces huge amounts of energy from small amounts of fuel, it holds greater promise for supplying more of our energy needs in the future.

Today, our nuclear energy comes from the process known as nuclear **fission**. In fission, the atomic nucleus of an element, such as uranium, is split. This splitting of the nucleus of an atom releases a large amount of energy, especially heat energy. To capture the release of this energy, a nuclear *reactor* is used. The reactor controls the splitting of the nuclei so that too much heat will not result. The heat is used to produce steam from water. The steam operates machines to generate electricity or to power submarines and other ships.

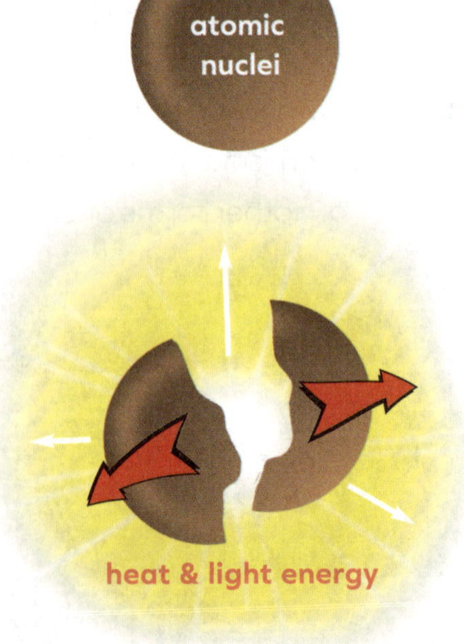

| Fission splits atomic nuclei to produce energy.

A nuclear power plant uses much less fuel than one using coal or oil. There is also much less pollution released into the atmosphere from a nuclear power plant. These are great advantages to using nuclear power.

There are some problems, however, in using nuclear power to supply our energy needs. Certain natural elements, such as uranium, are good sources of nuclear fuel. However, amounts of these elements are limited and they could be used up. Scientists continue to explore new ways to use other elements that are plentiful to make nuclear energy.

Another problem concerns the harmful radiation that is given off by atomic reactions. The power companies and scientists have worked hard to protect workers and the public from this harmful radiation. There are many protective devices used in nuclear power plants to provide safety and shut down the nuclear reactor if problems develop. However, there are accidents that have occurred at nuclear power plants. A major nuclear accident at a nuclear power plant could cause serious health problems over a large area for many people. Scientists, engineers, and public health officials are continually working to improve the safety and operation of nuclear energy facilities.

A third problem exists with nuclear energy. This involves the waste products from nuclear facilities. Fission plants produce hot waste water that may damage the environment. To help prevent this damage from *thermal pollution*, the power plants have large, expensive cooling devices to remove heat from the water before it is discharged to the environment. Much of this cooled water is reused in the power plant to keep the amount of discharged water low. Also, nuclear power plants generate radioactive wastes that must be disposed of in long-term disposal facilities deep underground. The *radioactive wastes* remain dangerous for long periods of time. The transportation and disposal of these radioactive wastes must be carefully controlled and monitored.

Despite the problems associated with nuclear power from fission, many people believe the benefits and potential future benefits of using nuclear energy far outweigh the problems that are associated with it.

Another type of nuclear energy that holds great promise for the future would use nuclear **fusion** to produce energy. Fusion involves the combining of atomic nuclei to form heavier nuclei. In this process, enormous amounts of energy are released. Nuclear fusion produces the heat and light of the sun and other stars.

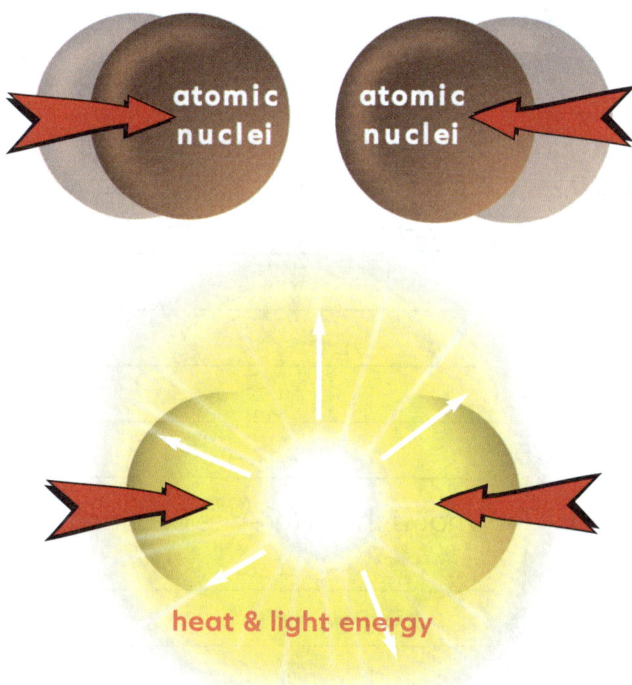

Fusion combines atomic nuclei to produce energy.

It also provides the explosive force in the hydrogen bomb. In these atomic fusion reactions, hydrogen nuclei are combined to produce helium.

Scientists and engineers are working on various ways to control nuclear fusion reactions to produce energy for our use. Experimental fusion reactors use forms of hydrogen for fuel. Since these forms of hydrogen are found in large quantities in the world's oceans, fusion could provide an unlimited source of fuel to supply our energy needs in the future. Nuclear fusion devices are also safer than those using nuclear fission. In addition, fusion does not create a waste disposal problem because most of the waste products from fusion reactions are not radioactive. At this point, however, fusion devices have not yet produced usable amounts of energy. More work needs to be done with nuclear fusion reactors to safely produce sufficient quantities of energy for the future.

Answer these questions.

3.19 What are the advantages of using nuclear energy instead of oil and coal to produce energy? ____

____

____

____

____

3.20 What are some problems associated with the use of nuclear fission to supply energy needs? ____

____

____

____

____

3.21 What is the difference between nuclear *fission* and nuclear *fusion*?

____

____

____

____

3.22 What would be the advantages in using nuclear fusion to supply our energy needs in the future? ____

____

____

____

____

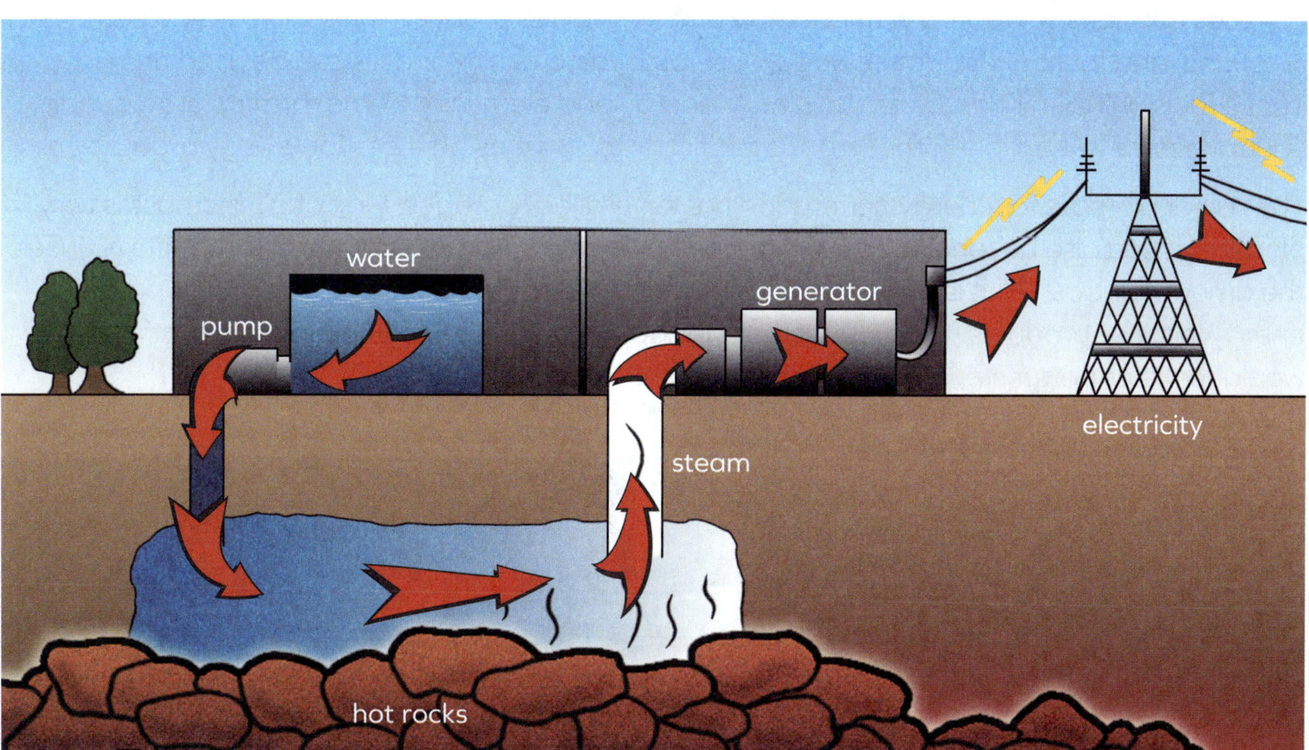

| Geothermal power plant

Geothermal energy. As you learned in the previous section of this LIFEPAC, the earth contains much heat below its surface. *Geothermal energy* is produced whenever water comes in contact with the hot rocks below the earth's surface. The hot rocks heat the water enough to turn part or all of it into steam. If wells are drilled into the earth to contact this hot water and steam, it can be pumped to the earth's surface. If no underground water and steam exist naturally, water can be pumped down through wells into the ground so that the water is heated by hot rocks. Then the hot water and steam can be used on the surface of the earth to generate electricity or to provide heat energy for other purposes.

Geothermal power is already being used in some places in the United States and elsewhere as a source of energy. It holds promise to provide energy to more people in the future. However, currently, geothermal energy can only be used in places where the hot rocks lie somewhat close to the surface. Scientists and engineers continue to explore ways to increase the efficient use of geothermal energy.

Biomass. One interesting fuel source for our energy needs in the future is called *biomass*. Biomass is any organic material that can be converted into energy or a source of energy. It includes many solid and liquid waste products; for example, garbage, scrap paper, and manure. Burning some biomass like solid and liquid wastes can produce heat energy and electricity. Many cities throughout the world already burn their trash to produce electrical power for their people. Some paper and lumber mills also burn waste wood to generate steam for their plants.

Biomass can also be treated with bacteria or chemicals to produce fuels such as synthetic gas, methane, and fuel oil. Manure, sewage, and solid wastes from landfills can be used this way. These fuels are then burned to obtain heat energy and electricity. Some farmers grow sugar cane, trees, seaweed, and other crops specifically to serve as biomass for energy production.

The use of biomass for energy generation has several advantages. First of all, biomass is very plentiful. It can also be renewed and replaced. In addition, burning our waste products reduces the amount of trash that is placed in landfills. Using waste products as fuel recovers potential energy in these products that would otherwise be wasted. The use of biomass in the future would make us better stewards of God's creation.

| A biomass manure plant; solid waste can be burned for heat energy to produce electricity.

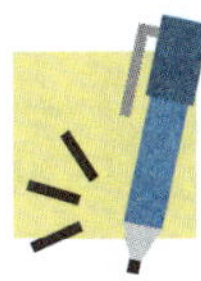

Answer *true* or *false*.

3.23 __________ Geothermal energy uses hot rocks beneath the earth's surface to heat water.

3.24 __________ Geothermal energy can be used anywhere in the world.

3.25 __________ The United States already has geothermal power plants in some places.

3.26 __________ Biomass materials include garbage, scrap wood, and seaweed.

3.27 __________ Some biomass can be treated with bacteria and chemicals to produce synthetic gas and methane for fuel.

3.28 __________ Burning our waste products increases the amount of trash placed in landfills.

3.29 __________ God wants us to be good stewards in our use of energy supplies.

Before you take this last Self Test, you may want to do one or more of these self checks.

1. ________ Read the objectives. See if you can do them.

2. ________ Restudy the material related to any objectives that you cannot do.

3. ________ Use the **SQ3R** study procedure to review the material:

a. **S**can the sections.

b. **Q**uestion yourself.

c. **R**ead to answer your questions.

d. **R**ecite the answers to yourself.

e. **R**eview areas you did not understand.

4. ________ Review all vocabulary, activities, and Self Tests, writing a correct answer for every wrong answer.

SELF TEST 3

Answer *true* or *false* (each answer, 2 points).

3.01 __________ Many of our energy supplies cannot be renewed or replaced.

3.02 __________ Wood is easier to use as a fuel than oil.

3.03 __________ Oil is used for political power by some countries.

3.04 __________ Air pollution from cars and power plants is still a problem today.

3.05 __________ Equipment used for solar energy is usually not expensive.

3.06 __________ Solar energy is difficult to store.

3.07 __________ Geothermal energy can only be used where hot rocks are near the surface.

3.08 __________ Nuclear energy provides a great amount of energy from a small amount of fuel.

3.09 __________ Biomass materials include garbage, scrap wood, and seaweed.

3.010 __________ Oil and coal supplies can be renewed.

3.011 __________ Burning our waste products decreases the amount of trash placed in landfills.

3.012 __________ More energy is supplied today from fossil fuels than from any other source.

3.013 __________ Energy cannot transform from one form to another.

3.014 __________ Forms of hydrogen in the oceans could be used as a source of energy in the future.

3.015 __________ The use of nuclear energy eliminates concerns about pollution.

Write the correct letter and word on each blank (each answer, 3 points).

3.016 Light rays from the sun are called __________ energy.

a. solar b. heat c. chemical

3.017 One of the major problems in using solar energy is __________ .

a. heat b. cost c. speed

3.018 Work is done when a force moves an object through __________ .

a. time b. a distance c. sound

3.019 __________ convert solar energy into electrical energy.

a. Geothermal pumps b. Solar cells c. Light guns

3.020 Today, our nuclear energy comes from a process called nuclear __________ .

a. boiling b. fusion c. fission

Match these items (each answer, 3 points).

3.021 __________ oil

3.022 __________ flint

3.023 __________ pollution

3.024 __________ gasoline

3.025 __________ stewardship

3.026 __________ reactor

3.027 __________ biomass

3.028 __________ joule

3.029 __________ intelligence

a. major problem with fossil fuels

b. unit of work

c. solar collector

d. garbage and scrap paper

e. provides 6 percent of the world's energy

f. 40 percent of energy supply

g. controls release of nuclear energy

h. provides spark with friction

i. major oil component

j. humans have it

k. caring for the earth's creatures and resources

Answer these questions (each answer, 4 points).

3.030 What are two advantages of using nuclear energy instead of oil and coal for energy?

a. ____

b. ____

3.031 What are two problems associated with the use of nuclear fission for energy?

a. ______________________________

b. ______________________________

Complete these items (each answer, 5 points).

3.032 What is the difference between nuclear *fusion* and nuclear *fission*?

____

____

____

____

____

3.033 Explain how geothermal energy is obtained as an energy supply.

____

____

____

____

Teacher check: Initials ____________

Score ____________ Date ____________

78/98

Before you take the LIFEPAC Test, you may want to do one or more of these self checks.

1. ________ Read the objectives. See if you can do them.
2. ________ Restudy the material related to any objectives that you cannot do.
3. ________ Use the **SQ3R** study procedure to review the material.
4. ________ Review activities, Self Tests, and LIFEPAC vocabulary words.
5. ________ Restudy areas of weakness indicated by the last Self Test.

NOTES

SCIENCE 506
RECORDS IN ROCK: THE FLOOD

Author:
Barry G. Burrus, M.Div, M.A., B.S.

Editor:
Brian Ring

Illustrations:
Brian Ring

Media Credits:
Page 3: © Val_Iva, iStock, Thinkstock; **4:** © bennyartist, iStock, Thinkstock; **7:** © Nadine Wickendon, Dorling Kindersley, Thinkstock; **9, 24, 40:** © Dorling Kindersley, Thinkstock; **11:** © Levent Konuk, iStock, Thinkstock; **18:** © Pink_frog, iStock, Thinkstock; **20:** © photostockam, iStock, Thinkstock; **22:** © Nadine Wickendon, Dorling Kindersley, Thinkstock; **31:** © LUNAMARINA, iStock, Thinkstock; **33:** © BibleArtLibrary, iStock, Thinkstock; **36:** © Corey Ford, iStock, Thinkstock; **37:** © sorincolac, iStock, Thinkstock.

804 N. 2nd Ave. E.
Rock Rapids, IA 51246-1759

RECORDS IN ROCK: THE FLOOD

Have you seen a picture or television image of a flood? Have you ever seen a real flood or lived through one? Sometimes, the tremendous amount of water is frightening. Water rises above the level where it is normally found. This extra water in a flood can cause damage and even threaten life. Floods can cause great damage, especially if they are major floods.

The Bible records the story of the greatest flood that has ever been on the earth. It was a flood so great that it destroyed almost every living thing on the earth. Only one man and his family lived through this great flood: Noah. Through Noah, God also saved many other kinds of birds and animals from the Flood.

Life on Earth after the Flood was somewhat different from the way it was before the Flood. In this LIFEPAC®, you will explore what the Bible says about life on earth *before* the Flood, *during* the Flood, and *after* the Flood. You will especially focus on the records of the Flood that God has provided, both in the Bible and in the physical parts of the earth.

Objectives

Read these objectives. These objectives tell what you should be able to do when you have completed this LIFEPAC. Each section will list according to the numbers below what objectives will be met in that section. When you have finished this LIFEPAC, you should be able to:

1. Describe Bible records of the earth before, during, and after the Flood.
2. Describe physical records of the earth's past.
3. Explain the relationship between Bible records of the Flood and physical records.
4. Identify changes in the earth after the Flood.

1. BEFORE THE FLOOD

God created everything that exists. We often wonder what it was like on Earth at the beginning of God's creation. What was it like many thousands of years ago on Earth? Fortunately, we have some records of what it was like long ago. One of those records is the Bible. The first eleven chapters of the Book of Genesis describe God's creation of the world and what happened in the early part of God's creation. We can call this the Bible Record of what happened long ago. The *Bible Record* in Genesis is especially important in understanding God's intention for human beings and what happened to human beings in the early part of God's creation.

One very important thing to remember about the Bible Record of long ago is that it is *inspired by God.* The Bible is the word of God. It was written by people who were inspired by God. It tells us the truth that God wants all people to know. By faith, we can know for certain that the Bible Record is true.

Objectives

Review these objectives. When you have completed this section, you should be able to:

1. Describe Bible records of the earth before, during, and after the Flood.
2. Describe physical records of the earth's past.
3. Explain the relationship between Bible records of the Flood and physical records.

Vocabulary

Study these new words. Learning the meanings of these words is a good study habit and will improve your understanding of this LIFEPAC.

data (dā' tə) or (dat' ə). Facts; things known; information.

descendant (di sen' dənt). Offspring; one born of a certain group or family.

evidence (ev'ə dəns). Facts; information and clues that make the truth clear.

fossil (fos' əl). Hardened remains of a plant or animal. A fossil can also be an imprint of a once-living plant or animal.

fossilized (fos'ə līzd). Made into a fossil.

indicate (in' də kāt). Point out; show; suggest.

intention (in ten' shən). The purpose of acting in a certain way.

mammoth (mam' əth). Very large, elephant-type animal that no longer lives on the earth. Mammoths had trunks, hairy skin, and long, curved trunks.

petrified (pet' rə fīd). Turned to stone. For example, tree remains that have turned to stone by the action of mineral-rich water are petrified.

records (rek' ərdz). Something that relates or recalls past events.

theory (thē ər ē'). An explanation based on thinking, reasoning, or observation.

thistle (this' əl). A plant that has prickly leaves and stem. Thistles are often considered weeds.

Note: *All vocabulary words in this LIFEPAC appear in* **boldface** *print the first time they are used. If you are unsure of the meaning when you are reading, study the definitions given.*

Pronunciation Key: h**a**t, **ā**ge, c**ã**re, f**ä**r; l**e**t, **ē**qual, t**ė**rm; **i**t, **ī**ce; h**o**t, **ō**pen, **ô**rder; **oi**l; **ou**t; c**u**p, p**u̇**t, r**ü**le; **ch**ild; lo**ng**; **th**in; /ŦH/ for **th**en; /zh/ for mea**s**ure; /u/ or /ə/ represents /a/ in **a**bout, /e/ in tak**e**n, /i/ in penc**i**l, /o/ in lem**o**n, and /u/ in circ**u**s.

The second main record that we have of what it was like on earth long ago can be called the *Physical Record*. This is the record that we can find in rocks, **fossils**, and other ancient remains from long ago. The Physical Record gives us **evidence** that we can see and touch. With this evidence of the Physical Record, scientists and other people attempt to explain what happened long ago and what life might have been like on earth. Sometimes these explanations from physical evidence are developed into a **theory**. These theories can sometimes be useful in helping to explain what happened long ago. However, a theory may or may not be true. A theory is simply man's attempt to explain—from physical evidence, observation, and reasoning—what happened long ago or how things came to be.

One of the most important events on earth of long ago, described in the Bible, is a great flood. It was so great that we call it *the Flood*. The events and record of the Flood are found in Genesis 6–9. In this LIFEPAC, you will examine the Bible Record and some parts of the Physical Record to look at life on earth before, during, and after the Flood. In this section of the LIFEPAC, we will explore the period before the Flood.

Write the correct word on each line.

1.1 The two main records we have of long ago are the a. ________________ Record and the b. ________________ Record.

1.2 The Book of Genesis is important in understanding God's ________________ for human beings.

1.3 By faith, we can know for certain that the Bible is ________________ .

1.4 Physical evidence of long ago can be found in rocks, ________________ , and other ancient remains.

1.5 A ________________ to explain what happened long ago is developed by people from the physical evidence, observation, and reasoning.

The Bible Record

The Bible tells us that God created everything that exists. He created everything in an orderly way. He created all of the plants and animals. God created man and woman as the greatest part of His creation. Above all creatures, man and woman were created in God's image. God also saw that everything He had created was good.

Unfortunately, man and woman were tempted by Satan (in the form of a serpent) and disobeyed God. As a result, sin, suffering, and death entered God's creation. Even after they sinned, God helped Adam and Eve by clothing them. However, God made them leave the Garden of Eden to dwell elsewhere on the earth. This is part of man's story before the Flood.

The Bible does not give us lots of physical details about His creation before the Flood. However, it is clear that many plants and animals as well as human beings were on the earth before the Flood. Let us take a look at some of the physical details of life on earth before the Flood according to the Bible Record.

Plants and animals. God created many types of plants. Grass, trees, and herbs grew abundantly. They grew well in order for humans and animals to have a food supply. God also planted a garden that grew much food. God placed Adam and Eve in this garden to take good care of it. God looked at everything that he had made and saw that it was very good.

As a result of the sin of Adam and Eve, we see that things changed among the plants and animals. God made the serpent crawl on his belly. New plants appeared: thorns and thistles. The thorns and **thistles** made life more difficult for the people. However, plant life continued to grow well.

A wide variety of animals was placed on the earth by God. Adam was able to name the animals. The Bible tells us that God made fish and birds. Cattle, reptiles, and wildlife roamed the earth. All of these animals were expected to reproduce to keep the earth filled. This was part of God's intention for the earth.

Many believe that human beings did not use animals for food before the time of the Flood. In Genesis 1:29-30, the Bible says that God gave the seed-bearing plants and seed-bearing fruits of trees for man to eat. God also gave plants for the animals to eat, too. We will see that only later, after the Flood, God gave animals to people to use for food.

| God placed Adam and Eve in the Garden of Eden to care for it.

Write the correct answer on each line.

1.6 The Bible has ____________ details about the physical world before the Flood.

a. no b. few c. many

1.7 Plants were created for ______________________________ according to the Bible.

a. only the garden of Eden

b. the whole earth

c. Adam and Eve

1.8 Life was made more difficult for people when ______________________________ started to grow.

a. thorns and thistles b. grass and herbs c. trees and thistles

1.9 Animals were to keep the earth filled through ________________________ .

a. reproduction b. photosynthesis c. roaming the land

1.10 The earth before the Flood had ________________________ of plants and animals according to the Bible.

a. only a few b. two of each kind c. a great number

Complete these activities.

1.11 List three types of plants that God created.

a. ______________________________

b. ______________________________

c. ______________________________

1.12 List four types of animals that God created.

a. ______________________________

b. ______________________________

c. ______________________________

d. ______________________________

Read Genesis 4:1-6:8

Human beings. God created humans in His own image. He placed them on earth to care for His creation. God told man and woman to reproduce and to have responsibility for all plant and animal life. After Adam and Eve sinned, they left the Garden of Eden. Children were born to them. The population of human beings began growing. Before the Flood, there were many people upon the earth, according to the Bible. Some of these people were even giants.

The Bible shows that people before the Flood must have been very intelligent. For example, God told Adam to name all of the animals (Genesis 2:19). That must have taken much understanding for Adam to do.

The Bible also shows that people before the Flood knew how to garden and farm (Genesis 2:15 and 4:2-3, 20). A man named Tubal-Cain knew how to make many kinds of tools out of bronze and iron (Genesis 4:22). A man named Jubal had many descendants who knew how to make and play musical instruments. People knew how to build houses and cities (Genesis 4:17). They also knew how to keep records of days, weeks, months, and years (Genesis 5). In other words, the people before the Flood had many talents and skills. They were intelligent, not ignorant.

God gave people before the Flood great intelligence. He also gave them a long life as the Bible Record shows (Genesis 5). Perhaps the long lifetime helped people to grow greatly in knowledge and increase their skills. The Bible shows that they used the gift of intellect that God had given them. They used their minds to sustain and improve their lives on earth.

But the Bible also shows that people on Earth continued to sin, and some people caused harm to others. Cain killed Abel. People grew in wickedness. Some people used their intelligence to plan terrible things. Things grew so terrible among men and women on earth that God was sorry He had made them. So, God planned to make a new beginning for His creation of Earth. He planned to use one man, Noah, to bring about this change. Noah was a man who walked in God's ways.

| Cain killed Abel.

Answer *true* or *false*.

1.13 __________ Some people had very long lives before the Flood.

1.14 __________ Giants lived on the earth before the Flood.

1.15 __________ Jubal named the animals.

1.16 __________ Tubal-Cain taught people how to work with thistles.

1.17 __________ People before the Flood used great minds for both good and evil plans.

1.18 __________ People before the Flood knew how to keep a record of time.

1.19 __________ People enjoyed music before the Flood.

1.20 __________ People never lived in cities until after the Flood.

SOLVE THE PUZZLE!

1.21 The following puzzle contains a key Bible quote for this section of the LIFEPAC. Follow these directions to solve the puzzle.

- ☐ 1. Begin at the arrow.
- ☐ 2. Draw a line from the first letter to the next.
- ☐ 3. You may go to the side, up, or down.
- ☐ 4. You may not go diagonally or skip a letter.
- ☐ 5. Continue with the line until you have all the words that form a complete verse.

1.22 Write the Bible quote here.

____

____

____

____

____

____

____

➤	A	N	D	E	V	S	A
V	E	W	G	R	Y	G	W
E	R	A	O	H	A	O	T
T	Y	S	D	E	D	O	I
H	H	A	T	H	M	D	D
I	T	A	E	D	A	O	L
N	G	N	D	B	E	H	

1.23 The quote is found in Genesis chapter 1. What verse is it? __________________

The Physical Record

God gave us a written record in the Bible about the times before the Flood. However, God has also provided another main kind of record for us about these times. This is the Physical Record found in rocks, fossils, and other ancient remains. We can learn much about these times of long ago from fossils and rocks. When these bits of **data** are considered together, we can tell something of what the earth was like. Although there are some similarities, the data from rocks and fossils tells us that the world before The Flood was different from our world in many ways. Let's consider some of the physical evidence from early times in the earth's history.

| Tyrannosaurus Rex

Plants and animals. Fossils show that long ago thickly growing trees and other plants covered great areas of the earth. Many of these plants were similar to those growing today except for size. **Petrified** wood and **fossilized** leaves show that earlier plants were of great size. This data also indicates that the earth had a rich cover of plants.

Records in rocks also show that the earth contained huge animals. Fossils of **mammoths** and dinosaurs have been found. Smaller animal fossils have also been discovered. The variety of animal species found in fossil form is greater than is on earth today. In addition, the fossils show that many animals of long ago seem to have been stronger and larger than their **descendants** today.

Fossils of plants and animals present an interesting fact. Fossils of mammoths have been discovered in every section of the earth except South America and Australia. Fossils of certain trees have been found in every section of the earth from the polar regions to the equator. From this data, it appears that most species could live anyplace on earth. Some people conclude that at sometime in the past the earth's climate was without seasons which were marked by large temperature changes. Therefore, the whole earth would have had a similar climate. The climate was warm enough to allow the earth to become rich in plant and animal life everywhere.

Define these words. Use the vocabulary from this LIFEPAC or a dictionary.

1.24 fossil ______________________________

____

1.25 petrified ______________________________

____

1.26 data ______________________________

____

1.27 descendants ______________________________

____

1.28 fossilized ______________________________

____

Human beings. Humans also lived on the earth before the Flood, according to fossil records. Fossilized human remains have been found that have been dated before the Flood. Some human fossils have been found that were located with mammoth bones and other ancient animal fossils. Yet, only a few human fossils have been found compared to the large number of animal and plant fossils. The Physical Record exists of man of long ago before the Flood, but there is not a lot of evidence.

Write the letter for the correct record before the statement.

a. Bible Record
b. Physical Record
c. Both Bible and Physical Records

1.29 __________ There were many animal species.

1.30 __________ Humans lived before the Flood.

1.31 __________ Climate was similar over the earth.

1.32 __________ God made Adam.

1.33 __________ Ancient animals were very large.

1.34 __________ Tubal-Cain worked with bronze and iron.

Complete the activities. An important reading skill is to compare and contrast ideas you have read about. When you compare, you find likenesses between ideas. When you contrast, you find differences between ideas. Often you can use this skill to compare or contrast ideas with things you know about.

In this activity, you will compare and contrast information that you have read so far in this LIFEPAC with what you know about the earth today.

1.35 The earth's climate

a. Compare: ____

____

____

____

b. Contrast: ____

____

____

____

1.36 Animal species

a. Compare: ______________________________

____

____

____

b. Contrast: ______________________________

____

____

____

1.37 Plant size

a. Compare: ______________________________

____

____

____

b. Contrast: ______________________________

____

____

____

Teacher check:

Initials ______________ Date ______________

Review the material in this section to prepare for the Self Test. The Self Test will check your understanding of this section. Any items you miss on this test will show you what areas you will need to restudy in order to prepare for the unit test.

SELF TEST 1

Match these items (each answer, 3 points).

1.01 __________ named the animals
1.02 __________ descendants played music
1.03 __________ killed Abel
1.04 __________ worked with bronze and iron
1.05 __________ records in rocks
1.06 __________ information
1.07 __________ indicate
1.08 __________ early animal
1.09 __________ how animals kept the earth filled
1.010 __________ tells the Flood story

a. Seth
b. dinosaur
c. point out
d. Adam
e. Jubal
f. thorns
g. Genesis
h. Tubal-Cain
i. fossils
j. data
k. Eve
l. Lamech
m. Cain
n. reproduction

Answer *true* or *false* (each answer, 2 points).

1.011 __________ There were definite seasons of large temperature changes on Earth before the Flood.
1.012 __________ Giants lived on Earth before the Flood.
1.013 __________ Mammoth fossils have been found only near the equator.
1.014 __________ More human fossils have been found than any other type of fossil.
1.015 __________ The Bible has a very detailed physical description of the earth before the Flood.
1.016 __________ Humans were placed on the earth to take care of it.
1.017 __________ There were no cities before the Flood.

1.018 __________ Plants were created only for the Garden of Eden.

1.019 __________ By faith, we can know that the Bible Record is true.

1.020 __________ Physical records show that God made Adam.

Write the following events in the correct order (each answer, 3 points).

Thistles began growing.
Most of the people were very wicked.
People invented methods of building and instruments for music.
Adam and Eve lived in the Garden of Eden.
God was sorry that he made humans who had become so wicked.

1.021 ______________________________

1.022 ______________________________

1.023 ______________________________

1.024 ______________________________

1.025 ______________________________

Write the letter of the correct answer on each line (each answer, 3 points).

1.026 The variety of animal species is __________ today compared with the variety before the Flood.

a. less b. about the same c. more

1.027 Some people believe that humans did not __________ before the Flood.

a. eat meat b. cook c. eat seeds

1.028 People before the Flood used their great minds for __________ .

a. good b. evil c. good and evil

1.029 Petrified wood is __________ evidence of ancient times.

a. physical b. Bible c. not

1.030 Evidence shows that most animals of the same species today are __________ than they were before the Flood.

a. smaller than b. larger than c. the same size as

Answer this question (this answer, 5 points).

1.031 Why did God want to make a new beginning with Noah?

____

____

____

____

____

____

Define these words (each definition, 5 points).

1.032 data ____

____

1.033 descendant ____

____

1.034 fossil ____

____

Teacher check: Initials ____________

Score ____________ Date ____________

80 / 100

2. THE FLOOD

God wanted to save Noah and his family from the great flood that He was preparing to bring upon the earth. Therefore, God spoke to Noah and told him what to do. Part of what God told Noah was to build a huge vessel called an ark. He also told Noah to take his family and two of every kind of living thing on the earth and enter the ark. Even though God was going to destroy every living thing upon the earth through the Flood, He planned to make a new beginning of life on Earth through one man: Noah.

In this section of the LIFEPAC, you will learn more about the details of Noah's ark and the Flood. You will read and study the Bible Record of the Flood to help you answer many questions. For example, what materials were used to build the ark? What was the size of the ark? How long did it take to build the ark? Why was Noah chosen to build it? How long did the Flood last? You will find the answers to these questions and many more in the Bible Record.

The Physical Record of the Flood is not widely understood by many people today. However, according to some scientists, physical evidence of the Flood has been found. Rocks and fossils indicate a time of great destruction. You will learn how scientists can use this data to tell of past events.

Objectives

Review these objectives. When you have completed this section, you should be able to:

1. Describe Bible records of the earth before, during, and after the Flood.
2. Describe physical records of the earth's past.
3. Explain the relationship between Bible records of the Flood and physical records.

Vocabulary

Study these new words. Learning the meanings of these words is a good study habit and will improve your understanding of this LIFEPAC.

archaeologist (är' kē ol' ə jist). One who studies the people, customs, and life of ancient times.

canopy (kan' ə pē). A covering over another object. A water vapor canopy may have existed over the earth's atmosphere before the Flood.

destruction (di struk' shən). Being destroyed; ruin.

dimension (də men' shən). Measurement of length, width, or height.

historian (hi stôr' ē ən). A person who studies history and becomes an expert in the knowledge of history.

moisture (mois' chər). Wetness or dampness caused by water or other liquids.

proportion (prə pôr' shən). Relation in size, number, amount, or degree of one thing compared to another.

resin (rez' n). A sticky substance that flows from certain plants and trees, especially fir and pine.

sacrifice (sak' rə fīs). To give up; an offering to God. Early humans burned animals as a way of worshipping God.

tradition (trə dish' ən). Idea, story, or belief handed down from parents to children or one generation to the next.

Pronunciation Key: hat, āge, cãre, fär; let, ēqual, tėrm; it, īce; hot, ōpen, ôrder; oil; out; cup, pu̇t, rüle; child; long; thin; /ŦH/ for then; /zh/ for measure; /u/ or /ə/ represents /a/ in about, /e/ in taken, /i/ in pencil, /o/ in lemon, and /u/ in circus.

The Bible Record

We are told in Genesis that God was very unhappy with the humans of Noah's time. Only Noah lived a life pleasing to God. Noah was instructed by God to build a large boat—the ark. God told Noah exactly how he was to build the ark.

The ark was made of gopherwood. "Gopherwood" is thought to mean the wood of the cypress tree, which was used for shipbuilding throughout the ancient Middle East. Cypress is an evergreen that provides strong wood from a large trunk and limbs.

The length of the ark was 300 cubits; the width was 50 cubits; and the height was 30 cubits.

For a long time Bible readers wondered just how large these **dimensions** were in modern measures. In the late 1800s, archaeologists discovered an ancient tunnel in Jerusalem. This tunnel had been built in the days of King Hezekiah (about 700 B.C.). At the entrance was an inscription that said the tunnel was 1,200 cubits long. The archaeologist measured the tunnel, which proved to be 800 feet long (54,000 centimeters). That meant that one cubit was one and a half feet, or 18 inches long (45 centimeters). Now, at last, Bible students knew that, at least in Hezekiah's day, the Hebrew cubit equaled about 18 inches (45 centimeters).

Some archaeologists have found reason to believe that there may have been more than one measure called a cubit, particularly in other countries of the ancient Middle East. However, no one has discovered evidence of a cubit smaller than 18 inches. We may safely believe that the cubit measure used by Noah was at least 18 inches (45 centimeters).

The dimensions of the ark were perfect for floating. The ark did not need a shaped bow (although it may have had one) as most ships need. The ark was designed for floating, not for going quickly through the water. Nevertheless, many modern cargo ships are built with the same proportions, because these **proportions** make the ships very steady in the water.

| A present-day model of Noah's ark

Work out these figures.

2.1 How long was the ark in inches?

300 (cubits) x 18 (inches) = ____________ inches.

2.2 How long was the ark in feet?

5400 (inches) ÷ 12 (inches) = ____________ feet.

2.3 How wide was the ark in inches?

50 (cubits) x 18 (inches) = ____________ inches.

2.4 How wide was the ark in feet?

900 (inches) ÷ 12 (inches) = ____________ feet.

2.5 What was the area covered by the ark?

450 (feet) x 75 (feet) = ____________ square feet.

2.6 The ark had three decks (floors). How much total area was in the three floors? Multiply the area covered by the ark by 3.

____________ square feet x 3 = ____________ square feet

2.7 A football field has 46,900 square feet.

The area covered by three decks of the ark is more than ____________ times the area covered by a football field.

After Noah had finished putting the ark together with the gopherwood boards, he had to make it watertight. God had given Noah instructions for this task. Noah used pitch, a waterproofing material, to coat it inside and outside. We do not know whether the **resin** from trees was used or tar from a tar pit. The Bible says that pitch was used both inside and outside of the boards. Such a large boat with such waterproofing would take a long time to complete. The building of the ark took Noah about 120 years, according to the time God gave to human beings before the Flood was to start (Genesis 6:3).

Noah was told what food supplies were needed. God asked Noah to take seven pairs of every clean animal and just one pair of the unclean animals. Noah, his wife, Noah's three sons, and their wives went into the ark. God sealed the door of the ark, and rain was sent to the earth.

Many Bible students believe that the earth had not seen rain before the Flood. Dews and mist provided **moisture**. Rivers, and other areas of moisture were on the earth but not rain. The first rain that God ever sent to Earth lasted 40 days and nights. The rains were not the only cause of the Flood. The Bible also says (Genesis 7:11-12) that in one day all the fountains of the great deep were broken up and the windows (floodgates) of heaven were opened.

The fountains of the deep must have been a large source of water beneath the earth's surface. One explanation of the fountains of the deep breaking up is an earthquake of such force that all the sources of underground water were laid open. This event would have provided a large source of water for the Flood. All of the water from these underground sources gushed up while the cloudbursts sent down water from the heavens. Some people believe that the water above the floodgates of heaven came from a large **canopy** of water vapor that surrounded the atmosphere of the earth. The initial rains upon the earth occurred when this vapor canopy was turned to liquid water and fell upon the earth. The rains also provided much of the water source for the Flood. All of this water that God brought on the earth was more than enough to cover the highest points of the earth that existed before the Flood.

Whether the water continued to come up from below, we do not know, but the heavy rains continued steadily for 40 days and 40 nights. The ark floated safely on the water. The people and animals were safe and dry inside.

After it stopped raining, the water covered the earth for a long time. Nearly a year passed before Noah, his family, and all the animals could leave the ark for dry land. Noah built an altar and sacrificed one of each kind of clean animal as an offering to God. All people, animals, and plants outside the ark had been destroyed by the waters. It was certainly a different world that greeted Noah and his family.

SCIENCE 506

LIFEPAC TEST

NAME ____________________

DATE ____________________

SCORE ____________________

SCIENCE 506: LIFEPAC TEST

Match these items (each answer, 3 points).

1. __________ Noah lived
2. __________ people used their intellects for evil
3. __________ seasons with climate changes the Flood
4. __________ God promised not to destroy the world by flood
5. __________ animals reproduced
6. __________ glaciers
7. __________ gravity
8. __________ some trees were much larger
9. __________ fewer mammoths lived
10. __________ reptiles lived
11. __________ deep ocean basins
12. __________ people gardened and farmed

a. before the Flood
b. after the Flood
c. both before and after

Answer *true or false* (each answer, 2 points).

13. __________ Some people lived a very long lifetime before the Flood.
14. __________ By faith, we know that the Bible Record is true.
15. __________ It is possible that animals were not used for food by humans before the Flood.
16. __________ Famines occurred throughout the earth before the Flood according to the Bible.
17. __________ The Bible has the only total world flood story known to man.
18. __________ Mammoth fossils show that animal life was centered around the equator.
19. __________ Much of the earth was probably covered by permafrost before the Flood.
20. __________ Glaciers could have been caused by the Flood.

21. __________ Leaf fossils have been found in coal deposits.

22. __________ No human fossils have been found with animal fossils.

23. __________ Changes in the surface of the earth continue today.

Complete these lists (each answer, 4 points).

24. List three forces that could have changed the earth's surface as a result of the Flood.

a. ____

b. ____

c. ____

25. List three ways landmasses shifted since the Flood.

a. ____

b. ____

c. ____

Write the letter for the correct answer on each line (each answer, 3 points).

26. The __________ cycle as we know it was formed after the Flood.

a. water
b. snow
c. fire

27. The Bible record and the physical evidence agree that __________ .

a. Adam named the animals
b. the whole earth has had a mild climate at one time
c. The Flood formed oil

28. Physical data supports the Bible record that __________ .

a. Jubal's descendants made musical instruments
b. dinosaurs lived on the earth
c. there was a time of worldwide destruction

29. The Bible __________ that glaciers were billions of years old.

a. does not forget
b. does not say
c. tells

SCI 506 LIFEPAC TEST

30. Physical evidence of long ago can be found in rocks, __________, and other ancient remains.

a. rivers

b. fossils

c. the atmosphere

31. The Bible __________ physical evidence about the Flood.

a. helps us understand

b. discounts

c. keeps us from using

Complete these statements.

2.8 Noah took about ______________ years to build the ark.

2.9 The Bible tells of ______________ people that went into the ark.

2.10 There were ______________ of each kind of unclean animal in the ark.

2.11 Before the Flood a. ______________________ and b. ______________________ gave moisture to the earth.

2.12 Noah kept the animals on the ark for nearly ______________ .

2.13 Noah sacrificed one of each kind of ______________ animal after he left the ark.

2.14 After the Flood ______________ with climate changes were new to the earth.

SOLVE THE PUZZLE!

2.15 This puzzle contains a key Bible quote for this section of the LIFEPAC.

Complete the puzzle as you did in the last section.
You may review the directions by turning back to the first puzzle

E	R	E	L	I	V	S	H	A	L
M	H	T	H	H	W	T	H	N	L
A	T	R	E	H	E	A	G	O	T
I	N	A	E	D	N	T	I	E	C
T	E	M	E	D	A	A	N	A	S
H	T	I	A	L	D	N	D	N	E
S	D	D	N	O	S	A	N	A	Y
E	E	H	D	C	U	R	D	D	A
V	R	A	N	M	M	E	T	N	I
E	S	T	A	E	R	A	N	D	W

2.16 Write the Bible verse here.

____

____

____

____

2.17 Find the verse in the chapters listed at the beginning of this section and memorize the verse. Recite the verse to your teacher.

Teacher check:

Initials ______________

Date ______________

Pretend that you are a newspaper reporter, and you are able to interview Noah.

2.18 What kinds of questions would you ask him?

a. ____

____

b. ____

____

c. ____

____

d. ____

____

2.19 Imagine how Noah might respond to your questions. Write a newspaper article about your imaginary interview. Take this LIFEPAC and your finished article to your teacher for a teacher check.

Teacher check:

Initials ______________

Date ______________

The Physical Record

What does science have to say about the Flood? No written account from people who lived at that time in history has been found. Scientists take clues from fossils, rock layers, and other deposits. They use all their skills and understanding to explain these clues. However, their answers vary. Some scientists point to physical evidence which they believe is from the Flood. Other scientists do not believe this evidence is from the Flood of Noah's time.

| The Flood could explain the quick way in which all life was destroyed.

Many deposits of bones have been located around the world. Some have been on mountainsides. Others were in deep cracks. Deep earth has covered some. Still others have been discovered in caves.

Very large bones, very small bones, and human remains have been found together. Herbivores, carnivores, and birds have been found at the same place. Even shells and fish bones were found among plant and tree remains. The bones have not been chewed, weathered, or burned.

Something must have happened to these animals at the same time. It could not have been fire. Disease could not have taken large numbers of such a wide variety of animals. Predators would have left evidence in the bones. Whatever happened must have been strong and long-lasting. It collected and carried huge and tiny animals to their deaths.

Could water have caused those deaths? Were some animals going up mountains to get away from a flood? Were others hiding in caves? Were others swept into deep cracks and some buried in mudslides caused by heavy rains and rising water? A huge flood seems to be a reasonable answer.

Perhaps oil and coal deposits could give us clues, too. Oil was formed from animals. Coal was formed from plants and trees. Great pressure and time helped form oil and coal. How did we get all the oil and coal that is deposited around the world? Did animals and trees fall into swamps that were later covered by rock? A great flood could have been responsible. The earth was full of huge plants and animals. They could have been swept as groups into great deposits. Then rocks and soil were pushed over the deposits by water. With time, pressure, and the right conditions, oil and coal could have been formed.

Leaf fossils in coal and fish fossils in oil tell an interesting story. Perfect remains have been found. These findings indicate that destruction was quick. Living things did not have time to decay. Change in the earth happened swiftly. These fossils have been found in coal and oil deposits around the world. Some scientists say that water covering the whole earth is the best explanation for these amazing discoveries.

Answer *true* or *false*.

2.20 ____________ Scientists vary in their beliefs about the Flood.

2.21 ____________ Some large deposits of bone have been found in mountains.

2.22 ____________ Most of the bones found in large groups have been chewed.

2.23 ____________ Disease killed all the animals at once.

2.24 ____________ Oil was formed from trees.

2.25 __________ Oil is mostly found in Iran.

2.26 __________ Coal was formed by pressure and fire.

2.27 __________ Large amounts of water could shift soil around.

Other oral or written records. Another type of "physical" evidence that exists about the Flood is found in the oral or written records of various cultures throughout the world. **Historians** have studied these **traditions** around the world. They have found that many of the tribes and nations of the world have a "flood story." These traditions are not new. They are very old. These stories were usually passed down from ancient times by word of mouth.

The American Indians believed in a great flood. The Chinese had a flood tradition. There were Siberian and Australian flood stories. Most of these groups did not know of the Bible; however, they all agreed on some points. They believed that the whole earth was covered by a great flood, a boat saved some people, and some people lived through the Flood.

Where did all these traditions get started? Could all the tribes be telling about the same flood? Do these other stories about a great flood support the Bible Record? Many people believe that all the stories are really about the same great flood—the Flood as recorded truly in the Bible. These traditions and stories provide further evidence for the Bible Record of the Flood.

LOOK IT UP!

2.28 Use the library or the Internet to find one of the ancient flood stories. Follow these directions.

1. Use these keywords to guide your research: legend, myth, flood, Siberian, Indian, Chinese, Mesopotamian, Gilgamesh Epic.
2. Choose a tradition to read about. ______________________________
   Name of country or group
3. Tell the story to a friend. ______________________________
   Friend's name

Teacher check:

Initials ______________ Date ______________

Answer these questions.

2.29 How does your story agree with the Bible Record?

____

____

____

____

____

2.30 How is your story different from the Bible Record?

____

____

____

____

____

2.31 How do you explain why there are differences in the explanations?

____

____

____

____

____

Teacher check:

Initials ____________________ Date ____________________

Review the material in this section to prepare for the Self Test. The Self Test will check your understanding of this section and will review the other sections. Any items you miss on this test will show you what areas you will need to restudy in order to prepare for the unit test.

SELF TEST 2

Answer *true* or *false* (each answer, 2 points).

2.01 ________ Genesis tells of great dinosaurs roaming the earth.

2.02 ________ Noah took about 50 years to build the ark.

2.03 ________ God told Noah how to build the ark.

2.04 ________ Floods were common before Noah's time.

2.05 ________ The story of oil formation is found in the Bible.

2.06 ________ There are ancient stories of a great flood in writings other than the Bible.

2.07 ________ Some physical evidence indicates that destruction of living things on earth was quick.

2.08 ________ A large flood could open cracks in rocks and deposit dead plants and animals there.

2.09 ________ Science can prove that Noah never lived.

2.010 ________ Large deposits of mammoth bones have been found with bones of small animals.

Match these items (each answer, 3 points).

a. Bible Record
b. Physical Record
c. both Bible and Physical Records

2.011 __________ large plants on early earth

2.012 __________ no definite seasons before the Flood

2.013 __________ bones on mountainsides

2.014 __________ fossils in oil

2.015 __________ destruction of life

2.016 __________ ark

2.017 __________ forty days and nights of rain

2.018 __________ large deposits of bones

2.019 __________ sacrifices given

2.020 __________ Noah

2.021 __________ giants on the earth

2.022 __________ men lived a very long time

Write the correct answer on each line (each answer, 3 points).

2.023 Animals kept the earth __________________ through reproduction.
a. populated b. overrun c. dangerous

2.024 The earth's climate was ____________ before the Flood.
a. cold b. rainy c. warm

2.025 Water covered the earth for nearly one ____________ after the Flood according to the Bible.
a. week b. month c. year

2.026 Dews and ____________ watered the earth before the Flood.
a. rains b. tears c. mists

2.027 Noah sacrificed one of each kind of ____________ animal after leaving the ark.
a. unclean b. clean c. old

2.028 Much ____________ was needed to form coal.
a. skin b. pressure c. wind

2.029 Oil was formed from ______________ .

a. animals b. plants c. fire

2.030 The study of __________________ is part of a historian's work.

a. math b. traditions c. photosynthesis

Define these words (each definition, 5 points).

2.031 petrified ____

2.032 accuracy ____

Answer these questions (each item, 5 points).

2.033 How does physical evidence show that a flood covered the earth?

____

____

____

____

2.034 Why do differences exist in flood traditions of various nations or tribes?

____

____

____

Teacher check: Initials ____________

Score ____________ Date ____________

80/100

3. AFTER THE FLOOD

According to some scientists, several changes in nature happened because of the Flood. The Bible Record suggests some changes, but few details are given. Many clues, however, are found throughout the Bible that help us understand the Flood results better.

New fossil discoveries help us learn more of the past. Research of glaciers and rock layers are adding more information. Studies of volcanoes, earthquakes, and shifting landmasses give deeper understanding of changes to the earth. Records in rock are helping us gain details of the earth's history. Some of the changes in the earth may have taken place during, or since, the Flood. You will explore some of these explanations in this LIFEPAC section.

Objectives

Review these objectives. When you have completed this section, you should be able to:

1. Describe Bible records of the earth before, during, and after the Flood.
2. Describe physical records of the earth's past.
3. Explain the relationship between Bible records of the Flood and physical records.
4. Identify changes in the earth after the Flood.

Vocabulary

Study these new words. Learning the meanings of these words is a good study habit and will improve your understanding of this LIFEPAC.

crust (krust). Outside covering.

erode (i rōd'). Wear down with time.

extinct (ek stingkt'). No longer living.

famine (fam' ən). A lack of food; starving. Famine sometimes occurs because of extended drought.

glacier (glā' shər). Large ice mass that constantly moves very slowly.
gravity (grav' ə tē). A force of nature that pulls things towards the earth's center.
permafrost (per' mə frost). Frost that does not thaw. Some land areas in the Arctic are frozen all year.

Pronunciation Key: hat, āge, cãre, fär; let, ēqual, tėrm; it, īce; hot, ōpen, ôrder; oil; out; cup, pu̇t, rüle; child; long; thin; /ŦH/ for then; /zh/ for measure; /u/ or /ə/ represents /a/ in about, /e/ in taken, /i/ in pencil, /o/ in lemon, and /u/ in circus.

The Bible Record

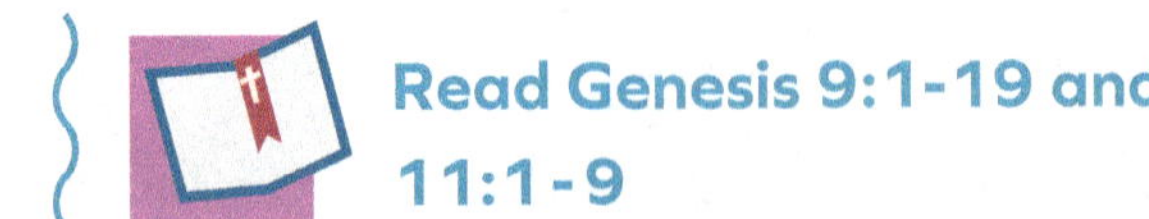

You have learned that the Bible tells of several changes in the earth as a result of the Flood. Seasons came to the earth. With seasons came planting and harvest time. Rain fell on the earth after the Flood. Plants, animals, and human lives were destroyed by the Flood.

Several more changes happened. The Bible gives us some clues. However, these new differences were not pointed out in detail. Perhaps the most important purpose of the Flood story is to show why it happened.

Earth. You can get an idea of what the earth was like following the Flood by reading about people's lives. The book of Genesis records many things about the way the earth was and the way people lived. A **famine** came to Abram (Genesis 12:10). Abram grew rich in cattle, silver, and gold (Genesis 13:2). We are told of a salt sea, a plain, wilderness, and mountain (Genesis, chapter 14). Animals were used for work (Genesis 24:10). Wells were used for water supply (Genesis 26:15).

Every part of the Bible has references to the earth and what it was like. The Bible tells of winds that wrecked ships, of fish that were plentiful, of the many kinds of trees that grew, of wheat, shrubs, grass, flowers, and weeds that were part of the earth's cover. Birds and wildlife filled the earth. All of these things were part of the earth after the Flood.

People. There were a number of changes in people after the Flood. Of course the Flood destroyed all people except Noah's family.

These people of Noah's family reproduced. The population grew. At first, all people spoke the same language. God caused people to speak in different languages after they started to build the Tower of Babel. The dividing by language caused people to move to other parts of the earth.

After the Flood, the life spans became much shorter (Genesis, Chapter 11). Today our oldest people do not reach even half the age of the early descendants of Noah.

People began to use animal meat for food (Genesis 9:3). Animals became fearful of people. All animals were counted upon to reproduce. Many of them increased their populations greatly.

Cities were built. Governments developed that had kings or other rulers. People learned how to make weapons and tools. Education and the use of writing came into use. The Bible tells us that skills advanced greatly as time passed.

When people tried to build the Tower of Babel, God divided them by creating many languages.

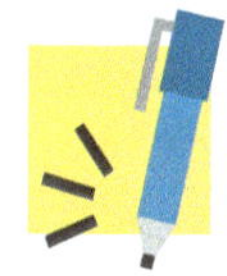

Answer *true* or *false*.

3.1 __________ The Bible gives clues about the earth after the Flood.

3.2 __________ The Bible tells how plants began to grow after the Flood.

3.3 __________ Genesis tells how the sea became salty.

3.4 __________ Abram caused a famine.

3.5 __________ As time went on after the Flood, people's life spans were longer than before.

3.6 __________ Animals were not as trustful of human beings after the Flood.

3.7 __________ Governments were set up as the world population grew after the Flood.

3.8 __________ People were scattered over the earth.

Answer these questions.

3.9 Why did God cause the Flood to happen?

____

____

____

____

____

3.10 What were some of the changes that happened to animals after the Flood?

____

____

____

____

____

SOLVE THE PUZZLE!

3.11 This puzzle contains a key Bible quote for this section of the LIFEPAC.

Complete the puzzle as you did in the earlier sections. You may review the directions by turning back to the first puzzle in Section 1.

D	A	N	F	O	R	A	N	O
U	I	D	E	B	L	T	E	F
O	T	S	H	A	L	O	K	A
L	C						O	C
H	E						V	E
T	N	T	E	E	M	N	A	N
W	I	M	S	A	N	T	B	E
O	B	Y	O	N	E	E	W	T
	➤	I	D	D	T	H		
	H	T	R	A	E	E		

More puzzle activities.

3.12 Write the Bible verse from Activity 3.11 and where it is found.

____

____

____

3.13 In your own words, tell what God's covenant was that He talked about with Noah after the Flood as recorded in Genesis 9:1-17.

____

____

____

____

Teacher check:

Initials ______________ Date ______________

The Physical Record

The Flood was very destructive to life on earth. There is physical evidence to show this is so. Did the Flood make changes to the earth itself? Some scientists believe that it did. These scientists are sure that physical evidence on Earth proves the waters did rise and fall during the Flood. This event left lasting evidence of its occurrence that continues to be discovered. The study of fossils, glaciers, and land movement has produced much data. You will consider some of this information.

Remains of living things. Many years ago, large fossil deposits were found in Arctic areas. Among the types of animals found were some bison and many huge woolly mammoths. Over a hundred years ago, a frozen woolly mammoth was discovered in Siberia. Its skin and muscles were not decayed. Its eyes and other organs were whole. Its stomach held undigested food. This food was of plants not presently growing in Siberia. In addition, the mammoth was in a standing position.

Since this first discovery of a frozen woolly mammoth, many other similar woolly mammoth remains have been found in Siberia, Alaska, and in other Arctic areas. Many explanations have been given for these strange finds. Some people thought that the mammoths were washed into cold areas by rivers. However, the mammoths were not decayed and were standing. Other people claimed that the mammoths were caught too far north by sudden winter storms. However, some of the mammoth remains were found in several feet of **permafrost**.

When did all of these mammoths die, and what was the cause of their deaths? It has not been shown conclusively that all of these mammoths died at the time of the Flood, nor even that they died at the same time. More study needs to be done. However, some scientists believe that their remains and the circumstances of their deaths are physical evidence for the sudden destruction of the Flood.

| Woolly mammoth

The mammoths could have been trapped by the waters of the Flood. Since fossil remains of other (not woolly) mammoths are found in every continent except two, it is possible that the climate during their time was warm and mild over the earth. Then, something very destructive happened to trap so many mammoths. Perhaps those found in Siberia were trying to get away from the approaching Flood waters. They may have stepped into water-softened soil and sunk in over their heads. Before decay set in, the water-protected mud cooled. Then it froze as water drained from the surface. The explanation of some scientists is that the earth's weather patterns changed following the Flood.

Fossils also show us some other things about ancient life that was different before and after the Flood. Some animals that lived before the Flood are no longer living. They are **extinct**. This fact suggests that the earth was so much different after the Flood that some animals could not survive. Maybe lack of enough food for some of the largest animals caused them to die out.

Plant fossils also show that some of the plants did not survive after the Flood changed the world. Also, most plants have not been able to grow as large as those before the Flood. Perhaps the changed weather conditions after the Flood made growth more difficult for the plants.

Write the correct answer on each line.

3.14 Some ________________ remains of mammoths have been found in the Arctic areas.

a. modern b. complete c. live

3.15 Large deposits of mammoth fossils have been found

____ .

a. nearly all over the world

b. only in the Arctic

c. mostly around the equator

3.16 Fossils show that some animals ________________________________ .

a. had not seen rain b. are extinct c. liked the cold

3.17 Plant fossils show that ____ .

a. plants lived in stone b. plants were perfect c. plants were larger once

Glaciers and other forces. Some scientists believe in a theory that layers of rock and soil were formed by glaciers. They believe in an ice age that covered the earth for millions or billions of years.

Other scientists disagree with that theory. These scientists say that too much physical evidence exists against the earth's **crust** being formed during such a long period of time. Yet, these scientists agree that glaciers were involved in shaping the earth's surface. They conclude that glaciers have been at work only since the Flood. Indeed, glaciers are present in part of the earth today.

| Today, glaciers can be found in Alaska.

Scientists can learn much by observing glaciers at work today. Glaciers **erode** and break down stone as they constantly move from the pull of gravity. They deposit materials in an organized pattern. However, today's glaciers are smaller compared to those that occurred long ago.

The Flood may possibly have given the glaciers a start. This is because the Flood may have started the *water cycle* as we know it today. With snow a part of the water cycle, huge glaciers and ice caps could have developed. The formation of glaciers could have explained where some of the water went after the Flood. The ice age could have been short as the earth settled into new conditions after the Flood.

Evidences were found of much volcano and earthquake activity during and after the Flood. Volcanic rock deposits and faults in rock layers show considerable activity took place as the earth struggled through changed conditions as a result of the Flood.

Complete these sentences.

3.18 Glaciers may have helped develop the earth's ______________________.

3.19 Large glaciers probably lasted a ______________ time.

3.20 The water ______________ started after the Flood.

3.21 Glaciers are constantly ______________________.

3.22 Volcanoes and ______________________ helped make changes in the earth.

3.23 Glaciers and icecaps store ______________.

Complete each activity. Here are some mammoths. Each mammoth has eaten a vocabulary word! The word is jumbled up. Help the mammoth digest its food by spelling each word correctly. After each unscrambled word, write its definition.

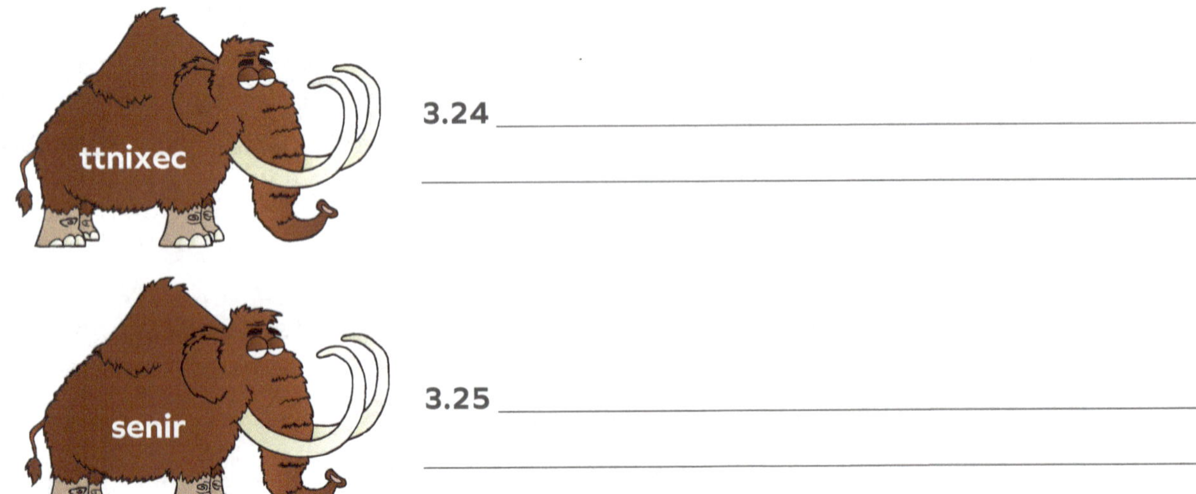

3.24 ____

____

3.25 ____

____

3.26 ____

____

3.27 ____

____

3.28 ____

____

3.29 ____

____

3.30 ____

____

3.31 ____

____

Complete this interview.

3.32 Scientists develop their ideas about glaciers through study and exploration. Nonscientists have difficulty knowing what to believe. An interview with an older person can help you learn how people develop conclusions.
Follow these directions. Check the box in front of each step as you complete it.

☐ 1. Think about three questions that you want to ask an older person about glaciers. Write the questions here.

____

____

____

☐ 2. Show your questions to your teacher.
☐ 3. Set up your interview with the older person and conduct the interview. Record the answers the older person gives you.
☐ 4. Write out your results on another sheet of paper.
☐ 5. Take the paper and this LIFEPAC to the teacher for a Teacher check.

Teacher check:

Initials ______________ Date ______________

Shifting land areas. Scientists have developed another interesting theory about the continents of the world. They believe that the landmasses of the continents are shifting. Evidence indicates that the Atlantic Ocean is growing larger and the Pacific Ocean is getting smaller. The American continents seem to be slowly drifting westward. Some scientists believe that this drift began with the Flood and continues to this day. Examinations of land boundaries and ocean floors show that the continents as we know them could have been one landmass (see Figures 1 and 2). The Flood could have started the continents drifting.

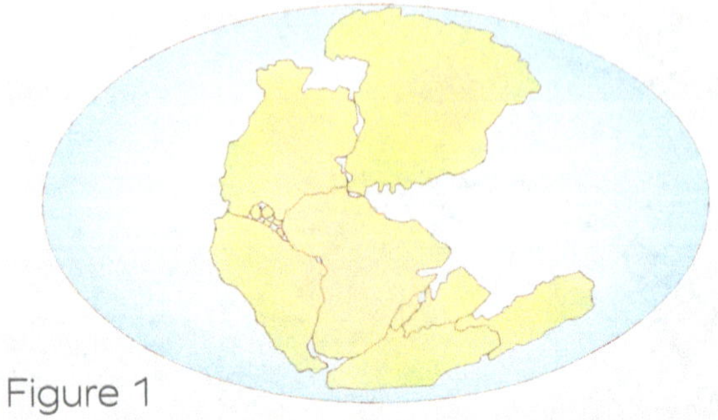

| Figure 1

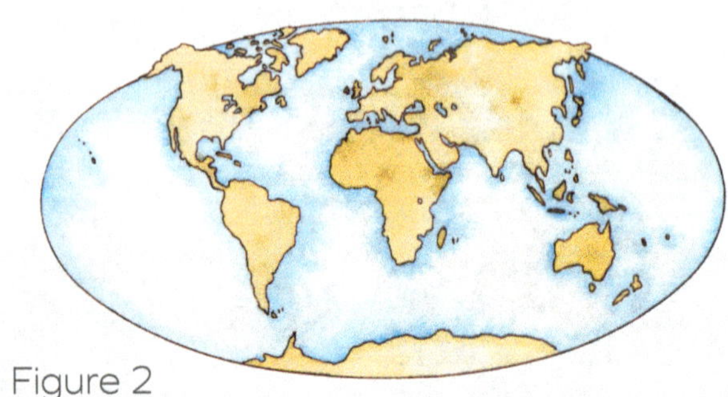

| Figure 2

The action of the Flood can also explain the development of many land forms. After the rains ended, the water did not continue to cover the earth. What happened to the water? **Gravity** pulled it to the lowest parts of the earth. In the great rush of water, the land and the water separated. Mountains were pushed up. Canyons were formed in the earth. Large, deep ocean basins were formed for the water to fill. Therefore, the waters flowed down the surface of the earth as the continents divided and ocean basins were deepened.

For the water to settle to new levels in the lowest areas probably took many years. During that time, glaciers were forming. The water cycle took effect. The water levels were becoming fixed, but the earth's land surface continued to change. Weather conditions and water pressure combined forces to perform the changes.

Soil on the surface shifted as a result of wind and rain. These forces could erode soil and rock rapidly. All of these forces are at work today and continue to change the earth's surfaces.

Match these items.

3.33 __________ getting larger

3.34 __________ drifting today

3.35 __________ pulled water to lowest places

3.36 __________ erode land surfaces

3.37 __________ contain frozen water

3.38 __________ helped form mountains

a. gravity
b. mitosis
c. glaciers
d. continents
e. water pressure
f. Continental Divide
g. Atlantic Ocean
h. wind and rain

Before you take this last Self Test, you may want to do one or more of these self checks.

1. ________ Read the objectives. See if you can do them.
2. ________ Restudy the material related to any objectives that you cannot do.
3. ________ Use the **SQ3R** study procedure to review the material:
   a. **S**can the sections.
   b. **Q**uestion yourself.
   c. **R**ead to answer your questions.
   d. **R**ecite the answers to yourself.
   e. **R**eview areas you did not understand.
4. ________ Review all vocabulary, activities, and Self Tests, writing a correct answer for every wrong answer.

SELF TEST 3

Answer *true* or *false* (each answer, 2 points).

3.01 __________ The Bible tells how the water drained from the land areas after the Flood.

3.02 __________ Noah lived to be over nine hundred years old according to the Bible.

3.03 __________ New languages formed after the Tower of Babel.

3.04 __________ There was a time of great destruction on the earth.

3.05 __________ The Bible tells of huge trees and thick forests before the Flood.

3.06 __________ Some animal and human fossils have been found together.

3.07 __________ Stories of a great flood are told among tribes around the world.

3.08 __________ The world climate was mild before the Flood.

3.09 __________ Oil was probably formed from animals.

3.010 __________ Petrified wood was once part of living trees.

Match these items. Some letters will be used more than once (each answer, 3 points).

3.011 __________ large sheets of ice

3.012 __________ wind erodes soil

3.013 __________ very hot

3.014 __________ water pressure helped form mountains

3.015 __________ continents drift

3.016 __________ these are slow moving

3.017 __________ sudden earth movements

a. glaciers

b. earthquakes

c. volcanoes

d. shifting landmasses

Define these words (each item, 5 points).

3.018 gravity ______________________________
____

3.019 erode ______________________________
____

3.020 data ______________________________
____

3.021 extinct ______________________________
____

Write the correct answer on each line (each answer, 3 points).

3.022 Distinct fall and winter occurred ______________ the Flood.
a. only before b. only after c. both before and after

3.023 That Adam named the animals is shown by (the) ______________ record(s).
a. physical b. Bible c. both Bible and physical

3.024 Animals were not ______________ before the Flood according to some Bible students.
a. tamed by humans b. eaten by humans c. liked by humans

3.025 Some animals were not able to survive the ______________ caused by the Flood.
a. rain b. changed earth c. mountains

3.026 Some complete mammoth remains were found in ______________ .
a. oceans b. volcanoes c. permafrost

3.027 Some fossils from very large ______________ have been found.
a. plants b. books c. houses

3.028 Snow began as part of the ______________ .
a. earthquakes b. volcanoes c. water cycle

3.029 Plants, animals, and ______________ were destroyed by the Flood.
a. human lives b. rocks c. glaciers

Answer these questions (each item, 5 points).

3.030 How do mammoth fossils and remains give clues to the nature of the earth when mammoths were alive?

____

____

____

____

____

3.031 What are some differences between glacier theories and Bible accounts of the Flood?

____

____

____

____

3.032 What happened to the waters of the Flood?

____

____

____

____

Teacher check: Initials ____________

Score ____________ Date ____________

80/100

Before you take the LIFEPAC Test, you may want to do one or more of these self checks.

1. ________ Read the objectives. See if you can do them.
2. ________ Restudy the material related to any objectives that you cannot do.
3. ________ Use the **SQ3R** study procedure to review the material.
4. ________ Review activities, Self Tests, and LIFEPAC vocabulary words.
5. ________ Restudy areas of weakness indicated by the last Self Test.

SCIENCE 507

RECORDS IN ROCK: FOSSILS

Author:
Barry G. Burrus, M.Div, M.A., B.S.

Editor:
Brian Ring

Illustrations:
Brian Ring

Media Credits:
Page 3, 23: © Aneese, iStock, Thinkstock; **4, 15, 18, 32:** © Marcio Silva, iStock, Thinkstock; **6:** © DC Colombia, iStock, Thinkstock; **9:** © Russell Shively, iStock Thinkstock; **12, 32:** © fkienas, iStock, Thinkstock; **15, 32:** © apollob66, iStock, Thinkstock; **19:** © woodstock, iStock, Thinkstock; **20, 36:** © Aysunbk, iStock, Thinkstock; **24:** © artisticco, iStock, Thinkstock; **30:** © DaracSem, iStock, Thinkstock; **32:** © Snowshill, iStock,Thinkstock; © Pi-Lens, iStock, Thinkstock; **39:** © Tigatelu, iStock, Thinkstock; **42:** © EcoPic, iStock, Thinkstock; **43:** © Sasha Samardzija, iStock, Thinkstock; **44:** © alice-photo, iStock, Thinkstock; **45:** © mj0007, iStock, Thinkstock; **47:** © JaysonPhotography, iStock, Thinkstock; © aleks0649, iStock, Thinkstock; **48:** © matthew grove, iStock, Thinkstock.

All maps in this book © Image Resources, unless otherwise stated.

804 N. 2nd Ave. E.
Rock Rapids, IA 51246-1759

RECORDS IN ROCK: FOSSILS

God created everything that exists. Fortunately, we have records preserved in rock and other materials of many of God's living things created long ago. These preserved records are called fossils. Fossils help us to learn about the types of living things that existed on the earth many thousands of years ago. As you learned in the previous LIFEPAC®, they are part of the physical record that God has given us in His creation.

In this LIFEPAC, you will learn much more about fossils. You will learn about the different types of fossils and where they may be found. You will also learn how fossils were formed long ago. Finally, you will learn what we can discover about times long ago by studying fossils.

Objectives

Read these objectives. These objectives tell what you will be able to do when you have successfully completed this LIFEPAC. Each section will list according to the numbers below what objectives will be met in that section. When you have finished this LIFEPAC, you should be able to:

1. Identify different fossil types.
2. Explain where fossils may be found.
3. Describe fossil identification procedures.
4. Use fossil clues in making inferences.

1. FOSSIL FORMATION

Fossils are very interesting to find and study. They are the hardened remains of plants or animals that lived long ago. Fossils can also be an imprint of a once-living plant or animal. For example, some fossils are leaves, wood, shells, and skeletons of plants or animals that were buried during the time of the great Flood of Noah. Others are tracks left by moving animals of long ago.

You might be surprised to learn that fossils are very common and easy to find. They are plentiful in nearly every state in the United States. There are probably many fossils where you live. These fossils come in a great variety.

In this section of the LIFEPAC, you will learn about the different *types* of fossils. You will also learn about the location of some major fossil deposits around the world. You will also learn where fossils could be expected to be found in your local area.

Objectives

Review these objectives. When you have completed this section, you should be able to:

1. Identify different fossil types.
2. Explain where fossils may be found.

Vocabulary

Study these new words. Learning the meanings of these words is a good study habit and will improve your understanding of this LIFEPAC.

amber (am′ bər). A hardened, yellowish material formed from the gum-like sap of cone-bearing trees.

carbonized (kär′ bə nīzd). Changed into carbon.

cluster (klus′ tər). A grouping together of things that are alike.

dissolved (di zolvd′). Became another form—usually liquid; faded away.

estimated (es′ tə mā′ təd). Made judgments or opinions; formed a good general answer by using data.

identified (ī den′ tə fīd). Named something; decided what something was by comparing.

imprint (im′ print). A mark pressed into a surface that was created by pressure.

mastodons (mas′ tə donz). Huge, prehistoric animals that resembled elephants and are now extinct.

mineral (min′ ər əl). A material gotten from the ground. It is not alive, but is a chemical.

mummification (mum′ mə fə kā′ shən). A process of forming fossils whereby animal or plant skin, tissue, or other parts are preserved by drying or the action of chemicals.

preserved (pri zėrvd′). Kept safe or protected.

prohibit (prō hib′ it). To prevent from doing something.

sediment (sed′ ə mənt). Material that settles to the bottom in liquid, such as dirt that has settled to the bottom of a river or lake.

similar (sim′ə lər). Somewhat alike.

shale (shāl). A type of fine-grained rock made from clay or mud.

sites (sīts). Places where something is located.

unearth (un ėrth′). To discover or dig up.

Note: *All vocabulary words in this LIFEPAC appear in* **boldface** *print the first time they are used. If you are unsure of the meaning when you are reading, study the definitions given.*

Pronunciation Key: h**a**t, **ā**ge, c**ã**re, f**ä**r; l**e**t, **ē**qual, t**ė**rm; **i**t, **ī**ce; h**o**t, **ō**pen, **ô**rder; **oi**l; **ou**t; c**u**p, p**u̇**t, r**ü**le; **ch**ild; lo**ng**; **th**in; /ŦH/ for **th**en; /zh/ for mea**s**ure; /u/ or /ə/ represents /a/ in **a**bout, /e/ in tak**e**n, /i/ in penc**i**l, /o/ in lem**o**n, and /u/ in circ**u**s.

Types of Fossils

Millions of fossils have been found by people in modern times. Some of these fossils are plants. Some are fossils of animals. Even human fossils have been found. Some fossils are just imprints of plants or animals. There are so many varieties of fossils that it is useful to classify them.

There are several ways to classify fossils, but one of the most useful ways is to classify them by type. You will now learn about four types of fossils: *print fossils, original-remains fossils, petrified fossils, and carbonized fossils.*

Print fossils. *Print fossils* are the most common type. They are the prints or impressions of a plant or animal that lived long ago. The actual remains of the plant or animal are no longer present in the fossil. Only an impression of the remains has been left in the rock. These print fossils are further categorized as either (1) *mold fossils* or (2) *cast fossils*. Let's consider each of these two kinds of print fossils and how they were formed. As we discuss each of these kinds of fossils, you will get a chance to make your own models of them!

A *mold fossil* was formed when a living thing was covered with **sediment** and died. Later, the sediment hardened into rock. The plant or animal within the sediment decayed and **dissolved**. Because the plant or animal no longer existed, a hollow area in the hardened sediment remained. The actual plant or animal parts were no longer present. However, the outer shape or impression of the living thing was left in the sediment. Therefore, the fossil looks like a mold of the original plant or animal.

Most of the mold fossils that have been found are prints of shells, bones, or wood. Skin, leaves, and soft plant or animal parts are not usually found as mold fossils. This is because the pressure of the sediment may have destroyed the softer parts before they could make an impression. Also, bones, shells, and wood do not dissolve or decay as quickly as do soft or delicate living things.

In the experiment that follows, you will observe how a mold of an object can be made. This would be similar to the way mold fossils were formed.

| A mold fossil is an impression of the remains of a plant, animal, or object.

EXPERIMENT 507.A MOLD FOSSIL COPY

View 507 Mold Fossil Copy: Grade 5 Science experiments video

You will examine what happens when a mold fossil is made.
Your result will not be a real fossil. It will be a copy of a mold fossil.

These supplies are needed:

a small plastic container (about 10 centimeters across)
modeling clay
a seashell or bone

Follow these directions carefully. Check the box when each step is completed.

- ☐ 1. Press the modeling clay into the bottom of the plastic container. The clay should be at least 1 centimeter thick.
- ☐ 2. Smooth the surface of the clay.
- ☐ 3. Carefully press the shell or bone into the clay. (If you use a shell, press the outside of the shell into the clay.)
- ☐ 4. Lift the shell or bone out of the clay. You should have a clear imprint remaining in the clay.
- ☐ 5. Keep your mold fossil copy from this experiment in a safe place to use in the next experiment.

Do this activity.

1.1 Draw a picture of your copy of the mold fossil.

Answer these questions.

1.2 How is your copy of a mold fossil like the shell or bone you used?

____

____

1.3 How is your copy of a mold fossil *different* from the shell or bone you used?

____

____

1.4 Why would this type of fossil be called a *print fossil*?

____

____

____

Teacher check:

Initials ______________ Date ______________

You have learned that one form of a print fossil is a mold fossil. Another form of a print fossil is called a *cast fossil*. The cast fossil is made after a mold fossil has been formed. A cast fossil forms when ground water containing dissolved **minerals** and other fine particles drains though the rock and sediment and into the mold that has been formed by a decayed or dissolved plant or animal. The minerals and fine particles in the water are deposited inside the mold. When enough minerals and fine particles are deposited to fill up the mold, a copy—or *cast*—of the original plant or animal is made. With time, the casts can harden, and a *cast fossil* is made.

| A cast fossil is a copy of the original.

Like the mold fossil, the cast fossil is not actually made up of the remains of the ancient plant or animal. Instead, it is an imprint or cast of the original. However, it is a true copy of the original. It is part of the physical record that God has given us of ancient plants or animals that once lived upon the earth.

EXPERIMENT 507.B CAST FOSSIL COPY

View 507 Cast Fossil Copy: Grade 5 Science experiments video

You will examine what happens when a cast fossil is made. Since you must make your copy of a cast fossil in a short time, you will not use minerals from ground water. Instead, you will use some molding plaster to make your *cast*. Your result will not be a real fossil. It will be a copy of a cast fossil.

These supplies are needed:

- the mold fossil copy from the previous experiment
- molding plaster
- a tin can and stick
- a jar of water

Follow these directions carefully. Check the box when each step is completed.

- ☐ 1. Prepare the molding plaster. Put some of the molding plaster into the can. Pour a small amount of water into the plaster. Stir the mixture with a stick. Add more water or plaster until the mixture is creamy, somewhat thick, and still liquid.
- ☐ 2. Pour the molding plaster mixture into the clay copy of the mold fossil that you made in the last experiment until the mold is completely filled.
- ☐ 3. Allow the molding plaster mixture in the mold to harden for at least an hour.
- ☐ 4. Remove the hardened plaster from the clay mold. This hardened plaster is your copy of a cast fossil.

Do this activity.

1.5 Draw a picture of your copy of the cast fossil.

Answer these questions.

1.6 How is your copy of the cast fossil like the original seashell or bone that you used earlier?

____

____

1.7 How is your cast fossil copy different from the original shell or bone?

____

____

1.8 Why would this type of fossil be called a *cast fossil*?

____

____

____

Teacher check:

Initials ____________________ Date ____________________

Original-remains fossils. The second type of fossil is called an original-remains fossil. Unlike the print fossils, the original plant or animal remains in an original-remains fossil did not decay or dissolve. Instead, an original-remains fossil contains the actual remains of the plant or animal. These plants and animals may have lived thousands of years ago.

An example of the original-remains fossil type is the mammoth found in Siberia. (You read about the mammoth and bison remains in Science LIFEPAC 506.) In that case, the actual remains of the mammoth were found in their completeness. The mammoth had not decayed at all. It had been protected from decay by the cold temperature of the permafrost in the Arctic region. This mammoth was one form of an original-remains fossil.

Original-remains fossils have been **preserved** in other ways, too. Some insects that lived long ago have been found perfectly preserved in **amber**, a hardened yellowish material from cone-bearing trees. These insects were completely formed and were not decayed at all. Their thin wings were protected unharmed. Their organs were not disturbed.

Another way that the original remains of ancient plants or animals have been preserved is by oil or coal deposits. Perfect remains of tiny fish and plants have been found in oil and coal deposits throughout the world. These remains were preserved by the presence of oil or coal around them. The pressure of the earth was not great enough to destroy the remains of the plants or animals. Therefore, they have become original-remains fossils.

| Insects preserved in amber

Occasionally, animal and plant remains are fossilized with little or no change through a process known as **mummification**. In this process, the animal or plant skin, tissue, or other body parts are preserved by drying or by the action of chemicals. These original-remains fossils are sometimes found in desert areas where the air is very dry.

Finally, the most common type of original-remains fossils is the hard parts of plants or animals that remain from long ago. These parts are usually shells or bones. They have been buried, and the soft parts of the plants or animals decay. Only the hard parts are preserved. Some of these bones and shells have been found deep under the ground. Others were in caves or near the surface of the earth. These remains are considered to be original-remains fossils.

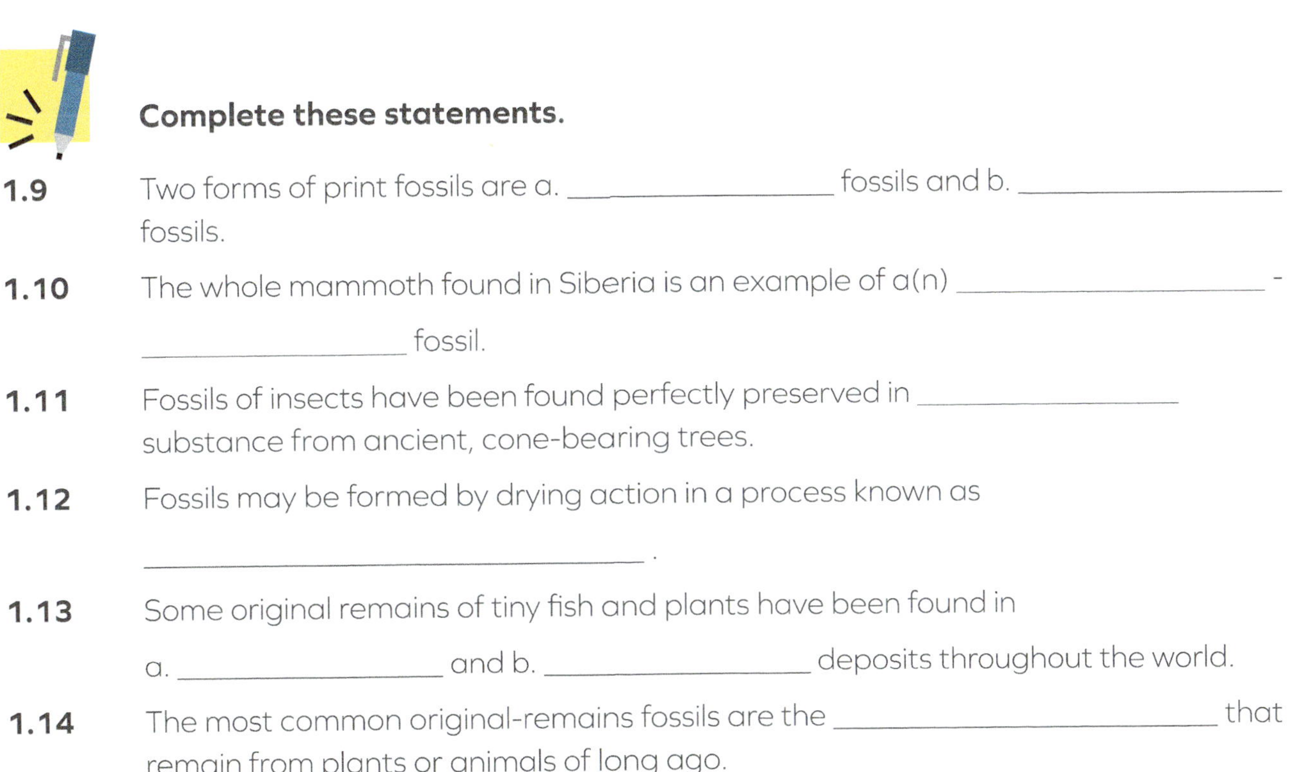

Complete these statements.

1.9 Two forms of print fossils are a. ________________ fossils and b. ________________ fossils.

1.10 The whole mammoth found in Siberia is an example of a(n) ________________ - ________________ fossil.

1.11 Fossils of insects have been found perfectly preserved in ________________ substance from ancient, cone-bearing trees.

1.12 Fossils may be formed by drying action in a process known as ________________________ .

1.13 Some original remains of tiny fish and plants have been found in a. ________________ and b. ________________ deposits throughout the world.

1.14 The most common original-remains fossils are the ________________________ that remain from plants or animals of long ago.

Complete these activities.

1.15 You learned about the mammoth remains found in Siberia and other Arctic regions in the previous LIFEPAC, Science 506. The mammoth story can be helpful to your understanding of original-remains fossils. In the space below, write what you remember about the mammoth that was discovered in Siberia more than 100 years ago.

____

____

____

____

____

1.16 Now refer to the Science 506 LIFEPAC to check your memory about the mammoth found in Siberia. Correct any mistakes, and add any missing information. Write your corrected statements in the space provided below.

____

____

____

____

Petrified fossils. The third type of fossil is called a *petrified fossil*. Petrified wood is the most commonly known fossil of this type. Many animal bones, shells, and teeth have been petrified, too.

How did *petrification* of plants and animals take place long ago? Basically, there were two ways, and minerals were involved in both ways. In some plant and animal remains, water containing minerals soaked into the pores of the original hard parts of the plant or animal. Some or all of the original hard parts remain, but they were greatly strengthened and preserved by the minerals in the water. This process is called *permineralization*.

Other petrified fossils form in a different way. In these cases, the minerals in the water totally replaced the original plant or animal. This process is called *replacement*. In replacement, two events happened at the same time. The water dissolved the compounds that made up the original material, while, at the same time, the minerals are deposited in their place. Petrified fossils that formed by *replacement* can have even microscopic details of the original hard part of the plant or animal preserved.

Carbonized fossils. The fourth type of fossil, called a **carbonized** *fossil*, was formed in an unusual way. Living tissues are made up of compounds of carbon and other chemical elements. As the decaying tissues of ancient plants or animals broke down into their chemical parts, most of the chemicals disappeared, except carbon. These decaying tissues left behind traces of carbon in the rock. Fossils formed by this process of *carbonization* usually show great details of the original living thing. Ancient plants, fish, and soft-bodied creatures have been preserved in great detail as carbonized fossils.

Carbonized fossils are usually found in areas where coal has been formed. They are less known than other types of fossils. However, carbonized fossils also give us information about life in the past. They are also part of God's physical record of the earth.

| Petrified tree trunk

| Carbonized fish fossil

Answer *true* or *false*.

1.17 __________ Petrified wood is the most common type of carbonized fossil.

1.18 __________ Minerals in water helped to form petrified fossils.

1.19 __________ In *replacement*, the minerals in water totally replace the original hard parts of a plant or animal.

1.20 ____________ Some petrified fossils contain hardened parts of the original plant or animal.

1.21 ____________ Carbonized fossils are usually found in areas where coal has been formed.

Write the correct answer on each line.

1.22 Petrified fossils are formed by minerals through ______________________________ .

a. permineralization or replacement

b. replacement only

c. carbonization

1.23 Petrified fossils formed by ________________________ can have microscopic details of the original hard parts preserved.

a. imprinting   b. replacement   c. carbonization

1.24 Living tissues are made up of compounds of ________________________ and other chemical elements.

a. acid   b. carbon   c. carbon dioxide

1.25 Carbonized fossils are formed from traces of ________________________ left in the rock.

a. carbon   b. zinc   c. water

Complete this activity.

1.26 This is a crossword puzzle. The words that will be used in the puzzle have been discussed in this LIFEPAC. Use the definitions below to identify the words and then write the words in the puzzle.

ACROSS

2. A kind of print fossil. It forms when minerals from water fill up a mold of a living thing.
3. Something that is left from a living thing after it dies.
6. Part of the physical record of ancient times. It was formed by a living thing.
7. A type of fossil that is formed by minerals, either by permineralization or by replacement.
8. A yellowish, gum-like material from ancient, cone-bearing trees that has hardened.

DOWN

1. A type of fossil formed from an imprint of a living thing.
2. A type of fossil formed from carbon left over from the original plant or animal.
4. A kind of print fossil. It forms from an imprint of the original plant or animal into sediment. The original material then dissolves or decays away.
5. A material usually contained in water that helps to form fossils.

Fossil Locations

There are many places around the world that are famous for the number or types of fossils that have been discovered there. Many millions of fossils have been discovered. It is very likely that there are also many fossils located within a short distance of your home, too. In this section of the LIFEPAC, you will learn about some of the more famous fossil deposit locations around the world. You will also have the opportunity to find out about other famous deposits of fossils. In addition, you will learn where it is likely that fossils may be found in your own local area.

Around the world. There are many places around the world where large deposits of fossils have been found. Some of these fossil locations are more famous than others. Just because they are famous, however, does not necessarily mean that they are more important. These fossil locations may be famous for other reasons. Perhaps that particular location was where fossils of a certain type were first found. Other famous locations hold unusual animals or have a great variety of species of plants or animals. Whatever the reason, certain deposits of fossils around the world have become more well known than others.

You will now learn something about the kinds and types of fossils found at some of these famous locations around the world. Please keep in mind that there are many other fossil finds besides the ones that will be discussed in this section of the LIFEPAC.

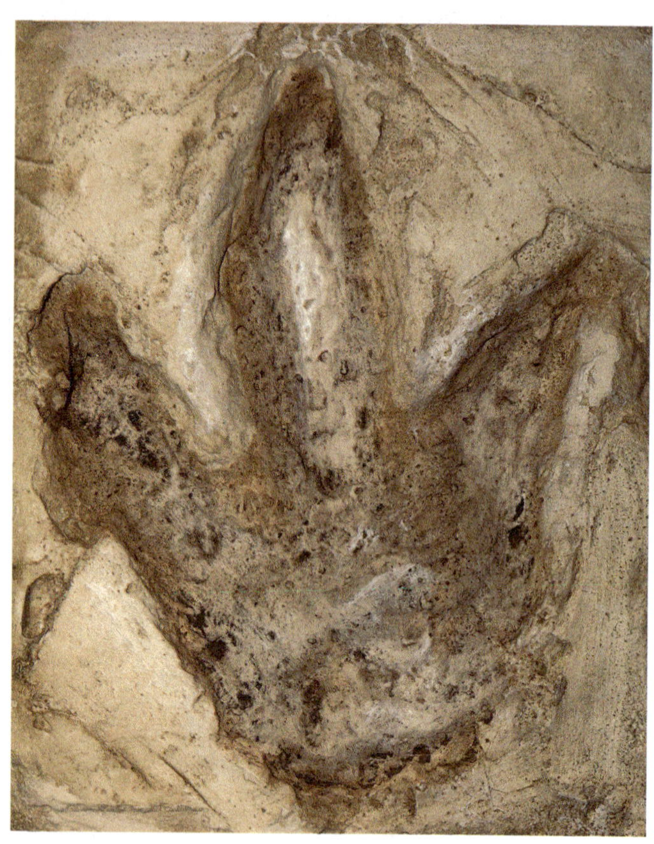

| Dinosaur footprint fossil

In Massachusetts, a great many dinosaur tracks were discovered. These tracks formed *print fossils*. Thousands of dinosaur footprints were found in Massachusetts in an area of red sandstone in the Connecticut River Valley. Scientists believe that the dinosaurs originally made tracks in mud. The prints later hardened and became stone.

Many dinosaur bones have been found in the Gobi Desert of Mongolia, a region that lies between China and Russia. In addition, dinosaur egg fossils were found. Some of these fossilized eggs held tiny dinosaur skeletons inside. Before this fossil discovery, people did not know that dinosaurs laid eggs.

In a fossil deposit near Florissant, Colorado, a great many species of plants and animals were found. Insect fossils, bird and fish skeletons, leaves, nuts, and blossoms have all been found there. These fossils were in layers of rock formed from volcanoes.

One of the best amber deposits containing original-remains fossils was found along the Baltic Sea in Northern Europe. The amber deposits contained the remains of many insects. Scientists were amazed to discover insects from every region of the earth in this single amber deposit.

The Cumberland Bone Cave in Maryland contains bones from hundreds of animals. Again, scientists found fossilized animal remains from different climates and environments. Some bones were from tropical animals. Other bones were from animals native to cold regions. Caves located only a few miles away held no fossils.

Several other interesting bone deposits have been found in other places around the world. In Sicily, large hippopotamus bone fossil beds were discovered. Near Agate Springs, Nebraska, a layer of rock contained thousands of unusual animal fossils. This collection of fossils is called a *bone bed*. Near the Green River in Wyoming, fossilized bones from animals larger than elephants were discovered. One of the most widely known fossil deposits in the world is in Los Angeles, California. It is called the La Brea Tar Pits. In this area, tar-like material bubbled out of several large holes, or pits. Sometimes bones would bubble out of the pits. Explorers began to realize that these bones were from animals that had become extinct. Then they learned that these tar pits held bones from many, many animals. Some plant remains were even preserved in the pits. Several of these pits were dug up. Complete animal skeletons were found. Remains from extinct animals were numerous. More than two hundred kinds of animals and plants were **identified**. Among the animals identified were saber-toothed tigers, giant wolves, sloths, **mastodons**, short-faced bears, and horses. These tar pits have been an excellent source of information about life in the past.

| Reconstructed mastodons at the La Brea Tar Pits

After the first frozen mammoth remains were discovered in Siberia, many more have been found. Complete mammoth remains have been found along the Lena River in Siberia. A number of mammoth remains have also been found along the northern coast of Alaska. Some people have **estimated** that as many as 5 million mammoth remains are still buried in permafrost!

Petrified wood fossils can be found in many places around the world. The Yellowstone Park region in Wyoming has some deposits. Perhaps the best-known location of petrified wood in the world is the Petrified Forest National Park in Arizona. Great **clusters** of petrified logs can be seen above the ground surface. The park extends for more than nine miles (15 kilometers) and petrified logs are lying about through most of the area.

Petrified bones, tusks, and teeth from mammoths and mastodons have been located in Alaska. When the Alaska Pipeline was constructed in the 1970s, chips of these petrified fossils were **unearthed** by the millions.

| Carbonized fossil of a fish

Coal mines and coal mine regions are the best **sites** for carbonized fossils. Some people even consider coal to be a large mass of fossil material. These people explain that coal comes from living things. Coal is made of the carbon that remains after the other parts of living things dissolve. The term *fossil fuels* comes from this idea. Both coal and oil are called fossil fuels. Well-preserved carbon fossils can be found in most coal mines, and coal mines are located throughout the world. The original structure of the living thing has been preserved as carbon in rock.

Some of the following activities about fossils around the world involve the use of maps. The information that you complete in the first items will be used to help you locate large fossil deposits on a world map. The information you have just covered in this LIFEPAC will help you answer some questions. You may also need to use an atlas, other reference books, or the Internet to help you complete the activities.

Write the name for the correct fossil location(s) on each blank.

1.27 Bone beds: ______________________________

1.28 Dinosaur bones and eggs: ______________________________

1.29 Petrified wood:

a. ______________________________

b. ______________________________

1.30 Hippopotamus fossil beds: ______________________________

1.31 Bone cave: ______________________________

1.32 Tar pits: ______________________________

1.33 Frozen mammoths:

a. ______________________________

b. ______________________________

1.34 Amber: ______________________________

1.35 Bones of animals larger than elephants: ______________________________

1.36 Petrified tusks, bones, and teeth: ______________________________

1.37 Dinosaur tracks: ______________________________

Classify these fossils by using your answers for the last exercise. Write the name of the location in the blank spaces.

1.39 Print (tracks): ______________________________

1.40 Original-remains:

a. ______________ b. ______________

c. ______________ d. ______________

e. ______________ f. ______________

g. ______________ h. ______________

i. ______________ j. ______________

1.41 Petrified:

a. ______________

b. ______________

c. ______________

1.42 On the world map below, locate the sites of the famous fossil deposits listed on the previous page. Place the symbols (shown in the **Key**) in the general area on the map where they would be found.

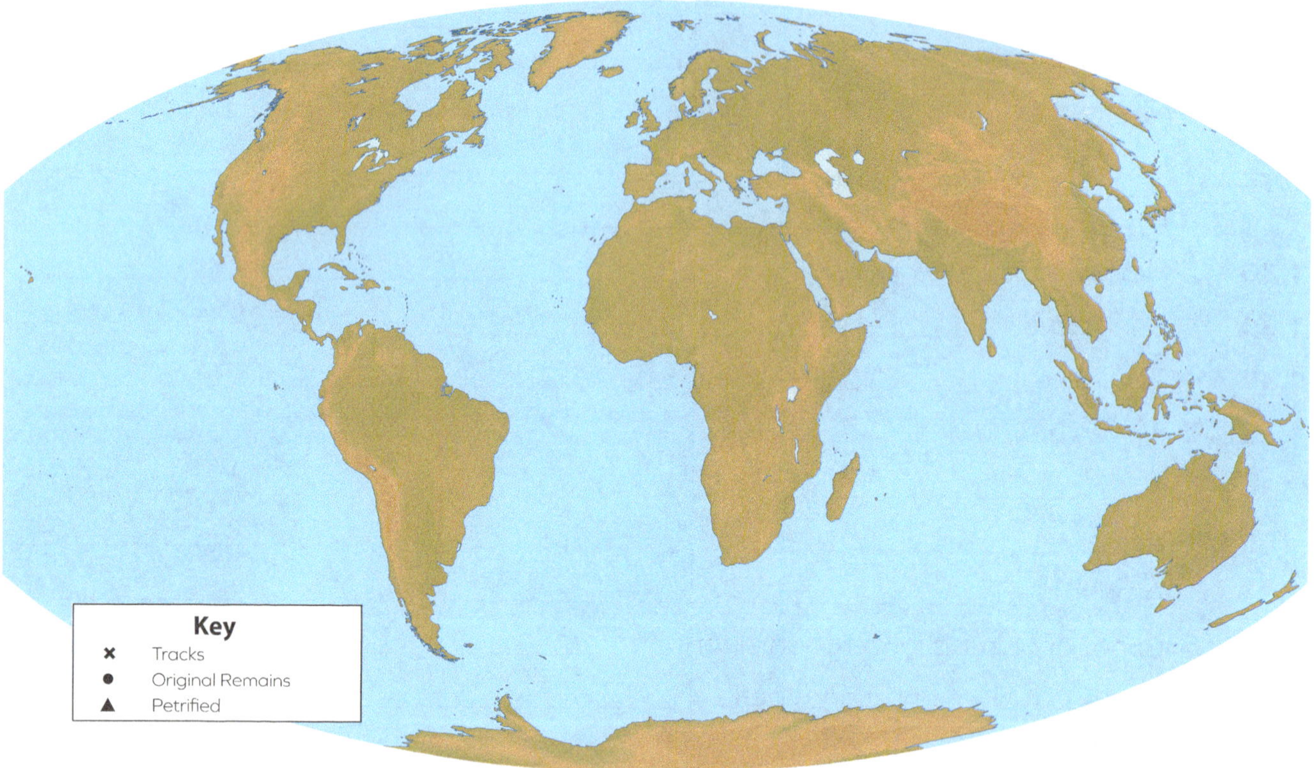

Complete this optional activity. There are other well-known fossil sites around the world that were not included in this LIFEPAC. In this optional activity, you can search several resources — such as the library or Internet or a museum — to locate some of these other major fossil deposits around the world. Perhaps you will find the locations of deposits that contain mold fossils, cast fossils, and carbonized fossils, too. When you have located several new sites, complete the activities below.

1.43 On another piece of paper, list the fossil deposit sites that you located.

1.44 On another piece of paper, classify the locations under the different types of fossils.

1.45 Add new symbols to the **Key** for the world map if needed. Then locate your additional "fossil finds" on the world map above.

Teacher check:

Initials ______________________ Date ______________________

Local deposits. You may be surprised to learn that you can find many fossils on your own. Anyone can find and keep fossils. You should be able to find fossils in almost any area of the United States. If you live in another country, the chances are very good that fossils are plentiful in your country, too!

| Dinosaur tracks in the Arizona desert

Of course, you probably have some questions. Where are the best places to look for fossils? What information is needed to find a fossil. In the rest of this section of the LIFEPAC, you will learn the answers to these questions.

Some places are better than others for possible fossil finds. Probably you would not find fossils lying on a paved playground or parking lot. Usually, houses, churches, and schools do not have yards where you would find fossils on the surface of the ground. Where might you look?

Fossils may be found along stream or river banks. Areas where there are many rocks may also have some fossils. Fossil prints may be in the rocks. They may be anywhere on the surface of the ground. They could be underground, too. Someone digging in the ground might bring a fossil to the surface. Sometimes the sites of new homes or buildings might be a good place to get fossils.

Some types of rocks are more likely than others to contain fossils. Limestone, **shale**, and sandstone may have fossils in them. These rocks were formed from sediments such as mud, clay, or sand. Shelled animals, fish, or leaves sometimes become trapped in these soft materials. Eventually, the sediments harden. The bones and shells are preserved, or prints of the original remains are formed. These rock types can be found over much of North America. They provide the best source of fossils for people who cannot go to a known fossil deposit site.

Fossil discoveries are made nearly every day. Most of them are common finds. They are fossils that are **similar** to other fossils from that area. Scientists would not expect to find complete mammoth remains outside an area of permafrost. Preserved bones are usually deep in the ground. Carbonized fossils would be found in or near coal mines. Petrified wood is not a common fossil found in most places.

Sometimes a rare fossil is found by people who are not looking for fossils. If care is not taken, the fossil may be damaged, and historical information may be lost. Perhaps you will discover a fossil that you think is rare. If you do, leave it where you found it. Report the find to a parent, teacher, or someone who can help you learn more about it.

Persons who want to look for fossils need to be careful when they choose their search area. Safety is important. Loose rocks, riverbanks, and new building sites can be dangerous. Permission from the landowners is important to obtain before searching for fossils. Landowners may not want fossil hunters disturbing their land. Digging may damage the environment. National parks usually have rules that **prohibit** fossil removal.

| Fossils may be underground.

Good stewardship of fossils is important, too. God has made it possible for fossils to be formed. If people are not thoughtful in hunting for fossils, they can do harm to the physical record of long ago that God has given to us. God wants us to be responsible for the earth and to care for it. If people thoughtlessly destroy fossils, they destroy evidence of former life and make it more difficult to learn of God's greatness.

Write the correct answer on each line.

1.46 Fossils may be most likely to be discovered ______________________.

a. along stream banks b. in trees c. in paved parking lots

1.47 Limestone, sandstone, and ______________________ are common rocks where fossils are found.

a. granite b. shoal c. shale

1.48 National parks usually ______________________ fossil removal.

a. prohibit b. encourage c. do not like

1.49 Prints of ______________________ are likely to be found in limestone.

a. mouse skin b. carbon c. fish skeletons

1.50 When you take care in choosing fossil search sites, you are ______________________.

a. preserving fossils

b. practicing good stewardship

c. selfish

Look for fossils.

1.51 There are several ways that you can look for fossils. In this activity, you will choose one of the ways listed below. Discuss these ways with your teacher, and together decide what you will do.

Our choice ______________________ ______________________

Initials Date

a. Talk to a parent, teacher, or another person who might know of fossil locations nearby. Plan a short trip to look for fossils. (Be sure to get permission from your parents and from the landowners.) Go to the site and look for fossils. Bring back anything that you believe is a fossil. Make a display for the room. Also, write an account of your experience of looking for fossils. (Later in this LIFEPAC, you may want to write about your find when you learn more about how to identify fossils.)

b. If a museum is in your area, you could help plan a tour of its fossil collections. Perhaps your family or school class could go on an outing together to the museum to observe the fossils. After visiting the museum, write a description of your favorite fossil display.

c. A visit to a famous fossil deposit site can be very interesting if it is possible. Plan a class or family trip to the deposit site. While you are at the site or upon your return, make drawings of some of the fossils. Write explanations about the drawings. Tell why these fossil finds were so important.

Teacher check:

Initials ______________________ Date ______________________

Use the library or Internet.

1.52 The following persons were important in making fossil discoveries. They have all contributed to knowledge about fossils. Choose one of these people to learn about. Use reference books, library books, and Internet sites about fossils to get your information.

Roy Andrews	Mary Anning	Baron Cuvier	Edward Cope
Rudolph Hauthal	W.W. Orcutt	C.H. Townsend	

Choose the person's most important fossil discoveries. Write a few paragraphs describing the work on another piece of paper. When you have done your best writing, copy it into the following space.

____

____

____

____

____

____

____

____

____

____

____

____

Teacher check:

Initials ____________ Date ____________

Review the material in this section to prepare for the Self Test. The Self Test will check your understanding of this section. Any items you miss on this test will show you what areas you will need to restudy in order to prepare for the unit test.

SCIENCE 507

LIFEPAC TEST

NAME ______________________

DATE ______________________

SCORE ______________________

SCIENCE 507: LIFEPAC TEST

Answer *true or false* (each answer, 2 points).

1. __________ Dinosaur tracks were found in Massachusetts.
2. __________ A cast fossil is one kind of petrified fossil.
3. __________ Ancient insects found in amber are original-remains fossils.
4. __________ Fossils are only found in a few places around the world.
5. __________ In *replacement*, the water replaces the original remains.
6. __________ Many fern fossils have been found.
7. __________ No fossils have been found of extinct animals.
8. __________ Dating of fossils by age is sometimes used to support theories of evolution.
9. __________ Comparisons of fossils is always possible.
10. __________ Fossils of soft-bodied animals are rarely found.
11. __________ A print fossil does not contain any of the original remains.
12. __________ Petrified tusks have been found.

Match these items (each answer, 3 points).

13. __________ mold fossil
14. __________ found in coal
15. __________ petrified fossils
16. __________ most common fossils
17. __________ mammoth fossil
18. __________ reconstruction
19. __________ incomplete remains
20. __________ "intelligent design"
21. __________ comparison
22. __________ method

a. rebuilding a skeleton
b. makes reading fossils hard
c. guided Creation and development of all things
d. a kind of print fossil
e. carbonized fossils
f. abundant at national park in Arizona
g. fungi
h. to decide or figure out
i. print fossils
j. found in Siberia
k. uses fossils and living things today
l. the way to do something

Write the letter for the correct answer on each line (each answer, 3 points).

23. Frozen mammoths have been found in ________ .
 a. Alaska b. Detroit c. Sicily
24. In the Gobi Desert, dinosaur ________ were discovered.
 a. feet b. bones and eggs c. tracks
25. Fossils may be formed by drying action in a process known as ________ .
 a. reconstruction b. hydration c. mummification
26. Limestone, sandstone, and ________ are common rocks where fossils are found.
 a. granite b. shoal c. shale
27. Christians can have a problem with identifying fossils by ________ .
 a. sight b. fossil type c. geologic age
28. Few ________ fossils have been found.
 a. seed-bearing plant
 b. fungi
 c. animal

Complete the lists (each answer, 4 points).

29. List three ways used to identify fossils:

a. ____________________

b. ____________________

c. ____________________

30. Name two kinds of print fossils.

a. ____________________

b. ____________________

Answer the questions (each answer, 4 points).

31. What is a fossil?

____

____

____

____

____

32. What is petrified wood?

____

____

____

____

____

____

SELF TEST 1

Answer *true* or *false* (each answer, 2 points).

1.01 __________ A paved parking lot is a good place to look for fossils.

1.02 __________ A cast fossil is one kind of carbonized fossil.

1.03 __________ Ancient insects preserved in amber are original-remains fossils.

1.04 __________ A print fossil does not contain any of the original remains.

1.05 __________ Dinosaur track fossils were found in Massachusetts.

1.06 __________ Minerals in water helped to form petrified fossils.

1.07 __________ Carbonized fossils are usually found in areas where coal has been formed.

1.08 __________ Fossils are only found in a few places around the world.

1.09 __________ Tar pits in Los Angeles contained many varieties of plant and animal fossils.

1.010 __________ Petrified tusks, bones, and teeth were found in Alaska.

1.011 __________ In *replacement*, the minerals in water totally replace the original hard part of the plant or animal.

Match these items (each answer, 2 points).

1.012	________	frozen mammoths	a.	print fossils
1.013	________	mold fossil	b.	original-remains fossils
1.014	________	bones in caves	c.	petrified fossils
1.015	________	found in coal	d.	carbonized fossils
1.016	________	permineralization		
1.017	________	tree rings can be seen		
1.018	________	most common fossils		
1.019	________	cast fossil		
1.020	________	preserved in amber		
1.021	________	skin stayed on some		

Write the correct answer on each line (each answer, 3 points).

1.022 Frozen mammoths have been found in ______________________.

a. Alaska b. Detroit c. Sicily

1.023 A large petrified wood deposit is found in ______________________.

a. Siberia b. Arizona c. Maryland

1.024 Some fossils are the ______________________ shells.

a. chemicals in b. shape of c. life in

1.025 Petrified fossils are formed by minerals through ______________________.

a. permineralization or replacement
b. replacement only
c. carbonization

1.026 In the Gobi Desert, dinosaur ______________________ were discovered.

a. eyes b. tongues c. eggs

1.027 Amber is hardened ______________________ material from cone-bearing trees.

a. gum-like b. bark-like c. needle-like

1.028 Animal and plant remains are fossilized with little or no change through a process known as ______________________.

a. carbonization b. photosynthesis c. mummification

1.029 An important thing to consider for those who hunt fossils is ______________________.

a. rain b. safety c. ease

Complete the following lists (each answer, 4 points).

1.030 List the four types of fossils.

a. ____________________

b. ____________________

c. ____________________

d. ____________________

1.031 List two kinds of fossil fuel.

a. ____________________

b. ____________________

Complete these items (each answer, 5 points).

1.032 Describe how a fossil might have been formed in sediment.

____

1.033 Explain how fossil hunters can be good stewards.

____

Teacher check: Initials ________

Score ________ Date ________

80/100

2. READING FOSSILS

Fossils are fun to find. You can have more fun with fossils if you know about fossil types. You can enjoy looking at fossils after you find them. They can tell us a great deal, too.

Almost like reading a book for information, you can *read fossils,* too! How can you *read* fossils? How can you find out what they are trying to tell us? This task is difficult when learning about fossils. Yet, it is very important to improve our understanding of God's creation. By reading fossils, we are learning from the physical record of the creation that God has given to us.

In this section of the LIFEPAC, you will learn about how fossils can be identified. You will explore difficulties in reading fossils. You will also consider judgments that can be made from fossils and fossil deposits.

Objectives

Review these objectives. When you have completed this section, you should be able to:

1. Identify different fossil types.
3. Describe fossil identification procedures.
4. Use fossil clues in making inferences.

Vocabulary

Study these new words. Learning the meanings of these words is a good study habit and will improve your understanding of this LIFEPAC.

accurate (ak′ yər it). To be careful; to make no mistakes.

boring (bôr′ ing). Changed into carbon.

conclusions (kən klü′ zhənz). Decisions or opinions reached through reason.

determine (di tėr′ mən). To decide or figure out.

evolution (ev′ ə lü′ shən). A process of change in a certain direction. It is also a name for several scientific *theories* about how life began and developed on the earth.

geological (jē′ ə loj′ ə kəl). Having to do with the science dealing with the layers of the earth; may include how rocks were formed and other features.

identification (īden′ tə fə kā′ shən). To make a decision about the name of something; telling of what something is.

incomplete (in kəm plēt′). Not finished; not done.

infer (in fėr′). To draw a conclusion through reason, by considering the known facts.

inferences (in′ fėr əns əz). The process of drawing a conclusion by logically considering the facts; a conclusion made through reason is an inference.

method (meth′ əd). The way to do something.

reconstruction (rē′ kən struk′ shən). To build or make again.

Pronunciation Key: h**a**t, **ā**ge, c**ã**re, f**ä**r; l**e**t, **ē**qual, t**ė**rm; **i**t, **ī**ce; h**o**t, **ō**pen, **ô**rder; **oi**l; **ou**t; c**u**p, p**u̇**t, r**ü**le; **ch**ild; lo**ng**; **th**in; /ŦH/ for **th**en; /zh/ for mea**s**ure; /u/ or /ə/ represents /a/ in **a**bout, /e/ in tak**e**n, /i/ in penc**i**l, /o/ in lem**o**n, and /u/ in circ**u**s.

Identification

When people first found animal bones at the La Brea Tar Pits in Los Angeles, they thought that these were just common bones. After many years, the bones were recognized as fossils. This kind of experience happened often in the past. People were not aware that they were finding fossils. Some of the fossils were destroyed or damaged. Others were lost. Many people did not know how to identify fossils. Fortunately, there is much more information about fossils and the identity of fossils today.

The **identification** of fossils can be done in many ways. You will now consider two rather simple ways to identify fossils: (1) by *fossil type* and (2) by *plant* or *animal type*. Let's consider each of these two ways to identify fossils.

Identity by fossil type. You have learned that there are several fossil types. You have also learned that certain fossil types are more likely to be found in some places than in others.

Fossils can be identified by their type. A mold fossil of a shell looks different than an original-remains fossil of a shell. Petrified wood does not appear the same as a cast fossil of wood. So some fossils can be classified by their fossil type just by sight.

Some fossils are harder to identify by type. Often, petrified bones look very much like the original bone. Someone who is not trained to tell the difference might be confused. A fossil expert would be able to **determine** the fossil type.

| Original-remains fossil

| Petrified fossil

| Carbonized fossil

| Cast fossil

| Mold fossil

Answer *true* or *false*.

2.1 __________ Some types of fossils look different from other fossil types.

2.2 __________ Some animal fossils do not look like fossils.

2.3 __________ Some fossils can be very hard to identify by type.

2.4 __________ A carbonized fossil of a fish skeleton would look very much like a mold fossil of a fish skeleton.

2.5 __________ To *determine* means to decide or figure out.

Identity by plant, animal, or living thing type. Another easy way to identify fossils is to determine the plant, animal, or living thing type to which they belong. Wood does not look like teeth. You can easily see a difference between a mold of a fish and the mold of a leaf. Fossils can be identified by the species to which the living thing belongs.

Those who identify fossils find it helpful if they know a great deal about plant and animal life. Since flowering plants today appear different from modern-day ferns, fossils of these two species could be classified as different types. Likewise, a bird is different from a reptile. So bird fossils would be unlike reptile fossils. However, single bones of these animals may look similar.

Animals in the same groups can be classified, too. For example, many sea animals have shells. Mollusks, such as snails and clams, could be grouped into different fossil identities. Their shapes are not alike.

You have learned about some animals with very soft bodies. Earthworms, flukes, and some insect larvae have no hard parts. Remains of these animals are seldom found as fossils. That is usually because their bodies were not hard enough to make an imprint in ancient sediments.

Complete this review activity. In Science LIFEPAC 502, you studied the *life cycles* of *plants, fungi,* and some *protists*. In Science LIFEPAC 503, you learned about the *life cycle of animals* and *animal-like protists*. Furthermore, you learned to classify these living things into some different groups. In the activities below, list two types of each group of living things. Refer to the appropriate LIFEPAC if you need help identifying these groups.

2.6 Seed-bearing plants:

a. ________________ b. ________________

2.7 Spore-bearing living things:

a. ________________ b. ________________

2.8 One-celled protists:

a. ________________ b. ________________

2.9 One-celled animal-like protists:

a. ________________ b. ________________

2.10 Egg-laying invertebrates:

a. ________________ b. ________________

c. ________________

2.11 Egg-laying vertebrates:

a. ________________ b. ________________

c. ________________

2.12 Live-bearing vertebrates:

a. ________________ b. ________________

Animals need plants for energy. Plants give off oxygen for animals to breathe. Plants are important for life to go on. God has blessed the earth with countless plants during the earth's history. The earth has been richly supplied with many plant species. Yet, the plant fossil record is less than that for animals. This is probably due to the fact that, in general, the plant bodies are much softer and more delicate than those of most types of animals. Fortunately, however, God has preserved some ancient plants as fossils so that we might learn more about His creation in the past.

Fossils from seed-bearing plants are common. They are often found in clay and other fine sediment. Pollen, seeds, cones, leaves, and stems can be identified as fossils. Flower fossils are very rare. However, a large deposit of tiny flower fossils was recently found in Sayreville, New Jersey. For most ancient flowers, their very soft parts were destroyed before they could become fossilized. Of course, petrified wood found in some places came from seed-bearing plants.

Many fern fossils have been located. The leaves of these spore-bearing plants were the plant parts fossilized most often. Few fungi fossils have been found. Perhaps the mold, mushroom, or toadstool bodies were crushed before they could be preserved.

God created many one-celled organisms, but only a few are in the fossil record. Some algae are preserved as fossils. However, fossils of certain algae types have not been discovered. These one-celled organisms were so delicate that they were unlikely to be preserved as fossils.

Complete these statements.

2.13 Petrified wood comes from ____________________-bearing plants.

2.14 There are many __________________________ organisms, but few fossils are found from that group.

2.15 There are few mushroom fossils because their bodies were too ____________________ to be preserved.

2.16 It seems that more fern ________________________ than other parts of the plant were fossilized.

2.17 When numbers are compared, ____________________ animal fossils have been found than those of plants.

2.18 Recently, fossils of tiny __________________ have been found in Sayreville, New Jersey.

The fossils of many animal species have been found. Some people think that fossils of far more animal species are still buried. Scientists attempt to classify animal fossils by body type; for example, fish fossils. Many of the animals that produced fossils are now extinct, so it is not always possible to find bodies of present-day animals that match those we find in fossils today.

Only a few fossils of one-celled animal-like organisms are common. They are protozoans that had attached to small shells. Most of them are on ocean floors. Some limestone deposits are mostly made up of these protozoan fossils.

The egg-laying invertebrates account for the largest variety of fossils. A great number of mollusks and shelled animals were formed into fossils. The strong, hard shells were harder to destroy. Also, they were water animals. This allowed them to be more easily deposited into sediments. They could be pushed into the soft mud, and their shells did not decay.

The soft-bodied worms were not as easily preserved as other invertebrates. Their fossils are rare. Some worm **borings** have been found. Insect fossils are rare, too. Fortunately, amber and other soft and sticky substances trapped ancient insects. They preserved the insects as original-remains fossils. However, insect bodies were not strong. They could easily be destroyed outside amber or other preservatives. So, an insect fossil find is important.

| Fish fossil

Skeletons of vertebrates are normal fossil finds. Print fossils of skeletons are common, too. Large and small fish were preserved in fossil form. Dinosaur fossils received much public notice. A wide variety of other reptile fossils are also known. Amphibians have also been identified as many fossils. They were fewer in number than the reptiles. Bird fossils are uncommon. Sea birds, divers, and larger birds that did not fly were more likely finds.

Mammal fossils are plentiful. Frozen mammoths, horse remains, rodent skeletons, and many other types of mammal fossils have been found. Mammals have a wide range of sizes and shapes. Fortunately, these features help them to be identified in fossils.

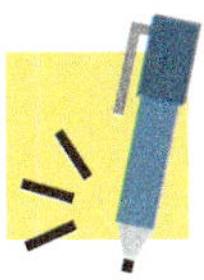

Answer *true* or *false*.

2.19 __________ Many varieties of protozoan fossils have been found.

2.20 __________ The bodies of mollusks were too soft, and few mollusk fossils were formed.

2.21 __________ Worm borings have been fossilized.

2.22 __________ Insect fossils are very common.

2.23 __________ Fossilized skeletons of mammals can be classified.

2.24 __________ Most reptile fossils are of dinosaurs.

2.25 __________ Most bird fossils seem to be those that could not fly and those that lived near water.

2.26 __________ A print fossil of a vertebrate is very rare.

Complete these activities.

2.27 Some plant and animal groups have difficult and interesting names. Your study so far has not included these terms. Choose one of the following names and complete the activities.

glyptodon	sanmiguelia	trilobite	ginko
aeger	dunbarella	unio	hesperonis
birch	eogyrinus	bothriolepis	belemnite
mesopsychopsis	stromatoporoid	rhynia	

a. Using reference books and/or the Internet, write a short article about one of these plants or animals (some of them are extinct).

b. Select a piece of drawing paper. Use the information you have found to sketch a picture of the plant or animal as it appeared when it was living. Write some information about the plant or animal on the picture. Display the picture in the room.

c. This activity is an optional addition to the picture. In one corner of the picture, sketch your idea of what a fossil from your plant or animal might look like.

Take this LIFEPAC and your article to be checked.

Teacher check:
Initials ______________ Date ______________

Identity by age. Another way to classify fossils is to identify the age in which the fossils may have been first deposited. However, using this **method** to identify fossils can be a problem for Christians. One reason is that the dating of fossils by age is sometimes used to support several theories of **evolution**.

| The earth has many layers of soil and rock

Some people use these theories of evolution to try to disprove the accounts of Creation and the Flood found in the Bible. Some of them even try to use science to prove that life did not begin with God as Creator. Instead, they say that life began as a natural, random, or accidental process over millions of years. They use the fossil record as one proof of their theories. Scientists know that the earth has many layers of soil and rock. Some people who support evolutionary theories reason that the fossils from the times longest ago would be in the lowest layers of soil and rock. They would classify fossils according to **geological** age of the soil and rock.

Other scientists would not use this method to identify fossils. Some of these scientists would be called *Creation* scientists. They would accept the Bible account of Creation and the Flood as true and accurate from a scientific standpoint. Most of them would also say that the earth is not millions of years old. They would say it is much younger, perhaps only several thousands of years old. Therefore, these Creation scientists say, the fossils could not belong to the geological ages identified by scientists who believe that the earth is millions—or even billions—of years old.

Creation scientists explain that the plant and animal life shown by fossils could have been on Earth at the same time. They say that the fossils would have been formed at the time of the Flood. They also explain that the different soil and rock layers found in the earth could have been formed as a result of the Flood. Many of them would say that the dating methods used to date ancient objects are not **accurate** or reliable. Creation scientists also point out that some "younger" fossils have been found in soil or rock layers *below* the "older" fossils.

In recent years, a number of scientists who are Christians have developed a theory called *Intelligent Design* to help explain Creation and the development of life on Earth. They point out that the complexity and intelligence built into DNA and the cells of living things cannot be accidental or random. Instead, these scientists say, it can be shown by scientific methods that an "intelligent design" guided the creation and development of all things that exist.

These scientists say that it was God who provided this "intelligent design." Some of these scientists would say that, although the earth and fossils might, indeed, be millions of years old, God created all that exists and guided the development of His creation.

Whom are we to believe? As you can see, scientists do not always agree. They have different explanations for the same thing. For example, scientists do not always agree on the effects certain chemicals or drugs have on the body. Explanations that scientists use to explain things can also change over time as new information becomes available.

As Christians, however, we believe that God has created everything that exists. We also believe that God has given us the Bible to show us the truth about His creation and how we are to live by that truth. We cannot accept evolutionary theories and explanations that would discount the existence of God or His creation of all that exists. We can be sure that God has given us both the Bible Record and the Physical Record of times long ago. This Physical Record includes fossils.

Write the correct answer on each line.

2.28 The methods of identifying fossils by age can be ____________ for Christians.

a. modern b. easy c. a problem

2.29 Some theories of ____________ hold that there is no God who began creation.

a. mathematics b. evolution c. photosynthesis

2.30 Some scientists attempt to classify fossils by ____________ age.

a. new b. geological c. old

2.31 Scientists who accept the Biblical account of Creation and the Flood are usually called ____________.

a. biologists b. Creation scientists c. evolutionists

2.32 Some scientists who are Christians have developed a theory called ____________ ____________ to explain the creation and development of life on earth.

a. Intelligent Design b. fossil formation c. relativity

2.33 Scientists do not always ____________ about the creation and development of life.

a. think b. agree c. talk

2.34 Christians ____________ accept evolutionary theories that discount the existence of God or His creation of all that exists.

a. can b. cannot c. sometimes

Complete this activity.

2.35 There has been much debate for more than a century about theories of evolution and the Biblical accounts of the Creation. Do some research with reference books, at the library, or with the help of the Internet to describe the different approaches to understanding how life developed on earth. Write a paper about this debate that will discuss the following questions:

a. When and how did the debate over theories of evolution begin?

b. What are some of the main points of Darwin's theory of evolution?

c. What do Creation scientists today say about some of the main problems with Darwin's theory of evolution? (Try to find at least 3 main problems.)

When you have written your paper, take it to your teacher to be checked.

Teacher check:

Initials ____________________ Date ____________________

Difficulties in Reading Fossils

Even though you find a fossil, you might have difficulty *reading* it. For example, it might be just part of a fossilized plant or animal. Much of the fossil remains might be missing. To get information from an **incomplete** fossil or remains could be a problem in identifying the fossil.

Making comparisons of fossils with living things today can be hard, too. What part is it? To what species did it belong? Could that piece be expected to come from other places? These questions can cause difficulty when reading fossils. Accurate fossil readings are not always possible. Let's discuss some more about problems that happen in fossil identification with *incomplete remains* and *comparisons* with living things today.

Incomplete remains. Only a few plants and animals were completely preserved as fossils. Most of them have parts missing. Skin, organs, flower petals, and other soft parts were usually not fossilized. Whole mammoths have been found; however, a complete dinosaur body has not been found. Complete bird, fish, plant, or worm bodies have not been found either.

Sometimes bits are so small or broken up that identity cannot be made. Using the small pieces for good information can be a hard task.

Any fossils could be broken or have missing parts. Some animals had fewer parts when they were alive. Their fossil parts may give more information. Animals with shells are examples. Other animals had many bones or teeth. Broken or missing parts may cause problems in reading those fossils.

Comparisons. How do we know that a certain fossil is from a fish? We must have data about fish first. Most fish skeletons have similar forms. Their bones can be compared. We try to read fossils by making comparisons. This can be done with any fossil.

It may seem easy to compare fossils to living things, but there are problems. What if the fossil animal is extinct? What if the bone looks like bones from many different animals? Identifying, or reading, the fossil can become very hard.

| Partial fossils make it hard to identify the original animal or plant.

Often fossils are found in places where they are expected. They can be compared with others nearby. Yet, people were surprised to find mammoths in Siberia. These animals did not compare with the kinds of animals expected there. Identification is even more difficult when a piece of a fossil or part of an animal is found in an unlikely place.

Write the correct answer on each line.

2.36 If a fossil is broken, it may be hard to ______________________ it.

a. see b. read c. pick

2.37 In fossil comparisons it helps to know about similar ______________________________ .

a. incomplete remains b. question c. living things

2.38 A difficulty in fossil comparisons is that the fossil may be from ______________________ plant or animal.

a. a large b. an old c. an extinct

2.39 One reason why most fossilized animals have incomplete remains is that parts like the ____________________ were not preserved.

a. skin b. teeth c. shells

2.40 Comparison using ____________________ can be very difficult

a. data b. questions c. broken pieces

2.41 Animal fossils can be ____________________ with other fossils nearby in order to identify them.

a. compared b. agree c. talk

Inferences

Each fossil has a story to tell. It is often the best physical evidence of life on earth long ago. Yet, that story is not often clear. No little note is on the fossil that says, "I am a skull of a horse." People must use the data they have to explain their new finds. Sometimes **inferences** can be made from small clues. If good inferences are made, **reconstruction** can take place.

Clues. You have learned of some clues that can be used to make inferences. Live animals give clues about fossils from the same species. The location of the fossil find can give clues when other fossils were found in the same area. Size and shape of parts help. Other bits of evidence give clues, too.

Even when the fossilized animal is thought to be extinct, the fossil part may be useful. Its size and shape can give clues to its environment. It may be related to other animals that have similar features.

Bones can give good clues. Animal forms can be explained from just fossil bones. Heavy or light bones would give clues about the animal's size and how it moved. A skull can tell of the animal's mouth. Then inferences about the animal's food can be made.

| Sabre tooth tiger skull

Casts and molds give good clues. Sometimes a complete skeleton or leaf is shown in the print. Comparisons can be made and inferences may be drawn about what life was like on the earth a long time ago. Clues about climate can be given. Warm weather plants and animal fossils have been found all over the world.

Complete this activity.

2.42 Look at this picture of a fossil. What are some clues you might use to make inferences? (Write only clues. Do not write inferences.)

a. ______________________________

b. ______________________________

c. ______________________________

d. ______________________________

e. ______________________________

Making conclusions. Clues give information so we can make **conclusions**. The clues might be thought of as data. We must decide what the clues mean. A conclusion is an attempt to bring meaning to data.

Conclusions are very useful. They help organize data. Yet, many conclusions in science may not be complete. Some of them may not be accurate. They should be viewed as the best decisions to be made for the present time. Conclusions can change when new data is produced. They may change when someone finds a new way to explain the data. Today we understand fossils in ways that people who lived long ago had not considered.

The scientist does not find it helpful to think of conclusions as *proof* of anything. Often people stop searching when they think they have the *right* answer. Being open to new information helps our knowledge to grow.

How can we best use clues to draw conclusions? How to use clues is a key question when dealing with fossils. Many fossils have been found. They were discovered in many places. They were preserved in different ways. People have several different beliefs about fossil development. The several ways conclusions are made becomes quite important.

Comparison using clues is a way to draw conclusions. If a shell fossil is found, it would be compared to animals with shells. Present-day shells that look most like the fossil might be a place to begin. Their species may be **inferred** from comparing them. Then conclusions may be made about the fossil from data on its species. Its life cycle might be inferred. Its foods could be determined. Its way of moving, its environment, and its way of giving birth may be concluded. Comparison to living animals would help us infer things about the fossil itself.

Conclusions can be made about past life on earth. Perhaps similar fossils are spread throughout the earth. From these facts scientists can infer that the original animals lived around the world. A variety of fossils from one deposit tell of the types of animals that lived in that area. With enough data, decisions are often more accurate.

Conclusions about the earth itself may be drawn. Rock types and layers where there are fossils tell us that something caused fossils to form. Things have happened to preserve different types of fossils. Conclusions about landforms, climate, and events can be made. Some scientists explain the Biblical Flood from fossil records.

Bones and teeth help us make conclusions. It is possible to infer what body part the bone is from by its shape. Bones have scars where muscles were connected. These scars can help decide where it was located in the body. The tooth types that were most used help us draw conclusions about food eaten.

We can make inferences about animal habits. Tracks and borings show how they moved. Body shape and size were important when animals developed eating and sleeping habits.

Sometimes comparison is not possible. For example, we know of no large dinosaur-like animals living today. Other data must be used to make conclusions. We infer that some of these animals were large. Dinosaur bones are often large. When they are pieced together, the result is a large animal. Inferences can be made through this reconstruction.

From a fossilized shark tooth, we can learn about the extinct Megalodon — enormous, prehistoric sharks.

Complete these activities.

2.43 Look back at activity 2.42. You listed five clues about the fossil. What are some conclusions you could make about these clues?

a. ____________________

b. ____________________

c. ____________________

d. ____________________

e. ____________________

2.44 Take this list to another person who has made conclusions for this activity. Compare conclusions. How were they different?

____

____

____

2.45 Why were they different?

____

____

____

Teacher check:

Initials ____________ Date ____________

Reconstruction. Much can be learned about past life when an animal is reconstructed from fossil parts. Inferences can be made after the reconstruction. Many things must be inferred while the parts are being joined.

In building the skeleton, the scientist places the bones in their original spots. Inferences are made from living animals that seem to be similar. Also, their position in the ground may give clues to how they fit together. Care must be taken not to mix bones from different animals. An unusual looking beast may result.

| Reconstructed skeleton and model

Often bones are missing. Inferences are drawn from live animals about these bones. Size, shape, and location are important. The scientist needs to allow space for missing bones or the skeleton will be less accurate. Sometimes missing bones are replaced by man-made bones.

Wire and screws are used to connect bones. Rods and wire support the skeleton in a lifelike position. Inferences from the bones help determine the animal form.

Another way to reconstruct fossils is to use the skeleton as a guide. A full-sized model is built. Inferences are used to help decide how the original animal looked. Muscles are filled in using bone-scar clues. Comparisons to similar living animals are made, too. Animals of certain types seem to have muscles and soft parts formed in similar ways. After the body is reconstructed, other parts are added. Skin, feathers, scales, or hair are placed as a result of inference. Color is also important.

Reconstructed skeletons or models are helpful. They give us ideas of size, shape, and function. They give us a better picture of life in the past than a pile of bones. You must remember that these models were built from inferences. These models are scientists' best conclusions. Yet, these reconstructions may not be completely accurate. New data may be found. Then changes in the skeletons or models need to be made.

Today, scientists also use computers to help make reconstructions of ancient animals. The use of computers is faster than building scale models. On computers, scientists can easily make changes as they investigate inferences from the fossil records. Fossils are important to help scientists make these reconstructions. We can use the information from reconstructions to learn more about God's creation, especially about times long ago.

Complete this activity.

2.46 Here is a drawing of a skeleton. Make some inferences about how the live animal may have looked. Use colored pencils to fill in the skeleton, creating features that reflect your inferences.

Teacher check:

Initials ____________________ Date ____________________

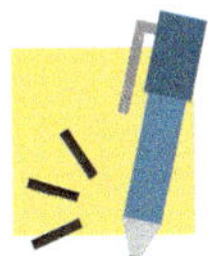

Complete these statements.

2.47 Scientists ______________________ skeletons by putting fossils together.

2.48 Missing bones can be replaced by __________________________ bones.

2.49 Sometimes _________________ are made that include skin and hair.

2.50 Often ______________________ must be drawn in order to rebuild skeletons from fossils.

2.51 Bone _________________ give clues about muscle sizes.

Complete this activity.

2.52 Suppose bones from two animals were found together. If people did not use data correctly, problems could develop during reconstruction. Draw a picture of a reconstructed animal where bones from two animals were used. Make the picture on another piece of paper. Display it in the classroom.

Teacher check:

Initials _____________________ Date ____________________

Before you take this last Self Test, you may want to do one or more of these self checks.

1. ________ Read the objectives. See if you can do them.
2. ________ Restudy the material related to any objectives that you cannot do.
3. ________ Use the **SQ3R** study procedure to review the material:
   a. **S**can the sections.
   b. **Q**uestion yourself.
   c. **R**ead to answer your questions.
   d. **R**ecite the answers to yourself.
   e. **R**eview areas you did not understand.
4. ________ Review all vocabulary, activities, and Self Tests, writing a correct answer for every wrong answer.

SELF TEST 2

Match these items (each answer, 3 points).

2.01 __________ fossil type
2.02 __________ determine
2.03 __________ seed-bearing plants
2.04 __________ flowers
2.05 __________ Creation scientist
2.06 __________ insects
2.07 __________ reconstruction
2.08 __________ incomplete remains
2.09 __________ clue
2.010 __________ comparison

a. fossils are rare
b. accepts the Bible account of Creation and the Flood
c. many found in amber
d. rebuilding a skeleton
e. one of the simple ways to identify fossils
f. to decide or figure out
g. fossils are common
h. makes reading fossils hard
i. absolute proof
j. believes in evolution
k. size and shape of fossil
l. uses fossil and living things today

Answer *true or false* (each answer, 2 points).

2.011 __________ Bones found at the La Brea Tar Pits in Los Angeles were immediately recognized as fossils.

2.012 __________ Fossils can be recognized by *fossil type* and by *plant or animal type*.

2.013 __________ Petrified bones rarely look like the original bones.

2.014 __________ Fossils of soft-bodied animals are rarely found.

2.015 __________ Many fern fossils have been located.

2.016 __________ A print fossil of a vertebrate is very rare.

2.017 __________ Dating of fossils by age is sometimes used to support theories of evolution.

2.018 __________ Some scientists say that an "intelligent design" guided the creation and development of all things.

2.019 __________ Incomplete remains of fossils are easy to identify.

2.020 __________ No fossils have been found of extinct animals.

2.021 __________ Comparisons of fossils are always possible.

Write the correct answer on each line (each answer, 3 points).

2.022 Few ______________________________ fossils have been found.
a. seed-bearing plant b. fungi c. animal

2.023 The largest variety of fossils comes from ______________________________ .
a. dinosaurs
b. flowers
c. egg-laying invertebrates

2.024 Scientists who support evolution usually classify fossils by __________________________ .
a. fossil type b. animal or plant type c. geological age

2.025 Creation scientists usually say that fossils were formed at the time of __________________________ .
a. the Flood b. Creation c. Abraham

2.026 If a fossil is broken, it may be hard to ________________________ .
a. see b. read c. pick

2.027 A way to reconstruct fossils is to use the _________________________ as a guide.
a. Bible b. skeleton c. rock layer

Complete this activity (each item, 5 points).

2.028 List the four types of fossils that you studied.
a. ____
b. ____
c. ____
d. ____

Answer these questions (each item, 5 points).

2.029 What are some problems that Creation scientists find with the conclusions of some evolutionists?

____

____

____

____

____

2.030 How can good inferences be made about fossils?

____

____

____

____

Teacher check: Initials ________

Score ________ Date ________

80/100

Before you take the LIFEPAC Test, you may want to do one or more of these self checks.

1. ________ Read the objectives. See if you can do them.
2. ________ Restudy the material related to any objectives that you cannot do.
3. ________ Use the **SQ3R** study procedure to review the material.
4. ________ Review activities, Self Tests, and LIFEPAC vocabulary words.
5. ________ Restudy areas of weakness indicated by the last Self Test.

SCIENCE 508

RECORDS IN ROCK: GEOLOGY

Author:
Barry G. Burrus, M.Div, M.A., B.S.

Editor:
Brian Ring

Illustrations:
Brian Ring

Media Credits:
Page 3: © Xavier Fargas, iStock, Thinkstock; **3, 13:** © bubaone, iStock, Thinkstock; **5:** © 1expert, iStock, Thinkstock; **8:** © Trifonenko, iStock, Thinkstock; **18:** © donvictorio, iStock, Thinkstock; **22:** © sittipong_srikanya, iStock, Thinkstock; **23:** © sonsam, iStock, Thinkstock; © nuinuii, iStock, Thinkstock; © Hemera Technologies, PhotoObjects.net, Thinkstock; **26:** © Andrey Burmakin, iStock, Thinkstock; **33:** © MartinM303, iStock, Thinkstock; **37:** © JohannaUnger, iStock, Thinkstock; **40:** © Jupiterimages, Photos.com, Thinkstock; **42:** © Dorling Kindersley, Thinkstock; **46:** © lukaves, iStock, Thinkstock; **48:** © anton_novik, iStock, Thinkstock; **53:** © PeterGinter, Digital Vision, Thinkstock.

All maps in this book © Image Resources, unless otherwise stated.

804 N. 2nd Ave. E.
Rock Rapids, IA 51246-1759

RECORDS IN ROCK: GEOLOGY

The earth is the home that God has created for us. It is a wonderful home. The earth has three main parts that we can normally see: the air around the earth, the waters upon the surface of the earth, and the solid part of the earth. This third part of the earth consists mainly of rock. It is very interesting to study. As you learned in the previous LIFEPAC®, fossils are found in the rocks of the earth. By studying the fossils found in the earth, we can learn much about God's creation and the physical record that He has given to us.

However, there are many other things about the solid part of the earth besides fossils that are interesting to study. For example, the rocks themselves are interesting. They come in many types, sizes, shapes, and colors. They can be fun to observe and collect. They can also help us learn more about God's creation and about the history of the earth.

In this LIFEPAC, you will learn more about the solid part of the earth. You will learn not only about the surface parts of the earth, but also about parts that lie deep within the earth. You will also learn about forces that change the solid parts of the earth and how the earth changes over time.

Objectives

Read these objectives. The objectives tell you what you will be able to do when you have successfully completed this LIFEPAC. Each section will list according to the numbers below what objectives will be met in that section. When you have finished this LIFEPAC, you should be able to:

1. Describe the earth's surface features.
2. Identify the main parts of the earth.
3. Describe the types of rock in the earth.
4. Describe the forces that change the earth's surface.
5. Tell how the surface of the earth is changing.

1. THE STRUCTURE OF THE EARTH

The earth is a very interesting part of God's creation to study. The study of the earth is called geology, and scientists who study the earth are called geologists. One of the things that *geologists* study is the *structure* of the earth. For example, they are interested in the size and shape of the earth. They also want to know more about the surface of the earth and what causes differences in the features of the earth's surface. They are also interested in what lies below the surface of the earth. All of these areas deal with the structure of the earth.

In this section of the LIFEPAC, you will learn more about the main features of the earth: its size, shape, and surface contours. You will also learn about the different layers of the earth and what lies below the surface of the earth. Finally, you will learn more about the kinds of rocks that are part of the surface of the earth and how to identify these rocks.

Objectives

Review these objectives. When you have completed this section, you should be able to:

1. Describe the earth's surface features.
2. Identify the main parts of the earth.
3. Describe the types of rock in the earth.

Vocabulary

Study these new words. Learning the meanings of these words is a good study habit and will improve your understanding of this LIFEPAC.

aggregates (ăg′ rĭ-gĭts). A clustered mass of individual particles held together. Rocks are aggregates of minerals.

cleavage (klē′ vj). The way in which something splits apart.

conglomerate (kən glom′ ər ət). Something made up of several different materials, such as a rock made up of different kinds of pebbles.

core (kôr). The central part of something. The part that is located at the center.

crust (krust). The outside rock layer that covers the earth.

dense (dens). Thickly or tightly packed together.

element (el′ə mənt). A basic substance made of atoms that are chemically alike.

equator (i kwā′ tər). An imaginary circle around the earth exactly halfway between the poles of the earth.

geology (jē ol′ə je). The study of the earth, both its physical parts and its history

granite (gran′ it). A very hard rock made of small particles of igneous rocks.

igneous (ig′ nē əs). Formed by great heat or actions of volcanoes.

landforms (land′ formz). The physical features of the earth. Mountains, valleys, and hills are landforms.

luster (lus′ tər). Degree of brightness of shine on a surface.

magma (mag′ mə). Melted material usually found deep inside the earth. It is made up of minerals.

mantle (man′ tl). The earth layer just below the crust.

metamorphic (met ə môr′ fik). Description of something that has changed form. A rock that has changed from one form to another.

minerals (mĭn′ ər-əls). The common solid materials found on Earth that make up rock. Their atoms are usually arranged in a regular pattern and form crystals.

pressure (presh′ ər). The force of weight pushing against or squeezing something.

sedimentary (sed ə men′ tər ē). Formed as materials settled to the bottom of a liquid.

silt (silt). Very fine mineral particles.

Note: *All vocabulary words in this LIFEPAC appear in* **boldface** *print the first time they are used. If you are unsure of the meaning when you are reading, study the definitions given.*

Pronunciation Key: h**a**t, **ā**ge, c**ã**re, f**ä**r; l**e**t, **ē**qual, t**ė**rm; **i**t, **ī**ce; h**o**t, **ō**pen, **ô**rder; **oi**l; **ou**t; c**u**p, p**u̇**t, r**ü**le; **ch**ild; lo**ng**; **th**in; /ŦH/ for **th**en; /zh/ for mea**s**ure; /u/ or /ə/ represents /a/ in **a**bout, /e/ in tak**e**n, /i/ in penc**i**l, /o/ in lem**o**n, and /u/ in circ**u**s.

Features of the Earth

Viewed from space, the earth appears as a large sphere (ball). It has vast patches of white clouds, blue oceans, and brown and green land areas. At the top of the earth is the North Pole, and the South Pole is near the bottom of the earth. The white areas surrounding the poles are large ice-covered landmasses. This view of the earth from space, showing its overall structure, is truly beautiful. Let's consider some details about the overall structure of the earth.

Size and shape. The earth is shaped like a large sphere. However, the earth is not perfectly round. It is slightly flattened at the poles. This means that the diameter of the earth measured from the North Pole to the South Pole is slightly less that the diameter across the middle of the earth at the **equator**. From pole to pole, the diameter of the earth is about 7,900 miles (12,714 kilometers). At the equator, the diameter of the earth is about 7,926 miles (12,756 kilometers). Therefore, the distance from pole to pole is 26 miles (42 kilometers) less than the diameter of the earth at the equator. This is why the earth is actually slightly flattened at the poles, although it may look perfectly round when viewed from far away in space.

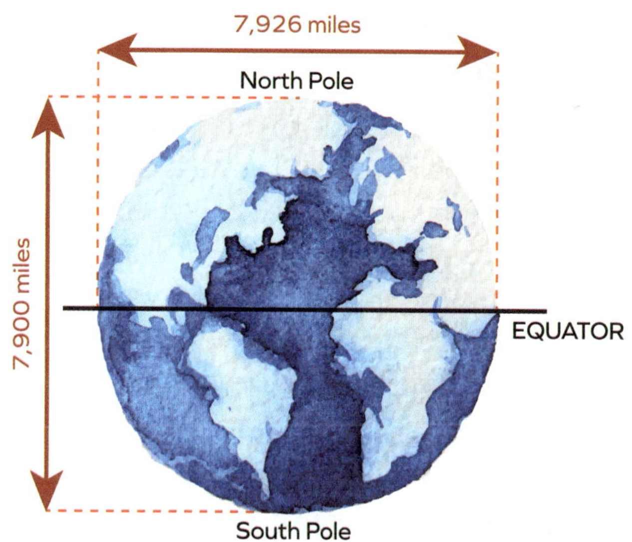

In the same way, the distance around the earth is shorter at the poles than at the equator. At the poles, the earth is 24,860 miles (40,008 kilometers) around. At the equator, it is slightly greater: 24,902 miles (40,075 kilometers) around. However, the equator is not actually the "fattest" part of the earth. The distance around the earth is greatest along a circle slightly south of the equator. Therefore, the earth's shape is a little like a pear, which has its fattest part just below its middle. But this bulge in the earth's shape is so small that the earth still looks like a perfectly round sphere when viewed from space.

| The Size and Shape of the Earth Vary Slightly. The "fattest" part of the earth from north to south is 24,860 miles around, and from east to west is 24,902.

It is interesting that long ago, some people thought that the world was flat. Unlike people today, they had no way to get above the surface of the earth to see it from afar. Furthermore, no one had traveled around the earth at that time to tell of its shape. People had no instrument to examine the shape of the earth. On the surface, the earth looked pretty flat, so it was easy to believe that the earth was flat.

| Today, an airplane can fly around the world in less than two days.

As time went on, people began to think of the earth as ball-shaped. They began to gain enough information to show that the earth was round. Finally, from 1519 to 1522, one of the five ships and crew that were in an expedition to the spice islands of South East Asia started by the explorer Ferdinand Magellan sailed completely around the world, proving the earth was round. After that, people began to think of the earth with new understanding.

The great size of the earth surprised most people. Most people were not aware of all the land areas of the world. They were also surprised by the large size of the oceans of the world, especially the Pacific Ocean. People thought the earth was smaller than it really was. Even Christopher Columbus believed the earth was smaller. When he reached America, he thought he had landed in India.

Today, it is common to think of a round earth. In fact, you have probably seen globes of the earth showing that the earth is a round sphere. You have probably also seen many pictures of the earth from space, showing that the earth is round. Most of the earth's surface has been explored today. All of this evidence makes it easy for us to accept that the earth is round.

In some ways today, people are beginning to think of the earth as "smaller." Even though the physical size of the earth is the same, it takes far less time to travel around the earth today. Magellan's original voyage around the earth took almost three years. Today, a jet airplane can travel around the world in less than two days. And astronauts can circle our earth in space in about 90 minutes! Furthermore, our modern communications allow us to be instantly in touch with people and events around the earth. For all of these reasons, we think of the earth as "smaller" today than it was a century or two ago.

Answer *true* or *false*.

1.1 __________ Viewed from space, the earth looks like a large sphere.

1.2 __________ The earth is slightly flattened at the poles.

1.3 __________ The distance around the earth is the same at the poles and at the equator.

1.4 __________ The diameter of the earth at the equator is about 7,926 miles.

1.5 __________ People long ago knew that the earth was round.

1.6 __________ A ship of Christopher Columbus was the first to sail around the earth.

1.7 __________ In some respects, people today view the earth as "smaller" than it was a century ago.

Landforms. When we view the earth near its surface, we see that the surface of the earth has many **landforms**. Hills, valleys, mountains, rivers, and plains are examples of different landforms. Other landforms include oceans, mesas, volcanoes, and gorges. Perhaps you have been on a mountain or seen an ocean. It is likely that you live near a lake or river. You live on and near various kinds of landforms.

People who climb mountains are often amazed by the great height of the peaks. Deep ocean floors are more than three and a half miles below the surface, with the deepest point—the Challenger Deep southwest of Guam—being almost seven miles down. It seems that the surface of the earth is not smooth at all. Landforms, such as the tallest mountains and the deepest parts of the ocean, can be very large when viewed close-up.

Globes are smooth. Pictures taken from outer space do not show great differences on the earth's surface. How can this be? The landforms are tiny when compared to the *total* earth surface. A piece of dust on a globe might compare to the highest mountain. A drop of water would be deeper than the deepest ocean. The earth is actually a smooth planet. Humans are so much smaller than landforms that small differences appear great to us.

Although the basic size and shape of the earth remain the same, the earth's landforms are constantly changing. Some changes happen slowly and others occur very suddenly. The changes in the earth's surface are important to us because they affect our lives and give us clues about the history of the earth.

508.A COMPARE AN ORANGE AND THE EARTH

You will view an orange at a distance and then close-up. Then you will compare what you see with landforms of the earth.

These supplies are needed:

orange
magnifying glass

Follow these directions carefully. Put a check in the box after each step is completed.

- ☐ 1. Place the orange on a table about 10 feet (3 meters) from you.
- ☐ 2. Sketch what you see in Figure 1. (Do not use the magnifying glass in this step.)
- ☐ 3. Bring the orange to your desk.
- ☐ 4. Observe it with the magnifying glass.
- ☐ 5. Sketch what you see in Figure 2.

| Figure 1

| Figure 2

Teacher check:

Initials ____________ Date ____________

Answer these questions.

1.8 List some likenesses in your observations. ______________________________

____

____

1.9 List some differences in your observations. ______________________________

____

____

1.10 Why were there differences in the two observations? ______________________________

____

____

1.11 Compare this observation with the earth and its landforms.

____

____

____

____

Complete this activity. Many landforms have names. For example, the Atlantic Ocean is a large body of water off the east coast of the United States. Write the names of famous landforms after the clues. You may use an atlas, other books, or the internet to help in this activity.

1.12 High, rocky range in Colorado. ______________________________

1.13 Deep river valley in northern Arizona. ______________________________

1.14 Large level area in central United States. ______________________________

1.15 Large body of water on the western border of Oregon. ______________________________

1.16 Long, wide river valley from Minnesota through Louisiana.

____

1.17 Body of water bordering Texas, Louisiana, Mississippi, Alabama, and Florida.

____

1.18 Honolulu is located on one of these landforms. ______________________________

1.19 Low mountains reaching from Georgia to Pennsylvania.

____

Use the Bible. Landforms are mentioned many times in the Bible. Sometimes the way they were formed is explained. Some verses compare certain landforms to something or someone else. Complete the following activities with a friend.

Friend's name ______________________________

1.20 Read Psalm 125:1–2. Discuss it together. How did the author use landforms to explain his ideas? ______________________________

____

____

1.21 Read Deuteronomy 11:10–12. What landforms did the new land have?

____

1.22 In Matthew 5:14, Christ used a landform to explain something important. What was He telling about? ______________________________

____

1.23 Find another Bible passage where a landform is used to help explain ideas.

Passage: ____________________

Tell how the landform helped explain the idea. ______________________________

____

____

____

Layers of the Earth

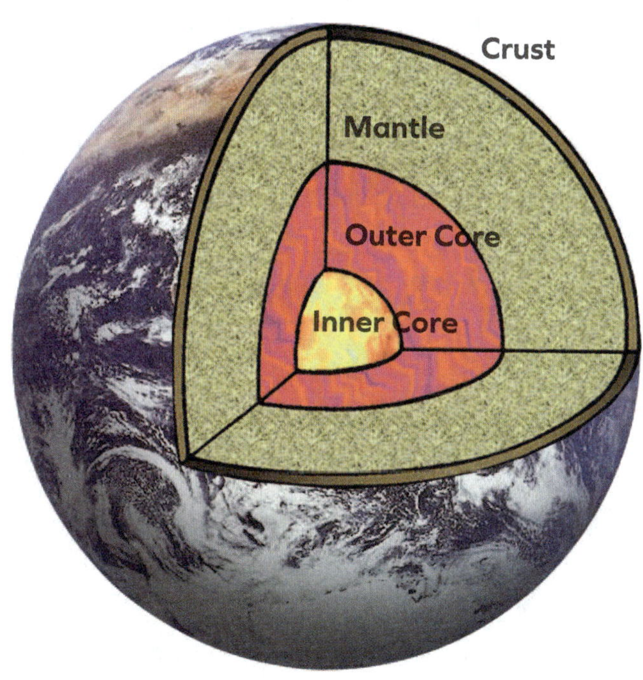

| Layers of the earth

The earth is round, large, and has landforms. These features help describe the earth, but what is the earth made of? Is it a solid sphere composed of water, soil, and rocks? The surface is important. The parts of the earth beneath the surface are also important.

Crust. The earth is made of several layers. The outer layer is known as the **crust**. Rocks and soil on the surface are part of the crust. Under the earth's land areas is a type of rock called **granite**. Granite is part of the crust layer. The crust is not the same depth all over the earth. The depth ranges from five to twenty miles (8 to thirty-two kilometers). The crust may seem like a deep layer to us. When compared to the whole earth, the crust is very thin. The crust supports all life on Earth.

The materials of the crust have less *mass* than the materials deeper in the earth. Scientists think that gravity pulls the heaviest material toward the center of the earth. The materials having less mass are left at the surface. Scientists also believe that the rocks of the crust are harder than the rocks deep in the earth.

Write the correct letter and answer on each line.

1.24 The crust could be as deep as thirty-two ______________________ thick.

a. kiloliters b. meters c. kilometers d. centimeters

1.25 The materials in the crust probably have less ________________ than those inside.

a. color b. mass c. strength d. height

1.26 The ____________________ of the earth is not part of its crust.

a. center b. surface c. water d. landforms

1.27 The Grand Canyon is a ______________________________ .

a. ocean b. volcano c. mountain d. landform

1.28 No ________________ exists below the crust.

a. life b. mass c. rock d. layers

Mantle. The layer below the crust is a thick layer of rock called the **mantle**. The mantle is much thicker than the crust. the mantle is thought to be about 1,800 miles (2,900 kilometers) deep.

No one has been inside the mantle because it is too far below the earth's surface. Scientists use special instruments to learn more about the earth's deeper layers. They have found that rocks in the mantle are very hot. The weight of the crust causes much **pressure** on the mantle. This pressure causes heat to build up. Some scientists also believe that chemical actions of certain rocks produce heat.

The rocks in the mantle are heavier than those in the crust, but they are not as hard. They are *not* connected in a solid mass. Filling the spaces between the rocks is a material called **magma**. Magma is a hot, melted material. Scientists believe the hot rocks of the mantle can shift. Sometimes the crust changes as a result of this movement.

Complete these statements.

1.29 The crust is ______________________________ than the mantle.

1.30 A hot material in the spaces between mantle rocks is ______________________________ .

1.31 The mantle's rocks are heated by ______________________________ on them.

1.32 Changes in the crust can happen if the mantle ______________________________ .

Complete this activity. Some words have several meanings. You have been using words that have more than one meaning. The dictionary tells how the meanings differ. Use the dictionary to help you find a different meaning for each of the following words. Then write a complete sentence using the new meaning.

1.33 mantle ______________________________

____

1.34 pressure ______________________________

____

1.35 gravity ______________________________

____

1.36 crust ______________________________

____

1.37 space ______________________________

____

1.38 mass ______________________________

____

Core. The earth's center is known as the **core**. It is surrounded by the mantle. The part of the core nearest the mantle is the *outer* core. At the very center of the earth is the *inner* core. Scientists believe the inner core is much different from the outer core.

The core is thought to be made of iron and nickel. This core material is probably melted in the outer core. Studies of the earth show that earthquakes send shock waves through the outer core. These waves move as if they were traveling through a thick, hot liquid. If the outer core is a melted mass, it would be able to flow slowly. Evidence shows that there are no solid rocks in the outer core. The outer layer of the core is about 1,400 miles (2.250 kilometers) thick.

The inner core is considered to be solid. Great pressure from the outer core, mantle, and crust seem to force the materials into a **dense** ball. The inner core is nearly 1,600 miles (2,600 kilometers) thick. Scientists believe the inner core is very hot—the temperature may be as high as 9,000 degrees Fahrenheit (5,000 degrees Celsius).

Match these items.

1.39 ________ very thin

1.40 ________ inner and outer

1.41 ________ at the surface

1.42 ________ between the center and surface

1.43 ________ earth's center

1.44 ________ melted iron and nickel

1.45 ________ magma flows between rocks

1.46 ________ soil and rocks usually are not melted

a. crust

b. mantle

c. core

Write a summary.

1.47 Sometimes it is important to write a summary of written items. To write a summary, you need to choose the most important ideas. Then write these ideas in a shortened form. Often a single paragraph can be used as a summary of several pages of a book.

In this activity, reread the section, "Layers of the Earth." Then write a paragraph as a summary for that section. (Write a first draft on another piece of paper before copying it into the LIFEPAC.)

____

____

____

____

____

____

____

____

____

____

____

____

____

____

____

____

____

____

Teacher check:

Initials ____________ Date ____________

Rocks on the Earth's Surface

The earth's crust is mostly made of rocks. They make up the hard, solid part of the earth. In most places, the rock of the earth is covered by a layer of soil. Trees, plants, and other living organisms usually grow in the soil, but sometimes they also grow on rock or in the cracks of rock. Soil itself is usually made up of tiny bits of rock combined with other organic materials from decayed plants and animals. Rock lies beneath the oceans, lakes, and rivers of the earth. Rock is also located under the polar icecaps.

Perhaps you have noticed as you travel on highways cut through the hills and mountains that there are different layers of rock exposed. Also, layers of rock can be observed where rivers have cut through rock to form canyons. The Grand Canyon in the United States is one of these places where many layers of rock are seen. There are also great cliffs of rock on seashores in places like Maine, or in countries like England and Norway. Even in some desert regions, rock cliffs and pinnacles of rock may be found among the vast stretches of sand.

| Layers of the Grand Canyon

What are rocks? Rocks are mostly **aggregates**, or combinations, of one or more **minerals**. The minerals in rock vary from rock to rock, producing different types of rock. You will learn more about the different types of rock later in this section of the LIFEPAC. However, the minerals themselves vary considerably. Before discussing the different types of rock, let's find out more about minerals.

Minerals. Every rock has minerals. Some rocks are made of several different types of minerals. There are about 3,000 different types of minerals, but only about 100 minerals are commonly found. Minerals include such common ones as rock salt and pencil "lead," and such rare minerals as gold, silver, and gems.

People who study minerals (*mineralogists*) use the term mineral to describe a substance that has four features. (1) A mineral is found in nature. Synthetic or man-made substances are not minerals. (2) A mineral has the same chemical makeup wherever it is found on the earth. Sand is not a mineral because samples of sand from different places on the earth have different chemical makeups. (3) The atoms of a mineral are arranged in a regular pattern and form solid units called *crystals*. Crystals have special forms and have flat sides called *faces*. Most crystals have six faces, but some have eight. There are six main kinds of crystals. (Some scientists split one of these kinds into two different ones, making a total of seven kinds of crystals.) (4) Almost all minerals are made up of substances that were never alive. The exceptions have undergone a transformation from living things to minerals over many years.

As you learned in a previous LIFEPAC of this Science series, living things contain minerals. When the living things die, the minerals can return to the earth. They are part of the *chemical cycle*. In Genesis 3:19, the Bible tells us, "...for dust thou art, and unto dust shalt thou return." A bone from a cow is not a mineral, but the cow's bone would contain minerals as part of it. If the bone decayed, the minerals in the bone would return to the earth.

Many minerals are actually **elements** that are found in nature. Copper is an element. Copper is also a mineral. The elements iron, tin, gold, silver, lead, and zinc are also minerals. All of these minerals can be found in rocks.

Laboratory tests can help identify the minerals contained in rocks. There are also other tests that can be used to identify minerals. Minerals' color, **luster**, streak, hardness, and **cleavage** are used to help identify them. (You will learn more about these characteristics of minerals later in this section of the LIFEPAC.)

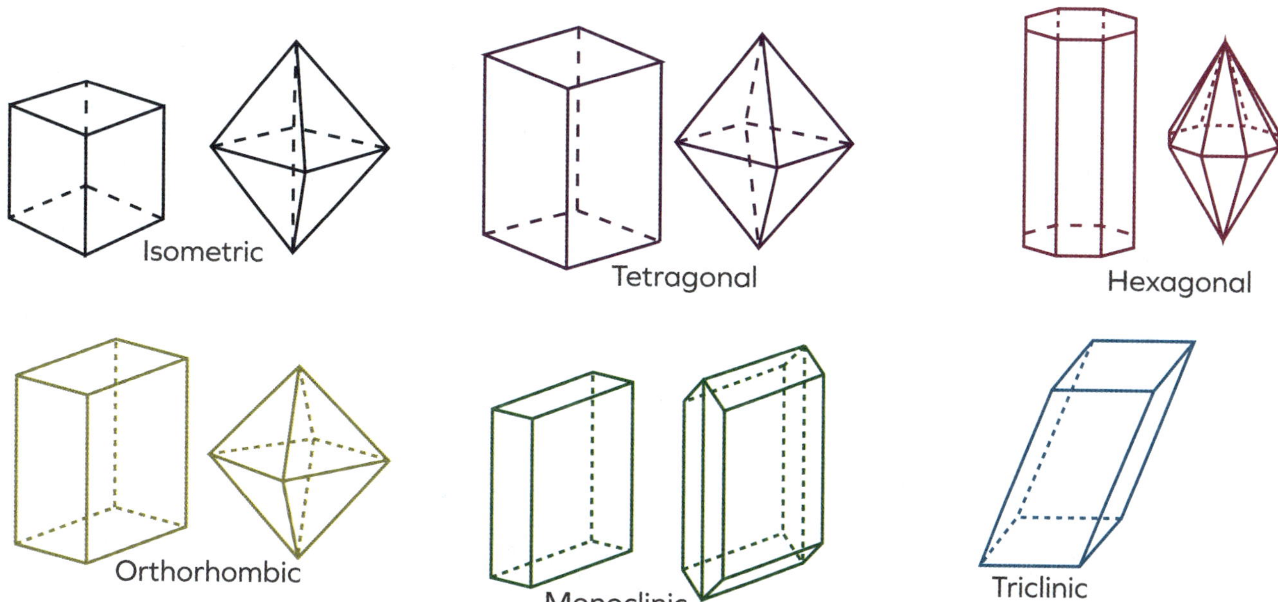

| Six main kinds of crystals

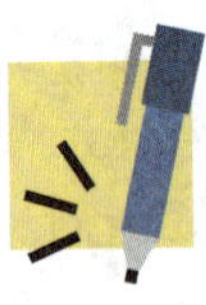

Complete this activity. Some of these items are minerals. Others are not minerals. Circle the items that are minerals. For those items that are not minerals, tell why they are not.

1.48 oak leaf ______________________________

1.49 aluminum ______________________________

1.50 nickel ______________________________

1.51 plastic bag ______________________________

1.52 pencil "lead" ______________________________

1.53 apple ______________________________

1.54 sand ______________________________

1.55 iron ______________________________

1.56 sulfur ______________________________

1.57 acorn ______________________________

Teacher check:

Initials ______________ Date ______________

508.B EXAMINE A MINERAL

You will examine a commonly found mineral—table salt—with a magnifying glass.

These supplies are needed:

small amount of table salt
colored paper
magnifying glass

Follow these directions carefully. Check the box when each step is completed.

- ☐ 1. Sprinkle a small amount of salt on the colored paper.
- ☐ 2. Use the magnifying glass to examine the salt.
- ☐ 3. Draw one piece of salt in the box at the side.

Teacher check:

Initials ____________ Date ____________

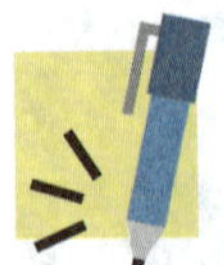

Write the correct letter and answer on each line.

1.58 The salt was shaped like a ______________________ .
a. crystal b. ball c. star d. sphere

1.59 It had ______________________ sides.
a. curved b. fat c. flat d. crooked

1.60 Each piece of salt had ______________________ sides.
a. six b. eight c. thirteen d. ten

1.61 Salt is ______________________, and is likely to be found in limestone.
a. found in nature b. man-made
c. made from living things d. dense

Kinds of rocks. All rocks are different. Shape and size are often the most obvious differences. Crystal structure and patterns also make them different. Some rocks contain different minerals than others. All rocks can be grouped into three main kinds of rocks. They are **sedimentary**, **igneous**, and **metamorphic**. The mature earth God created may have had each of these kinds in it. Since then, some rocks change and new ones form.

| Layers of sedimentary rock

Sedimentary. The sedimentary rocks are the most common rocks on the earth's surface. Sedimentary rocks are formed by natural forces. Sediment builds up on the earth. Rock chips, soil, **silt**, and other minerals form these sediments. Often water or air moves sediment to new areas. The sediments may pile up in low or protected places. After a while the pressure of water or other sediment forces the lower sediment together. Water carries natural cements through the sediments. This cement glues the sediment together and it hardens into rock.

Many of our sedimentary rocks were probably formed at the time of the Flood. The water that covered the whole earth probably carried many sediments that became rock. Today sedimentary rocks form very slowly.

| Conglomerate rock

Sedimentary rock is found in *layers*. The layers look like they were built one by one on top of another. Some of the layers appear very thin. Other layers seem very thick. Even within one small rock, layers can be seen.

Shale is a very common sedimentary rock made of very tiny grains of clay. Since the grains of clay are small and light, they are found under quiet water. *Sandstone* is similar to shale, but it contains larger grains of sand. Sandstone is found near shores and in valley floors. **Conglomerate** is a sedimentary rock formed when a mass of large pebbles are cemented together.

Limestone is formed from a dissolved mineral known as lime. Sometimes clays are mixed with lime. Most limestone is found in warm seawater or where a sea was once located. Coral and chalk are types of limestone.

Complete this activity.

1.62 Identify the "sediments" as either conglomerate, shale, or sandstone by writing the term under each box.

__________ __________ __________

Complete this activity.

1.63 The following rocks contain interesting elements. Instead of minerals, these elements are really other words we use for rock. The words are not written correctly. They are jumbled. Your task is to write them the correct way. Notice the beginning letter is in boldface (ck**r**o = rock).

a. note**s** ____________ b. beel**p**b ____________

c. lit**s** ____________ d. dan**s** ____________

e. re**b**loud ____________ f. var**g**el ____________

g. blobe**c** ____________

Teacher check:

Initials ____________ Date ____________

Igneous. Heat and pressure can force magma toward the earth's surface. When magma gets near enough to the surface to cool down, it forms igneous rock. Sometimes magma pours out onto the surface through volcanoes and cools rapidly. If gas is in the magma, it produces a light, bubbly igneous rock. Magma does not always reach the surface. Beneath the surface, it cools more slowly, forming large crystals. The slowest cooling magma forms the largest crystals. Two common igneous rocks are granite and basalt.

Metamorphic. A third kind of rock is the metamorphic rock. Heat and pressure can cause a rock to change from one form into another. The rock produced by the change is termed metamorphic. Both igneous and sedimentary rocks can be changed to metamorphic rock.

The change to a metamorphic rock is both a physical and chemical change. The physical change causes the rock to look different from before. You have learned that a chemical change causes a new material to form. A new rock that looks different and has different minerals is formed. Some more common metamorphic rocks include slate and marble. Each metamorphic rock comes from a certain type of rock. Marble was once limestone. Slate was formed from shale. Neither marble nor slate would come from any other rocks.

Match these items.

1.64 __________ slate
1.65 __________ from packed clay
1.66 __________ has bits of sand
1.67 __________ was once shale
1.68 __________ cooled magma
1.69 __________ quartz
1.70 __________ limestone
1.71 __________ chemical change is important
1.72 __________ settling is important
1.73 __________ chalk
1.74 __________ most of surface rocks
1.75 __________ granite
1.76 __________ can come from volcanoes
1.77 __________ conglomerate

a. sedimentary rock
b. igneous rock
c. metamorphic rock

Identifying rocks. People have identified rocks for many years. Certain rocks were considered precious. Other rocks were used for tools. Today we have many reasons to identify rocks. Jewelry is often made from rare rocks. Metals from rocks are used for many things. Useful items come from iron. Money and jewelry are made from gold and silver. Some people make stone fireplaces. Limestone is used by farmers to improve the soil. Identifying rocks is important to help us understand the earth's history.

How can you identify rocks? You have learned that rocks can be placed in three main groups. It is easy to learn which rocks fit in these groups, but it is difficult to be more detailed. The variety of rocks is great.

| Geologist examining luster of a rock

Several things can help identify rocks. Guidebooks and encyclopedias give clues and data about many rocks. Today, there is also a great amount of information about rocks, minerals, and gems on the internet. Information from all of these resources can be used to help identify rocks.

Knowledge of where rock deposits are located can also help in identifying rocks. Rocks can be seen in many places. Road cuts, mines, beaches, and deserts are common sites for rocks. Mountainsides, stream beds, and other landforms provide many different rocks. Sometimes these landforms are sources for information. Large areas may show layers or other deposits. Rocks that are too big to move can be identified and grouped also.

Finally, simple ways to *test* rocks can be used to identify them. There are five basic physical tests that are useful for rocks. One physical test for rocks is to check their *color*. Certain kinds of rocks always have a similar color. Other kinds of rock may vary in color.

Another test involves studying the rock's *luster*. *Luster* is how light reflects from the rocks' surfaces. Some rocks have a dull luster. A metal-like luster may be seen in other rocks.

A third test considers a rock's *streak*. The mark left by rubbing a rock against a very hard surface is called *streak*. The amount of the rock left on the hard surface and the color of the mark help identify the rock.

The *hardness* of a rock can also be tested. Any soft rock can be scratched by one that is harder. Diamond is the hardest rock. A diamond will scratch all other rocks. Hardness scales can be found in guidebooks or online.

The fifth simple test to help identify rocks is *cleavage*. Rocks have different ways of splitting or cracking known as *cleavage*. Certain rocks break into blocks. Some have a grain like surface when they split. Sometimes curved surfaces are left on rocks after they are broken. Still other rocks split into flat sheets.

Complete this list.

1.78 List five physical tests for identifying rocks.

a. ______________________________

b. ______________________________

c. ______________________________

d. ______________________________

e. ______________________________

Use the library or internet.

You will need a friend for this activity.

Friend's name ______________________________

The following list includes names of many rocks. Your partner and you should each choose one rock to learn about.

obsidian	marble	albite	steatite
mica	galena	pyrite	mercury
topaz	apatite	tufa	jasper
calcite	garnet	diopside	gneiss

My choice: ____________________ Friend's choice: ____________________

Use the library or internet to get as much information as you can about your rock. Then answer the following questions.

1.79 What are some important characteristics of your rock?

____

____

____

____

____

1.80 How is your rock similar to your partner's rock? ____________________

____

____

____

____

1.81 How is your rock different from your partner's rock? ____________________

____

____

____

____

Teacher check:

Initials ____________ Date ____________

Go on a rock hunt.

1.82 Here are several activities that will help you learn more about rocks. They can be done at home. (You may get someone there to help you.) Choose at least one of these things to do. Put a check next to the activity you choose. After you make your choice, take this page to your teacher. Discuss your decision with your teacher before starting to work. Select a goal for the completion date.

____________________ goal date ____________________ actual completion date

☐ 1. Choose a natural rock deposit near your home. It may be a roadcut, stream bed, cliff, or large rock. Draw a diagram of the deposit on poster paper. Include written explanations. Bring the poster to school for display.

☐ 2. Hunt for ten rocks you think are different kinds. Try the "hardness test" on your rocks. Hardness is a measure of how easy it is to scratch a mineral. Soft rocks can be scratched with your fingernail. Harder rocks are scratched by a steel knife, blade, or pin, and the hardest rocks resist scratching by all materials except diamond—the hardest mineral known to man. Place them in order from softest to hardest. Number them from one to ten. Glue these rocks to a piece of cardboard for display at school.

☐ 3. Find as many different kinds of rocks as possible. Use a guidebook or other resources to help you identify them. Using paper or cardboard, make a display of your rocks. Glue them to the display paper and write their names next to the rocks. You might also include an interesting fact about each rock. Find a place to display your project.

Teacher check:

Initials ____________________ Date ____________________

Review the material in this section to prepare for the Self Test. The Self Test will check your understanding of this section. Any items you miss on this test will show you what areas you will need to restudy in order to prepare for the unit test.

SELF TEST 1

Match these items (each answer, 3 points).

1.01 __________ a large sphere
1.02 __________ Magellan
1.03 __________ diameter at poles
1.04 __________ landforms
1.05 __________ mantle
1.06 __________ core
1.07 __________ minerals

a. hills, valleys, rivers, plains
b. layer below crust
c. at earth's center
d. earth viewed from space
e. commanded first ship to sail around earth
f. about 3,000 types
g. a common sedimentary rock
h. discovered America
i. 7,900 miles
j. 24,902 miles

Answer *true* or *false* (each answer, 2 points).

1.08 __________ People long ago thought the earth was flat.
1.09 __________ The earth is perfectly round at the poles.
1.10 __________ You would have to travel some distance to see a landform.
1.011 __________ Granite is part of the crust layer of the earth.
1.012 __________ The materials of the crust have less mass than materials deeper in the earth.
1.013 __________ The outer layer of the earth's core is about 1,400 miles.
1.014 __________ Sand is an example of a mineral.

SCIENCE 508

LIFEPAC TEST

NAME ____________________

DATE ____________________

SCORE ____________________

SCIENCE 508: LIFEPAC TEST

Answer *true or false* (each answer counts 2 points).

1. ____________ The earth's surface remains the same.
2. ____________ The earth is slightly flattened at the poles.
3. ____________ Weathering causes slow changes in the earth's surface.
4. ____________ The distance around the earth is greatest at the equator.
5. ____________ Folding is often the result of the movement of the inner earth.
6. ____________ Tidal waves can be caused by earthquakes.
7. ____________ The diameter of the earth at the poles is about 1,000 miles.
8. ____________ The deepest part of the ocean is about seven miles below the surface.
9. ____________ Erosion cannot be caused by gravity.
10. ____________ Growing plants can break rocks.

Match these items (each answer, 3 points).

11.	________ landforms		a.	igneous
12.	________ minerals		b.	move large quantities of soil
13.	________ Magellan		c.	land areas are squeezed together
14.	________ volcanoes		d.	at earth's center
15.	________ color		e.	shaped like a sphere
16.	________ glaciers		f.	hills, valleys, mountains, rivers
17.	________ floods		g.	led first ship around the earth
18.	________ Earth		h.	about 3,000 types
19.	________ folding		i.	produce lava
20.	________ core		j.	drag rocks underneath
21.	________ crystal		k.	physical test on rocks
			l.	sedimentary
			m.	regular structure of atoms

Label this diagram (each part, 3 points).

22. This diagram is a cross section of the earth. Write the correct name of the layer on the line.

a. ______________________________

b. ______________________________

c. ______________________________

d. ______________________________

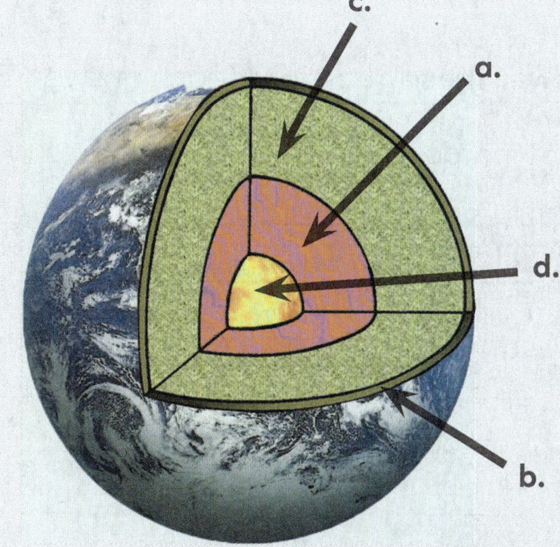

Write the correct letter and answer on the line (each answer, 3 points).

23. Astronauts in space can travel around the earth in about ________________ .

a. 90 minutes b. 12 hours c. 1 day d. 2 days

24. A common sedimentary rock made of tiny grains of clay is ________________ .

a. limestone b. slate c. shale d. granite

25. Sedimentary rocks were probably formed at ________________________ .

a. the time of the Flood b. mountain tops
c. great expense d. ancient forests

26. The San Andreas Fault is in ________________ .

a. Hawaii b. California c. Maryland d. New York

27. Forces that change landforms can also change ______________________ .

a. mountains b. energy c. living conditions d. oceans

Complete this activity (each answer, 2 points).

28. List five physical tests for identifying rocks.

a. ____
b. ____
c. ____
d. ____
e. ____

Answer these questions (each answer, 5 points).

29. How do landforms change as a result of earthquakes? ____________________
____
____
____
____

30. How do living conditions change as a result of erosion? ____________________
____
____
____
____

Draw this diagram (this answer, 5 points).

1.015 Draw a diagram of the earth. Label the main parts using these terms: *inner core, outer core, mantle, crust*.

Write the correct letter and answer on each line (each answer, 3 points).

1.016 ______________________ is a very common sedimentary rock made of tiny grains of clay.

a. Limestone b. Slate c. Shale d. Granite

1.017 Many sedimentary rocks were probably formed at the time of ______________________ .

a. Earth's creation b. the Flood

c. Adam d. Abraham

1.018 Marble rock was once ______________________ .

a. shale b. limestone c. granite d. wood

1.019 One physical test for rocks is to check their ______________________ .

a. size b. weight c. color d. flatness

1.020 Melted rock from a volcano is called ______________________ .

a. lava b. magma c. strength d. faulting

1.021 The earth's landforms are ______________________ .

a. always the same b. constantly changing

c. very rare d. mainly mountains

1.022 ________________ have special forms and have flat sides called *faces*.

a. Landforms
b. Crystals
c. Aggregates
d. Elements

Complete these activities (each answer, 3 points).

1.023 Name three landforms.

a. ________________
b. ________________
c. ________________

1.024 List five physical tests for identifying rocks.

a. ________________
b. ________________
c. ________________
d. ________________
e. ________________

Answer these questions (each answer, 5 points).

1.025 How are igneous rocks formed? ________________

____

____

____

1.026 How are metamorphic rocks formed? ________________

____

____

1.027 How are sedimentary rocks formed? ________________

____

____

Teacher check: Initials ________

Score ________ Date ________

80 / **100**

2. CHANGES IN THE EARTH

Volcanoes, earthquakes, floods, and glaciers are powerful natural forces. They can change the shape of the earth's surface. The changes may be sudden and far-reaching as at the time of the Flood. The earth also reshapes itself in less evident ways.

The earth changes every day. The mountain you climb changes. Beaches, hills, rivers, and deserts all change. Even the soil you walk on is different from the past. Changes in the earth's surface are not easy to see. A mountain looks the same from year to year. We can map land areas because their coastlines remain much the same. Over a long period of time, the shape of all landforms changes.

How do these changes take place? What powerful forces are at work? You have already learned about one kind of slow change—the formation of rocks. Another kind of change, the wearing away of soil and rock, also occurs.

Scientists have observed the forces that change the earth. They have set up experiments to test theories about the earth's changing surface. Their studies have given them a better understanding of how the earth changes. By looking at past changes, it is possible to predict how the earth might change in the future.

In this section you will learn about the forces that change the earth's surface. These forces are all part of God's creation that shape the earth today.

Objectives

Review these objectives. When you have completed this section, you should be able to:

4. Describe the forces that change the earth's surface.
5. Tell how the surface of the earth is changing.

Vocabulary

Study these new words. Learning the meanings of these words is a good study habit and will improve your understanding of this LIFEPAC.

channel (chan′ əl). A passage for water to flow through. The deepest part of a waterway.

contract (kon trakt′). Tighten or draw together.

delta (del′ tə). A deposit of soil and sand at the mouth of a river or stream.

erosion (i rō′ zhən). A wearing or washing away process that usually takes place slowly and regularly.

expand (ek spand′). To swell or increase in size.

explosion (ek splō′ zhən). A loud bursting noise caused by the blowing up of something.

faulting (fôl′ ting). The result of rock layers breaking or cracking, with part of the layer pushed down or up.

glacier (glā′ shər). A large ice mass formed from snow in cold areas or high mountains.

lava (lä və). Melted rock flowing from a volcano. Lava is made of materials from below the earth's crust, but includes some rocks and steam from the crust.

volcanic (vol kan′ ik). Caused by a volcano or like a volcano.

weathering (weth′ ər ing). The action of air, water, and temperature on the surface of the earth.

Pronunciation Key: h**a**t, **ā**ge, c**ã**re, f**ä**r; l**e**t, **ē**qual, t**ė**rm; **i**t, **ī**ce; h**o**t, **ō**pen, **ô**rder; **oi**l; **ou**t; c**u**p, p**u̇**t, r**ü**le; **ch**ild; lo**ng**; **th**in; /ŦH/ for **th**en; /zh/ for mea**s**ure; /u/ or /ə/ represents /a/ in **a**bout, /e/ in tak**e**n, /i/ in penc**i**l, /o/ in lem**o**n, and /u/ in circ**u**s.

Surface Forces

Many changes within the earth result from things that happen on the surface. The forces that cause these changes are at work all the time. They can cause slow changes or sudden, large changes.

Weathering. Change brought about by forces of weather is known as **weathering**. Wind, rain, and temperature are part of weather. The weather is a force in breaking down rocks. Weathering does not cause fast changes in the earth's surface.

Wind. The force of the *wind* can cause movement. You have seen it move kites and leaves. You may have seen dust blowing in the wind. When wind blows one thing into another, weathering can take place. For example, if sand is blown into large rocks, the large rocks will wear away in time.

Rain. Rain is another force that works slowly. The force of raindrops on certain rocks causes them to wear down. Rain also can cause a chemical change in some rocks. The water combines with the minerals in the rock to break it down.

| Wind erosion

Temperature. Have you seen rocks with natural cracks in them? Changing temperatures can cause a rock to crack. Each day when the sun shines on the rock, its surface is heated. Heat causes the surface to **expand** slightly. The inside of the rock does not heat up as fast as the outside of the rock. The inside of the rock stays cooler. At night, the surface cools down and **contracts**. The expanding and contracting weakens some places on the surface and a crack develops.

Temperature and water can be responsible for further splitting of rocks. If water gets into a crack in a rock and the temperature drops below the freezing point, the water will freeze and expand. After some time, the rock may be weak enough to break or chip into pieces.

Write the correct letter and answer on each line.

2.1 Weathering breaks down rock and is caused by ______________ forces.
a. armed
b. mantle
c. weather
d. strong

2.2 Wind wears down rocks by blowing ______________ them.
a. sand against
b. ice on
c. gently on
d. rocks toward

2.3 Raindrops can wear away the ______________ of rocks.
a. surface b. mantle c. outer core d. inner core

2.4 Rocks can be weathered by expanding and ______________.
a. contacting b. contracting c. compacting d. conducting

2.5 When ______________ forms in rock cracks, they may split wider.
a. dust b. wind c. rain d. ice

2.6 Weathering is usually a very ______________ process.
a. tiring b. dangerous c. slow d. rapid

Erosion. Often, part of the earth's surface is moved from one place to another. This movement is known as **erosion**. Erosion is one of the results of weathering. Gravity, wind, and water also cause erosion.

| Water and wind erosion

The wind moves soil and sand. Strong winds can cause sand or dust storms. Even mild wind can carry away soil. Wind erosion usually happens when plant life no longer holds the soil in place. Many deserts were formed by wind erosion.

Running water is a powerful moving force. Gravity pulls rainwater downward from higher parts of the earth. Sand and soil are carried with the water and deposited in low areas. Water can wash sand and soil into the river to be carried until the river slows down. The sand and soil may be taken to the end of the river to form a **delta**.

Movement of sand and soil is not the only way running water erodes the earth. Running water is also a cutting force. Valleys can be washed out by moving water. Rushing water can widen rivers or cut them deeper into the earth. The sand and rocks carried by running water can wear away the rocks beneath the river and at its edges.

Glaciers move along valleys cutting a wider and deeper channel.

Sometimes floods cause erosion. Floods carry soil from one place and deposit it in a different place. New river **channels** are sometimes carved by floods.

Glaciers. A glacier is a large moving mass of ice and snow. A glacier can be found in high mountains or other cold areas of the earth. As it moves, a glacier has an effect similar to water erosion.

Glaciers usually move through valleys. The valleys are left wider and deeper. Rocks are broken apart and jammed against each other. Under the weight of the moving ice and snow, rocks are ground down. Scratches and scrapes can easily be seen on rocks that have been in glaciers. Large glaciers can drag soil and rocks great distances.

As glaciers melt, the water carries rocks and soil away. Usually the smaller particles are moved the farthest downstream. Large hills can be formed from the materials deposited by melting glaciers.

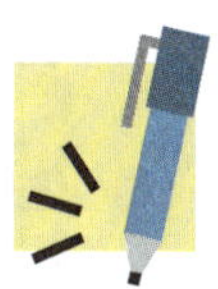

Complete these statements.

2.7 Moving air, moving water, and ______________________ can cause erosion.

2.8 The movement of the earth's surface by the wind, water, and glaciers is ______________________ .

2.9 Rock can be worn away by running ______________ .

2.10 Glaciers are located in a. ______________________ or b. ______________________ .

2.11 Wind can cause dust ______________________ that carry away soil.

2.12 Large rocks can be dragged along by ______________ .

508.C EROSION

View 508
EROSION: Grade 5
Science experiments
video

Using a mixture of soil, sand, and pebbles on an inclined board, you will see how water can cause erosion of the earth's surface.

These supplies are needed:

plastic tub or metal pan
mixture of soil, sand, large and small pebbles
glass of water
short board

Follow these directions carefully.. Put a check in the box after each step is completed.

☐ 1. Place the board inside the container. Have one end resting on the edge of the container, and the other end resting on the bottom (see the illustration below).

☐ 2. Place the mixture of soil, sand, and pebbles on the board.

☐ 3. Make a groove in the surface of the mixture from top to bottom. (Do not make the groove go all the way to the board.)

2.13 Explain what you think will happen if you pour water down the board.

____

____

☐ 4. Pour water slowly down the groove. (Use more water if needed.)

2.14 Sketch the results in the box.

Top View of Board

Side View of Board

2.15 What happened to the pebbles?

2.16 What happened to the sand?

2.17 What happened to the soil?

2.18 Compare your prediction with the actual results.

2.19 How does this experiment show what happens to soil and rocks in natural water erosion? ____

____

____

____

____

Teacher check:

Initials ____________________ Date ____________________

Living things. Weathering and erosion are nonliving forces of nature that can wear away rocks. Living things can also be involved in the process of wearing away rocks.

Have you ever seen a rock with plants growing from a crack? Is it possible for small trees or shrubs to grow from rock cracks?

You have learned that bean seeds swell when placed in water. Other seeds expand in water also. As seeds grow, their roots get larger and spread out. This growth can take place in cracks of rocks. As the roots grow larger, they force their way into the rock and enlarge the cracks.

Growing plants are a force in breaking down rocks. Plants grow slowly, and it may take years to break a rock apart. People can cause changes in the earth's surface. These changes can be slow or can happen in a very short time.

Every day you help make slow changes to the earth. Walking breaks up the soil and grinds rocks together, wearing down the earth. If you kick rocks or pick them up, you are moving them from one place to another. Perhaps you have stepped in mud and carried the wet soil on your feet to another place.

| The pioneers changed the landscape by making wagon tracks, *even through rocks*!

Some of the American pioneers made changes that helped erosion take place faster. The establishment of trails and the clearing of land for farming removed the protection that plants gave to prevent erosion. The early settlers also learned how to slow down erosion with new conservation methods because soil was important to them.

You can daily observe how humans change the earth. Direct changes to the earth involve building, farming, and road construction. To landscape around a house is one example of a change. Building roads is another way to change the earth's surface. When engineers build roads they carve out mountainsides and move whole hills. Sometimes river channels have to be moved, and ditches built beside the roads.

Farmers also cause changes. They dig wells and build dams for collecting water. Plowing the soil and removing the rocks from fields also change the surface.

Answer *true* or *false*.

2.20 __________ Plants often carry rocks from one place to another.

2.21 __________ Rocks can be split by plants.

2.22 __________ Humans take longer to change the earth's surface than plants take.

2.23 __________ People can move soil without knowing it.

2.24 __________ Walking can help wear away rocks.

2.25 __________ Building a road usually causes some change in the earth's surface.

2.26 __________ Humans can do things that will help erosion work faster.

Complete this observation activity.

2.27 In this activity, you will look for the ways humans have changed the earth's surface near your home or school. Go to the window of your classroom (or just outside the door of your home or school). List the ways people changed the earth's surface.

____

____

____

____

Compare your list with a friend's list.

Friend's name ________________________________

Discuss the lists. (You may add or subtract items.)

2.28 Select the most important change. ____________________

Why do you think it was the most important? ____________________

____

____

Teacher check:

Initials ____________________ Date ____________________

Forces from under the Surface

Surface forces can cause many changes in the earth, but additional changes come from underground forces. You have learned that deep inside the earth is movement. At times, the movement inside the earth causes great and sudden surface changes. Some forces work so slowly to change the earth that the results cannot be seen from day to day.

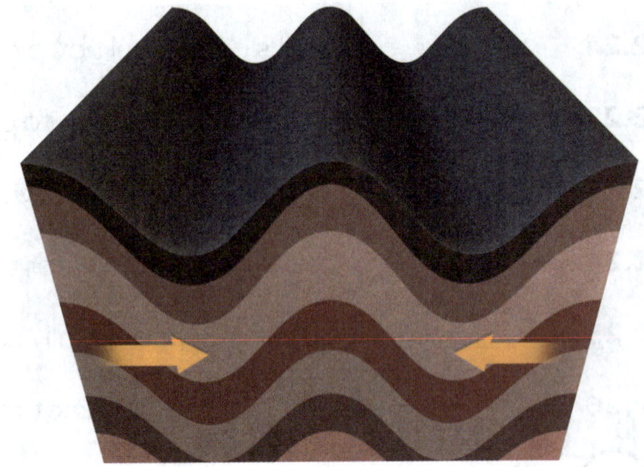

| Folding

Folding and faulting. The earth's crust is always in motion. In some places the crust is sinking while other areas of the crust are rising. Sometimes the underground motion causes a twisting of the land. Most of these movements occur over a period of many years. Scientific instruments can measure the motion. Scientists can observe the movement of the earth over a long period of time.

Folding is often the result of the movement of the inner earth. When some parts of the layered crust push against each other to bend and twist the rock layers, the result is a folded layer of rock. Some parts are pushed up or forced downward. Layers of rock overlap each other. Sometimes fresh roadcuts show how layers have folded.

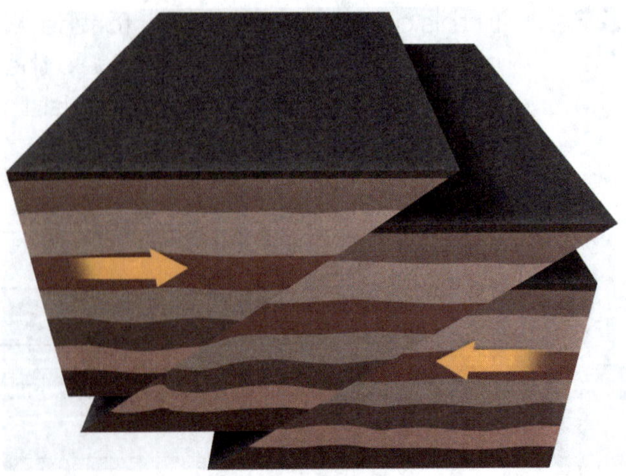

| Faulting

Usually **faulting** works along with folding. A *fault* is a crack in the layers of the earth's crust. The cracked layers slip by each other to cause a raising of the land. Faulting can result from the pushing or pulling of folding. Scientists also believe that magma may cause faults. As magma moves in the mantle, pressure could crack the crust and push layers up. The stretching would break them apart. Some faults reach deep into the earth and stretch long distances across the surface. The famous San Andreas Fault in California stretches for about 800 miles (1,280 kilometers) across the state.

| The San Andreas Fault in California

Write the correct letter and answer on each line.

2.29 The crust is always ______________________ slowly.

a. molting b. moving c. molding d. mending

2.30 A crack or split in rock layers is ______________________ .

a. a fault b. a mistake c. a fold d. a glacier

2.31 Sometimes folding forces layers to ______________________ .

a. bend b. age c. melt d. harden

2.32 Some scientists believe that ______________________ can cause enough pressure on landmasses for folding and faulting.

a. minerals b. moving magma

c. freezing d. erosion

2.33 The type of rock found in layers is ______________________ rock.

a. sedimentary b. igneous c. metamorphic d. magma

Use the library or internet.

2.34 Look up the location of some other well-known fault lines in the United States. See 1.79 and2.49. Select three of them and draw their locations on a map of the United States.

Teacher check:

Initials ______________________ Date ______________________

Complete this activity. Some words have several meanings. You have been using words that have more than one meaning. The dictionary tells how the meanings differ. Use the dictionary to help you find a different meaning for each of the following words. Then write a complete sentence using the new meaning.

2.35 contract ______________________________

____

____

2.36 channel ______________________________

____

____

2.37 fault ______________________________

____

____

2.38 crack ______________________________

____

____

2.39 change ______________________________

____

____

Teacher check:

Initials ____________ Date ____________

Earthquakes. An earthquake is a powerful force. The whole surface shakes at an earthquake site. Rumbling sounds can be heard. Cracks form in the ground. The land on each side of the crack moves in different directions. An earthquake may last only a few minutes, or the action could continue for several weeks. Earthquakes can cause great damage in cities or towns.

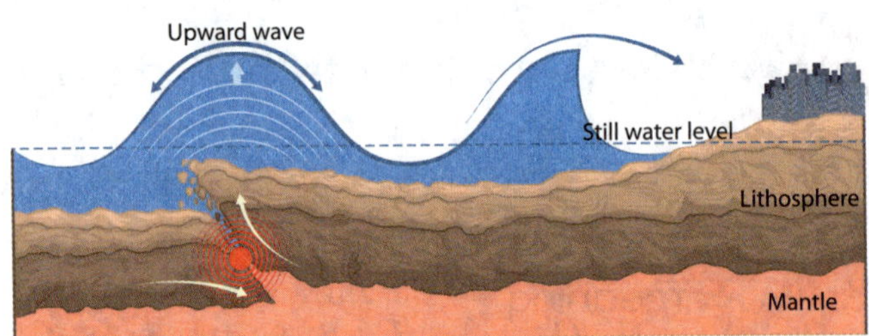

| An earthquake on the ocean floor can cause a tsunami (tidal wave).

In addition to shaking or cracking the surface, larger earthquakes often cause other problems. Landslides have resulted from earthquakes. *Tidal waves* are formed by the movements of underwater earthquakes. (A tidal wave, sometimes called a tsunami, is a large, destructive ocean wave.)

Scientists do not agree about the causes of earthquakes. They learn about them through the use of sensitive instruments. Their instruments have shown that the shock waves caused by earthquakes reach through the mantle and core of the earth.

Earthquakes usually occur along fault lines. Some of the largest earthquakes have been where deep faults are located. Sometimes the moving blocks of rock catch on each other during an earthquake. Pressure and slow crust movement cause the blocks to break loose again later. Then there is another earthquake.

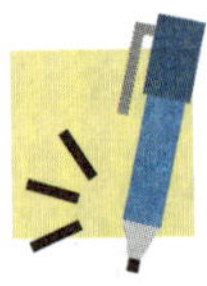

Answer *true* or *false*.

2.40 __________ Some earthquakes have caused landslides.

2.41 __________ Scientists are sure about the causes of earthquakes.

2.42 __________ Earthquakes usually happen at fault lines.

2.43 __________ Scientific instruments have shown that shock waves from earthquakes move long distances.

2.44 __________ Earthquakes can cause wide cracks in the earth's surface.

Use the Bible.

Acts 16:25-34 tells how Paul and Silas experienced an earthquake. Read these verses. Then answer the following questions.

2.45 Where were Paul and Silas? ______________________

2.46 What happened during the earthquake? ______________________

2.47 How did other people respond to that earthquake? ______________________

2.48 How did Paul and Silas make good use of the earthquake experience?

Volcanoes. Magma usually stays below the earth's crust under great pressure. Sometimes this very hot material can slowly flow into cracks of the crust.

The hot magma can break through layers of rock, or it can squeeze between the layers. The magma may cool off in the crust before it reaches the surface. Igneous rocks such as granite are formed from magma. Upper layers of rock may be pushed upward. Ridges of igneous rock are formed.

Volcanic activity occurs when a passage forms from the mantle to the earth's surface. **Lava** flows out onto the surface. This activity can result in a raging volcano. As the hot material bursts through the crust, rocks dissolve. Water forms steam. Part of the magma becomes gases. Lava, steam, rocks, and gases pour out over the surface with great rumbling sounds. The lava appears to glow with heat, but it is not on fire. In time the lava cools. More lava flows out over the cooler lava. A cone shape forms.

Lava does not always flow easily. Sometimes it cools down before it reaches the surface. Flow becomes slower. Pressure builds up causing **explosions**, and the lava blasts out over the surface.

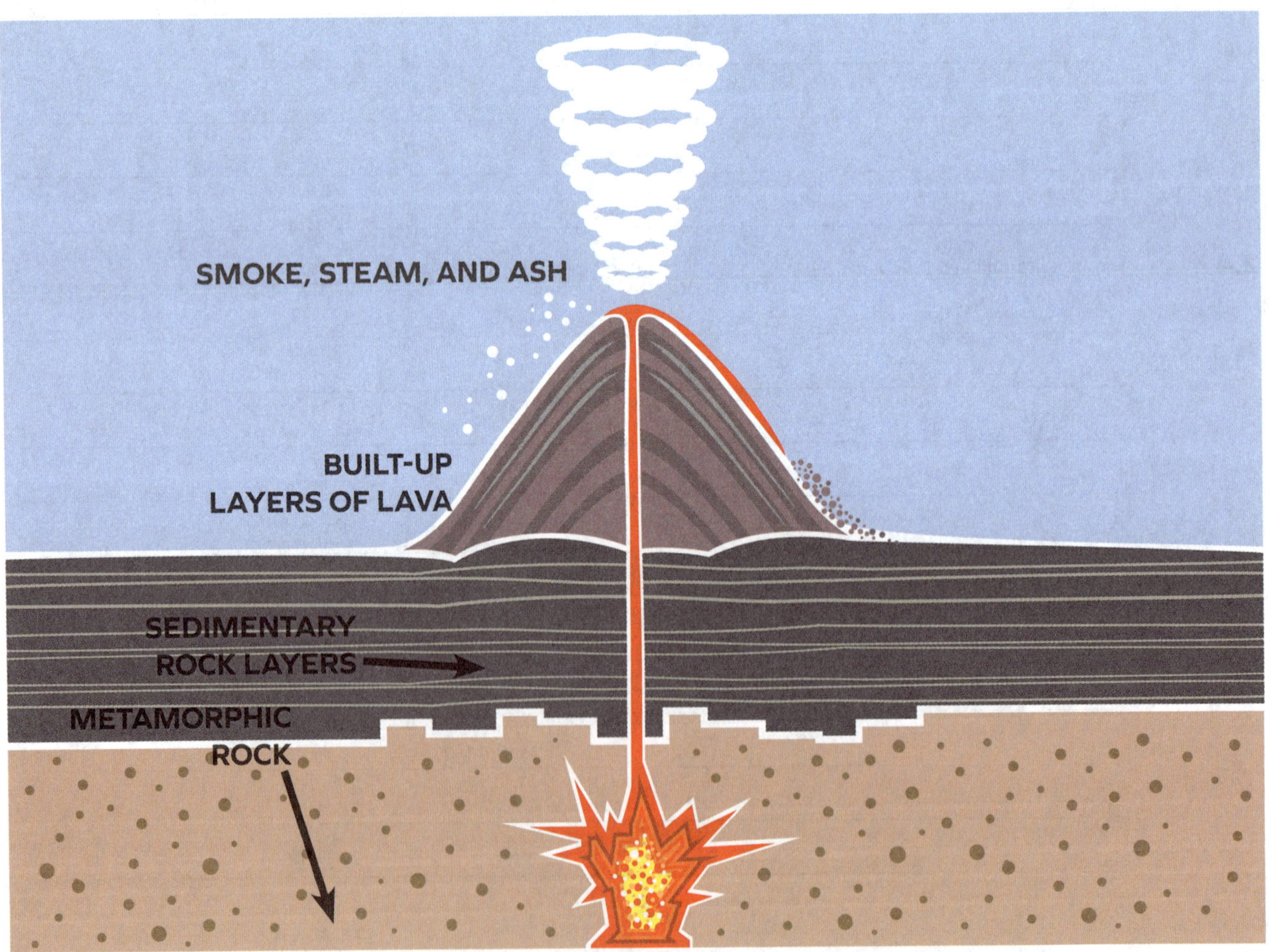

| Volcanic Cone

Use the library or internet. People have been interested in volcanoes for many years. Some volcanoes have been named. Other volcanoes formed in mountains or areas that already had names. The following list of names include some sites of famous volcanoes. Use the library or internet to learn more about these volcanoes.

Vesuvius	Pompeii	Lassen Peak, California
Etna	Krakatoa	Paricutin, Mexico
Fujiyama	Cotopaxi, Ecuador	Mauna Loa, Hawaii
Mount St. Helens, Washington		

2.49 Choose one of these volcano sites to learn about.

My choice is ______________________________.

After reading as much as you can, write a short summary of the information you found. Take this page and your summary to your teacher or parent for a check.

____
____
____
____
____
____
____
____
____
____
____
____
____

Teacher check:

Initials ____________________ Date ____________________

Write the correct answer on each line.

2.50 The ______________________________ flows out of a volcano.

a. magma b. mantle c. lava d. silt

2.51 Water can form ______________________________ inside a volcano.

a. rocks b. cones c. steam d. ice

2.52 Sometimes ______________________________ occur in volcanoes.

a. explosions b. fires c. ridges d. cleavage

2.53 Hot magma may ______________________________ itself between layers.

a. form b. melt c. dissolve d. squeeze

2.54 Lava may be ______________________________ .

a. sedimentary b. hot or cold c. ageless d. contracted

Results of Forces

Natural forces on the surface change the earth's features. Forces from within the earth are always at work to cause changes. What are the results of these changes? How are landforms and conditions affected by the changes? We will explore these questions in the remainder of this section of the LIFEPAC.

Changing landforms. The forces that change the earth help develop landforms. Some forces build and other forces tear down landforms.

Weathering is a force that wears away landforms. The weathering process breaks landforms into smaller units. Effects of heat, cold, and wind all cause mountain rocks to break down. Rain may soak into clay to cause landslides. Slowly mountains wear away.

Erosion carries on the tearing-down process. Materials from the higher landforms are eroded away. Deep channels are cut into the land. Erosion also builds. The water carries sand and soil toward the sea. As the water slows, it deposits its load. Sand and soil settle to the sea floor. Slowly it builds up, and new areas of land form.

Whole landforms are moved by *glaciers*. Valleys are widened and deepened. New hills and ponds are formed. The land appears completely changed.

Plants crack open rocks. Plants break down landforms, but they are also important in slowing erosion. Roots hold soil in place. Stems and roots slow down water as it runs down hills during rains.

People make decisions that produce changes. They can decide to use methods for keeping soil in place. Sometimes builders move complete landforms. When new highways are built, hills can be removed. Low areas are built up. Dams are constructed to hold back water.

| Several forces at work on landforms

Some scientists believe that present-day mountains were under deep water at one time. This was true at the time of the Flood. Many sediments were deposited, and soon after that many mountains were probably formed by the folding process. Pressure from the sides and below helped thrust huge masses of land upward. Faults in the layers of rock also caused some big sections to tip. One side of a faulted mountain is a long slope. The other side of the mountain has jagged features. Other land areas were also formed by faulting.

We think earthquakes are a tearing-down force. Trees, buildings, animals, and even people can be lost through earthquakes. Pressure from the inner earth may force land upward along fault lines. Some earthquakes have caused land surfaces to tilt. Lakes can be formed in this way.

When hot magma squeezes between rock layers, landforms can change. Hills and mountains have been formed from moving magma. Volcanoes have been important in making landforms. Cone structures can be seen from recent volcanoes. Scientists have learned that volcanic activity occurred over much of the earth. Volcanoes had much to do with shaping the earth's surface.

None of these natural forces works alone. While some are building, others are tearing down the same landforms. You can see erosion breaking down mountains and filling rivers with the soil. Landforms keep changing.

All of these changes are rather small and short term. Some forces have caused great changes. Earthquakes cause big changes to the land and the people who live in the affected area. Homes are destroyed. Land is changed. Sometimes cities or farming areas are covered by water from a newly formed lake.

The Flood caused many landforms. How quickly did our landforms develop? Today many scientists use observations to make estimates. They say that it took millions of years to build the earth as we know it. Other scientists disagree. These are Creation scientists. They believe that the great Flood caused many of the present landforms. The Flood was very powerful. The Flood set forces in motion that probably carved many of the features we see today. The landforms would not be millions of years old. They would be younger than that—merely thousands of years old. God has used various forces throughout history to shape the landforms that we see today.

Match these items.

2.55	________ bending a rock layer	a.	weathering
2.56	________ magma pushes between rock layers up onto the surface	b.	erosion
2.57	________ carries material someplace else	c.	people
2.58	________ mostly a wearing down process	d.	folding
2.59	________ causes sections of the crust to tip	e.	faulting
2.60	________ soil and sand build up in low places	f.	volcanic activity
2.61	________ can make decisions to tear down or build up		
2.62	________ leaves cone-shaped forms		

Use the Bible. Bible authors often used the words rock or stone to help explain their ideas. They used the words to compare one thing to another. Explain what they were comparing in these passages.

2.63 Psalm 42:9 ____

____

____

____

2.64 Proverbs 17:8 ____

____

____

____

2.65 1 Samuel 2:2 ____

____

____

____

2.66 Jeremiah 5:3 ______________________________

____

____

____

2.67 Matthew 7:25 ______________________________

____

____

____

2.68 Job 41:24 ______________________________

____

____

____

Changing living conditions. The same forces that change landforms can also change living conditions. Life is affected in many ways by changed landforms.

At times, wind and erosion forces carry good soil away. Without good soil plants do not grow well. Crops are poorer. Less food is produced. When the soil is improved, chances for producing more food are increased. Sometimes desert areas can grow better crops through irrigation. If men use good farming methods, erosion can be prevented.

| Lack of rain causes drought, and land can't produce crops.

Decisions about use of the land are important. Some methods of cutting lumber and farming encourage erosion. Stripping every tree off a hillside increases erosion. Leaving a few trees to hold down the soil will prevent erosion. New farming methods have been developed to preserve the soil. By tilling the soil and planting the crops at right angles to the flow of water, erosion is prevented.

Flooding is a major problem in some areas because it moves large quantities of soil. Scientists know that much of our dry land was under water at one time. When the earth's crust shifted, forming mountains and oceans, big changes came to the places where the water animals lived. They could no longer live in the same places.

Certainly the earth continues to change in many ways. God created the earth with the power to change. He designed the earth as a changing place.

Answer *true* or *false*.

2.69 __________ Most plants can grow better when soil is carried away by erosion.

2.70 __________ Human decisions about controlling erosion have very little effect on living conditions.

2.71 __________ Earthquakes can greatly change living conditions where they take place.

2.72 __________ Changes in landforms that affect large areas do not really affect living conditions.

2.73 __________ Some farming practices encourage erosion.

This exercise will help you use the vocabulary words. Each of the following sentences has a word or words underlined. Replace the underlined word with a vocabulary word. Write the word on the line.

2.74 ____________________ The <u>great sheet of ice</u> moves slowly down the mountain.

2.75 ____________________ The <u>hot volcanic material</u> flowed over the surface.

2.76 ____________________ Great <u>loud noises</u> rocked the countryside.

2.77 ____________________ The soil was lost by <u>washing away</u>.

2.78 ____________________ <u>Cracking</u> of rock layers can cause earthquakes.

2.79 ____________________ The ice began to <u>push out</u> against the rock until the rock broke.

Before you take this last Self Test, you may want to do one or more of these self checks.

1. ________ Read the objectives. See if you can do them.
2. ________ Restudy the material related to any objectives that you cannot do.
3. ________ Use the **SQ3R** study procedure to review the material:
   a. **S**can the sections.
   b. **Q**uestion yourself.
   c. **R**ead to answer your questions.
   d. **R**ecite the answers to yourself.
   e. **R**eview areas you did not understand.
4. ________ Review all vocabulary, activities, and Self Tests, writing a correct answer for every wrong answer.

SELF TEST 2

Match these items (each answer, 3 points).

2.01	________	erosion prevented	a.	volcanoes
2.02	________	moves large soil quantities	b.	folding
2.03	________	earth sometimes splits apart	c.	living things
2.04	________	lava flows	d.	river
2.05	________	land areas are squeezed together	e.	flooding
2.06	________	drag rocks underneath	f.	good farming methods
2.07	________	rock layers develop cracks	g.	earthquakes
2.08	________	wind blows sand against rocks	h.	minerals
2.09	________	plants split rocks	i.	streak
2.010	________	landform	j.	glaciers
			k.	faulting
			l.	weathering

Answer *true* or *false* (each answer, 2 points).

2.011 ________ The earth changes every day.

2.012 ________ Weathering causes fast changes in the earth's surface.

2.013 ________ The force of raindrops on certain rocks causes them to wear down.

2.014 ________ Gravity, moving air, and water cause erosion.

2.015 ________ A glacier is the hard rock under the poles' icecaps.

2.016 ________ Growing plants cannot break rocks.

2.017 ________ Folding is often the result of the movement of the inner earth.

2.018 ________ Faulting usually works along with folding.

2.019 ________ Earthquakes never cause tidal waves.

2.020 ________ When hot magma squeezes between rock layers, landforms can change.

Write the correct answer on the line (each answer, 3 points).

2.021 The same forces that change landforms can also change ________________.

a. mountains b. energy c. living conditions d. oceans

2.022 Some methods of ________________ encourage erosion.

a. swimming b. cutting lumber c. identifying rocks d. faulting

2.023 Change in the earth's surface by forces of weather is known as ________________.

a. folding b. faulting c. weathering d. downloading

2.024 Heat causes the surface of rocks to ________________.

a. wear b. expand c. decay d. shine

2.025 Many ________________ were formed by wind erosion.

a. glaciers b. mountains c. earthquakes d. deserts

2.026 Soil and sand can be taken to the end of a river to form a ________________.

a. delta b. peat bog c. dam d. highway

Draw these diagrams (each answer, 5 points).

2.027 An example of folding.

2.028 An example of faulting.

Complete these statements (each answer, 3 points).

2.029 The earth is slightly ____________________ at the poles.

2.030 Granite and quartz are ____________________ rocks.

2.031 A melted material in the mantle of the earth is called ____________________.

2.032 The core of the earth is thought to be mostly iron and ____________________.

Answer these questions (each item, 5 points).

2.033 How were igneous rocks formed? ____________________

2.034 What is a mineral? ____________________

Teacher check: Initials ________

Score ________ Date ________

80/100

Before you take the LIFEPAC Test, you may want to do one or more of these self checks.

1. ________ Read the objectives. See if you can do them.
2. ________ Restudy the material related to any objectives that you cannot do.
3. ________ Use the **SQ3R** study procedure to review the material.
4. ________ Review activities, Self Tests, and LIFEPAC vocabulary words.
5. ________ Restudy areas of weakness indicated by the last Self Test.

NOTES

SCIENCE 509
CYCLES IN NATURE

Author:
Barry G. Burrus, M.Div, M.A., B.S.

Editor:
Brian Ring

Illustrations:
Brian Ring

Media Credits:
Page 3: © Digital Vision, Thinkstock; **5:** © Stocktrek Images, Thinkstock; **7:** © Ingram Publishing, Thinkstock; **7, 44:** © Dorling Kindersley, Thinkstock; **9:** © Ilin Sergey, Hemera, Thinkstock; **10:** © Fotovika, iStock, Thinkstock; **11:** © mj0007, iStock, Thinkstock; **12:** © venusphoto, iStock, Thinkstock; © amana productions inc, Thinkstock; **14:** © teptong, iStock, Thinkstock; **16:** © Ivary, Thinkstock; **17:** © ttsz, iStock, Thinkstock; © zkifuk, iStock, Thinkstock; **21:** © rgoldston, iStock, Thinkstock; **25:** © Stocktrek Images, Thinkstock; **29:** © benmoat, iStock, Thinkstock; **30:** © nicomenijes, iStock, Thinkstock; © Ivan Proskuryakov, Hemera, Thinkstock; **31:** © Cinema Hope Design, iStock, Thinkstock; © Mikhail Dudarev, Hemera, Thinkstock; **36:** © Natalia Lukiyanova, iStock, Thinkstock; **37:** © Andrew_Mayovskyy, iStock, Thinkstock; **38:** © Artiom Ponkratenko, Hemera, Thinkstock; **39:** © mapichai, iStock, Thinkstock; **40:** © PIKSEL, iStock, Thinkstock; **42:** © irska, iStock, Thinkstock; **43:** © solarseven, iStock, Thinkstock; **46:** © maria flaya, iStock, Thinkstock; **48:** © stock_shoppe, iStock, Thinkstock; © Jupiterimages, Creatas, Thinkstock; **55:** © IgOrZh, iStock, Thinkstock; **58:** © egal, iStock, Thinkstock; **60:** © Fodor90, iStock, Thinkstock.

804 N. 2nd Ave. E.
Rock Rapids, IA 51246-1759

CYCLES IN NATURE

God has created and designed our world with great love, care, and wisdom. He has placed a great amount of order within His creation. We can also observe that there are many ordered *cycles* within God's creation. These signs of God's order and creation's cycles are all around us in nature. For example, in previous LIFEPACs, you learned about the water cycle, carbon cycle, and chemical cycle in nature. You also learned about life cycles of plants and animals. Yet, there are many more cycles than these in God's creation. The four seasons of the year—spring, summer, fall, and winter—are one example. The seasons change, yet they return again in a cycle from year to year.

In fact, the substance of all things that we can sense and observe — called *matter*—goes through change. Matter can also go through cycles. In this LIFEPAC®, you will study more about matter and the properties of matter. You will learn about the structure of matter and how matter changes. You will also learn about other cycles in nature—like the seasons of the year. Finally, you will learn more about God's order in all things that He has created.

Objectives

Read these objectives. The objectives tell you what you will be able to do when you have successfully completed this LIFEPAC. Each section will list according to the numbers below what objectives will be met in that section. When you have finished this LIFEPAC, you should be able to:

1. Identify the properties of matter.
2. Tell about the changes in matter.
3. Describe the structure of matter.
4. Explain the relationship between matter and the cycles of nature.
5. Describe some natural cycles.
6. Explain Bible accounts of God's order in creation.

1. MATTER

God created everything that exists, both seen and unseen. All that is seen includes the physical universe. Things that are unseen include spiritual beings, like the angels. Our focus in this LIFEPAC will be on things seen — the physical universe that God created. Every *thing* in the physical universe consists of *matter*. Matter is the substance of which all things in the physical universe are made. From the smallest living cell to the greatest galaxy in the universe, all things are made of matter.

You are surrounded by matter. You stand on it. You breathe it. In fact, your physical body is made of matter. All objects consist of matter. They may differ a great deal in size, shape, and appearance, but they all consist of matter.

Matter has *properties*. Some properties of matter are *common* to all matter. Other properties are *special* or specific to each kind of matter. This means similar types of matter have certain special characteristics that are common to all other matter of the same kind. For instance, all matter composed of the metal iron has similar characteristics, or *special properties*. These special properties help us to **distinguish** one kind of matter from another. You will learn more about common properties and special properties of matter in this section of the LIFEPAC.

Matter can *change*. Matter changes in many ways, including form, shape, and state. The changes in matter are very orderly because of the properties of matter. You will learn more about changes in matter in this section of the LIFEPAC.

All matter has *structure*. Matter consists of tiny particles that give matter its basic structure. You will learn more about the particles of matter and the motion of these particles in this section of the LIFEPAC.

By studying the *properties*, *changes*, and *structure* of matter, you should better understand the importance of matter in the cycles of nature. You should also be able to better appreciate the loving care and order that God has put into His creation.

Objectives

Review these objectives. When you have completed this section, you should be able to:

1. Identify the properties of matter.
2. Tell about the changes in matter.
3. Describe the structure of matter.
4. Explain the relationship between matter and the cycles of nature.

Vocabulary

Study these new words. Learning the meanings of these words is a good study habit and will improve your understanding of this LIFEPAC.

atom (at' əm). The small particle that makes up molecules. Each atom is unique for a chemical element.

brittleness (brit' l nəs). The physical property of being broken easily or of being broken with a snap.

characteristics (kar' ik' tə ris' tiks). Special features of something that help set one thing apart from another.

combustibility (kəm bus' tə bil' ət ē). The ability of a material to burn. It is a chemical property of matter.

conduct (kən dukt'). To channel through; heat or electricity can be channeled through conductors.

conservation (kon' sər vā' shən). The state of not being used up.

density (den' sə tē). The condition of being closely packed together. It is the amount of matter in a given volume of material.

displace (dis plās'). To take the place of something else.

distinguish (dis ting' gwish). To perceive as being separate or different.

exist (eg zist'). To be; to have being.

hydrogen (hī' drə jən). A colorless element commonly found in gas form. It burns easily, and its mass is less than all other elements.

inertia (in er' shu). To remain still if still, or continue moving if moving unless acted upon by an outside force.

molecule (mol' ə kyül). The smallest part of matter that can still exist without a chemical change. It is made up of atoms of elements.

normally (nôr' mə lē). In a regular way; commonly.

symbol (sim' bəl). Something that stands for, or represents, something else.

volume (vol' yəm). The amount of space taken up by matter.

Note: *All vocabulary words in this LIFEPAC appear in* **boldface** *print the first time they are used. If you are unsure of the meaning when you are reading, study the definitions given.*

Pronunciation Key: h**a**t, **ā**ge, c**ã**re, f**ä**r; l**e**t, **ē**qual, t**ė**rm; **i**t, **ī**ce; h**o**t, **ō**pen, **ô**rder; **oi**l; **ou**t; c**u**p, p**u̇**t, r**ü**le; **ch**ild; lo**ng**; **th**in; /ŦH/ for **th**en; /zh/ for mea**s**ure; /u/ or /ə/ represents /a/ in **a**bout, /e/ in tak**e**n, /i/ in penc**i**l, /o/ in lem**o**n, and /u/ in circ**u**s.

Properties of Matter

All matter has *properties*. These properties are the **characteristics** of matter. They are the various ways in which we describe matter. Some of these properties are *common* to all matter. Other properties are *special* or specific to each kind of matter. Let's explore these common and special properties of matter.

| Solids, liquids and gasses behave differently when put in containers.

Common properties. All matter in the universe has some common properties. Three of these common properties are **volume**, *mass*, and **inertia**. We can describe any matter as having volume, mass, and inertia. Let's first consider the property of volume.

Volume is the space taken up by matter. In fact, some scientists define matter as anything that occupies space. Objects of small volume do not take up much space. Objects with larger volumes take up more space. Does a tiny ant take up space? Yes. Its volume is small, though. An elephant has much more volume than an ant and takes up more space.

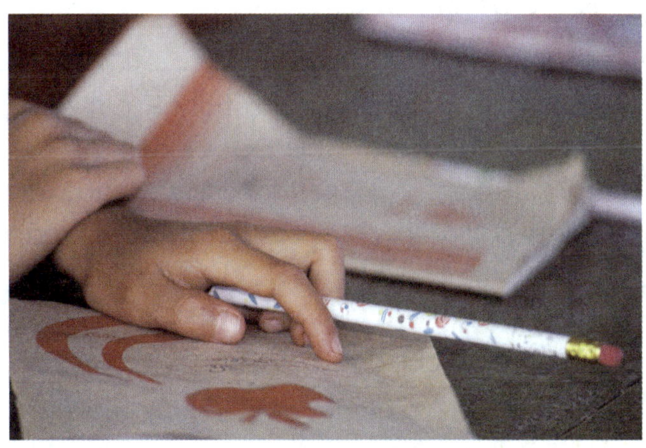

| Your hand and your pencil cannot occupy the exact same space together.

Volume is measured in units like pints, liters, gallons, cubic feet, or cubic meters. For example, when your parents or friends fill their car with 10 gallons of gasoline, they are putting a certain volume of gasoline into the car's gas tank. The volume of the gasoline is 10 gallons. It would occupy 10 gallons of space in the gas tank. Can two objects occupy the same space at the same time? Try this exercise to find out. Place your pencil on a desk. Now try to put your hand in exactly the same place. Can you do it? No. The pencil is taking up space so that your hand cannot occupy the exact same space. Two objects cannot occupy the same space at the same time. However, two objects can occupy the same space at different times. If you remove your pencil from the desk, you can rest your hand in the exact same place that the pencil previously occupied. In this case, we say that you **displace** the pencil with your hand. The volume of your hand now occupies part of the space formerly occupied by the volume of the pencil. In the experiment that follows, you will learn more about volume and how one object might displace another object.

509.A VOLUME

View 509 **VOLUME EXPERIMENT:** Grade 5 Science experiments video

You will use two marbles of different size to demonstrate how the volume of an object can be measured by displacing the same volume of another substance (in this case, water).

These supplies are needed:

- a tall, thin glass jar or a graduated cylinder
- water
- small marble
- large marble
- masking tape
- pen, pencil, or marker
- ruler with centimeter markings

Follow these directions carefully. Put a check mark in the box when each step is completed. (NOTE: If using a graduated cylinder, there is no need to make markings on tape with a ruler. Simply use some of the markings already imprinted on the cylinder for your measurements and record them on a sheet of paper for each step. Proceed with step 3 below.)

☐ 1. Place a piece of masking tape on the jar from top to bottom.

☐ 2. Using a ruler to measure, make marks one centimeter apart on the strip of tape, from bottom to top.

☐ 3. Pour water into the jar until it reaches your fifth mark.

☐ 4. Carefully drop the small marble into the water. Put a small mark on the tape where the new water level is located. Label it "X."

☐ 5. Remove the small marble. Make sure the water level is the same as step 3. Add more water if necessary.

☐ 6. Drop the large marble into the water. Put another mark on the tape where the water level is located. Label it "Z."

Answer these questions.

1.1 Why did the water level change when you dropped the marbles in the water?

____

____

____

1.2 Which marble caused the most change in water level?

____

____

Complete this activity.

1.3 Compare the volume of the two marbles.

____

____

____

Mass is a second common property of all matter. The quantity of matter in an object is called its *mass*. Mass is measured in units such as grams and pounds (mass). The mass of an object will be the same no matter where it is measured.

Mass should not be confused with an object's *weight*. The weight of an object of a given mass is directly related to the earth's gravitational pull on the object. Therefore, an object's weight can change depending upon the pull of gravity on the object. Since the force of gravity decreases as one moves away from earth, the weight of the object would also decrease as one moves away from earth. For example, a person with a mass of 75 pounds (mass) would weigh 75 pounds (force) on Earth; however, that person would weigh very little in outer space. That same 75 pound person would weigh about 12 pounds (force) on the moon because the force of gravity on the moon is less than that on Earth. However, the person would still have the same mass—75 pounds (mass)—whether on the earth, in outer space, or on the moon.

| A balance measures the mass of an object.

The mass of an object is usually measured on a balance by comparing it with another object of known mass. The mass tells us the amount of matter present in the object.

The third common property of matter is called *inertia*. All matter has inertia. This means that it resists any change in its condition of rest or of motion. Inertia means that an object remains still if still or continues moving if moving, unless acted upon by an outside force. For example, if you place a book on your desk, the book will remain still on your desk unless some force acts upon it to remove it. The inertia of the book at rest makes it remain at rest. Inertia keeps it from moving.

On the other hand, inertia will keep a moving object moving until another force acting upon it causes it to slow down or stop. For example, if you kick a soccer ball into the air, inertia keeps the ball moving until it hits something (like someone's foot) or the force of gravity pulls the ball to the ground.

| Inertia can keep a body in motion.

Complete this list.

1.4 What are three common properties of all matter?

a. ____________________

b. ____________________

c. ____________________

Write the correct letter and answer on each line.

1.5 The substance of all things that we can sense and touch is called ______________ .

a. matter b. volume c. color

1.6 The space taken up by matter is called ______________ .

a. mass b. volume c. a box

1.7 All matter has ______________ .

a. cells b. seeds c. properties

1.8 The quantity of matter in an object is called its ______________ .

a. volume b. mass c. measure

1.9 ________________ means that matter resists any change in its condition of rest or of motion.

a. Inertia b. Toughness c. Stillness

1.10 The ________________ of an object measures the pull of gravity on its mass.

a. stability b. weight c. inertia

Special properties. There are many kinds or varieties of matter in the universe. One kind of matter differs from another kind. For example, a rock differs from cheese. Both a rock and cheese differ from water. Therefore, there are some properties of matter that are specific to the different kinds of matter. These are called *special properties* of matter.

There are two main categories of special properties of matter: (1) *physical properties* and (2) *chemical properties*. Let's explore each of these special properties of matter.

Physical properties help us to recognize different kinds of matter by the five senses. Our sight, smell, touch, taste, and hearing allow us to distinguish between a great variety of matter. For example, by sight, we can recognize gold by its *color*. It would look different from silver because silver has a different color than gold. Therefore, *color* would be a physical property of matter. Another physical property using one of the five senses would be *odor*. We could tell the difference between gasoline and water by the odor of each.

There are other physical properties that can be used to distinguish matter of different kinds. An important one of these other physical properties is **density**. Density is the amount of mass in a given volume of matter. It is measured in units like pounds (mass) per cubic foot or kilograms per cubic meter. Density is a physical property that varies among different kinds of matter. For example, the density of steel metal would be much greater than the density of cork. There would be more mass in a cubic inch of steel than in a cubic inch of cork because the density of steel is greater than that of cork.

Brittleness is another physical property of matter. Suppose you threw a ball through a closed window. What would happen? The glass in the window would break into many pieces, but the ball would not break. By easily breaking into many pieces, the glass shows that it has the physical property of *brittleness*. Like other physical properties, brittleness differs from one kind of matter to another.

| The glass breaks because of its brittleness.

Two other physical properties of matter will be mentioned before we go on to the chemical properties of matter. One of these is *solubility*. This is the ability of one kind of matter to dissolve in another. For example, some materials will more readily dissolve in water than others. We would say that the materials that dissolve more readily would have greater solubility than the others. Another important physical property of matter is its ability to **conduct** heat or electricity. This physical property is called *conductivity*. Copper wire is an example of matter that has a higher conductivity than many other materials. Both heat and electricity are easily conducted through copper.

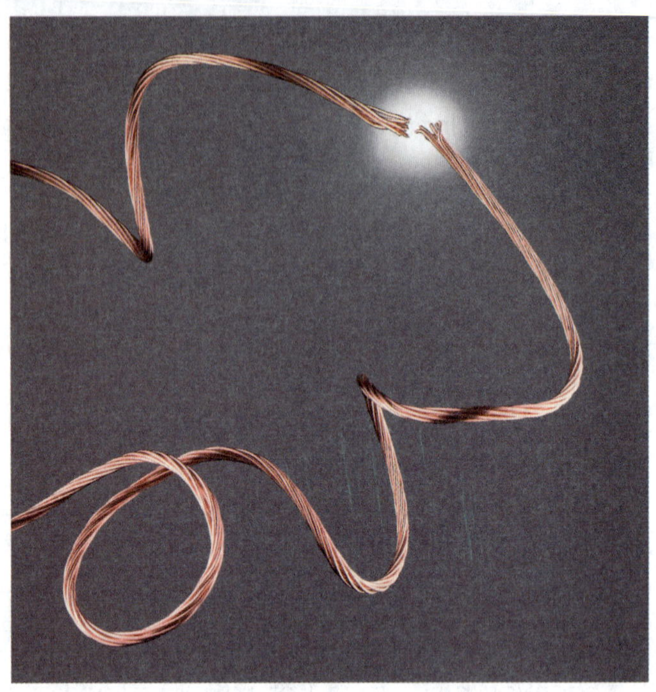

| Copper conducts both heat and electricity.

| A drop of ink showing its solubility in water.

509.B DETERMINE A PHYSICAL PROPERTY

View 509 DETERMINE A PHYSICAL PROPERTY: Grade 5 Science experiments video

You will determine the identity of a physical property of matter in this experiment.

These supplies are needed:

- 2 glass containers of water
- small piece of wood (toothpick)
- spoonful of sugar
- spoon or stir stick

Follow these directions carefully. Put a check mark in the box when each step is completed.

☐ 1. Place the wood in one container of water. Stir it around.

☐ 2. Place the sugar in the other container of water. Stir it around.

Answer these questions.

1.11 What happened to the wood?

____

1.12 What happened to the sugar?

____

1.13 What physical property of matter is involved in this experiment?

____

____

1.14 Which material is greater in this physical property? ____________________

Teacher check:

Initials ________________ Date ________________

Answer *true* or *false*.

1.15 __________ Our five senses can help us to recognize some of the physical properties of matter.

1.16 __________ Color and odor are examples of common properties of all matter.

1.17 __________ Density is the amount of mass in a given volume of material.

1.18 __________ Brittleness is a physical property that differs from one kind of material to another.

1.19 __________ The ability of one kind of matter to dissolve in another is called *conductivity*.

1.20 __________ Copper wire has a high electrical conductivity.

As you have learned, physical properties are one kind of special property of matter. A second special property of matter involves the *chemical properties* of that particular matter. Chemical properties of matter describe how a substance acts when it undergoes chemical change. All matter has chemical properties. Some of these chemical properties of matter cannot be observed unless that material is tested. Let's consider a couple of examples of chemical properties of matter.

One well-known chemical property of matter is the *ability to burn*. This chemical property is sometimes called **combustibility**. You have probably seen wood, paper, and candlewicks burning. These materials can burn easily when a flame of fire touches them. When materials burn, they combine with oxygen to produce other chemicals. There is a chemical change in the original material. Other materials have a very low combustibility. For example, rock will not burn when a normal flame touches it.

Another chemical property found in some materials is the *ability to rust*. Have you ever seen a nail or a piece of metal containing iron that was left outdoors for some time? More than likely, the material had formed a reddish brown coating on it. This coating is called *rust*. Rust forms when iron in the metal combines with oxygen in moist air to form iron oxide. The iron oxide is the rust. Therefore, the metal undergoes a chemical change when rust is formed. Many other materials do not form rust. Plastics and rubber are examples of matter that do not form rust. Therefore, the ability to rust is a chemical property that differs from one material to another.

| Rust is an iron oxide coating.

Complete these lists.

1.21 What are two kinds of special properties of matter?

a. ____________________

b. ____________________

1.22 What are two kinds of chemical properties of matter?

a. ____________________

b. ____________________

Answer these questions.

1.23 What is the combustibility of matter?

____

____

____

1.24 What is "rust" and how does it form?

____

____

____

1.25 How can you weigh more on the earth than you would on the moon and still have the same mass in both places?

____

____

____

1.26 Would your density be the same on the earth as it would be on the moon? __________
Explain your answer.

____

____

____

Changes in Matter

Matter can change. In fact, we see cycles in nature because matter changes. God has designed all matter in the universe to be able to change. Normally, matter can be changed in two basic ways: *physical changes* and *chemical changes*. We will explore both types of changes in this section of the LIFEPAC.

| Clouds are water in gas state (water vapor). When cooled, the cloud produces rain (liquid state).

Physical changes. Matter undergoes many physical changes. Physical change happens to matter whenever it changes in *size*, *shape*, or *location*. For example, breaking a rock into smaller pieces would change the size of the rock. Cutting off a slice of margarine would change the size of the stick of margarine. Rolling out a piece of modeling clay would change the shape of the clay. Pouring water from a glass into a bowl would change the shape and location of the water. All of these changes represent physical changes.

In previous LIFEPACs, you have studied other physical changes occurring in nature. Plants and animals change in size through growth. Living things change when they move, breathe, or reproduce. The earth's crust changes, too.

Rocks are formed in sediment. Rocks wear away by weathering. Mountains are changed by folding and faulting. These changes are also examples of physical changes of matter in nature.

Another important physical change to matter happens when it changes its *form* or *state*. Normally, matter is found in three states: *solid*, *liquid*, or *gas*. Matter can change from one state to another; for example, from a solid to a liquid. In a way, matter has a cycle when it changes from one state to another and back again. When ice melts and forms water, it changes state from a solid to a liquid. If the water is now heated, it forms steam—which is water in the gas state. If the steam is cooled, it returns to water. If it is cooled further, it freezes and becomes ice again. Therefore, the water cycles from solid to liquid to gas and back again. This is a cycle of nature.

Many things that we see around us are **normally** solid. Your pencil is in a solid state. Your chair is solid, too. Things that are solid usually have a fixed form and shape. If you simply move a solid to another location, it will still have the same form and shape as before. As you learned previously, a solid can be changed physically by breaking it into smaller pieces or changing its size or shape. However, it will still be solid.

A material will change from solid to liquid state by adding heat to it and changing its temperature. If ice is heated to just above 32 degrees Fahrenheit (0 degrees Celsius), it will melt into water. A solid metal spoon will become liquid metal if it is heated to a temperature hot enough for it to melt. You may remember from a previous LIFEPAC that magma is the liquid form of certain rocks. The magma is at a very hot temperature! Some solids require much more heat than other solids to change to the liquid state. It takes much more heat to change solid rocks to liquid than it does to change ice into water.

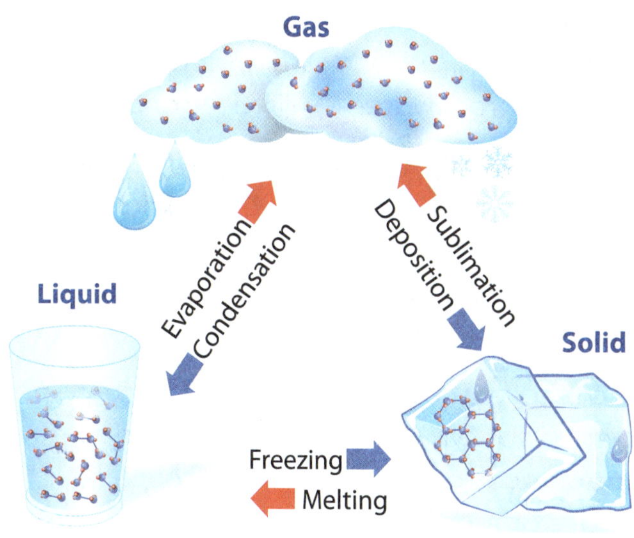

| Matter can change from one state to another.

Some materials in nature are normally in liquid form. Water is a good example. Liquids do not have a fixed shape or form. Liquids take the shape of the container in which they are held. Liquids usually change shape when they are moved from one location to another since the container will be different. A liquid will change to another state by adding or taking away enough heat.

| Nitrogen is a gas at room temperature but a liquid at very cold temperature.

If enough heat is added to water to raise its temperature to 212 degrees Fahrenheit (100 degrees Celsius), it will boil and turn to steam—or water in the gaseous state. However, if enough heat is removed from water, it will freeze and become ice—water in the solid state.

Finally, some matter is normally in the gaseous state. The air around us is gas. In fact, air consists of several gases mixed together, mainly nitrogen gas and oxygen gas. You should also recall that water is found in the air. This water found in air has evaporated from oceans, lakes, and other bodies of water on earth as part of the water cycle in nature. This water in the gaseous state found in air is also called water vapor.

A gas takes the shape and size of its container. A gas does not have a fixed shape and size of its own. A gas can be changed to a liquid by removing heat from the gas. For example, if oxygen in the air is cooled low enough, it becomes liquid oxygen. Liquid oxygen is sometimes used in industry and to provide combustion in rockets.

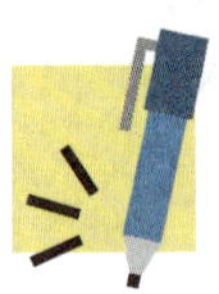

Complete these statements.

1.27 Matter that has its own size and shape is in the _______________ state.

1.28 Matter that takes the size and shape of its container is in the _______________ state.

1.29 Adding enough heat to a solid will change it to the _______________ state.

1.30 Removing enough heat from a gas will change it to the _______________ state.

1.31 Changing matter from one state to another is a _______________ change.

1.32 Matter changing states is an example of a _______________ in nature.

509.C WATER IN LIQUID STATE

View 509
WATER IN LIQUID STATE: Grade 5 Science experiments video

Water will be poured into four different types of containers in order to demonstrate some things about liquids.

These supplies are needed:

a baby food jar or similar small container
4 other differently shaped clear containers (see examples below)

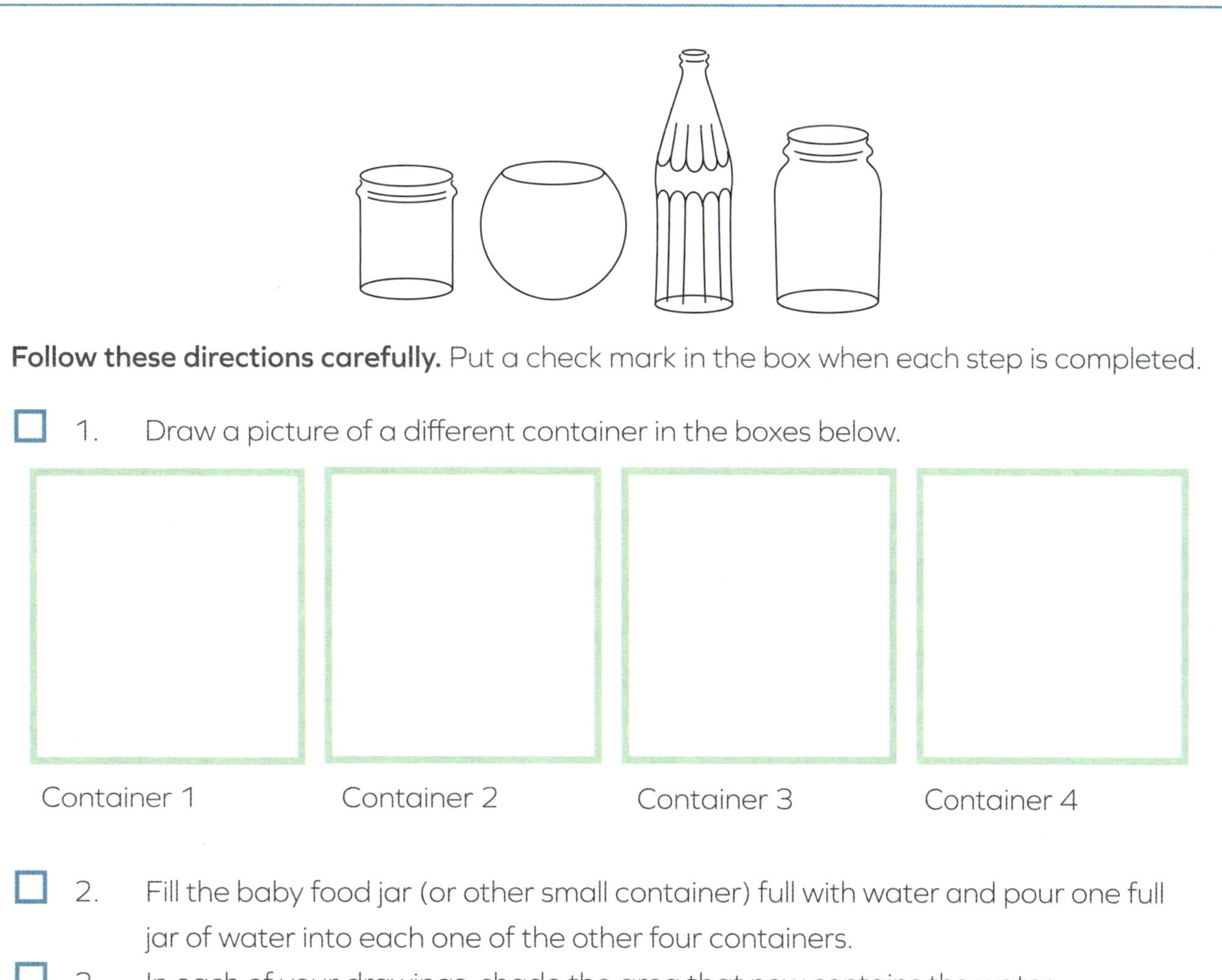

Follow these directions carefully. Put a check mark in the box when each step is completed.

☐ 1. Draw a picture of a different container in the boxes below.

Container 1 | Container 2 | Container 3 | Container 4

☐ 2. Fill the baby food jar (or other small container) full with water and pour one full jar of water into each one of the other four containers.

☐ 3. In each of your drawings, shade the area that now contains the water.

Complete these activities.

1.33 Compare the water level in each of the containers.

1.34 Compare the volume of water in each of the containers.

1.35 Compare the shape of the water in each of the containers.

1.36 Why is the water level different for some of the containers?

1.37 What does this experiment show about matter in the liquid state?

Complete this activity.

1.38 Place each of the following items under the correct state in which it normally occurs.

pencil	steam	fingernail	cookie	needle
ink	hammer	cotton	milk	blood
gasoline fumes		apple juice		oxygen

Solid	**Liquid**	**Gas**
____________	____________	____________
____________	____________	____________
____________	____________	____________
____________	____________	____________
____________	____________	____________
____________	____________	____________

Chemical changes. As you read previously in this section, burning and rusting cause *chemical changes* in matter. Chemical changes are much different than physical changes in matter. In chemical changes, the matter transforms into a different kind of matter. The chemical makeup of the material changes. However, physical changes in matter can also occur at the same time as chemical changes occur.

| Rusted iron chains

When paper is burned, it is no longer paper. It changes into another material—mainly carbon ash. When iron gets rusty, it is no longer pure iron. It changes into a new material—iron oxide, or "rust." The paper and iron change into new materials. The new materials will have different physical and chemical properties. They will usually look, smell, or feel differently than their original forms, because the matter has been changed both chemically and physically.

Answer *true* or *false*.

1.39 __________ When water is changed into steam, a chemical change occurs.

1.40 __________ Physical change and chemical change can happen at the same time.

1.41 __________ Sometimes new materials are not formed during chemical change.

1.42 __________ Burning only causes a physical change in paper.

1.43 __________ Rust is not the same material as iron.

509.D CHEMICAL AND PHYSICAL CHANGES

View 509 **CHEMICAL AND PHYSICAL CHANGES:** Grade 5 Science experiments video

NOTE: This experiment should be done with adult supervision.

____
Adult Signature

You will burn a candle and observe any physical and chemical changes that occur.

These supplies are needed:
- candle in candle holder
- large glass plate or pan
- match or lighter

Follow these directions carefully. Put a check mark in the box when each step is completed.

☐ 1. Light the candle with the match. Observe it for several minutes. Answer Activity 1.44.

☐ 2. *Be careful not to burn your hand in this step.* Hold the glass plate (or pan) about a decimeter (or 3-4 inches) above the flame. What happens? Record your observation in Activities 1.45 and 1.46.

☐ 3. *Be careful not to burn your hand in this step.* Hold the glass plate (or pan) just above the flame for a short time. What do you observe?
Record these things in Activities 1.47 and 1.48.

1.44 List the changes you observe taking place in the candle.

____

____

____

1.45 What happened to the plate when held about a decimeter (or 3–4 inches) above the flame?

____

____

____

1.46 What caused this particular thing to take place?

____

____

____

1.47 What happened to the plate when held just above the flame?

____

____

____

1.48 What do these results show?

____

____

____

1.49 List all the changes that took place in this experiment.
Label them *ch* (chemical) or *ph* (physical).

____

____

____

| The total mass before and after burning is the same.

Conservation of matter. You have seen things burn. You have observed ice melting. Perhaps you have seen glass break. What happens to the matter during all these changes? Is matter lost? Is it used up?

Matter often appears to be lost when it changes. For example, when paper burns, it seems like only a small amount of ash is left. The ashes are much smaller in volume than the original paper. The paper appears to have been destroyed. However, the matter has not been lost in this case. The matter has changed to different materials. The same amount of mass remains as before.

Scientists have learned how mass is not lost through burning. They have conducted experiments with burning to show this **conservation** of matter. The scientists use an airtight container to conduct the experiments so that no mass can escape from it. The mass of the matter to be burned and the mass of the air inside the container are measured. Then the material is burned within the container. After burning, the mass of the burned matter (the ashes), the unburned matter, the gases, and smoke is measured. The scientists always find that the total mass inside the container is exactly the same before burning and after burning. Chemical changes do not change the total mass of materials. There is *conservation of matter* during chemical changes.

The same results happen during physical changes of matter. When matter changes from one state to another, the total mass is conserved. For example, when water is boiled, the level of water in the container appears to get lower. It appears that there is less mass of the water as it boils. However, experiments conducted in airtight containers show that no mass is lost when water boils and changes from the liquid to gas state. One kilogram of water could be changed into steam inside an airtight container. However, the mass of the resulting steam would also be one kilogram. No mass is lost or destroyed during the boiling of water. There is *conservation of matter* during physical changes and changes from one state to another.

The earth has a certain amount of matter. Matter cannot be created or destroyed by nature. Except for the small amounts of mass sent into space by rockets and the mass changed in nuclear reactions (described in the next part of this section), the same amount of mass exists on Earth today as did 100 years ago! This same amount of mass cycles through nature constantly on Earth. Matter changes from one state to another and from one material to another. This cycle of matter in nature is an ongoing process. This cycle of matter in nature is even necessary for life to continue on Earth.

| Earth is the same mass as 100 years ago.

If no matter is created or lost, how did it get here on Earth? This question has puzzled people for many years. Yet, the answer is found in the Bible. The Bible says that God created the earth. God created all the matter that exists today. It is the same amount of matter that existed when God created the earth long ago. Matter was created once by God. It has been cycling constantly through nature ever since.

Write the correct letter and answer on each line.

1.50 Matter is not created or destroyed when it ______________________ .

a. changes state b. is made c. is lost

1.51 The ______________________ of matter means that matter is not created or destroyed.

a. conservation b. consecration c. concentration

1.52 A thousand years ago, the same amount of ________________ was on earth as today.

a. oil b. volume c. mass

1.53 When water changes state from a gas to a liquid, the ________________ of the water remains the same.

a. mass b. color c. volume

1.54 Matter ______________________ lost when it burns.

a. does get b. does not seem to be c. appears to get

Complete these activities.

Sometimes it is necessary to make *predictions* after reading some information. To predict accurately, the reader must understand the information. The prediction is made as a result of the understanding. A prediction is more than a guess. A prediction is based upon information understood by the person making the prediction. However, the person making the prediction is not certain of the results. After an event happens and the results are certain, a prediction can be tested for accuracy.

In this activity, you will make some predictions. Your predictions will be based on the information contained in the section you have just finished reading titled *Conservation of matter*. Read the next experiment (Experiment 509.E). Then *predict* the answers to the questions below.

1.55 How will the ice change?

____

____

____

1.56 How will the mass of the ice respond to the change?

____

____

____

1.57 Why will the mass respond in this way?

____

____

____

509.E CONSERVATION OF MATTER

View 509 CONSERVATION OF MATTER: Grade 5 Science experiments video

Using an equal-arm balance to measure mass, you will see if conservation of matter occurs when ice melts.

These supplies are needed:

- equal-arm balance (see illustration below)
- ice cube
- 2 baby food jars with equal mass
- dropper
- 2 baby food jar lids with equal mass

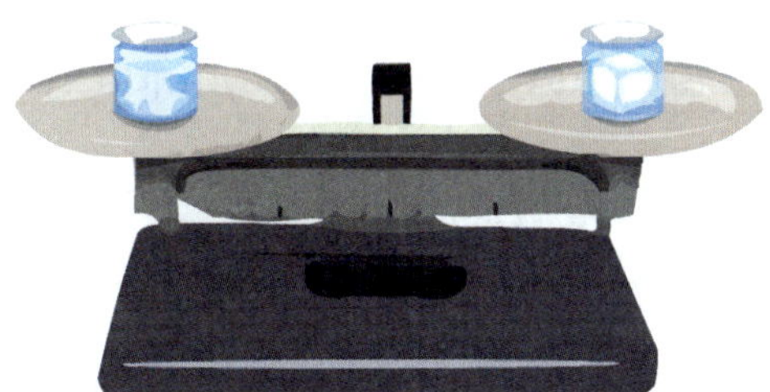

Follow these directions carefully. Put a check mark in the box when each step is completed.

- ☐ 1. Place the ice cube in one jar. Tightly close the lid. Put the jar on one side of the balance.
- ☐ 2. Pour some water into the remaining jar. Place it on the other side of the balance. Put the lid beside the jar on the balance pan.
- ☐ 3. Use the dropper to add or remove water from the jar until the balance is equal. Place the lid tightly on the jar or water.
- ☐ 4. Allow the ice to melt in the closed jar. You may go ahead to the next step while the ice is melting.
- ☐ 5. Go back and review your predictions in Questions 1.55, 1.56, and 1.57. Change your predictions, if necessary. Then, when the ice is melted, complete the questions and activities.

Answer these questions.

1.58 What happened to the mass of ice after it melted?

____

____

____

1.59 Why did this thing happen?

____

____

____

Complete this activity.

1.60 Compare the results of this experiment with your earlier predictions.

____

____

____

Use the Internet or library.

1.61 A French scientist named Antoine Lavoisier made some important observations. Use the Internet or library to learn more about him. On another piece of paper, write a summary of his observations and findings. Explain how his studies relate to your study of matter. Take this LIFEPAC and your summary to your teacher for a teacher check over this section.

Teacher check:

Initials ____________ Date ____________

Matter and energy. In 1905 a German-born scientist named Albert Einstein developed some mathematical formulas to explain the relationship between mass and energy. For several centuries before Einstein developed his formulas (contained in his "special theory of relativity"), scientists believed that matter could neither be created or destroyed. However, Einstein showed that matter can be changed into energy and energy into matter.

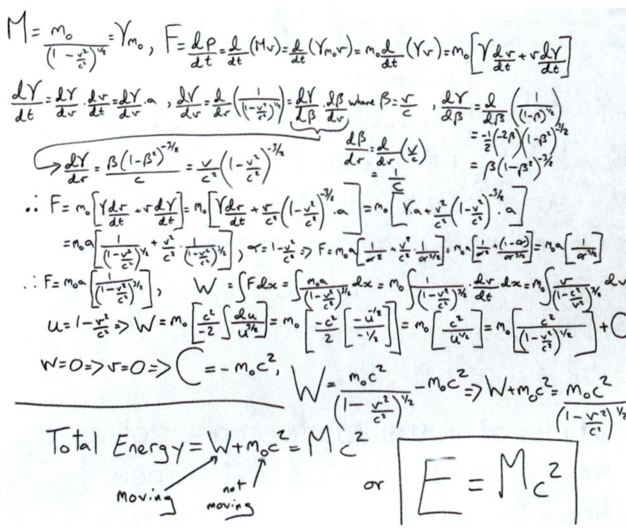

| Einstein's special theory of relativity

In a previous LIFEPAC, you studied the *transformation of energy* and learned that chemical changes can give off heat and light, as in the process of fusion in the sun. Einstein's formulas showed that whenever a chemical change occurs to give off heat and light, then the substances that changed must have lost some mass. However, in all the normal chemical reactions that have taken place in factories, laboratories, and homes in history, the total amount of mass lost so far is too small to be significant! Einstein's formulas show that measurable quantities of mass are changed into energy only in nuclear reactions such as those that occur in nuclear reactors and atomic bombs. Since Einstein's work in the 20th century, scientists now speak of a *law of conservation of mass and energy* which states: "Neither mass (matter) nor energy can be created or destroyed, but each may be converted into the other." Isn't it amazing that God has even created a cycle between matter and energy!

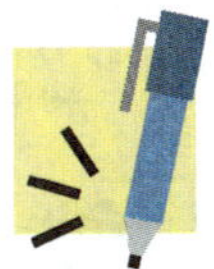

Match these items.

1.62 __________ mass

1.63 __________ volume

1.64 __________ conductivity

1.65 __________ Lavoisier

1.66 __________ Einstein

a. a special physical property of matter

b. a special chemical property of matter

c. measures inertia

d. the quantity of matter

e. the space taken up by matter

f. showed conservation of matter

g. showed relationship between matter and energy

Structure of Matter

What is the basic substance of matter? How is matter structured? In the remainder of this section of the LIFEPAC, you will study the basic structure of matter. You will learn about the basic particles that make up all matter. You will also learn about some ways these particles are in motion.

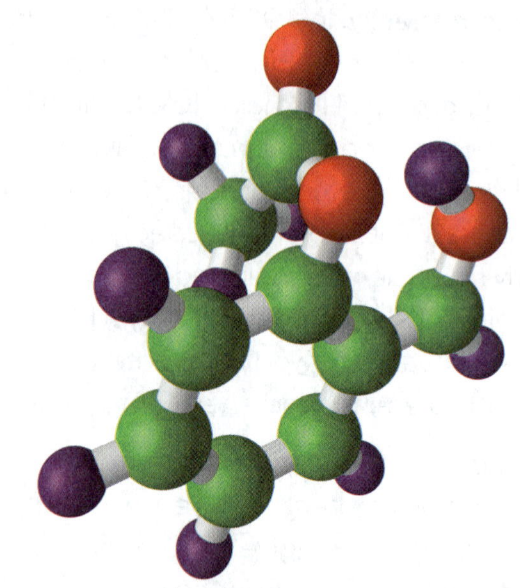

| Molecule model

Particles of matter. Matter consists of basic particles called **molecules**. You learned in a previous LIFEPAC that all living things are made of cells and that most cells are microscopic. Well, molecules are much smaller than cells. In fact, cells are made up of these very small particles of matter called molecules. These molecules are so tiny that only the largest of them can be seen with the most powerful electron microscopes!

Molecules are the smallest bits of matter that can **exist** without a chemical change. They are the smallest particles into which a substance can be divided and still have the chemical identity of the original substance. Water is made up of water molecules. One drop of water contains billions of water molecules. If one molecule from that drop of water was separated from the rest, it would still be water. However, if that one water molecule was divided further, it would no longer be water. It would be something else.

Each molecule of matter is made up of particles that are even smaller. These smaller particles are called **atoms**. Atoms are very, very tiny. They are more than a million times smaller than the thickness of a human hair! Atoms are the basic building blocks of all matter. They form the most basic substances of nature called the chemical *elements*. There are about 103 chemical elements. Copper, **hydrogen**, carbon, and oxygen are examples of common elements.

When atoms of elements combine, they form molecules. Atoms join together in different ways to make millions of different kinds of molecules. One example is the water molecule. Each water molecule contains three atoms. Two of these are hydrogen atoms, and the other one is an oxygen atom. Since the chemical **symbol** for hydrogen is "H" and the chemical symbol for oxygen is "O," water is sometimes written as H_2O.

| A water molecule is H_2O.

This means that the water molecule has two atoms of hydrogen and one atom of oxygen. All molecules can be represented by the chemical symbols for the number and types of atoms contained in each molecule. Carbon dioxide, for example, is written as CO_2 and contains one atom of carbon (C) and two atoms of oxygen (O). Water and carbon dioxide are examples of *chemical compounds*. They are called chemical compounds because they are made up of molecules that are formed by the combination of different atoms.

| CO_2 being emitted from a factory

Both molecules and atoms can combine in chemical reactions to form other chemical compounds. Compounds can also split in chemical reactions to form elements and other compounds. The new compounds or elements from chemical reactions have different chemical properties than the original elements or compounds. As compounds are formed or split, matter is cycled through nature.

Motion of particles. Molecules are always in motion. They are so tiny that we cannot see them move, but they are always moving. Molecules are in motion when the material is in the solid, liquid, or gas state.

In solids, the molecules are grouped very close together. The molecules hold their positions, but they still move around very fast. Even though the whole solid material keeps a fixed size and shape, the tiny molecules within the material are moving ever so slightly and at a very fast rate.

| Melted gold (liquid) is poured into a mold. When the gold cools, it becomes a solid bar.

When heat is transferred to a solid material, the molecules within the material begin to move faster and farther apart. Eventually, when enough heat is transferred to the solid material, it becomes a liquid. The molecules of a liquid are farther apart and move faster than those in a solid.

If still more heat is transferred to the liquid material, the molecules move even faster and farther apart. When enough heat is transferred to the material, it becomes a gas. Molecules in a gas are very far apart and move very fast. The molecules of a gas material are farther apart and move faster than the same material in liquid state.

Whether matter is in solid, liquid, or gas state, the molecules of the material are moving. You cannot see them move because they are so small. However, you can observe their movement in other ways. For example, when your family members prepare popcorn to eat, the molecules moving from the heated popcorn can be smelled in other parts of your house! Also, the heat absorbed by ice cream causes its molecules to move faster and farther apart, and the ice cream begins to melt. The motion of particles within matter helps to continue the cycles in nature.

Complete these statements.

1.67 ______________________ are the smallest particles of matter that can exist without a chemical change.

1.68 ______________________ form the most basic substances of nature called the chemical elements.

1.69 Chemical ______________________ are made up of molecules that are formed by the combination of different atoms.

1.70 Molecules are always in ______________________ .

1.71 Molecules in the liquid state move ______________________ than in the solid state.

1.72 A gas has molecules that move faster and are ______________________ than in the liquid state.

1.73 The motion of particles helps to continue the ______________________ in nature.

Review the material in this section to prepare for the Self Test. The Self Test will check your understanding of this section. Any items you miss on this test will show you what areas you will need to restudy in order to prepare for the unit test.

SELF TEST 1

Match these items (each answer, 3 points).

1.01 ________ color
1.02 ________ volume
1.03 ________ odor
1.04 ________ mass
1.05 ________ density
1.06 ________ inertia
1.07 ________ brittleness
1.08 ________ measurement
1.09 ________ solubility
1.10 ________ liquid

a. common property of matter
b. special property of matter
c. not a property of matter

Answer *true* or *false* (each answer, 2 points).

1.011 ________ Matter is the substance that we can sense and observe.
1.012 ________ Matter does not go through change or cycles.
1.013 ________ All matter in the universe has some common properties.
1.014 ________ Ten gallons of water is a measurement of its mass.
1.015 ________ An object's weight is always the same as its mass.
1.016 ________ Inertia causes an object at rest to remain at rest.
1.017 ________ Density is the amount of mass in a given volume of material.
1.018 ________ Changing from liquid to gas is a chemical change.
1.019 ________ Gas molecules of material move slower than those of a liquid of the material.

Write the correct answer on each line (each answer, 3 points).

1.020 An example of a physical change in a material is ________________.

a. breaking it b. rusting c. a nuclear reaction

1.021 An object in motion will keep moving because of its ________________.

a. size b. speed c. inertia

1.022 The ability to conduct heat is a ________________ property of matter.

a. chemical b. physical c. common

1.023 The chemical symbol for water is ________________.

a. H_2O b. CO_2 c. CH_2

1.024 A chemical ________________ is made up of all the same atoms.

a. element b. compound c. shape

1.025 Matter can ________________ when it changes from one state to another and back again.

a. disappear b. be created c. cycle

List the three common states of matter (each answer, 3 points).

1.026 ________________

1.027 ________________

1.028 ________________

Complete these statements (each answer, 3 points).

1.029 Matter that has its own size and shape is in the ________________ state.

1.030 Changing matter from one state to another is a ________________ change.

1.031 A ________________ change always produces new materials.

1.032 When matter changes from one state to another, the total mass is ________________.

1.033 ________________ form the most basic substances of nature called the chemical elements.

Answer these questions (each answer, 5 points).

1.034 What is the *law of conservation of mass and energy*?

____

____

____

____

1.035 How can heat change matter from a solid to a liquid to a gas?

____

____

____

____

____

____

____

____

____

____

____

____

Teacher check: Initials ______________

Score ______________ Date ______________

80/100

SCIENCE 509

LIFEPAC TEST

NAME ______________________

DATE ______________________

SCORE ______________________

SCIENCE 509: LIFEPAC TEST

Answer *true or false* (each answer counts 2 points).

1. __________ When water is changed into steam, a chemical change occurs.

2. __________ Rust is not the same material as iron.

3. __________ Decay is part of a cycle of matter.

4. __________ All matter in the universe has some common properties.

5. __________ An object's weight is always the same as its mass.

6. __________ Liquid molecules move slower than those of a solid of the same material.

7. __________ Day and night show a balance in the cycle of nature.

8. __________ A comet is a star with a tail.

9. __________ The earth exists because of the precise amount of matter given by God.

Match these items (each answer, 3 points).

10. __________ water in gas state

11. __________ each kind of atom is called a(n)

12. __________ molecules are made up of these

13. __________ molecules grouped close together

14. __________ causes molecules to separate farther

15. __________ two or more kinds of atoms together

16. __________ earth's tilt causes it to receive these

17. __________ head of a comet

18. __________ only a few comets have this part

19. __________ matter that is brought into the body

20. __________ crystals of water

21. __________ vapor state of matter

a. atoms
b. compound
c. coma
d. snow
e. solid state
f. element
g. cold
h. heat
i. slanted rays
j. gas state
k. food
l. tail
m. vapor

List these items (each answer, 4 points).

22. List the common properties of matter.

a. ______________________

b. ______________________

c. ______________________

Write the correct word(s) on each line (each answer, 3 points).

23. A special property of matter is ______________________ .

a. volume b. density c. measurement

24. Matter changes from one state to another when ______________ is added or removed.

a. mass b. heat c. inertia

25. When something burns, ________________ material is formed.

a. old b. no c. new

26. The liquid state of matter takes the ________________ of its container.

a. place b. heat c. shape

27. Matter is ________________ through nature.

a. created b. cycled c. lost

28. An object in motion will keep moving because of its ________________ .

a. size b. speed c. inertia

29. The chemical symbol for carbon dioxide is ______________ .

a. H_2O b. CO_2 c. CH_2

30. The Biblical reference to wind being cycled is ________________________ .

a. Job chapter 18 b. Genesis chapter 3 c. Ecclesiastes chapter 1

Answer these questions (each answer, 5 points).

31. What is the *law of conservation of mass and energy*?

____

____

____

____

____

____

32. How does the water cycle show precision in God's creation?

2. OTHER NATURAL CYCLES

Matter has special structure. Matter has properties and can change in many ways. Yet, matter is conserved when it changes. There is order in the way matter is cycled through nature.

The characteristics of matter cause many other cycles of nature. These cycles also show order in God's creation. We can make predictions based on our knowledge of each cycle.

Objectives

Review these objectives. When you have completed this section, you should be able to:

4. Explain the relationship between matter and the cycles of nature.
5. Describe some natural cycles.

Vocabulary

Study these new words. Learning the meanings of these words is a good study habit and will improve your understanding of this LIFEPAC.

atmosphere (ăt′ mə sfîr′). Air around the earth.

coma (kō′ mə). Cloud-like head of a comet.

Pronunciation Key: hat, āge, cãre, fär; let, ēqual, tėrm; it, īce; hot, ōpen, ôrder; oil; out; cup, pu̇t, rüle; child; long; thin; /ŦH/ for then; /zh/ for measure; /u/ or /ə/ represents /a/ in about, /e/ in taken, /i/ in pencil, /o/ in lemon, and /u/ in circus.

Seasons

Out of the four seasons—winter, spring, summer, and autumn—which one is your favorite? Every part of the earth has seasons. However, the winter where you live may not be as warm as some places. Your winter may not be as cold as some other spots on earth. You know that each season comes once a year. We go through the seasons cycle each year.
What are the characteristics of the seasons where you live?

Description. Winter is generally thought to be the coldest time of the year. Days seem shorter. Sometimes snow falls. Winter is much warmer near the equator than near the poles.
However, wintertime is colder than other seasons almost everywhere.

The days seem to get longer and warmer in spring. Often there is much rain in the spring season. Near the equator, spring seems very short.

Summertime is the warmest part of the year. Summer days are longer. Summer is warm enough near the poles for some of the snow to melt. Yet, the ground remains frozen.

In autumn, the days begin to get cooler and shorter. The weather cools down earlier near the poles. Autumn at the equator is short. It is often similar to spring.

When England is having winter, Kansas has winter. However, when Kansas is having winter, Brazil is having summer. All of the world north of the equator has winter at the same time. Places south of the equator have summer when those north of the equator have winter.
The seasons are opposite on opposite sides of the equator.

| Seasons

Answer *true* or *false*.

2.1 __________ Idaho has winter, but Florida does not.

2.2 __________ We can predict that autumn will follow summer.

2.3 __________ We can predict that summer days will be longer than winter days.

2.4 __________ Autumn is a longer season at some places than at others.

2.5 __________ The South Pole and North Pole have winter at the same time.

Use the Bible.

There are many references to the seasons in the Bible. Summer and winter are mentioned. Read Proverbs 26:1 and Mark 13:28, then answer these questions.

2.6 How are summertime and a fool compared? (Proverbs)

____

____

2.7 How can people predict summer is near? (Mark)

____

____

Causes. Why do we have the cycle of seasons? One reason is that the earth is tilted on its axis. The earth moves around the sun. The earth's tilt causes part of the earth to receive the sun's rays more directly. When the earth is tilted toward the sun, it is summer for that part of the earth. Six months later, the tilt causes the same part of earth to receive more slanted sun rays. For the part of the earth tilted away from the sun, it is winter. However, it is summer on the other side of the equator.

| The atmosphere absorbs some of the suns rays.

Slanted rays cover a larger area and are spread out. Matter receives less energy from the slanted rays. At the same time, the **atmosphere** keeps the slanted rays from bringing as much heat. Some heat energy is absorbed before it reaches the earth.

The days are also shorter in wintertime. So the sun's rays have less time to heat the matter.

How is matter affected by the rays from the sun? Heat causes molecules to move faster. Some matter changes to liquid or gas. With less heat from the sun, some liquids change to solid and some gases become liquid.

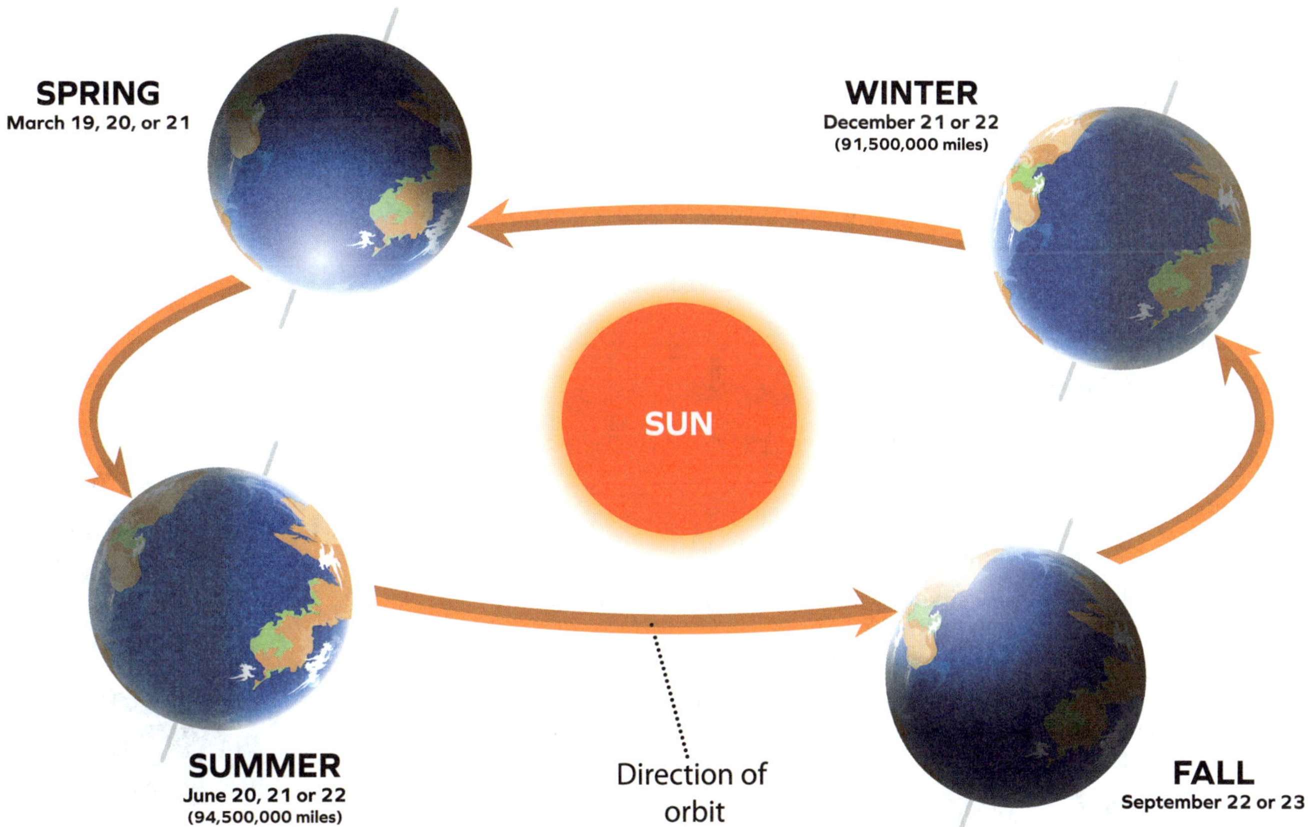

509.F EARTH'S MOVEMENT AROUND THE SUN

View 509 **EARTH'S MOVEMENT AROUND THE SUN:** Grade 5 Science experiments video

Using a globe of the earth, you will see how the earth's movement around the sun allows different seasons of the year.

This is needed:
globe with a tilted axis

Follow these directions carefully. Put a check mark in the box when each step is completed.

☐ 1. Choose a partner to help with this observation.

____

(Name)

☐ 2. Sit in a place where there is plenty of room on all sides.
Have your partner hold the globe at your eye level
about 33 feet (10 meters) in front of you.

☐ 3. Have your partner turn the globe so you can see
North America and South America.
Draw a simple diagram of your observation in Figure 1.

☐ 4. Have your partner move the globe to your left.
The position of the axis must not change.
Have your partner spin the globe so you see North America and South America.
Record what you see in Figure 2.

☐ 5. Have the globe moved behind you.
Do not change the axis. Turn around so you can see.
Record what you see of North America and South America in Figure 3.

☐ 6. Have the globe moved to your right.
Keep the axis pointing in the same direction as before.
Record what you see of North America and South America in Figure 4.

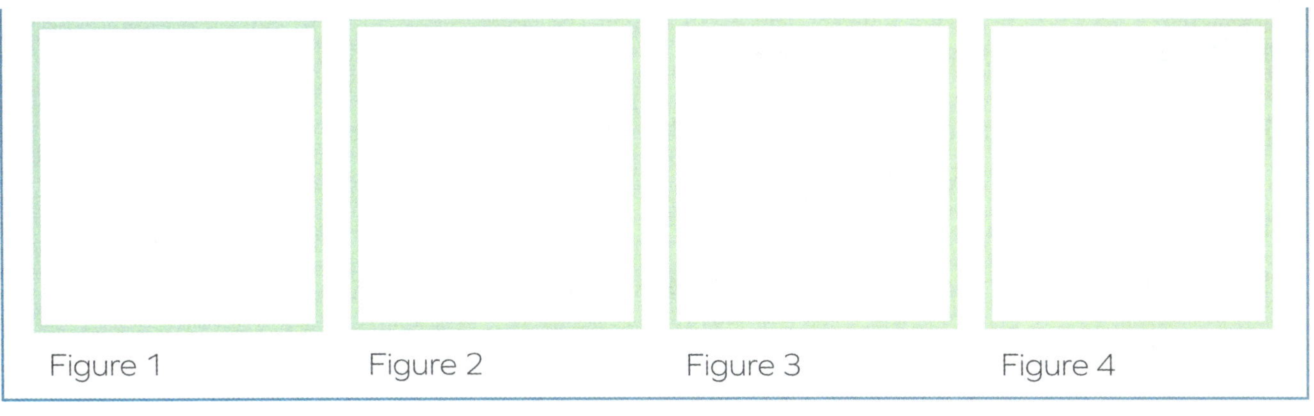

Answer these questions.

2.8 How did each new position change your view of North America and South America?

____

____

____

____

2.9 What did your observations show?

____

____

____

____

2.10 What part of the solar system did you represent?

____

____

____

2.11 In which figure would North America be having summer?

____

____

____

____

Complete these statements.

2.12 Summer happens in Vermont when the sun's rays hit it more ______________________ than any other time of year.

2.13 The days are shortest during the ______________________ season.

2.14 In some places when water molecules lose heat, ______________________ forms.

2.15 More heat gets through to the earth in the summer because the ______________________________ absorbs less heat.

Comets

For many years people feared comets. They did not understand what comets were. Some terrible stories were told about comets. Today we know some things about comets, but some things are still a mystery.

Description. A comet is not a star with a tail. A comet is matter that orbits around the sun. Scientists believe that the elements forming this matter are like those on Earth. Scientists do not agree about which elements are included in a comet's makeup. Several theories have been suggested based on observation and reason.

A comet usually has four parts. The cloud-like head is called the **coma**. In the center of the head, a nucleus is located. A well-known feature is the tail. However, most comets do not have the tail. Scientists also believe comets are surrounded by a cloud of hydrogen.

Each year several new comets are discovered. Most comets cannot be seen without a telescope. Comets are too far away to be seen by the eye alone. Some of them are too small to be easily seen. Comets often appear as a cloud of reflecting material or fuzzy stars. Tails develop only when the comets get near the sun.

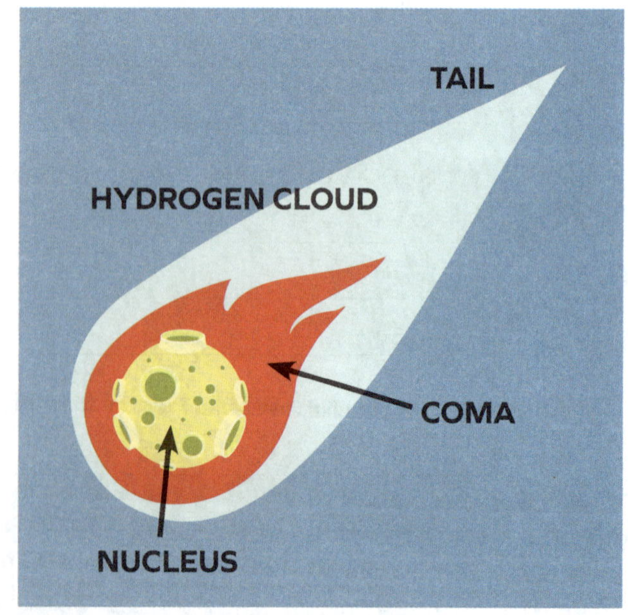

| Parts of a comet

Comets move across the sky. Yet, because comets are so far away, they do not appear to be moving. Their progress can be seen by comparing the position from night to night. Some people mistake "shooting stars" (meteors) for comets. A great difference exists between comets and meteors. Meteors are solid objects. Comets appear to have more gases and to be much less dense. The tail is especially thin. Also, the tail is usually pointing away from the sun.

| A comet in space

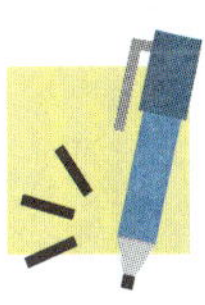

Write the correct letter and answer on each line.

2.16 The makeup of comets is ______________________________ .

a. different b. not agreed upon c. clearly known

2.17 Sometimes ______________________________ are mistaken for comets.

a. shooting rapids b. shooting flares c. shooting stars

2.18 The cloud-like head of a comet is called a ______________________________ .

a. tail b. comma c. coma

2.19 The matter in comets is believed to have similar ______________________________ as are on earth.

a. elements b. cells c. density

2.20 The tail is ______________________________ feature of most comets.

a. an unknown b. a bright c. not a

2.21 To observe most comets, you must use a ______________________________ .

a. microscope b. magnifying glass c. telescope

Cycle of comets. If comets move, where are they going? At one time people thought they were heavenly bodies passing by the earth. Observers found that the same comets seemed to return regularly. They concluded that these comets must have an orbit around the sun.

After much data was recorded, the orbits of many comets were discovered. Some orbits were as short as three years. One of the most famous comets, Halley's Comet, returns every seventy-six years. Some orbits bring their comets nearer the sun than other orbits. These comets get very bright and some develop a tail.

The orbit of a comet is really another cycle. The comet follows a regular pattern around the sun. The amount of time taken for each comet to complete its orbit can be predicted.
Much information about comets remains to be discovered. By studying the order of their cycles, scientists have gained much understanding of comets.

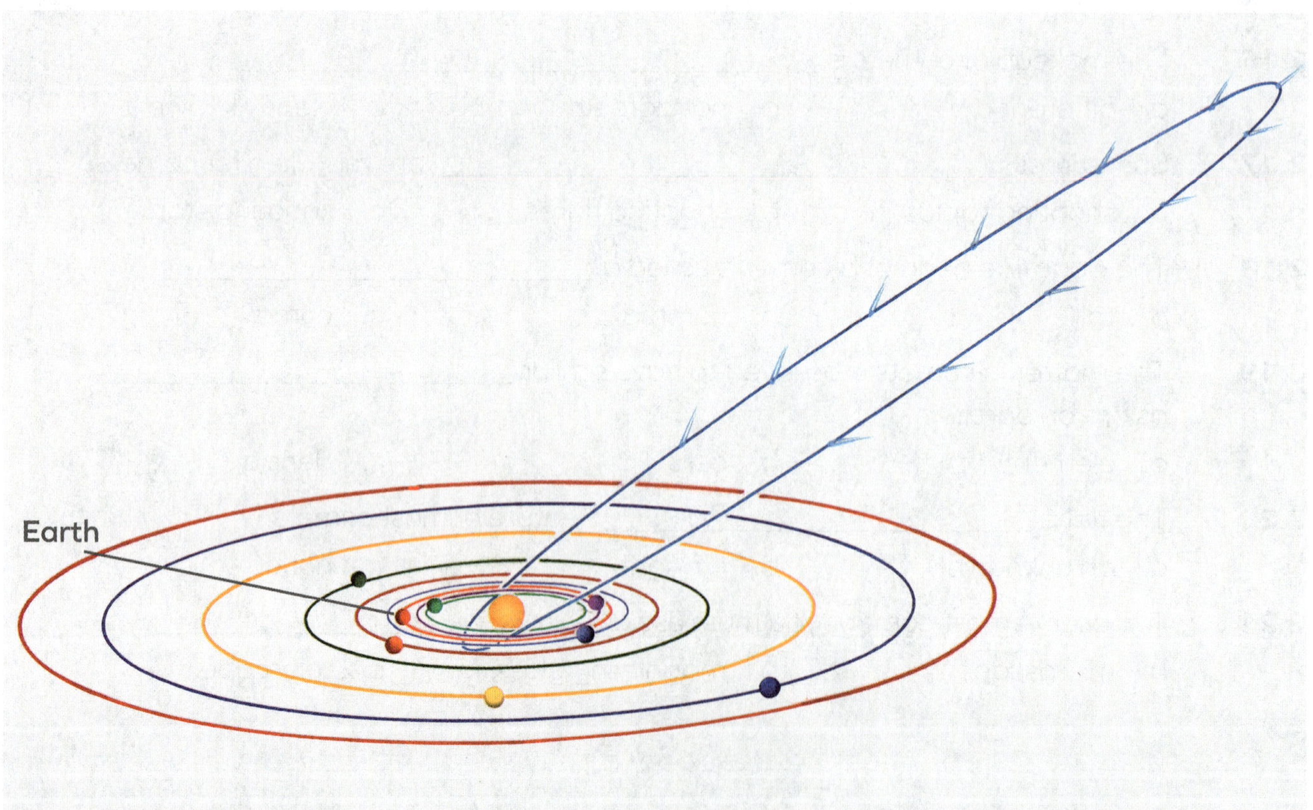

| The path of Halley's Comet in relation to our solar system

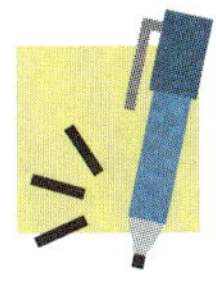

Answer *true* or *false*.

2.22 __________ All comets have the same length orbits as other comets.

2.23 __________ The orbit of a comet is one of nature's cycles.

2.24 __________ Comets orbit around the earth.

2.25 __________ Some comets get brighter at certain times in their orbits.

2.26 __________ Predictions of the return of comets are very difficult to make.

Use the Internet or library.

Over 6,000 comets have been discovered and studied. When a new comet is located, it is often named after the person who sights it first.

The following names are names of comets. Use the Internet or library to help you learn more about one of these people and comets.

Encke	Lubos Kohoutek	William Herschel
Edmond Halley	Tempel	Faye
Tsutomu Seki	Tuttle	Whipple
Kaoru Ikeya	Charles Messier	Shoemaker-Levy

2.27 Choose one of these comets or discoverers or select one you know about. Read as much as possible about your choice.

Name of my choice ____

2.28 On another paper write a report about the comet or the person who discovered it. When you have finished the report, take your paper and this LIFEPAC to your parent or teacher to check.

Teacher check:

Initials ____________________ Date ____________________

Life

Cycles in nature are important to life on earth. Life on earth couldn't continue without comets or seasons. The cycling of matter must happen for life to go on. Other cycles support life. You have studied about some of them. Now you will consider these cycles from another point of view. The order of nature is shown in these life-supporting cycles.

Formation and decay. A plant or animal life cycle includes birth, reproduction, and death. This life cycle causes each species to survive. The bodies of these living things are in a cycle, too. These bodies are formed, grow, die, and decay. This cycle happens over and over. Both plants and animals are involved in this cycle.

Each body is composed of matter. Life begins as one cell produced by a parent. After fertilization a body begins to grow for a multi-celled plant or animal. Matter is brought into the body in the form of food. The matter is changed chemically, and work is done. This work produces new cells, so some of the matter stays with the body. More and more matter is added to the body until it is mature. This process also produces the cells for fertilization.

| Every living thing has a life cycle.

When death occurs, the body decays. Bacteria in the soil helps the decaying process. These bacteria work on the body's matter to change it chemically. Some of the matter is returned to the soil where it can be used as food or nutrients for plants. The plants make new cells with the matter and the cycle continues. The conservation of matter happens during this cycle.

Complete these statements.

2.29 Living things are part of a cycle of ______________________ and decay.

2.30 Bacteria help the ______________________ process.

2.31 Matter makes a ______________________ in the body and work is done.

2.32 Each of the body's cells is made up of ______________________ .

2.33 Plants bring in ______________________ as nutrients from the soil.

Complete this activity.

2.34 In the following space, draw a diagram showing how matter cycles through bodies in the formation and decay process. Use an animal or plant in your diagram.

Teacher check:

Initials ______________ Date ______________

Water, carbon, and chemical cycles. You have learned that life depends on water, carbon dioxide and oxygen, and chemicals. You may recall that there are natural cycles for these things. Each of these materials is composed of matter. Matter is cycled through nature through these cycles.

The sun evaporates water from soil, oceans, lakes, plants, and animals. Water vapor is mixed with air. Clouds are formed. Rain falls to Earth from the clouds. These sentences give a simple explanation of the water cycle. What causes this water cycle to work?

Water is a chemical compound of hydrogen and oxygen. Water is the liquid form of this kind of matter. When air around water is warm, molecules of water change into the gas form. The molecules become part of the air. This process is known as *evaporation*. Warm air rises, and the evaporated water rises with the air.

Water vapor is always in the air near the earth's surface. Sometimes a great deal of moisture is in the air. Other times, it is said the air is "dry." Perhaps the sky has no clouds, but water vapor is still in the air.

Air can only hold a certain amount of water at a given temperature. When the air cools to a level called the *dew point*, clouds are formed. These clouds are very small droplets of water. The matter has returned to liquid form.

Sometimes the clouds continue to cool. Then the water droplets condense around small bits of dust. The droplets join other droplets and become heavier. Rain is a result.

| Dew forms in early morning or evening.

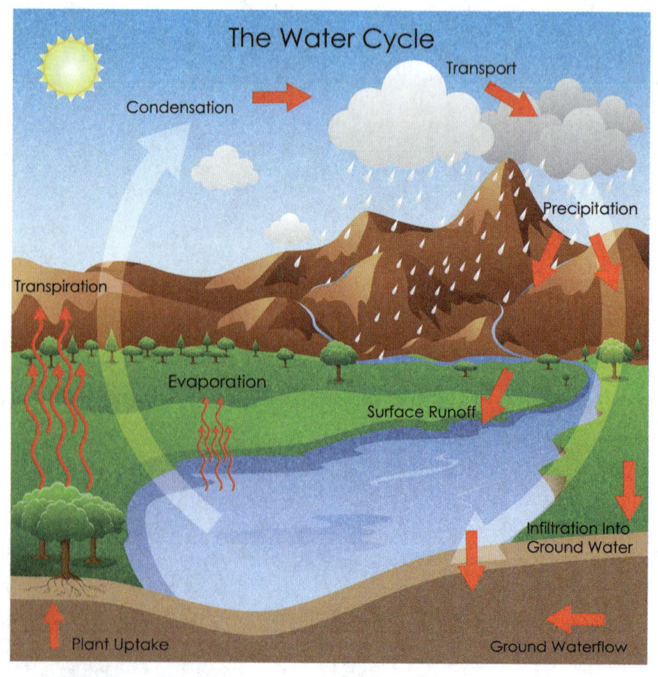

If the air is very cold, the liquid droplets change to the solid form. Ice crystals drop from the sky. These crystals are known as snow. Sometimes the air is cold enough that the crystals reach the ground. However, the snow may pass through warm air before it reaches the ground. Then the solid form melts into liquid and the earth receives rain.

Complete these activities.

You use the context of a word when you use other words or sentences to help understand new words or phrases. In the section you have just finished reading, some of the words and phrases gain meaning from the context.
Use the context to help complete the following activities.

2.35 Explain the meaning of these words or phrases.

a. the air is dry ______________________________

____

b. dew point ______________________________

____

c. ice crystals ______________________________

____

d. droplets ______________________________

____

2.36 If you did not have the context for this sentence, you might understand it differently. What else could it mean? "Ice crystals drop from the sky."

____

____

____

____

____

____

509.G EVAPORATION OF WATER

View 509 **EVAPORATION OF WATER:** Grade 5 Science experiments video

You will check the effect of temperature on the evaporation of water.

These supplies are needed:

graduated cylinder or a kitchen measure for small amounts of liquid
2 identical plastic storage containers about 3 inches square and 1 inch deep
funnel

Follow these directions carefully. Put a check mark in the box when each step is completed.

- ☐ 1. Pour 2 ounces or 1/4 cup (60 milliliters) of water into each container. Label them COLD and HOT.
- ☐ 2. Place one container in a cool place (refrigerator, if possible).
- ☐ 3. Place the other container in a warm place (near a heater or in the sun).
- ☐ 4. Every day check the amount of water in each container. Pour the water from the container into the liquid measure (use the funnel if necessary). Record the information in Chart 1. Return the water to the container, and repeat this step with the other container.
- ☐ 5. Repeat step 4 each day until Chart 1 is completed. Continue with *Review your ideas* in this LIFEPAC while this experiment is in progress.
- ☐ 6. Answer questions 2.37 and 2.38 about this experiment after you have finished Chart 1

CHART 1: AMOUNT OF WATER

DATE	HOT	COLD
1.		
2.		
3.		
4.		
5.		

2.37 What happened to the amount of water in each pan?

____

____

2.38 What do the results of this experiment show about water evaporation?

____

____

____

Review your ideas.

2.39 Carbon dioxide and oxygen are part of the carbon cycle. Chemicals are involved in the chemical cycle. Science LIFEPAC 504 briefly described these cycles as they related to life needs. Reread those sections of Science LIFEPAC 504. Choose either the carbon cycle or chemical cycle to write about.

In your own words, explain how the cycle functions. Relying on your understanding of matter, tell how the properties and changes in matter cause the cycle to operate.

____

____

____

____

____

____

____

____

____

Teacher check:

Initials ______________ Date ______________

Review the material in this section to prepare for the Self Test. The Self Test will check your understanding of this section and will review the other section. Any items you miss on this test will show you what areas you will need to restudy in order to prepare for the unit test.

SELF TEST 2

Answer *true or false* (each answer, 2 points).

2.01 ________ The earth is warmed most where the sun's rays are most slanted.

2.02 ________ Summer is longer in some places than in other places.

2.03 ________ Nights are shortest in summer.

2.04 ________ North America and South America have spring at the same time.

2.05 ________ Ground near the South Pole remains frozen the year round.

2.06 ________ Scientists agree on the makeup of comets.

2.07 ________ The comet's tail is very dense material.

2.08 ________ Warm air rises, taking moisture with it.

Match these items (each answer, 3 points).

2.09 ________ cloud-like comet head

2.010 ________ 76-year orbit

2.011 ________ number of comets discovered

2.012 ________ brings water vapor into the air

2.013 ________ ice crystals in the air

2.014 ________ small droplets of water

2.015 ________ common property

2.016 ________ determined by the size of an object

2.017 ________ made up of atoms

2.018 ________ changes the chemical makeup of matter

2.019 ________ necessary to evaporate water

2.020 ________ number of different kinds of elements

a. snow
b. coma
c. clouds
d. Encke's Comet
e. over 6,000
f. burning
g. about 103
h. volume
i. evaporation
j. energy
k. inertia
l. Halley's Comet
m. molecules

Write the correct letter and answer on each line (each answer, 3 points).

2.021 We can ____________________ that summer will follow spring.

a. predict b. edict c. predicate

2.022 The earth is tilted on its _______________ which helps cause seasons.

a. axle b. axes c. axis

2.023 As comets get near the sun they appear ________________________ .

a. brighter b. darker c. often

2.024 Clouds form when air cools to the ____________________________ .

a. rain drops b. gas form c. dew point

2.025 Even when the air is "dry," ____________________________ in the air.

a. water vapor is b. clouds are c. crystals are

2.026 The water cycle functions because the matter in water changes ______________________ .

a. forms b. properties c. minerals

2.027 Rusting is an example of a ____________________ change.

a. physical b. chemical c. common

2.028 A broken cup is an example of a ________________________ change.

a. physical b. chemical c. common

Complete this activity (each answer, 4 points).

2.029 Write the correct forms of matter on the lines.

least heat a. ______________ b. ______________ c. ______________ most heat

Answer these questions (each answer, 6 points).

2.030 Why are changing seasons a cycle of nature?

____

____

____

____

2.031 Why is a comet's orbit considered a cycle?

____

____

____

____

Teacher check: Initials ____________

Score ____________ Date ____________

80/100

3. GOD'S ORDER

Cycles in nature are evidence of order in the world. Properties of matter make it possible to describe how things function. We know what things can be done, and we know what things are physically impossible. Decisions can be based on our knowledge of natural cycles.

The observed evidence of order is helpful in understanding the earth. It is also helpful to consider how God was purposeful in creating an orderly system. This consideration of God's order can bring greater meaning to being alive. Your life is not just a result of matter cycling. Rather, it is a result of a great design by God.

In this section, you will learn what the Bible says about the balance, precision, and nature in the creation. Sometimes the Biblical writers used these natural things to explain an important idea. The description of nature shows God's part in its creation.

Objectives

Review this objective. When you have completed this section, you should be able to:

6. Explain Bible accounts of God's order in creation.

Vocabulary

Study these new words. Learning the meanings of these words is a good study habit and will improve your understanding of this LIFEPAC.

precise (pri sīs'). Exact or careful.

precision (pri sizh' īn). To be exact or accurate.

Pronunciation Key: hat, āge, cãre, fär; let, ēqual, tėrm; it, īce; hot, ōpen, ôrder; oil; out; cup, pu̇t, rüle; child; long; thin; /ŦH/ for **th**en; /zh/ for mea**s**ure; /u/ or /ə/ represents /a/ in **a**bout, /e/ in tak**e**n, /i/ in penc**i**l, /o/ in lem**o**n, and /u/ in circ**u**s.

Balance

Matter was created by God in the beginning of our universe. Isaiah suggested that God created things that we know as matter (Isaiah 40:12). He said that God measured how much water, sky, and soil were needed. This suggests that God was very careful as He created the earth. He planned a balance of different types of matter.

Ecclesiastes 1:4-7 shows that this balance includes cycles of nature. Life, day and night, wind, and water are examples of cycles. These cycles are ongoing and are important to the earth.

Use the Bible.

Read Isaiah 40:12 and Ecclesiastes 1:4-7.
Using these passages, complete the following activities.

3.1 Where did God measure the waters?

____

3.2 What did God do with the mountains and hills when He made them?

____

3.3 How do each of the following things cycle according to Ecclesiastes?

a. generations ______________________________

b. sun ______________________________

c. wind ______________________________

d. rivers ______________________________

Follow these directions to complete this activity.

3.4 The following puzzle contains a key Bible quote for this section of the LIFEPAC.

1. Begin at the arrow.
2. Draw a line from the first letter to the next.
3. You may go to the side, up, or down.
4. You may not go diagonally or skip a letter.
5. Continue with the line until all the letters have been used, and you will have a complete verse.

↓	S	T	D	S	
D	O	T	U	O	
W	O	H	O	L	C
T	N	K	U	H	E
H	E	N	C	T	F
	B	A	I	S	O
	A	L	N	G	

3.5 Write the Bible quote here.

____

____

3.6 This verse is part of a verse found in Job chapter 37.
Write the last part of the verse here.

____

____

____

3.7 What does this verse tell about God and His creation?

____

____

____

Precision

Why is there such a good balance in nature? Did God toss some matter together to get an earth? No. There is much precision in the earth and everywhere on the earth. Life exists because of exact measures of matter and the properties of this matter. The earth is made up of matter. The earth exists because of the **precise** amount of matter.

The Bible gives several examples of how God was precise in His creation of the earth. Job used the water cycle to show God's precision (Job 36:27–28). God causes the drops of rain to be small enough to pour down, but the rain lasts only as long as water vapor is in the air. Job also says that enough rain exists for humans to survive.

Jeremiah gave clues about how God could be precise in His creation (Jeremiah 10:12–13). Jeremiah said that God made the earth with power. He set up the world by using wisdom. The heavens were stretched out by God's good judgment.

Surely God was wise and powerful enough to be careful in designing the earth. The earth has plenty of those things needed to support life (Psalm 104:1–24). He provided water and land to support life. Humans were given control over other living things. Man was given use of everything created. Yet all living things were also controlled by natural forces.

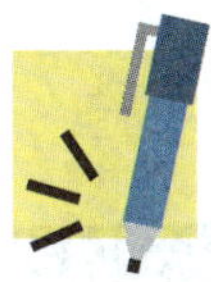

Write the correct letter and answer on each line.

3.8 Job showed that God was precise in His creation of the ______________ cycle.
a. water b. chemical c. carbon

3.9 Jeremiah said that God stretched out the heaven with ____________________ .
a. power b. wisdom c. good judgment

3.10 The earth has enough ____________________ to support life.
a. moons b. water c. age

3.11 God's design for the earth included __________________________________ .
a. controls over it b. careless creation c. too much matter

3.12 The balance in nature is ________________________ by the precision of God's creation.
a. stopped b. caused c. weakened

Use Psalm 104:1–24 to complete these activities.

3.13 God created several things for a purpose. What purpose did the following items have?
a. grass ____
b. herb ____
c. bread ____
d. high hills ____

3.14 Day and night controlled life in different ways.
How did the Psalmist view the difference between lions and man?
____
____

3.15 Make a poster. Choose something that you think shows God's precision in creation. Make a picture of this thing on a large piece of paper. Use Psalm 104:24 as a caption. Display the poster in your classroom.

Teacher check:
Initials ____________________ Date ____________________

Chemical Nature

You have studied that matter is composed of chemical elements. Your physical body is made up of matter, so your body has chemical elements. These elements are brought into the body through foods and the air you breathe. Some of the elements go out of the body through waste. Many elements will return to the earth after death occurs. The physical body will decay and elements will go back to the soil.

The Biblical account of Creation tells of this chemical nature of matter. Genesis 3:19 explains that we are *dust*. Dust is matter. Dust is composed of chemical elements. The dust in the Genesis statement would really be the chemical elements in the physical body. The precision and balance of the creation allows the elements of dust to be cycled.

| We are as dust.

Complete these statements.

3.16 Chemical elements can be brought into the body through ______________________ .

3.17 The Bible uses the word ______________________ to mean chemical elements.

3.18 The decay of a body allows chemical elements to ______________________ .

3.19 The elements can be cycled because of the a. ______________________ and b. ______________________ of God's creation.

Before you take this last Self Test, you may want to do one or more of these self checks.

1. ________ Read the objectives. See if you can do them.

2. ________ Restudy the material related to any objectives that you cannot do.

3. ________ Use the **SQ3R** study procedure to review the material:

a. **S**can the sections.

b. **Q**uestion yourself.

c. **R**ead to answer your questions.

d. **R**ecite the answers to yourself.

e. **R**eview areas you did not understand.

4. ________ Review all vocabulary, activities, and Self Tests, writing a correct answer for every wrong answer.

SELF TEST 3

Match these items (each answer, 3 points).

3.01 __________ wind is cycled

3.02 __________ dust to dust

3.03 __________ cycles show this in creation

3.04 __________ not created at present

3.05 __________ God made Earth with power

3.06 __________ water cycle shows precision

3.07 __________ humans control some of the creation

3.08 __________ everything functions properly

3.09 __________ God measured soil and water

3.010 __________ gives Earth its chemical nature

a. Genesis chapter 3
b. Psalm 104
c. Job chapter 36
d. Jeremiah chapter 10
e. Ecclesiastes chapter 1
f. Amos chapter 12
g. Isaiah chapter 40:12
h. elements
i. chemical
j. balance
k. matter
l. precision

Answer *true or false* (each answer, 2 points).

3.011 __________ Snow forms when clouds cool to the dew point.

3.012 __________ Water vapor is not usually seen.

3.013 __________ The mass of an object is how much volume it has.

3.014 __________ A gas and solid can take up the same space.

3.015 __________ We can predict that summer will follow spring.

3.016 __________ Inertia is a property of water vapor.

3.017 __________ Matter cycles through nature.

3.018 __________ The carbon cycle does not really involve matter.

3.019 __________ An atom is the smallest particle of matter that is still matter.

3.020 __________ When matter is being burned, it is not being conserved.

Write the correct letter and answer on each line (each answer, 3 points).

3.021 Some comets do not have a ______________________ .

a. tail b. coma c. nucleus

3.022 Comets move in ______________________ around the sun.

a. a straight line b. an orbit c. an axis

3.023 The makeup of comets is ______________________ .

a. well-known b. easily observed c. not certain

3.024 The earth is warmed most where the sun's rays are most ______________________ .

a. slanted b. direct c. tilted

3.025 Warm air takes moisture with it as it ______________________ .

a. rises b. drops c. evaporates

3.026 Burning is a chemical ______________________ .

a. cycle b. change c. element

3.027 A liquid form of matter has less heat than when it is in ______________________ form.

a. solid b. molecule c. gas

3.028 When two or more different molecules join together, ______________________ is formed.

a. an atom b. an element c. a compound

Complete these statements (each answer, 3 points).

3.029 Winter usually has ______________________ days than summer days.

3.030 As comets get near the sun, they appear ______________________ .

Complete these exercises (each answer, 5 points).

3.031 Explain how the water cycle functions because of change in matter.

____

____

____

____

____

____

3.032 Why are formation and decay considered a cycle of nature?

____

____

____

____

____

____

3.033 What is the meaning of the *conservation of mass*?

____

____

____

____

____

____

3.034 Explain how Ecclesiastes 1:4-7 relates to cycles and balance in nature.

____

____

____

____

____

____

Teacher check: Initials ____________

Score ____________ Date ____________

80 / 100

Before you take the LIFEPAC Test, you may want to do one or more of these self checks.

1. ________ Read the objectives. See if you can do them.
2. ________ Restudy the material related to any objectives that you cannot do.
3. ________ Use the **SQ3R** study procedure to review the material.
4. ________ Review activities, Self Tests, and LIFEPAC vocabulary words.
5. ________ Restudy areas of weakness indicated by the last Self Test.

NOTES

NOTES

NOTES

SCIENCE 510
LOOK AHEAD

Author:
Barry G. Burrus, M.Div, M.A., B.S.

Editor:
Brian Ring

Illustrator:
Brian Ring

Media Credits:
Page 3: © m-gucci, iStock, Thinkstock; **5:** © Stocktrek Images, Thinkstock; **10:** © andegro4ka, iStock, Thinkstock; **11:** © Dole08, iStock, Thinkstock; **17:** © blueringmedia, iStock, Thinkstock; **18:** © Micha? Adamczyk, iStock, Thinkstock; **21:** © cynoclub, iStock, Thinkstock; **24:** © john shepherd, iStock, Thinkstock; **25:** © mycola, iStock, Thinkstock; **27:** © Mike Watson Images, moodboard, Thinkstock; **32:** © Zoonar RF, Thinkstock; **33:** © Nadine Wickenden, Dorling Kindersley, Thinkstock; **34:** © LUNAMARINA, iStock, Thinkstock; © Eric Thomas, Dorling Kindersley, Thinkstock; **37:** © Hemera Tecnologies, PhotoObjects.net, Thinkstock; **38:** © artisticco, iStock, Thinkstock; **41:** © bubaone, Thinkstock; **43:** © walencienne, iStock, Thinkstock; **44:** © Jupiterimages, Photos.com, Thinkstock; **51:** © Dzhulbee, iStock, Thinkstock; **52:** © Ivan Cholakov, iStock, Thinkstock; **53:** © Digital Vision, Thinkstock; **55:** © sv-time, iStock, Thinkstock;**57:** © Leonid Karchevsky, iStock, Thinkstock; **59:** © stock_shoppe, iStock, Thinkstock

804 N. 2nd Ave. E.
Rock Rapids, IA 51246-1759

LOOK AHEAD

One of the best ways to prepare for what is ahead is to have a good knowledge of what you have covered. This LIFEPAC® is something like that. You will review much of the material that you have covered in the previous nine science LIFEPACs of this series. You will cover many of the same ideas in this LIFEPAC, but they will be presented somewhat differently. The previous topics will be related in new ways in this LIFEPAC. This LIFEPAC will give an *overview* of the topics previously covered in order to help you "look ahead" as you learn more about God's wonderful creation in the future.

This LIFEPAC can also help you to consider ways to use your information wisely. By knowing more about science, you can make better decisions on how to be a good steward of the world as God created it and meant it to be.

You will not have new vocabulary in this LIFEPAC. Instead, you will review the vocabulary presented in some of the previous nine LIFEPACs. You will do several creative activities, and you will continue to use the Bible. Some questions may not have the answers given in the text of this LIFEPAC. You may need to refresh your memory by returning to earlier LIFEPACs. By covering the material in this LIFEPAC in a new way, you will be strengthened in your new science knowledge and better able to "look ahead" to the future.

Objectives

Read these objectives. The objectives tell you what you will be able to do when you have successfully completed this LIFEPAC. Each section will list according to the numbers below what objectives will be met in that section. When you have finished this LIFEPAC, you should be able to:

1. Describe types of plants and animals.
2. Explain the relationship of cells to living things.
3. Describe the balance of nature.
4. Explain geological records.
5. Compare physical records and Biblical records of the earth's past.
6. Identify types of energy and work.
7. Tell about the order in matter, its structure, properties, and changes.

1. LIVING THINGS

God has created a rich variety of living things on the earth. Scientists today classify all living things into five *kingdoms*: (animals, plants, fungi, protists, and monerans). Examples of living things in each of these five kingdoms is given in Table 1. These living things are all around us: on the land, under the ground, in the water, and in the air. All living things are made of the basic unit of living things: a cell. Some living things consist of only one cell and are called *unicellular* organisms. Other living things consist of many cells and are called *multicellular*. All living things go through life cycles: they are born, reproduce, and die.

The cells of all living things have some similar parts. Every cell has a cell membrane and protoplasm (or cytoplasm) within the membrane. Some cells contain only these two parts and are called *prokaryote* cells. Bacteria, which are monerans, are an example of living things that contain only prokaryote cells. Many other cells contain three basic parts. These cells contain a cell membrane, cytoplasm, and a nucleus. These 3-part cells are called *eukaryote* cells. Unicellular organisms can be either prokaryote cells or eukaryote cells. All multicellular living things consist of eukaryote cells.

In this section of the LIFEPAC, you will examine the relationship of cells to living things, especially plants and animals. You will also review various types of plants, animals, fungi, protists, and monerans. Finally, you will learn more about the natural and human influences that impact the balance of nature.

Objectives

Review these objectives. When you have completed this section, you should be able to:

1. Describe types of plants and animals.
2. Explain the relationship of cells to living things.
3. Describe the balance of nature.

TABLE 1. CLASSIFYING LIVING THINGS

KINGDOM	CELL TYPE	FOOD	EXAMPLES
Animals	multicellular	obtains from outside sources	worms, insects, fish, birds, mammals
Plants	multicellular	produces their own	moss, trees, flowering plants
Fungi	unicellular or multicellular	obtains from outside sources	mushrooms, yeast, molds
Protists	unicellular or multicellular	produces their own and obtains from outside sources	protozoa, paramecium, green algae, red algae
Monerans	unicellular or multicellular	engulfed from outside sources	bacteria, blue-green algae

The Life of Plants, Fungi, Protists, and Monerans

The cells of all living things are alike in some ways. For example, all cells have cell membranes and protoplasm. Yet, there are also important differences among living things of the five kingdoms. These differences among cells cause living things of one kingdom to function somewhat differently from those of another kingdom. Even within the same kingdom of living things, differences in the structures of cells cause the living things to function differently. Let's now look at some common and some different features of the cells of plants, fungi, protists, and monerans. We will especially examine some important differences among plants.

Cells. In most plant and fungi cells, there is a fourth part of the cell: the *cell wall*. Cell walls surround the cell membrane. Cellulose in the cell walls helps to make the plants and fungi more rigid. Plants and fungi need rigid cell walls in order to stand and keep shape. Otherwise, they would be lying on the ground. By having cell walls, plants and fungi do not need skeletons or hard shells.

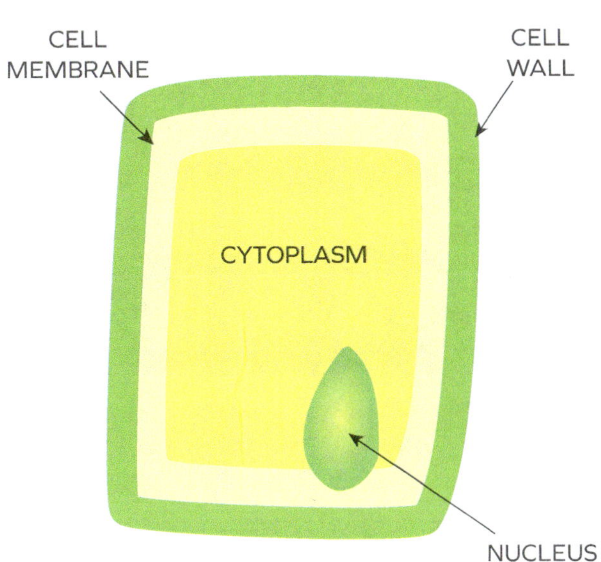

| Plant and fungi have a cell wall surrounding the cell membrane.

Plant cells, along with the cells of some protists and monerans, contain *chloroplasts*. These chloroplasts are some of the tiny parts of a cell within the cytoplasm called *organelles*. The chloroplasts contain *chlorophyll*—a green pigment. Chlorophyll absorbs energy from the sun. Fungi do not have chloroplasts nor chlorophyll. Only plants and some protists and monerans (like green algae) contain chlorophyll. The chlorophyll is what gives plants their green color.

When sunlight shines on the chlorophyll within living things, *photosynthesis* takes place. In photosynthesis, the energy from the sun is used by the chlorophyll to combine carbon dioxide and water in the plant. This process forms oxygen and sugars that are used within the plant for food. The oxygen is released from the plant to the atmosphere as a product of photosynthesis. The oxygen released from the plants is used by other living things, mainly animals and human beings, in order to breathe.

As part of God's plan for living things, only plants and some protists and monerans go through the process of photosynthesis. They receive energy directly from the sun and store this energy in their cells during photosynthesis and the production of "food" and oxygen. Other living things, like animals and fungi, cannot receive their energy directly from the sun. They must use the energy stored in plants or some protists and monerans for food in order to receive energy.

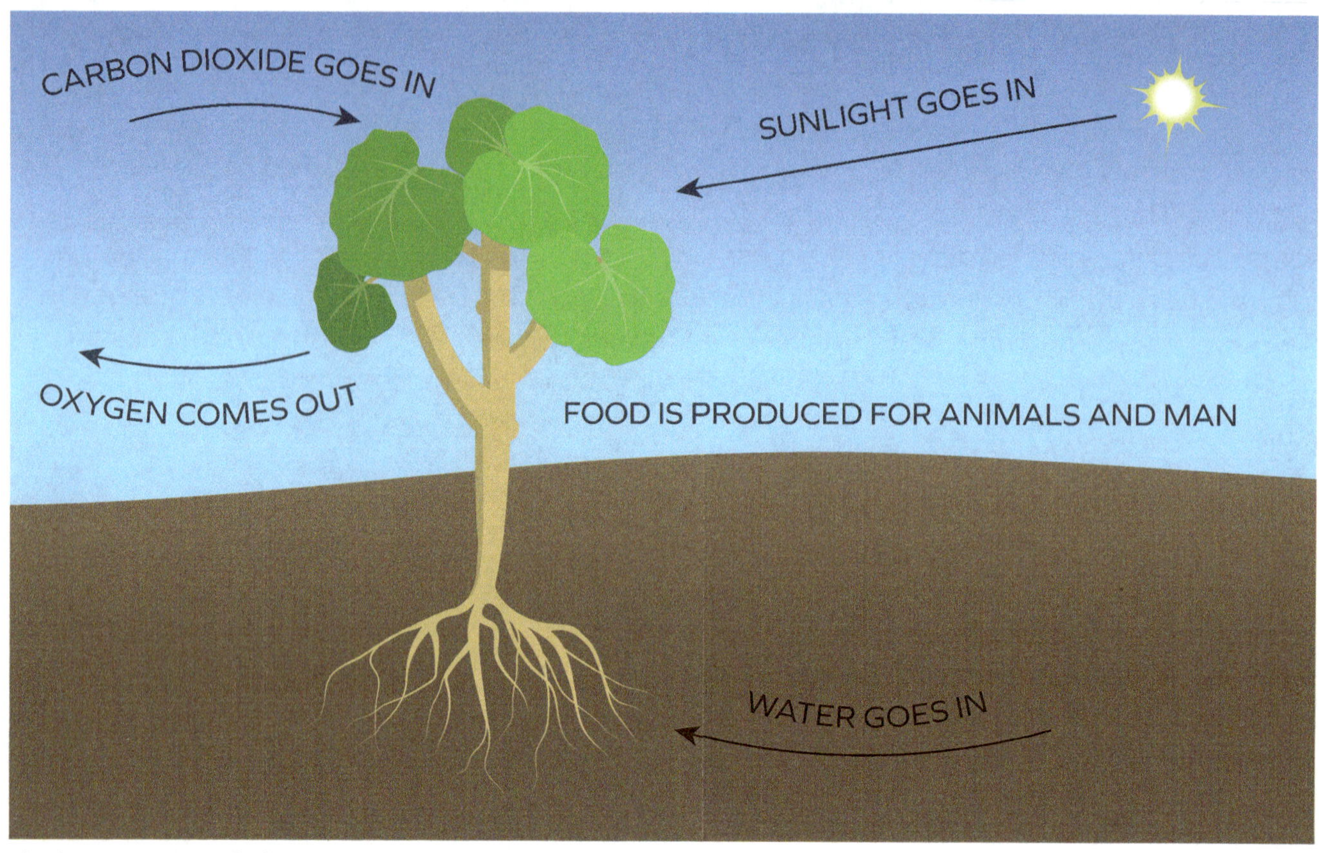

| The process of photosynthesis

Cells in plants or fungi that perform a similar function are called *tissue*. Plants and fungi have epidermal, connective, storage, and supportive tissues. Connective tissues carry needed materials through the plant or fungus. Storage tissues store food.

Write the correct letter and answer in the blank.

1.1 Some living things consist of only one cell and are called ______________________ organisms.

a. multicellular b. unicellular c. regular

1.2 Three-part cells are called ______________________ cells.

a. prokaryote b. eukaryote c. complex

1.3 In most plant and fungus cells, there is a fourth part of the cell called the ______________________.

a. protoplasm b. cavity c. cell wall

1.4 The chloroplasts within a cell contain ______________________, a green pigment.

a. proteins b. chlorophyll c. oxygen

1.5 In ______________________, the energy from the sun is used by the chlorophyll to combine carbon dioxide and water in the plant.

a. photosynthesis b. hydration c. oxidation

Complete this list.

1.6 List the five kingdoms of all living things.

a. ______________________ b. ______________________

c. ______________________ d. ______________________

e. ______________________

Do this activity. In the first two LIFEPACs of this series—Science 501 and Science 502—you learned many new vocabulary words. Some of these vocabulary words are listed below; however, the letters in these words are scrambled within the little "cells" below. Unscramble the vocabulary words and write them correctly within the cell. Note that the first letter of each correctly spelled word is in bold print. After you have written the word correctly, write the definition on the lines following the cell.

1.7 lel**c** ______________________

____

1.8 selulo**c**l ______________________

____

1.9 leco**n**ulus ______________________

____

1.10 lemy**x** ______________________

____

1.11 sitseus ______________________________

1.12 igfnu ______________________________

1.13 sytea ______________________________

1.14 ressop ______________________________

Types of plants, fungi, protists, and monerans. Each living organism must reproduce if its species is to survive. Its method of reproduction helps determine its *classification* among the kingdoms of living things. For example, some plants are seed-bearing, and other plants are cone-bearing. Each plant type includes many varieties of plants. These plants often look very different. They have different parts, and their life cycles may vary greatly.

Seed-bearing plants reproduce by means of a seed. The seed is formed only after an egg from the plant has been fertilized by sperm. The fertilized egg grows into an embryo through *mitosis*, a process in which the cells of the organism grow, split, and divide. A seed coat is formed around the embryo.

| An avocado is a seed-bearing plant.

In a flowering plant, the seed is surrounded by the flower's ovary. The ovary becomes fruit. In a cone-bearing plant, the seed grows inside the female cone. The cone functions much like fruit, but it is not considered a fruit.

| Certain pine trees are cone-bearing plants.

The seeds of both flowering and cone-bearing plants begin to grow when they fall to the ground and are covered by soil. Warmth and water help the new plants to mature. The life cycle continues as these plants mature into adults and produce new seeds.

Spore-bearing plants do not produce seeds. They reproduce by means of spores. Ferns are an example of plants that reproduce by spores. Spores of fern plants do not grow into adult plants. They grow into tiny green plants through mitosis. Then, the egg cells and sperm cells are formed. After fertilization, embryos begin to develop. These embryos grow into adult ferns.

Many types of fungi also reproduce by spores. The spores in fungi function somewhat differently than they do in plants. Spores are released into the air by the parent fungus. When they settle onto something warm and damp, they begin to grow. They grow into adult fungi through mitosis.

Many one-celled organisms reproduce by giving up part of themselves. The parent organism divides into two new cells. Each new organism cell can perform all the functions needed to survive. Algae, which may be either protists or monerans, divide through mitosis. The algae cell grows and reproduces in a short time. Yeast, a type of fungus, reproduces through budding. Colonies of yeast cells may be connected, but each yeast cell is a separate organism. Reproduction of yeast happens very fast in warm, damp conditions.

| Different Types of Algae

1.15

Draw a diagram.

In this space, draw a diagram of a flowering plant. Label the parts. Use arrows to show what happens during reproduction. (You may need to use the Science 502 LIFEPAC for review.)

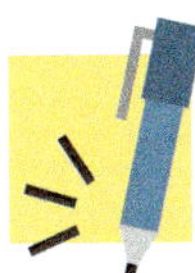

Match these items.

1.16 __________ sperm
1.17 __________ stamen
1.18 __________ mitosis
1.19 __________ sac
1.20 __________ cone near top of tree
1.21 __________ ovary
1.22 __________ seed
1.23 __________ hyphae
1.24 __________ anther
1.25 __________ pistil
1.26 __________ egg cell
1.27 __________ fruit
1.28 __________ larger cone
1.29 __________ stigma
1.30 __________ pollen

a. male part
b. female part
c. neither male nor female

Complete this activity.

1.31 Mitosis is important for the growth of cells and for reproduction. Budding is also a form of reproduction. In the spaces below, describe what happens in these processes.

a. mitosis ____

____

____

____

____

b. budding ____

____

____

____

____

Life of Animals and Animal-Like Protists

The cells of animals have a similar general structure. All animal cells are eukaryote cells; that is, they have a cell membrane, cytoplasm, and nucleus. Yet, there are many variations in the cells of animals. Size, shape, and specific inner structure determine whether animal cells are part of muscle, blood, bone, or other tissues. The animals cells are joined together to make a specific organism. Each organism is part of a species of animal. All of these species survive through reproduction.

Many animal species exist. They may be classified in several ways. One way to classify animals is to group them according to whether or not they have a backbone. Thus, animals are either vertebrates (with a backbone) or invertebrates (no backbone). Within these two groups are animals of various types. God placed a great variety of animals on the earth!

Cells. The cells of animals do not have to be rigid like those of plants and fungi. Thus, animal cells do not need cell walls. Also, animals do not undergo photosynthesis. They have no chloroplasts or chlorophyll within their cells.

Animal cells need to vary in size and shape because of the functions they perform. Blood cells must be round and unattached in order to move throughout the body system. Epithelial cells need to be long and thin to cover the body's surface. All of these cells are joined together to form tissues and the animal's body.

Animal cells function somewhat similar to those of plants and fungi. They take in food and store it. They use the food stored in cells for survival. However, animal cells use oxygen and give off carbon dioxide. In plants, it is just the opposite because photosynthesis takes in carbon dioxide and produces oxygen.

Animal tissues include epithelial, connective, muscular, and nervous tissue. In each of these tissues, the cells are similar and are grouped to perform similar body functions. Muscle tissues help move the body. Nervous tissues carry messages. Connective tissues join and support all of the body's cells. Epithelial cells cover the body and protect it. Linings within the body are also made of epithelial cells.

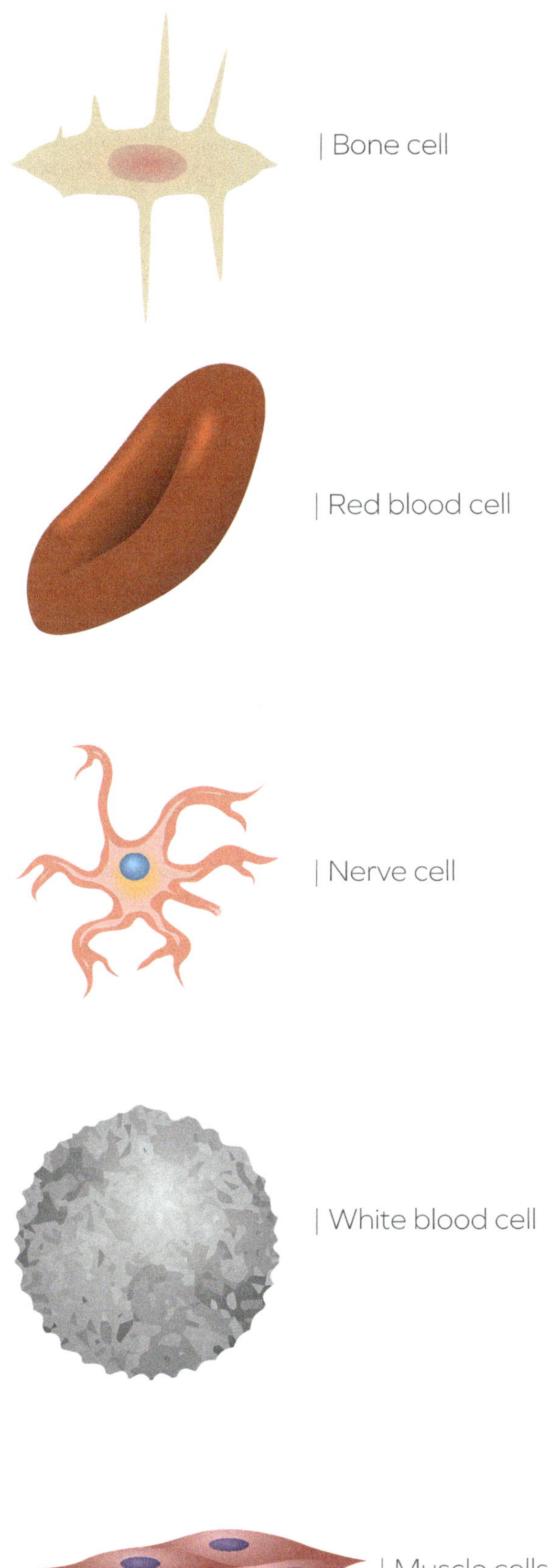

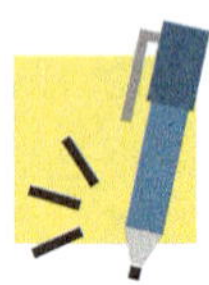

Write *true* or *false*.

1.32 __________ Animal cells take in oxygen and give off carbon dioxide.

1.33 __________ Animal cells contain chloroplasts.

1.34 __________ Photosynthesis is the same as mitosis.

1.35 __________ Food is stored in animal cells.

1.36 __________ Epithelial cells are skin cells.

1.37 __________ Cells in a tissue do not perform a similar function.

1.38 __________ The size and shape of cells can indicate what they do.

1.39 __________ Invertebrates have a backbone.

Use the Internet or library.

1.40 Organs of animal bodies are composed of tissues. These organs function in special ways. Use the Internet or library to learn more about one of the body's organs or tissues. Then write a summary of your findings. Include ideas about the importance of cell size and shape for organ or tissue function. Here is a list of some animal organs or tissues. Choose one of these or one of your own choice.

heart	eye	liver	bone	muscle
nerve	brain	ear	stomach	cartilage
blood	gland	skin	nose	lung

Teacher check:

Initials ____________________ Date ____________________

Types of animals and animal-like protists. Animals can be classified as invertebrates or vertebrates. Some protists have animal-like qualities, such as the ability to move from place to place and the ability to take in oxygen and give off carbon dioxide (like animals do). All of these living organisms—animals and animal-like protists—go through a life cycle involving birth, reproduction, and death.

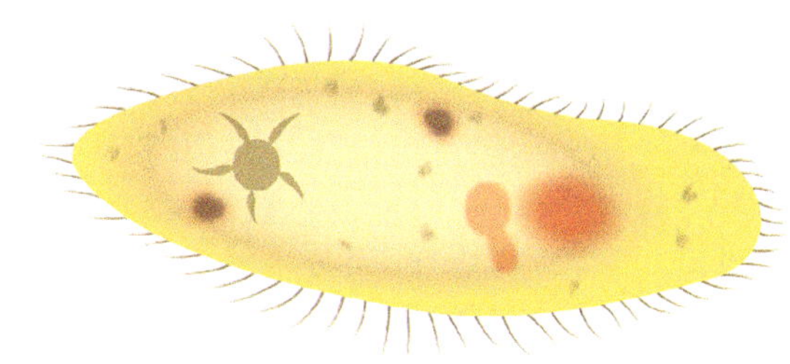

| Paramecium

Protozoans are one type of animal-like protists. These organisms obtain food through their cell membranes. In much the same way, their waste passes back through the membrane of their cell. Through a process called osmosis, oxygen passes into the cell of the protozoan, and carbon dioxide is released from the cell.

Reproduction in most protozoans occurs through mitosis. The nucleus of the parent cell divides. Cytoplasm surrounds each new nucleus. Then the two parts of the cell divide and split, forming two new offspring. Other types of protozoans reproduce through budding. Some protozoans reproduce by forming spores. Still others show the beginnings of sexual reproduction, requiring a male and female parent. God has provided an amazing variety of reproduction in these tiny creatures!

Invertebrate animals can be classified as insects, worms, or mollusks. These creatures do not have backbones. All of these groups of invertebrates are egg-layers; however, each of these groups differs in body structure. Some stages in the life cycle are also different from group to group.

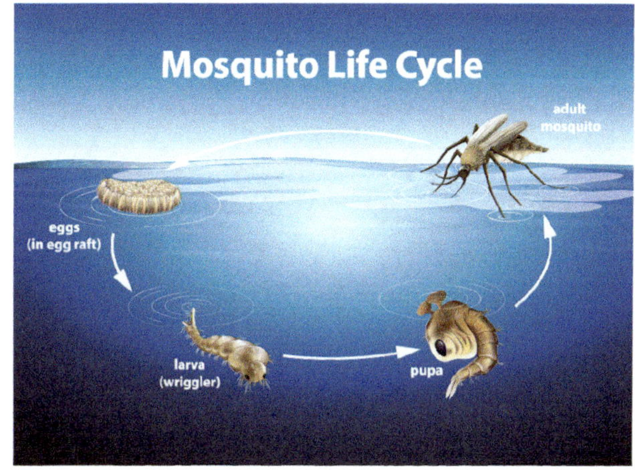

The beginning of insect reproduction occurs when the female forms eggs in her ovaries. Sperm from a male are deposited in another special part of her body. When the female lays her eggs, the sperm fertilize them. After hatching, the new insects undergo a growth stage. A few insects grow into adults when a tiny copy of the parent is hatched (for example, the silverfish). Other insects go through a nymph form before becoming adults (like the cricket). Some insects are hatched into larvae, change into pupae, and finally become adults. (The housefly is an example.)

Worms come in many varieties. The most commonly known worm is the earthworm. Tapeworms, flatworms, roundworms, and leeches are other types of worms. Worm eggs are fertilized inside the female body (or, for an earthworm, the female part of the body).

Then the eggs are released before they are hatched. Many baby worms are copies of their parents. However, some worm species (such as the tapeworm) hatch into larvae. These larvae need a host (such as a cat) in order to survive. During this stage, the larvae are called parasites. Later, they become adult tapeworms and continue to be a parasite requiring a host.

| The octopus is a mollusk.

Mollusks are soft-bodied invertebrates that have no bones. Most species of mollusks grow hard shells to protect themselves. Snails, clams, and oysters are examples of hard-shelled mollusks. Some mollusks, like the squid and octopus, do not have a hard, outer shell for protection.

Some mollusks' eggs are fertilized inside the females' bodies. Other mollusk species lay their eggs before fertilization. The eggs are in small cases when they are laid. Larvae are hatched. Some mollusk larvae come out of the cases and must find a plant or animal host until they reach adulthood. Other mollusk larvae remain in the case and come out as young adults. Shells are grown by some mollusk larvae, but most mollusks grow their main shell during the adult stage.

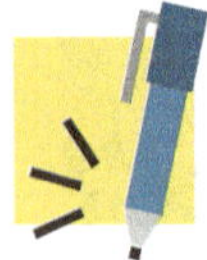

Complete this list.

1.41 On another piece of paper, list the names of as many animal-like protists, insects, worms, and mollusks as you can. When you have finished, write your total numbers in the spaces below.

The number of names on my list is:

Animal-like protists ______________

Insects ______________

Worms ______________

Mollusks ______________

Use the Internet or library.

1.42 Now use the Internet, other books, or the Science 503 LIFEPAC, to find the names of other animal-like protists, insects, worms, and mollusks. Using your list in number 1.41 plus the additional names that you discover, write the names of the various creatures in the table below. (You may not have room for all of them that you find. Choose those that have different features.)

	ANIMAL-LIKE PROTISTS	INSECTS	WORMS	MOLLUSKS
A.				
B.				
C.				
D.				
E.				
F.				
G.				
H.				
I.				
J.				

Teacher check:

Initials ____________________ Date ____________________

Complete these vocabulary activities.

1.43 What is the difference between mitosis and osmosis? ______________________

____

____

____

____

1.44 How are hosts and parasites related? ______________________

____

____

____

____

1.45 How are pupae, larvae, and nymphs similar? ______________________

____

____

____

____

1.46 How are pupae, larvae, and nymphs different? ______________________

____

____

____

____

Vertebrates are animals with backbones. Their backbones and other bones form their skeletons. Skeletons give shape to the bodies of these animals and protect their internal organs. All vertebrates are multicellular. They have many varieties of bodies and differing life cycles. Fish, amphibians, reptiles, and birds are egg-laying vertebrates. Mammals are vertebrates that are live-bearing.

Fish are vertebrates that live in the water. They use gills to breathe. Most fish are egg-layers. Their eggs are laid by females and then fertilized by the sperm of males. After fertilization, the parents do not stay near the eggs. The eggs hatch into tiny copies of the parents. A few of the adults grow into adulthood and reproduce. Several fish species are live-bearing. The parents do not care for or protect the offspring.

Amphibians live part of their lives in the water like fish, but then change and live part of their lives on land. This process of change is called *metamorphosis*. Frogs are an example of amphibians. Their eggs are laid and fertilized in the water. After the eggs hatch, the new offspring appear more like fish than their parents. During this part of their life cycle, the amphibians live like small fish and cannot survive out of the water. Soon, the amphibians begin to change and grow lungs and legs. Tails disappear, and the offspring now appear more like their parents. They can no longer live underwater without coming to the surface for air.

Reptiles are vertebrates that are covered with scales, or plates, for protection. Reptiles include alligators, lizards, snakes, and turtles. They usually live near water but cannot breathe underwater. Female reptiles lay their eggs on land rather than in water. Once they lay their eggs on the land, they do not stay near the nest to warm or protect their eggs. Newborn baby reptiles usually look like the parents, except their scales or plates are not yet hard.

Birds are the only animals that have feathers. All birds have wings, and almost all of them can fly. They have two legs. Their eggs are fertilized when still inside the females' bodies. Shells of the fertilized eggs become hardened before the female lays them. Parents need to keep the eggs warm and moist before hatching.

Newborn birds are nearly helpless and are fed and protected by the parents. As the baby birds grow and become stronger, they look more like their parents. Before long, they are pushed from their nest and learn to survive on their own.

Mammals are a very important group of vertebrates. They differ from almost all other animals in several important ways. Among these differences, only female mammals are able to nurse their babies with the milk they produce, and only mammals have hair. There are a great variety of mammals. They differ greatly in sizes, shapes, and life styles. Mammal embryos develop inside the female bodies. The *gestation period* of embryo development varies among mammals. Mother mammals produce milk to feed their offspring. Baby mammals are very weak at birth and need the care, protection, and training of their parents.

Draw a diagram.

1.47 In this space, draw a diagram of the life stages of a frog. Label the parts and stages. (You may need to refer to the Science 503 LIFEPAC.)

a. Define each word below as it is used in the study of animals.
b. Write a sentence using the word in another way.

1.48 plate

a. ____

____

b. ____

____

1.49 scale

a. ____

____

b. ____

____

Write the correct letter and answer in the blank.

1.50 A ____________________ has a backbone.

a. vertebrate b. worm c. mollusk

1.51 Amphibians live part of their lives like ____________________ .

a. birds b. fish c. carrots

1.52 Mammal mothers produce ____________________ for their young.

a. bones b. milk c. friends

1.53 Fish eggs are usually laid and fertilized ____________________ .

a. underwater b. in the warm sand c. on hosts

1.54 Newborn birds could not survive without ____________________ .

a. milk b. parasites c. parents

1.55 An example of a reptile is a(n) ____________________ .

a. tiger b. alligator c. bear

Balance of Nature

God has planned that all living things depend upon one another. Plants need animals to survive. Animals need plants to survive. All living things need energy. Some organisms need oxygen. Others need carbon dioxide. These life-supporting needs can be supplied from one organism to another. When the life needs of all living things in an area of the earth are met, we say that there is a *balance of nature*.

The balance of nature is influenced by many sources. Disease, weather, fire, and human beings affect the balance of nature. Some of these influences can cause all members of a certain animal or plant species to die or to move to another area of the earth. Let's examine some natural influences and some human influences on the balance of nature.

Natural influences. Plants receive energy from the sun. This energy is stored in green plant cells to be used later by the plants. Plants are also a source of energy for other living things that consume the plants.

Green plants are called *producers* because they are the main living things that produce food. Animals, fungi, and some other plants cannot make their own food. They must receive food from green plants. Examples of producers are grass and trees.

Organisms that receive their energy directly from plants are called *primary consumers*. These primary consumers can digest green plants or the seeds from green plants and receive energy from the food stored in plants. However, some animals cannot digest plants. They must eat other animals to receive food and energy. These animals are called *secondary consumers*.

| A primary consumer (cow) gets energy from a producer (grass).

Another group of organisms that contribute to the balance of nature are called *decomposers*. Bacteria and fungi are examples of decomposers. Decomposers feed on the waste products or dead bodies of other plants or animals. Decomposers receive their energy from the cells of those other sources.

Producers, consumers, and decomposers are parts of *food chains* in nature. These food chains are important to the balance of nature everywhere. Only a certain number of higher-order consumers (secondary consumers, third-level consumers, etc.) can be supported in a certain location, or *ecosystem*. A growth in the number of higher-order consumers could kill off many primary consumers. If that happened, certain plants would begin to be too numerous.

The higher-order consumers would begin to starve, and the balance of nature would be upset.

However, the balance of nature would eventually be restored. This is because more higher-order consumers would begin to die. Then, the primary consumers would be more likely to survive. Their numbers would grow. More plants (the producers) would be eaten, and the balance of nature would be restored.

| When the water cycle prevents a producer (grass), from surviving it can affect the whole food chain.

The *water cycle* also influences the balance of nature. Plants and animals need water to survive. Cytoplasm contains water, and the water helps the cells of living things do their work. Photosynthesis in green plants also depends upon water. Without the water cycle functioning correctly, plants could not get enough water. Thus, when a drought occurs, plants can die. When it rains too much, plants can be flooded and destroyed. All of life is affected by too little or too much rain.

Life also depends upon the *carbon cycle*. Plants use the carbon dioxide given off by animals. Animals need the oxygen given off by plants. When one of these needs is not filled, both plants and animals have problems. Sometimes this exchange between plants and animals occurs underwater. God has planned that there be a great balance of nature in all of His creation.

Complete these activities.

1.56 Why are baboons, sparrows, and human beings considered both primary and secondary consumers? ____

____

____

1.57 Why are there more primary consumers than secondary consumers?

____

____

____

____

____

1.58 Describe a food chain in an environment near you. (You may need to refer to the Science 504 LIFEPAC to complete this activity.)

____

____

____

____

List some general characteristics of the following groups of organisms that are special to each group.

1.59 producers ______________________________

____

____

1.60 primary consumers ______________________________

____

____

1.61 secondary consumers ______________________________

____

____

1.62 decomposers ______________________________

____

____

Write *true* or *false*.

1.63 __________ The food chain is part of the balance of nature.

1.64 __________ Cytoplasm is made up largely of water.

1.65 __________ Drought could affect the balance of nature.

1.66 __________ The lack of oxygen in a lake could cause problems for the animal life of that lake.

1.67 __________ Photosynthesis depends upon water.

1.68 __________ Green plants are the only producers.

1.69 __________ An oversupply of secondary consumers could cause the numbers of other forms of life to become smaller.

Human Impact on the Balance of Nature

Human influences. Human beings can also affect the balance of nature. God has given us the ability to make decisions. We can decide to preserve nature or destroy it. These decisions can be very important for the balance of nature. Loss of life and pollution can be the results of wrong decisions.

| Clearing land for construction affects the plants and animals in that area.

Even the decisions to build homes or clear land can affect the balance of nature. Some species can no longer survive after land is cleared or homes are built. Other plants and animals may increase in numbers with such human-caused changes. In such circumstances, human beings may need to become *predators* in order to keep the balance of nature.

Plant and animal life are affected by pollution. Waste chemicals in the air can slow growth in plants and cause problems with photosynthesis. Lungs of animals can be harmed and lives shortened. Chemicals polluting the water can cause similar problems for plants and often poison animals. These human influences work against the natural balance of nature.

God has given human beings responsibility for life (Genesis 1:28). We have been told to care for other living things. God wants us to be good *stewards* of His creation. Our choices determine whether or not we will have good stewardship of these things.

How can you be a good steward of plants and animals? Good stewardship would involve being careful. For example, you can properly dispose of waste products and recycle materials if possible. You can conserve natural resources like water. You can walk or ride a bicycle instead of taking a car or truck. You can decide not to bother animals in nature or their nests. You can hunt or fish within the law. You may need to feed some animals or kill others because you, too, are part of the balance of nature. It is not always easy to determine what would be the best way to be careful, but God will help you make the right choices as you pray to Him and ask for guidance.

Write the correct letter and answer on the blank.

1.70 Good stewardship involves ______________________ things.
a. polluting b. wasting c. caring for

1.71 Human beings ______________________ predators.
a. never are b. sometimes are c. should not kill

1.72 Pollution is not caused by ______________________ .
a. photosynthesis b. chemicals c. human beings

1.73 One way to ______________________ nature is to recycle wastes.
a. destroy b. be good stewards of c. upset

1.74 The balance of nature is sometimes helped by ______________________ decisions.
a. human b. animal c. plant

Use the news.

1.75 Newspapers and magazines often contain articles about pollution or other ways that human beings influence the balance of nature. Look for some of these articles in recent newspapers or magazines. Write a summary of one of the articles. Include ideas about the effects of human beings on the balance of nature. Explain why you think these effects are good or bad. Give your completed summary and this LIFEPAC to your teacher.

Teacher check:
Initials ______________ Date ______________

Review the material in this section to prepare for the Self Test. The Self Test will check your understanding of this section. Any items you miss on this test will show you what areas you will need to restudy in order to prepare for the unit test.

SELF TEST 1

Match these items (each answer, 3 points).

1.01 __________ bacteria
1.02 __________ mammal
1.03 __________ insect
1.04 __________ flowering
1.05 __________ blue-green algae
1.06 __________ amoeba
1.07 __________ reptile
1.08 __________ fruit
1.09 __________ yeast
1.10 __________ cone-bearing

a. moneran
b. animal-like protist
c. seed-bearing plant
d. fungi
e. egg-laying invertebrate
f. egg-laying vertebrate
g. live-bearing vertebrate

Write the correct letter and answer on the blank (each answer, 5 points).

1.011 All living things may be classified into ____________________ .
a. five kingdoms b. plants or animals c. mammals

1.012 A(n) ____________________ organism has many cells.
a. unicellular b. multicellular c. moneran

1.013 In ____________________ , the energy from the sun is used by the chlorophyll in a green plant to combine carbon dioxide and water.
a. osmosis b. photosynthesis c. migration

1.014 Only mammals have ____________________ .
a. wings b. shells c. hair

Label this diagram (this question, 10 points).

1.015 Use these words to label the diagram of a food chain: primary consumer, decomposer, secondary consumer, producer.

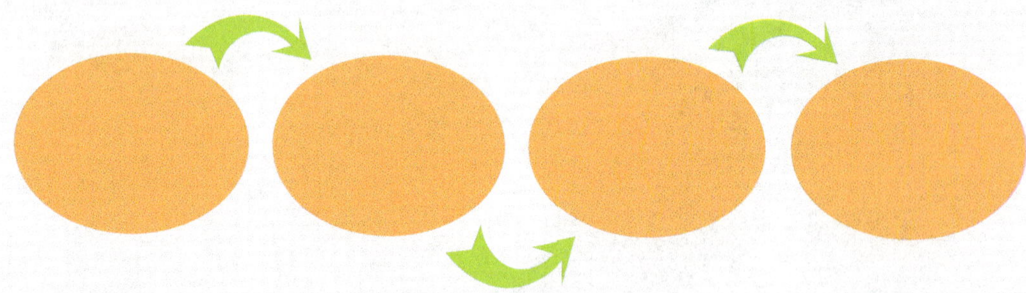

Write *true or false* (each answer, 3 points).

1.016 __________ Flowering plants produce seeds for reproduction.

1.017 __________ Prokaryote cells have three basic parts.

1.018 __________ Fish care for and nourish their young after birth.

1.019 __________ Animal cells contain chloroplasts.

1.020 __________ Mollusks are a type of fish.

1.021 __________ Only plants and fungi have cell walls.

1.022 __________ The balance of nature depends upon the water cycle.

1.023 __________ Birds are the only animals that have feathers.

1.024 __________ Humans cannot affect the balance of nature.

1.025 __________ Riding a bicycle instead of taking a car can show good stewardship.

Complete these activities (each answer, 5 points).

1.026 Explain how the carbon cycle is important to the balance of nature.

____

____

____

____

____

____

1.027 Why is mitosis important to plants and animals?

____

____

____

____

____

____

Teacher check: Initials ____________

Score ____________ Date ____________

80/100

2. THE EARTH

As stated in the beginning of this LIFEPAC, it is helpful to look at what was covered in the past in order to help prepare for what lies ahead. People have been interested in the history of the earth for a long time. They want to know what happened in the past and how living things came into existence.

Many theories and stories of the earth's formation and development have been given over the years. Some of these stories and theories have become outdated or have proven they are impossible. The story and explanation of earth's beginning and development as recorded in the Bible has lasted for several thousand years. Other explanations have been developed by some scientists over the past 200 years.

Why is the earth's past explained in so many different ways? No person living today was able to observe Earth's beginnings. No records of the earliest times were written as they happened. We must get our information today from evidence we can gather from physical records and from written material recorded after these events happened. As Christians, we can trust that the record written down in the first eleven chapters of the Bible was *inspired by God*. It is a written record of what God wanted us to know about the earliest times of life upon Earth.

Evidence about the history of the earth can come from many sources. You will examine *records of life* by studying the Bible and by reviewing information on fossils. In addition, the story of the Flood in the Bible and the science of geology can be helpful in learning more about *records in rock*.

Objectives

Review these objectives. When you have completed this section, you should be able to:

4. Explain geological records.
5. Compare physical records and Biblical records of the earth's past.

Records of Life

Read Genesis chapters 1–8 to learn more about living things and changes that happened on Earth.

Both the Biblical record and the physical record in fossils and rocks show that the earth has contained living things for a long time. The Bible tells about changes that happened to life on earth as a result of the Flood. Fossil records also show that life was not always as we know it today.

Bible Record. The Bible contains a written record of the earliest life on Earth. It tells us that God created the earth and everything in the earth. God placed human beings on earth to care for the life He had made. A great many other things, including plants and animals, filled the earth. God made human beings the stewards of all these things.

The people who lived before the Flood learned many trades. They were able to farm, build, work with metals, and play musical instruments. These people used their intelligence to improve life on Earth. At the same time, people chose to destroy life and property. They chose to disobey God. Lives were taken. Terrible things were planned. Because of the wickedness that came on Earth through the sin of human beings, God decided to have a fresh beginning for life on Earth.

The Bible explains that Noah lived a life pleasing to God. God chose Noah to help Him make a new beginning on Earth. God told Noah to build an ark. When the ark was completed, Noah took food supplies on board. He also took seven pairs of clean animals and one pair of unclean animals onto the ark. Noah's family also entered the ark. Then God shut the door to the ark.

After Noah, his family, and all the pairs of creatures were safely inside the ark, God caused the waters of the deep and the floodgates of heaven to bring forth water upon the earth. It rained for the first time upon the earth. The rain lasted forty days and forty nights. The great Flood happened. Animals, plants, and human beings outside the ark on the earth could not survive the great Flood. Only the animals and people in Noah's ark were saved from drowning.

After nearly a year in the ark, some land had dried enough for Noah, his family, and the animals to leave the ark. The earth had changed. Seasons began. The earth continued to have rain and snow. Life began again. Perhaps seeds and spores that floated on the waters settled in the earth for the start of new plants.

Some scientists believe that fossil deposits were formed as a result of the Flood. Perhaps animals tried to escape the onrushing waters. They crowded together until there was nowhere to go. The great pressures of the water may have caused the land to heave and move. This movement could have trapped animals and covered plants.

Physical evidence exists that long ago the earth's climate was much the same all over the world. The Bible suggests the same idea by reporting that the seasons began after the Flood (Genesis 8:22). This fact can possibly explain why remains of similar species were found in many places all over the world.

| Shell fossil

SCIENCE 510

LIFEPAC TEST

NAME ______________________

DATE ______________________

SCORE ______________________

80
100

SCIENCE 510: LIFEPAC TEST

Match these items (each answer, 3 points).

1. __________ unicellular
2. __________ cytoplasm
3. __________ chloroplasts
4. __________ yeast
5. __________ mitosis
6. __________ balance of nature
7. __________ original-remains
8. __________ work
9. __________ metamorphic
10. __________ solubility

a. contain chlorophyll
b. cell division
c. transformation of energy from one form to another
d. a form of chemical energy
e. organism has only one cell
f. liquid within cell membrane
g. a type of fungus
h. life needs are met
i. a type of plant
j. a type of fossil
k. a physical property of matter
l. a type of rock

Write *true* or *false* (each answer counts 2 points).

11. ______________ Green plants are primary consumers.
12. ______________ Bacteria are a form of animal-like protists.
13. ______________ Mollusks are a type of invertebrate.
14. ______________ Natural and human influences affect the balance of nature.
15. ______________ The Bible is one of the records of life.
16. ______________ Physical evidence suggests that long ago the climate was much the same all over the earth.
17. ______________ Growing plants can split rocks.
18. ______________ Noah took one pair of clean animals into the ark.
19. ______________ Kinetic energy is energy that is stored.

20. ____________ God wants human beings to be good stewards of energy sources.

21. ____________ Molecules sometimes stop their motion.

22. ____________ When water changes from liquid to steam, a chemical change occurs.

Complete this diagram (each answer, 2 points).

23. Draw a diagram of the earth's layers and use these labels:

outer core	mantle	crust	inner core

Write the correct letter and word(s) on each line (each answer, 5 points).

24. A(n) ________________________ has no backbone.
a. invertebrate b. vertebrate c. mammal

25. A fox is a ________________________ .
a. producer
b. secondary consumer
c. decomposer

26. All living things may be classified into ________________________ .
a. five kingdoms b. protozoans c. multicellulars

27. In a ________________ fossil, only carbon is left from the original remains.
a. print b. mold c. carbonized

28. Earthquakes usually happen at ______________ lines.
a. fold b. fault c. power

29. Cycles of nature are an example of ________________________ .
a. mitosis b. chemical changes c. God's order

Complete these activities (each answer, 5 points).

30. Describe at least two ways that mammals differ from all other animals.

____
____
____

31. Explain how human influences affect the balance of nature.

____
____
____
____
____
____
____
____
____
____

Some scientists believe that oil and coal were formed slowly, over billions of years. Other scientists suggest that the Flood caused changes in the earth's surface that resulted in oil and coal. The great destruction of plant and animal life would have supplied the oil and coal deposits. Tremendous pressure of water and shifting rocks may have helped to form oil and coal over a shorter period of time. It is also possible that God created the earth with oil and coal in it.

Complete these sentences.

2.1 The builder of the ark was ________________ .

2.2 Noah took ______________________ pair(s) of clean animals on board the ark.

2.3 Land may have heaved under the __________________________ of the water from the Flood.

2.4 Evidence exists that before the Flood the _____________________ was similar over the whole earth.

2.5 The Flood may have been responsible for formation of a. ______________________ and b. ________________________ .

Be creative in this story-writing activity.

2.6 You will need a partner to complete this activity.

____

Partner's Name

Follow these directions and complete the activities. Check the box when each step is completed.

☐ 1. Discuss the following questions. Think of as many ideas as you can for each question.
   a. What was life like for people before the time of the Flood?
   b. What was life like for animals before the time of the Flood?
   c. Where did animals get their food?

☐ 2. Consider what it would have been like to be an animal in the early days of the earth. Discuss these ideas.
   a. Who would be your friends?
   b. Who would be your enemies?

☐ 3. Suppose you were an animal living at the time when Noah was building the ark. Discuss these ideas.
   a. What do you think about Noah's actions?
   b. What are people saying about Noah?
   c. What are you hoping for when it comes time to fill the ark?
   d. How would you feel if you were chosen for the ark?
   e. What things might happen to you if you were not chosen for the ark?
   f. What things might happen to you if you were chosen for the ark?

☐ 4. Choose an animal that may have lived during Noah's time. On a separate sheet of paper, write about what happened to it during the Flood. (The animal may be on the ark, or it may not have been chosen.) Use your imagination.

☐ 5. When the story is finished, read it to your partner.

☐ 6. Have your partner check the story with you to help make corrections.

☐ 7. Take this LIFEPAC and your paper to the teacher for a teacher check.

Teacher check:

Initials _______________ Date _______________

Fossils. Fossils are part of the physical record of life that God has given us. Fossils tell of life in the past. Both animal fossils and plant fossils have been found. These fossils have been discovered all over the world and are of several different types.

Types of fossils. Print fossils were formed by the imprints of bodies in soft sediment. When the sediment hardened and the bodies decayed, the outer shapes remained. These are mold fossils. Sometimes, minerals filled the spaces left from the decayed bodies. After hardening, the minerals became another kind of print fossil—the cast fossil.

| Plant fossil

Original-remains fossils are plants and animals that were trapped in the earth long ago and have not decayed. Mastodons have been discovered frozen in permafrost. Amber has preserved some insects. Shells and bones have been found underground, too.

Petrified fossils are really rock. They are made of minerals that have replaced the original matter. The new substance looks very much like the material that was replaced.

Carbonized fossils represent another type of change in the bodies of plants or animals. Instead of decaying, another process caused everything to dissolve except the carbon in the bodies. The carbon is left in the rock and shows many details of the original plants or animals.

Fossils have been discovered in many types of deposits. Large groups of each type of fossil have been identified in various sites around the world. Individual fossils can be found almost anywhere on the earth. The most common fossils are those found in limestone, shale, or sandstone.

Fossils are fun to find. It may be easy to unearth and to classify fossil types. It is, however, more difficult to make inferences about early life from fossil clues.

Reading fossils. We can read fossils more easily when we have knowledge of present-day plants and animals. Then, comparisons may be made. All fossils could be grouped according to species, because of similar shape or special parts. However, many species were not preserved. Their parts were too soft, and they perhaps were crushed before they could be fossilized.

When parts are missing, it is difficult to identify fossils. Sometimes pieces are broken. Often, parts from several animals are found together. Some fossils of extinct animals also have been unearthed. Some fossils have been located in areas where the species would not be expected to live. All of those who want to read fossils face these difficult problems.

In spite of many difficulties, some scientists have learned how to read fossils well. They use every bit of data from the fossil: its location, the shape of its parts, and living things. These people use every possible clue to make inferences about the environment. From the available clues, the size and shape of animals, how they moved, and what they ate can be inferred. Even inferences about climate are possible.

Scientists sometimes have to infer from fossils how a species may have looked.

Inferences can be used to draw conclusions about early life. Understanding of the prehistoric earth is improved by these conclusions. Inferences also are used in another way. Animals may be reconstructed from the fossil parts. Scientists use inferences to reconstruct skeletons or create models of prehistoric creatures. Computer models can be used to help in this process. These reconstructions help our understanding by giving us a picture of early life.

Write the correct letter and answer on the blank.

2.7 Commonly found fossils are of the ____________________ type.

a. petrified b. print c. carbonized

2.8 Undecayed plants and animals of long ago are ____________________ fossils.

a. original-remains b. permafrost c. cast

2.9 It is difficult to read fossils, especially when ____________________.

a. all the parts are present

b. the animal is extinct

c. it is the only animal in the deposit

2.10 A clue that can be helpful about a fossil is its ____________________.

a. location b. speed c. conclusion

2.11 Information about the ______________________ the prehistoric earth can be inferred from fossils.

a. languages on b. climate of c. knowledge of people on

Explain these terms as related to fossils.

2.12 inference ______________________

____

____

2.13 reconstruction ______________________

____

____

Complete this puzzle.

2.14 This puzzle contains eight vocabulary words from Science LIFEPAC 507. The words are also found in this review section on fossils. Begin in any space. Move from box to box in any direction until the word is formed. (Boxes always touch the next box on the corner or side.) You may move vertically, horizontally, or diagonally. List the words on the lines.

O	H	A	E	N	U
D	T	R	N	S	S
O	S	A	I	T	E
N	H	L	M	B	R
E	T	E	I	L	A
D	I	I	F	E	D

a. ______________________ b. ______________________

c. ______________________ d. ______________________

e. ______________________ f. ______________________

g. ______________________ h. ______________________

Records in Rock

Hills, valleys, mountains, rivers, and oceans are landforms that cover the earth. The earth is large, and these landforms are tiny in comparison. The earth is always changing. It did not always appear as it does today. Sometimes the changes were small. Large changes resulted from great forces. The science of geology also tells of the earth's history, makeup, and changes.

The Flood. The Bible describes the Flood. We can infer that changes in the earth resulted from the Flood. Many clues in the Bible point to a changed world following the Flood. Inferences can be made that oceans were deepened and continents pushed up (Read Psalm 104:5–9 to find some evidence). The huge Flood could have caused sediments to be deposited in layers.

Perhaps glaciers began as a result of the Flood. Glaciers may have eroded stone and broken it into smaller pieces. Organized deposits of rock may also have been left by glaciers. Volcanoes and earthquakes were probably active around the time of the Flood, too. Creation scientists, who believe that the Bible indicates what happened long ago, find that the Flood helps them to explain much of the geological evidence that others cannot explain.

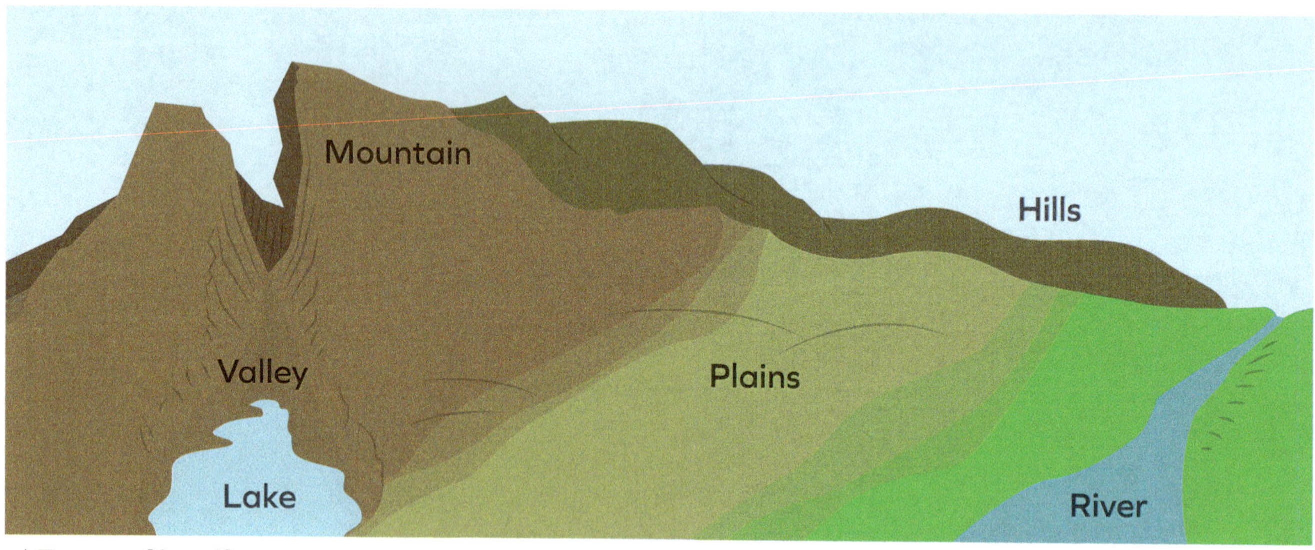

| Types of landforms

Write *true* or *false*.

2.15 __________ The Bible has much direct information which tells us how the earth changed after the Flood.

2.16 __________ The Bible explains how glaciers got their start.

2.17 __________ Earthquakes may have been active during the time of the Flood.

2.18 __________ The earth's landforms are changing.

2.19 __________ Psalm 104 suggests that the Flood changed the surface of the earth.

Geology. The earth has three main parts. The crust is a thin surface layer. Just below the crust is a thick mantle layer. In the center of the earth is a section called the core. The core has two parts—the outer core and the inner core.

The crust is the earth's layer that supports life. Rocks and soil are part of the crust and make up the crust's landforms. These materials probably have less mass than those deeper inside the earth.

The crust and its features cause pressure on the mantle. The pressure causes heat to build up in the mantle rocks. Chemical reactions may also cause some heat. Scientists believe that hot magma flows between mantle rocks. Shifting of the mantle materials also occurs. These shifts sometimes cause surface features to change.

The core is believed to be very hot. Its material is probably iron and nickel. The outer core seems to be magma with no solid rocks. The inner core is considered a dense ball of very hot materials. No one is certain of the makeup of the mantle and the core, but inferences have been made from scientific tests.

The earth's surface is easier to describe accurately. It can be observed in closer detail. The rocks are made up of minerals. These rocks can be classified according to how they were formed.

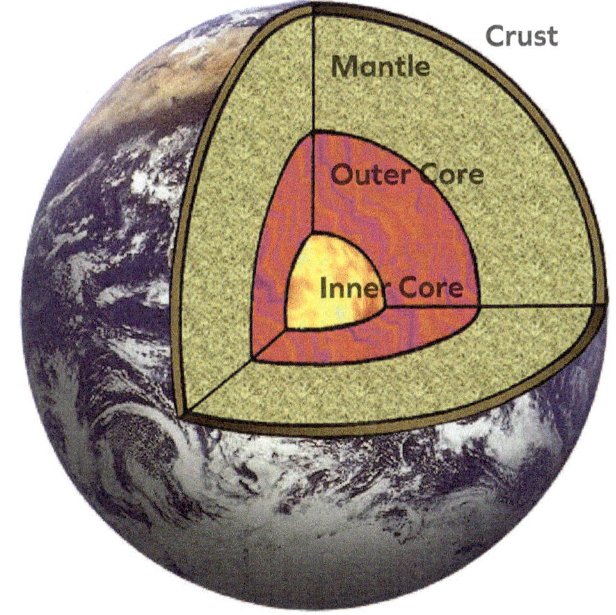

| Layers of the earth

Sedimentary rocks can be found in layers. They were formed when sediment was washed into low areas of the crust. Pressures of water and soil and natural cements caused the sediments to harden as layers. Igneous rocks come from magma that has cooled. Metamorphic rock is a type of rock that has changed from one form into a different form. The change is both physical and chemical.

Rocks can be identified by several methods. Guidebooks give clues and data about rocks. Knowledge of rock deposits also can be helpful. Laboratory tests on chemicals in rocks can help in identification. Simple observation tests can be used to identify rocks. These tests check for color, luster, streak, hardness, and cleavage of the rocks.

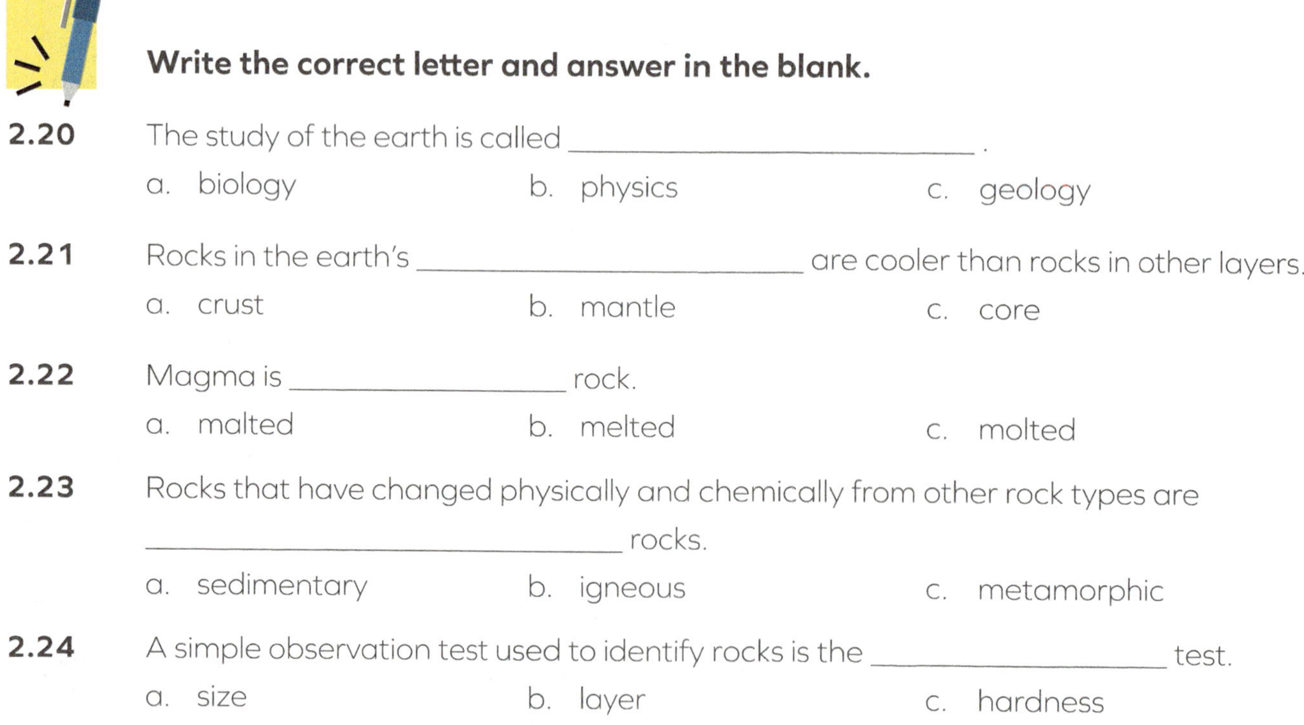

Write the correct letter and answer in the blank.

2.20 The study of the earth is called ______________ .

a. biology b. physics c. geology

2.21 Rocks in the earth's ______________ are cooler than rocks in other layers.

a. crust b. mantle c. core

2.22 Magma is ______________ rock.

a. malted b. melted c. molted

2.23 Rocks that have changed physically and chemically from other rock types are ______________ rocks.

a. sedimentary b. igneous c. metamorphic

2.24 A simple observation test used to identify rocks is the ______________ test.

a. size b. layer c. hardness

Complete this activity. Select a rock from your teacher's rock supply. Use guidebooks, your knowledge, and other sources of information to help you decide what type it is. Try to further identify it if possible.

2.25 This rock is ________________________________ .

a. sedimentary b. igneous c. metamorphic

2.26 I identify the rock as ____________________________________ .

After identification, think about the rock's history.
How was it formed? Where might it have formed? What events did it experience?

On a separate piece of paper, write a short description of the rock's journey (as you imagine it) from its formation to the present time. When you finish your creative description, take your paper and this LIFEPAC to your teacher for a teacher check.

Teacher check:
Initials ____________________ Date ____________________

How has the earth changed with time? Powerful forces are constantly at work to change features. These forces can build up and tear down landforms. Some of the forces work slowly. Other forces have sudden and far-reaching effects. These forces have been observed for centuries. Scientists use observations of them to make inferences. Some of the theories about how the earth changes have been tested. Changes and forces can be described. However, ideas about how the earth changed long ago and which forces were most involved in the changes are different.

| Weathering sometimes creates unusual formations like this arch.

Weathering wears away the earth's surface. Wind, rain, and temperature cause rocks to reshape, chip, or crack. Sometimes, chemical action caused by rain helps to break down rocks.

Wind and rain also can cause erosion. Soil and sand can be moved from place to place. The earth's surface changes when valleys are cut deeper by running water, or when floods deposit sediment in low places. Erosion tears down some areas by removing soil and sand. However, other areas are built up by erosion when these materials are deposited.

Glaciers are large, moving masses of ice and snow. They usually move through valleys. Under the weight, rocks are worn down. Valleys are widened. After the ice melts, hills and lakes remain.

Plants and animals also change the earth's surface. Sometimes, growing plants split rocks. Soil is worn down by animals. Human beings change the landscape by farming, building roads, and moving small landforms.

The earth's surface can be changed by forces below it. Folding, faulting, earthquakes, and volcanoes have changed the earth greatly in the past. Forces are at work today causing changes to the earth.

Some areas of land are slowly sinking, while other areas are rising. Folding is one cause of this movement. Some of the layers in the crust push against each other. This pushing causes layers to bend, break, and overlap. Faulting often occurs along with folding. Faults are cracks in rock layers, and the pressures of folding can push one of these layers past another. Some scientists believe that our present mountains and land areas were formed by folding and faulting.

Earthquakes also change the surface. They shake whole areas and sometimes cause a shifting of rock layers. Earthquakes usually occur at fault lines. Some land areas have been tilted by earthquakes. Lakes, too, have been formed by earthquakes.

When hot magma is forced from the earth's mantle up through the crust, a volcano may result. Lava flows out and cools. A cone structure forms from the cooled lava. Many landforms also have been formed by magma that did not reach the surface. The magma squeezed between rock layers and cooled. Some hills and mountains were formed this way.

Even things from outer space can alter the landscape, like an asteroid hitting the earth.

Complete these activities.

2.27 Expanding and contracting are important to the weathering process. Explain the meaning of these words.

a. expanding ______________________________

____

b. contracting ______________________________

____

2.28 How do expanding and contracting work together in the weathering process?

____

____

____

____

Complete these lists.

2.29 List the forces that change the surface of the earth.

Surface Forces	**Forces from below the Surface**
a. ______________	e. ______________
b. ______________	f. ______________
c. ______________	g. ______________
d. ______________	h. ______________

Complete these activities. Follow these directions. Check the box when each step is completed.

2.30 This activity may be done near school or as a home project. You may ask someone to work with you.

☐ 1. Select a landform to observe. ______________________________
My landform

☐ 2. Use any information or knowledge available to list ways the landform may have developed. Consider the forces involved.

☐ 3. Write your ideas in a short description of the landform. Tell how you think it was formed, and how it has changed.

☐ 4. Copy your description neatly on a separate sheet of paper.

Teacher check:

Initials ____________________ Date ____________________

Complete this maze.

2.31 This maze is of a volcano. Start at the arrow on the top of the cone. You will come out at one of the arrows at the bottom.

Review the material in this section to prepare for the Self Test. The Self Test will check your understanding of this section and will review the other sections. Any items you miss on this test will show you what areas you will need to restudy in order to prepare for the unit test.

SELF TEST 2

Write *true* or *false* (each answer, 2 points).

2.01 ________ Animals are not a force in changing the earth's surface.

2.02 ________ Folding can cause mountains to rise.

2.03 ________ Water erosion can cause some rivers to cut deeper.

2.04 ________ Growing plants can split rocks.

2.05 ________ People sometimes remove landforms.

2.06 ________ Chemical tests can be used to identify rocks.

2.07 ________ Materials toward the earth's center probably have less mass than those on the surface.

2.08 ________ Rocks are made up of minerals.

2.09 ________ The Bible tells of great earthquakes at the time of the Flood.

2.010 ________ Noah took one pair of each animal into the ark.

Write the correct letter and answer on the blank (each answer, 5 points).

2.011 A glacier can ________________________ as it moves.
a. crush stone b. cause drought c. create life

2.012 Earthquakes usually happen at ________________ lines.
a. fault b. fold c. luster

2.013 Volcanoes pour out ________________ .
a. hot water b. ice c. lava

2.014 Sedimentary rock is found in ________________________ .
a. granite b. the earth's center c. layers

2.015 Temperature is part of the ________________________ process.
a. aging b. weathering c. folding

Match these items (each answer, 3 points).

2.016 __________ print fossil
2.017 __________ original-remains fossil
2.018 __________ petrified fossil
2.019 __________ carbonized fossil
2.020 __________ landform
2.021 __________ igneous
2.022 __________ metamorphic
2.023 __________ sedimentary
2.024 __________ cleavage
2.025 __________ geology

a. hardness
b. from physical and chemical changes
c. sandstone
d. from magma
e. study of energy
f. helps identify rocks
g. undecayed plant or animal
h. replaced by a mineral
i. only plants
j. imprint of plant or animal
k. oil
l. mountain
m. only carbon remains
n. science of the earth

Complete this list (each answer, 5 points).

2.026 List the main earth layers.

a. ______________________________

b. ______________________________

c. ______________________________

Answer these questions (each answer, 5 points).

2.027 How could the Flood have been responsible for the formation of fossils?

____

____

____

2.028 How could the Flood have changed landforms? ______________________

____

____

____

Teacher check: Initials ________

Score ________ Date ________

80/100

3. ORDER IN CREATION

God has created everything that exists. He has also put great order into all of His creation. Natural cycles—like the seasons, the phases of the moon, day and night, and the orbits of comets—are evidence of the order in the creation. Plants, animals, and the balance of nature are the results of God's divine intelligence. The structure of the earth itself shows the order of God's creation.

All things that take up space are made of matter. Matter cycles through nature. Energy is also provided by God. Energy is necessary for life to exist upon earth. Both matter and energy show the order of God's creation.

Objectives

Review these objectives. When you have completed this section, you should be able to:

3. Describe the balance of nature.
6. Identify types of energy and work.
7. Tell about the order in matter, its structure, properties, and changes.

Energy

God designed all living things to need energy in order to survive, grow, and perform the activities of life. Energy is one of the most basic parts of God's creation. We can see God's order in energy and the way it is used and transformed. Energy is defined as *the ability to do work*. Energy is used for work being actively performed or it can be stored for use at a later time. Many forms of energy exist. Energy can be transformed from one form to another.

| The sun provides light and heat energy.

Forms of energy. Energy that is stored is called *potential* energy. Anything that has the possibility of moving or of causing movement has potential energy. When anything is in motion, it has *kinetic* energy.

Our main source of energy is the sun. The sun's energy comes to us in the forms of heat energy and light energy. The sun's energy can be stored in matter on the earth. For example, you have learned that the sun's energy can be stored in green plants as food. When the food is used by the cells of the plant for growth, or when it is consumed by other living things for nourishment, the stored energy in the food is released to do work.

Chemical energy is another form of energy. It can be stored in matter such as paper, wood, oil, and coal. These things may be burned to release the chemical energy stored in them. Chemical energy changes to heat energy during burning. For example, the burning of logs provides heat from a campfire. Chemical energy can also be transformed to heat energy without burning. When certain chemicals are mixed together, heat is given off.

Mechanical energy is another form of energy. Whenever anything moves, it has mechanical energy. The rubbing together of two objects can transform mechanical energy into heat energy. Collision of two objects also releases heat energy from mechanical energy.

Light energy comes from the sun. Burning also produces light energy. When light radiates off matter, heat energy can also be produced.

Electricity is another form of energy. Electricity can flow through matter as a current, or it can be generated by mechanical energy, as in a hydroelectric dam. Electricity can also come from chemical energy, as in a battery. In some ways, electricity can be transformed into other forms of energy, such as mechanical energy. Lightning is also a type of electrical energy.

Sound energy is a form of energy that can come from mechanical, chemical, or electrical energy. Sound energy can also be transformed into mechanical and heat energy. The sound of an explosion can move matter. That movement can cause heat.

When energy changes from one form to another, it is not lost. It is conserved. However, the usefulness of energy to do work may be lost in some cases. For example, some scientists believe that some of the heat that results from energy transformation cannot be transformed back into another form. Today, we also know, through nuclear physics and the work of a scientist named Albert Einstein, that energy can be converted to matter and matter can be converted to energy.

Energy transformations are constantly taking place. When one change takes place, it is possible for several more to happen at the same time. A burning piece of wood may cause sound, light, heat, and mechanical energy to be produced. These forms of energy soon may be changed to other forms. The transformations of energy continue. They are a sign of God's order and design in the universe.

| A fire produces sound, light, heat, and potential mechanical energy.

Complete these sentences.

3.1 ______________________ is the ability to do work.

3.2 The two basic forms of energy are potential energy and ______________________ energy.

3.3 A ______________________ of energy takes place when energy changes from one form to another.

3.4 Energy is not ______________________ when it changes from one form to another.

3.5 Most of earth's energy comes from the ______________________.

3.6 Energy can be stored in green plants as ______________________.

3.7 Rubbing objects together changes ____________________ energy into heat energy.

3.8 ____________ wood can produce heat, sound, light, and mechanical energy.

Complete these activities. (You may need to refer to the Science 505 LIFEPAC.)

3.9 Explain how friction is involved in energy transformation. ____________________

____

____

____

____

____

3.10 What is meant by *solar energy*? ____________________

____

3.11 The following list contains some energy transformations. Think of the common changes for each of these items. (**HINT:**—An example of *mechanical* to *light* might be two pieces of moving flint causing a spark when they hit each other.)

a. mechanical to sound ____________________

b. light to chemical ____________________

c. electrical to light ____________________

d. sound to mechanical ____________________

e. chemical to mechanical ____________________

f. heat to mechanical to heat ____________________

Energy and work. *Work* is done when a force moves an object by a distance. Energy supplies the force needed to move objects through a distance. Work is also done when matter changes shape or form. Energy is also used in this process. In fact, energy is transformed when work is done. Work can also be defined as the result of the transformation of energy from one form to another.

Since energy is being constantly transformed, work is going on all the time. Work is being done when paper burns. Work is being done when a bat hits a ball. Your body cells are even doing work while you are asleep. How? The stored energy in the food you eat is being "burned" to give off energy to make your body grow, to build new cells, to help you breathe, and to make your heart to pump. These are all examples of the transformation of energy-producing work.

Is work being done if nothing is moving? For example, is fuel in a gasoline tank doing work? Is a pencil lying on a desk doing work? The answer is no. Work is only done when something moves and there is a transformation of energy. However, both the fuel in the gas tank and the pencil on the desk have energy. They have potential energy. They have the potential to do work. Work will be done if the fuel burns or the pencil rolls off the desk.

Not all work is useful work. Sometimes the work produced by transformation of energy is wasted. Wasting work is a problem especially when the energy source cannot be easily renewed. For example, oil is one of our energy sources that cannot be easily renewed. If oil is not used efficiently, much of the work produced from oil is wasted. While oil is useful in doing work, we need to cut down on the wasteful use of oil. It is also good to develop other renewable sources of energy to do work.

God gave people the responsibility for energy use. We have the intelligence to make decisions about how we use energy. We can be good stewards by using energy sources wisely. Today, there is more understanding about energy and work than ever before. This understanding and concern need to grow for us to become better stewards of God's creation.

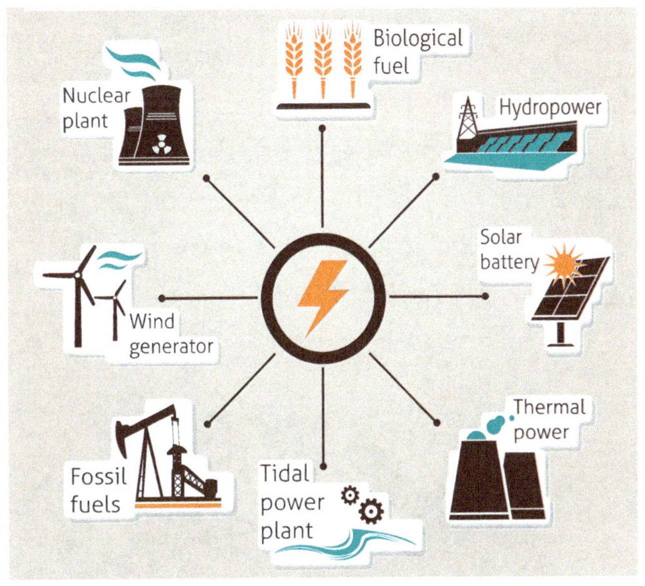

| We have to utilize many forms of energy.

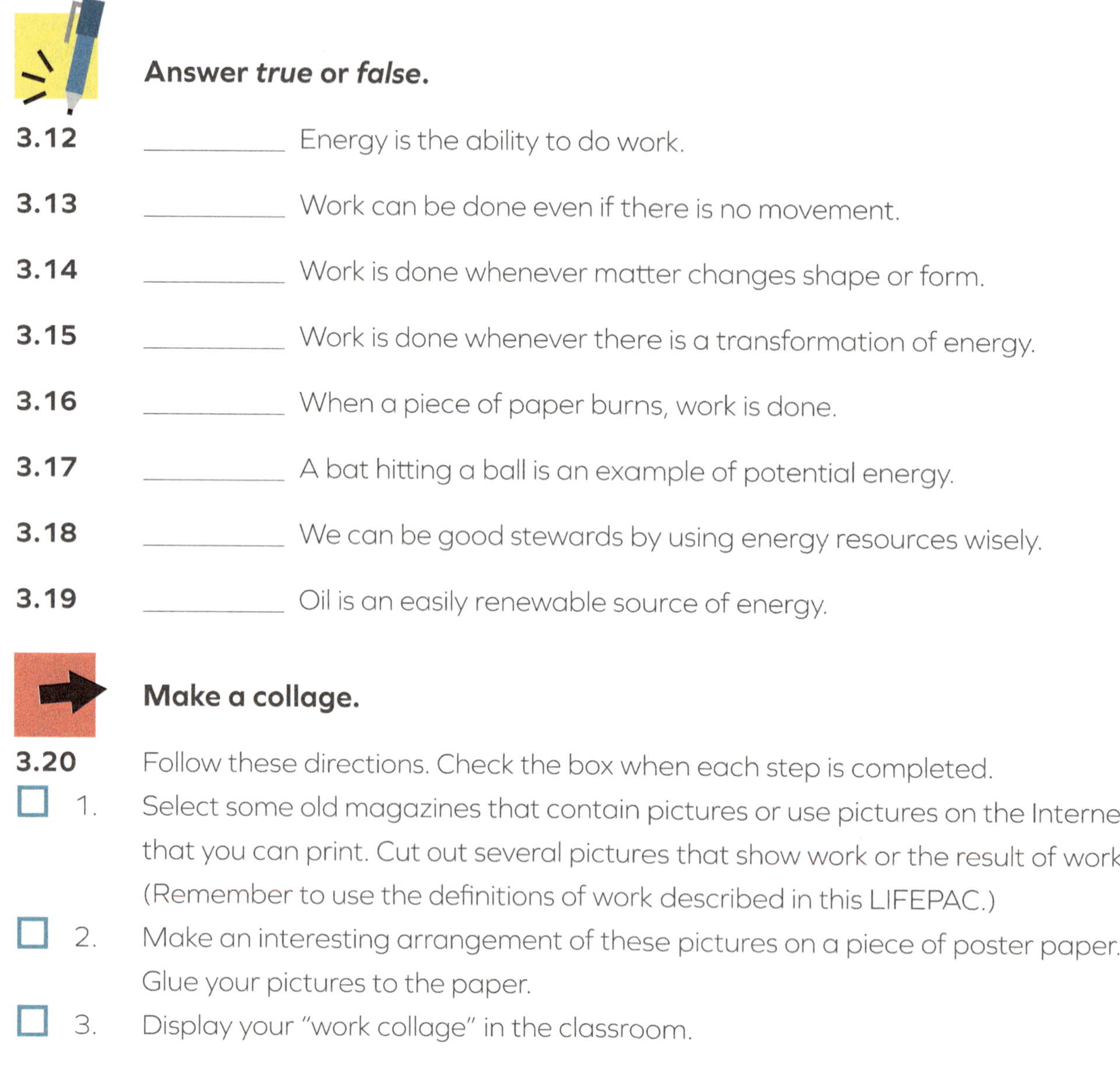

Answer *true* or *false*.

3.12 __________ Energy is the ability to do work.

3.13 __________ Work can be done even if there is no movement.

3.14 __________ Work is done whenever matter changes shape or form.

3.15 __________ Work is done whenever there is a transformation of energy.

3.16 __________ When a piece of paper burns, work is done.

3.17 __________ A bat hitting a ball is an example of potential energy.

3.18 __________ We can be good stewards by using energy resources wisely.

3.19 __________ Oil is an easily renewable source of energy.

Make a collage.

3.20 Follow these directions. Check the box when each step is completed.

☐ 1. Select some old magazines that contain pictures or use pictures on the Internet that you can print. Cut out several pictures that show work or the result of work. (Remember to use the definitions of work described in this LIFEPAC.)

☐ 2. Make an interesting arrangement of these pictures on a piece of poster paper. Glue your pictures to the paper.

☐ 3. Display your "work collage" in the classroom.

Teacher check:

Initials ____________________ Date ____________________

Matter

Another way that God's order is shown in the universe is in *matter*. Everything in the physical universe is matter. Matter is anything that takes up space. Matter has properties. Some properties are common to all matter. Other properties are special to each kind of matter. Matter can change. Because it can change, matter can be cycled through nature. As it does this, we can observe God's order in creation. Matter also has structure. The structure of matter is also a sign of God's orderly universe.

Structure and properties. Matter consists of tiny particles that give matter its basic structure. *Molecules* are the smallest bits of matter that can exist without a chemical change. Each molecule of matter is made up of even smaller particles called *atoms*. Atoms are the basic building blocks of all matter. Atoms form the most basic substances of nature called the chemical *elements*.

Molecules and atoms form the basic structure of all matter. The way that atoms of elements bind together to form molecules determines the different types of matter. There are millions of different types of molecules. Molecules and atoms can combine in chemical reactions to form other kinds of molecules.

Molecules are always in motion. You cannot see the molecules move because they are so small, but even in solid materials, the molecules are moving. Adding heat to matter causes molecules in matter to move faster and farther apart. If enough heat is added to a solid, a liquid will form. If even more heat is added to the material, eventually a gas will form. Solids, liquids, and gases are three states of matter. Materials can cycle from solids to liquids to gases and back again. God's order is in the structure of matter.

All matter has some common properties. Common properties of all matter include mass, volume, and inertia. Mass is the amount of matter present. Volume is the space that matter takes up. Inertia is a property of matter that causes it to stay at rest if it is at rest or to stay in motion if it is in motion.

Matter also has special properties that depend upon the kind of matter present. The two main categories of special properties are (1) physical properties and (2) chemical properties. Color, odor, density, brittleness, solubility, and conductivity are examples of physical properties of matter. Chemical properties include the ability to burn (or combustibility) and the ability to rust. All of these special properties vary according to the type of matter present.

| Atoms and molecules form all matter.

Matter can change. It can change physically and chemically. Physical changes happen whenever matter changes size, shape, or location. For example, breaking a rock into smaller pieces would change the size of the rock. As discussed above, matter changes physically when it changes state from solid, liquid, or gas. With physical change, the kind of matter present stays the same. Water molecules that change from solid to liquid are still water molecules.

Chemical change in matter is different. When chemical changes happen, new substances are formed. The molecules are different. The new substance may also have different properties than the old substance.

Like energy, matter is not lost when it is changed or transformed. Both matter and energy are conserved during changes. However, matter can be changed into energy and energy can be changed into matter. *The law of conservation of mass and energy* states: "Neither mass (matter) nor energy can be created or destroyed, but each may be converted into the other." God's order is in the forms and changes of matter and energy.

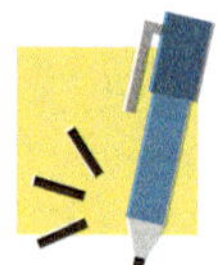

Match these items.

3.21 ________ matter
3.22 ________ molecules
3.23 ________ atoms
3.24 ________ elements
3.25 ________ solid, liquid, gas
3.26 ________ mass
3.27 ________ color
3.28 ________ ability to burn
3.29 ________ matter and energy
3.30 ________ rock breaking

a. basic substances of nature, composed of atoms
b. amount of matter
c. chemical property of matter
d. taste
e. anything that takes up space
f. basic building blocks of all matter
g. smallest bits of matter that exist without chemical change
h. ability to rust
i. states of matter
j. physical property of matter
k. conserved during changes
l. physical change in matter

Write a description.

3.31 Describe a common property of matter taking up space and explain what it is.

____

____

____

____

Cycles. The properties and structure of matter permit cycles of nature. Matter can go through many cycles. Since matter changes but is usually conserved, it cycles through nature in an orderly way.

The water cycle in nature functions because water changes states easily. Job 36:27-28 suggests that the water cycle was well-planned by God. The precision involved is important. For example, if the water would evaporate at a higher temperature, the earth would not receive rain.

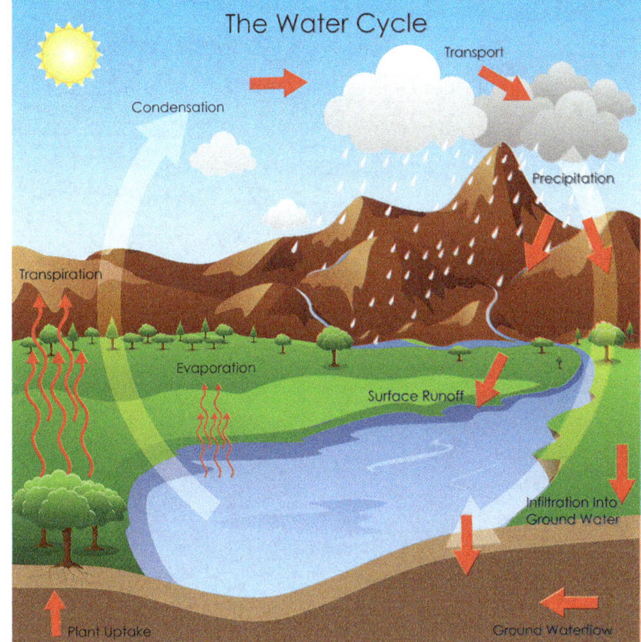

The cycle of seasons is dependent upon the molecules of matter. Direct sunlight in summer warms the molecules in matter. Then the molecules move faster. The heat is absorbed by matter and stored. Therefore, the summer has warmer conditions in nature. In winter, the sun's rays are slanted on the earth's surface. Less heat is absorbed in matter. Colder conditions result.

God's plan for a balance of different types of matter is shown in Ecclesiastes 1:4-7. Several important natural cycles are discussed. Cycles of life, day and night, wind, and water are ongoing. They are important to the earth. They show forth God's order in creation.

Fill in the blanks.

3.32 How does the water cycle show God's precision in nature?

____

____

____

3.33 Why is matter important to cycles of nature?

____

____

____

3.34 What are some of the cycles mentioned in Ecclesiastes chapter 1?

____

____

____

Use the Bible.

3.35 Read Isaiah 40:12. God created a balance of nature. Cycles in nature operate as a result of this balance. It is suggested that God measured the kinds of matter as He created them. List those things Isaiah said that God measured and how God measured them.

a. ______________________________

b. ______________________________

c. ______________________________

d. ______________________________

e. ______________________________

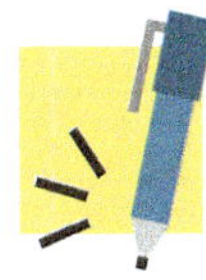

Complete these activities about comets. You studied the cycle of comets in the Science 509 LIFEPAC. If needed, restudy that section of the LIFEPAC to fill in the blanks below.

3.36 The comet follows ________________ around the sun.
a. the moon b. the earth c. an orbit

3.37 Not all comets have ____________ .
a. heads b. tails c. matter

3.38 Comets do not appear to be ________________ .
a. moving b. still c. real

3.39 Comets are ________________ than meteors.
a. closer to earth b. smaller c. less dense

3.40 The ______________ comets are those that come nearest to the sun.
a. biggest b. oldest c. brightest

3.41 The amount of time of each known comet's cycle can be ________________ .
a. predicted b. unknown c. less than a day

3.42 Many comets have been given the names of ____________________ .
a. the Zodiac b. geologists c. their discoverers

Before you take this last Self Test, you may want to do one or more of these self checks.

1. ________ Read the objectives. See if you can do them.
2. ________ Restudy the material related to any objectives that you cannot do.
3. ________ Use the **SQ3R** study procedure to review the material:
   a. **S**can the sections.
   b. **Q**uestion yourself.
   c. **R**ead to answer your questions.
   d. **R**ecite the answers to yourself.
   e. **R**eview areas you did not understand.
4. ________ Review all activities and Self Tests, writing a correct answer for every wrong answer.

SELF TEST 3

Write the correct letter and answer in each blank (each answer, 5 points).

3.01 Energy that is stored is called ____________________ energy.
a. variable b. potential c. kinetic

3.02 Whenever anything moves, it has ____________________ energy.
a. chemical b. heat c. mechanical

3.03 When a force moves an object by a distance, ______________ is done.
a. work b. energy c. a cycle

3.04 We can be ____________________ if we use energy wisely.
a. negligent b. good stewards c. carefree

Match these items (each answer, 3 points).

3.05 __________ energy
3.06 __________ matter
3.07 __________ chemical energy
3.08 __________ atoms
3.09 __________ density
3.010 __________ solid, liquid, gas
3.011 __________ water cycle

a. basic building blocks of all matter
b. shows God's precision in design
c. photosynthesis
d. anything that takes up space
e. the ability to do work
f. chemical change in matter
g. physical property of matter
h. states of matter
i. can be stored in paper, wood, oil, and coal

Answer *true or false* (each answer, 2 points).

3.012 __________ All comets have the same time cycle.

3.013 __________ When energy is changed from one form to another, it is not lost.

3.014 __________ No work is done when an energy transformation takes place.

3.015 __________ Sound is a form of energy.

3.016 __________ Energy transformations are constantly taking place.

3.017 __________ God gave people responsibility for energy use.

3.018 __________ Matter cannot change.

3.019 __________ Molecules are always in motion.

3.020 __________ The chemical elements are made up of complex molecules.

3.021 __________ When water changes from a solid to a liquid, a chemical change occurs.

3.022 __________ The cycle of seasons is dependent upon the molecules of matter.

3.023 __________ Isaiah 40:12 shows that God created a balance of nature.

3.024 __________ Lightning is a type of electrical energy.

3.025 __________ Our main source of energy is the sun.

Complete these lists (each item, 3 points).

3.026 List the three main states of all matter.

a. __________________ b. __________________ c. __________________

3.027 List four physical properties of matter.

a. __________________________ b. __________________________

c. __________________________ d. __________________________

Complete these activities (each answer, 5 points).

3.028 Explain what is meant by the *inertia* of matter.

____

____

____

____

3.029 Explain what is meant by the *law of conservation of mass and energy*.

____

____

____

____

____

Teacher check: Initials ________

Score ________ Date ________

80/100

Before you take the LIFEPAC Test, you may want to do one or more of these self checks.

1. ________ Read the objectives. See if you can do them.
2. ________ Restudy the material related to any objectives that you cannot do.
3. ________ Use the **SQ3R** study procedure to review the material.
4. ________ Review activities, Self Tests, and LIFEPAC vocabulary words.
5. ________ Restudy areas of weakness indicated by the last Self Test.

NOTES

NOTES

NOTES

NOTES